JUL 20

RED
NOVEMBER

RED
NOVEMBER

Will the Country Vote Red for Trump or Red for Socialism?

JOEL B. POLLAK

CENTER
STREET®

NEW YORK   NASHVILLE

Center Street
Hachette Book Group
1290 Avenue of the Americas, New York, NY 10104
centerstreet.com
twitter.com/centerstreet

First Edition: July 2020

Center Street is a division of Hachette Book Group, Inc. The Center Street name and logo are trademarks of Hachette Book Group, Inc.

The publisher is not responsible for websites (or their content) that are not owned by the publisher.

Library of Congress Cataloging-in-Publication Data has been applied for.

ISBNs: 978-1-5460-9984-0 (hardcover), 978-1-5460-9969-7 (ebook)

Printed in the United States of America

LSC-C

10 9 8 7 6 5 4 3 2 1

For Maya and Alexander

CONTENTS

PREFACE

This book tells the story of the 2020 Democratic Party presidential primary, the most left-wing primary in the history of American presidential elections. I began work on the book in early 2019, when there were roughly two dozen candidates. I followed those candidates on the campaign trail throughout the debates, the impeachment of President Donald Trump, and the sudden outbreak of the coronavirus pandemic in the late winter of 2020, just after Super Tuesday.

The book was completed in early May 2020, when former vice president Joe Biden had all but secured the presidential nomination of the Democratic Party.

Biden was not the most left-wing candidate in the field, which was dominated by "progressives," including Biden's main rival, "democratic socialist" Senator Bernie Sanders (I-VT). Yet Biden was arguably the most left-wing Democratic Party nominee ever. Former president Barack Obama, endorsing his former running mate, declared: "Joe already has what is the most progressive platform of any major-party nominee in history."[1]

On every single issue, Biden had been forced, by his rivals and by his party's voters, to adopt policies far to the left of his lifelong positions. He endorsed almost every "democratic socialist" priority and program. He wanted "Medicare for All" to be a choice, and proposed a "Green New Deal" with more generous deadlines than those demanded by the far

ix

left. Otherwise, there were few distinctions. Like Sanders, Biden saw the 2020 election as an opportunity "to fundamentally transform" America.[2]

It remained to be seen whether Biden would, in fact, be the nominee, given growing concerns about his age. By the end of April, many political analysts had begun to suspect that the party would find a way to replace Biden with another candidate. "Neither party has ever had to replace someone at the top of the ticket," observed the respected political data website FiveThirtyEight.com,[3] but the possibility was real.

New concerns arose when Biden faced allegations that he had sexually assaulted a staffer, Tara Reade, in a Senate hallway in 1993. He denied the accusations, but Democrats who had insisted in recent years that all women had the right to be believed were increasingly uncomfortable with their presumptive nominee.

Biden had already promised that his running mate would be a woman, but some women urged that he be replaced. "Democrats need to begin formulating an alternative strategy for 2020—one that does not include Mr. Biden," wrote Elizabeth Bruenig of the *New York Times*.[4]

No one could even be sure what the election itself would look like. Democrats pressed for a national mail-in ballot, ostensibly for fear of exposing voters to the coronavirus in polling places; Republicans fretted over the possibility of fraud. President Donald Trump promised to return to his trademark campaign rallies, but it was unclear when, or whether, large public gatherings would be safe again.

Whatever the outcome, one thing remained true: the Democratic primary had been the most radical contest the country had ever seen. Trump, arguably, had governed as the most conservative president since Ronald Reagan—or Calvin Coolidge. The choice American voters faced in November 2020 had never been more stark—or more consequential.

The book you are about to read has been a labor of love. I hope you will enjoy reading it almost as much as I enjoyed writing it.

Pacific Palisades, California
May 12, 2020
18 Iyar/Lag BaOmer, 5780

ONE

INTRODUCTION

"Nothing is more interesting than revolution, or should I say insurrection,
because all the imagery of revolution comes from insurrection,
which is a different thing.
"Everything we want in a society is what we find brought out in people in
the moment of insurrection.
"This is the moment the true socialist worships and thinks will be
incarnated in the society on the morning after."
—Norman Rush, *Mating: A Novel*[5]

"FIGHT THE POWER"

Nine days before the virus canceled all the rallies, I stood on a media riser in a crush of bodies, fighting for a camera angle as Bernie Sanders stooped over a podium to address tens of thousands of people in a crowded-to-capacity hall that would, by month's end, become an Army field hospital.

I could almost understand the appeal of it all. I could feel the tug on my heart, so many years later.

I could feel the urge to vote for Bernie Sanders, "democratic socialist."

1

If you had told me, as a college student, twenty-five years before, that a presidential candidate would emerge who would embrace a visionary idea of what a perfect society could be; that he would be a veteran of the civil rights movement, one with years of practical experience at nearly every level of government; that he would be Jewish, like me, yet embraced by African American icons from Cornel West to Public Enemy, the latter about to take the stage with him; there is no question that I would have voted for him, volunteered for him, joined the throng of sign-waving supporters standing before him.

"We are not just a campaign, we are a multi-generational, multiracial grassroots movement," he said.[6]

"We are going to stand together, black and white, Latino, Native American, Asian American. We all going to stand together, gay and straight.... So let us go forward.... Let's transform this country," he concluded. The crowd roared.

The theme of the March 1, 2020, rally, one of the last before the crucial Super Tuesday primary vote, was "Fight the Power"—one of Public Enemy's most celebrated and controversial songs.

In my junior year of high school, sometime in late 1992 or early 1993, I had been kicked out of the school library for a week for shouting "Fight the Power!" as I watched a stern-faced, gray-haired librarian notorious for draconian discipline walk one of my friends through the reading room.

(It turned out he had simply been helping my friend find a book.)

"Fight the Power" was an odd look for a presidential campaign, especially that of a major-party front-runner. It was a bold throw-down, a brash statement that Bernie Sanders, 77, was not going to "pivot" back toward the center, was not going to pander to the moderates or the independents—that he was going to remain every bit the socialist revolutionary he had always been.

Onstage, the rappers took their places, with two dancers in military fatigues and tactical vests. It almost looked like a Third World coup had taken place.

Chuck D, the venerable 59-year-old prophet of hip-hop, addressed the crowd over the mic. "Put your fist in the air if you believe in truth to power, and truth in the first place!" he exhorted.[7]

Dedicating his performance to his father and grandfather, he explained his support for Sanders. "It's about truth, and connecting yourself to a fucking agenda you can feel, instead of sitting on the couch, not doing a goddamned thing."

Paying for health care, he said, was a "struggle in this damn country." Likewise with paying for child care. And "climate control," he said, "resonated with me."

"You got to get your ass up and vote for something," he added. "I don't do this shit much, but listen to me. Time to grow up, and somebody got to put the big-ass pants on."

The crowd cheered. A few moments later, the beat kicked in, and the song started again. It was "Bring the Noise," another Public Enemy classic—minus the charismatic Flavor Flav, the group member famous for wearing a giant clock around his neck beneath flashing gold teeth.

(Flav had been expelled from the group earlier that day for refusing to join the rest of the group in backing Bernie Sanders.[8] He said he did not want Public Enemy to be the "soundtrack of a fake revolution."[9] Every revolution, real or fake, has its purges.)

It was crazy—but also fun. I could feel the beat moving my feet, feel the urge to lose myself in the bouncing crowd. This is what I once had dreamed politics could be, the moment of insurrection, America's true revolution.

And just two days hence, on Super Tuesday, if the polls were right, it would take over the Democratic Party, like it or not—for better or for worse.

In many ways, it already had.

Whether he won or not, Bernie Sanders and his supporters had shaped the 2020 Democratic Party presidential field into the most left-wing group of candidates in American history, one in which even the supposedly "moderate" candidates were proposing ideas that had been considered too radical for mainstream politics a decade before.

They would either bring their party to ruin—or usher in a new United Socialist States of America.

BACK IN THE USSA

Thirty years after the end of the Cold War, socialism had become the key issue in the 2020 presidential election.

How had it become so dominant, at least among Democrats? And what did it mean for America's future?

This was not merely a case of Republicans labeling Democrats and their policies as "socialist" to paint them as too extreme. As Sanders himself often delighted in pointing out, many of the social policies now taken for granted by many Americans were once derided by conservatives as "socialist."

In any other year, perhaps, the "socialist" label could have been easily dismissed as partisan hyperbole. Even in 2016, when Sanders ran a strong campaign for the Democratic Party nomination, he and his supporters were seen as a minority, a left-wing fringe, not representative of the party. He was not even a Democrat.

But by 2020, his ideas had been adopted, at least in part, by nearly every single Democratic presidential candidate. And he had been joined on Capitol Hill by a new cohort of self-proclaimed democratic socialists whose policies had reframed the American political debate.

Democrats could not deny that socialism was on the ballot. A few criticized it—notably, Mike Bloomberg, the billionaire former three-term mayor of New York City, who entered the race late and was seen by many moderate Democrats as their party's only hope. He called Sanders's proposals "communism"—not just "socialism"—adding that they "just didn't work."[10]

But many Democrats, if not most, embraced or at least accepted the party's leftward shift.

In an election where Democrats had a good chance of making Trump a one-term president, the party's embrace of socialism meant that two things were possible.

One possibility was that the Democratic Party was about to repeat the mistakes of 1972 and 1984, when it nominated candidates who lost the general election in landslides largely because they were too far to the left of the American electorate. Senator George McGovern (D-SD), running on an antiwar platform, lost every state except Massachusetts, and the District of Columbia, to President Richard Nixon;[11] former vice president Walter Mondale, running on a pledge to raise taxes, won only his home state of Minnesota, and DC, against President Ronald Reagan.[12]

The other possibility was that the American people were about to elect the first socialist government in the country's history—with explicit plans for radical and irreversible changes to the Constitution, the law, the economy, the health care system, immigration policy, national security, and American society in general.

Even the candidates who claimed *not* to be socialists embraced their rivals' socialist policies.

Senator Elizabeth Warren (D-MA) adopted Sanders's health care plan, "Medicare for All," and joined him in promising to eliminate private health insurance. She added a wealth tax, proposing to confiscate 2 percent of what the richest Americans had saved after paying taxes in the past—though critics pointed out that the idea was likely unconstitutional.[13]

Former vice president Joe Biden, who led the polls throughout the early months of the campaign, was the most left-wing front-runner in American political history. He promised to raise taxes immediately, end the use of fossil fuels, and use federal taxpayers' money to pay for abortions, among other proposals. He wanted to make Medicare for All voluntary, not mandatory. And, like his rivals, he proposed to make health care free for illegal aliens.

If President Donald Trump was failing, if his rhetoric and style were so intolerable, a middle-of-the-road candidate with moderate policies and minimal qualifications would have sufficed. Instead, Democrats proposed socialism—albeit a "democratic" version—as the alternative.

To hear Sanders describe it, American society was so broken that only socialism could fix it. The economy, he said, was working for billionaires, but not for "working-class people"—whom, he said, "are suffering under incredible economic hardship, desperately trying to survive."[14] The United States, he pointed out repeatedly, was the only industrialized nation not to guarantee government-funded health care to all of its citizens. And Trump, a member of the billionaire class, who appeared to defy all political boundaries and conventions, represented a creeping authoritarianism that only socialism could smash.

Other Democrats might not have seen the country in such dark and dire terms. But in the early days of the campaign, Trump looked vulnerable.

Perhaps Democrats were so confident of victory that they sought to seize the opportunity to enact the sweeping changes that they had only dared dream about or whispered to each other quietly, beyond the hearing of journalists (who agreed with them) or conservatives (who would object). Perhaps Trump's own disruptive victory had shown them that the old political constraints did not apply.

Or perhaps Democrats, too, were victims of an ongoing political change that they had long encouraged but could no longer control.

FROM LEFT TO RIGHT

I witnessed that change firsthand—though my own political transition was in the opposite direction.

When I cast my first vote in 1996, as a 19-year-old Harvard sophomore and a self-identified radical leftist, I wrote in Ralph Nader's name on my Illinois absentee ballot. By the time I graduated law school in 2009, I was a Tea Party conservative Republican.

I had grown up in the Chicago suburb of Skokie, which was disproportionately Jewish (like me) and also conventionally liberal. In high school, I was inspired by *The Autobiography of Malcolm X*, which I had found on display in that school library during Black History Month. I found the story captivating despite the protagonist's brief descent into anti-Semitism. Here was a man struggling to find the truth, adjusting his views over time through the benefit of experience but grappling with great questions about race and justice and fairness and freedom.

These themes resonated with my sense of historical guilt. I had been born in South Africa, and though my family immigrated to the United States when I was just eight weeks old, I felt more and more conscious of the burden of that history.

I approached the high school's "Afro-American club" and asked to join—not on the basis of my South African roots but simply as a white student who wished to learn more. Cautiously, the club's president accepted me.

I arrived at Harvard at the same time as the charismatic African American Studies professor Dr. Cornel West. I took his class "Race, Nation, and Democracy," which took in the broad sweep of left-wing thought and radical politics. I was mesmerized and took the worldview of the class as essentially correct—that the United States was a country of noble ideals but with an evil, continuing legacy of white supremacy. I wrote breezy, agitprop term papers such as one calling for what I called "transformative communication"—an argument for *more* left-wing bias in the media, the better to encourage Americans to support radical change.

My turn to the right was not inevitable. It began subtly—during college, in fact. Armed with utopian visions and ambitious goals, I had worked and volunteered for several left-wing causes, in each case finding that political reality did not quite conform to my ivory-tower visions. In class, working toward my degree in environmental science, I noted my professors backing policy recommendations that they, and I, knew were somewhat ahead of scientific "consensus."

Still, when I left Harvard, I thought of myself as something of a radical progressive. I won a fellowship to study in South Africa—a country that fascinated me not only because of my roots but also because it was in the throes of a miraculous political transition from apartheid to democracy. The new African National Congress (ANC) government had adopted many of the radical policies I favored.

It was in South Africa that my political shift began in earnest. It was impossible to ignore that however well-intentioned the country's left-wing policies were, many of them were failures in practice. The country's aggressive affirmative action policies, for example, often hurt the very people they were aimed at helping. Forcing white teachers to take early retirement, for example, meant that black children in public schools generally received a *worse* education than they would have before the end of apartheid.

When the second Palestinian intifada started in the Middle East in September 2000, the ruling ANC sided with the Palestinians, embracing what I knew to be a false narrative of Israel as an apartheid state. I found myself debating senior members of the government I had admired—who, when presented with incontrovertible facts, declared them to be unimportant.

Eventually, I became a speechwriter for the country's center-left opposition party, the Democratic Alliance. When I returned to the United States for law school, I still thought of myself as a Democrat. But my views felt out of step—especially after the left opposed Senator Joe Lieberman (D-CT), an observant Jew, in his 2006 reelection primary. His crime had been supporting President George W. Bush's War on Terror.

If there was no room for Joe Lieberman, I thought, there was no room for me. (Democrats underestimate just how much their intolerance of dissent drives people away.)

I confronted the fact that I had previously thought of Republicans as racist, greedy, and intolerant. I was none of those things.

But my ideas—about individual liberty, about the dangers of big government, about the importance of the Constitution—lined up with the conservatives.

I made the switch. And eventually, after running a bold but unsuccessful campaign for Congress in my hometown in 2010, I found my way to Breitbart.

THE GUY FROM BREITBART

This book emerged as the result of my political coverage of the 2020 Democratic presidential primary for Breitbart News. Breitbart.com is a conservative website founded by my friend and mentor, the late Andrew Breitbart.

Andrew grew up as a West Los Angeles liberal and was only introduced to conservative talk radio through his future father-in-law, the legendary actor Orson Bean.[15] As he noted in his memoir, *Righteous Indignation: Excuse Me While I Save the World*,[16] Andrew began to see through the politically correct pieties with which he had surrounded himself.

Andrew befriended and worked for Internet news pioneer Matt Drudge, who wanted not only to create an alternative to the mainstream media but also to beat it at its own game. Drudge broke the story that President Bill Clinton had been having an affair with an intern—a story that mainstream outlets had spiked and that led to his impeachment, though not his conviction or removal from office.

In the years that followed, Andrew spread his wings. He helped Arianna Huffington set up the left-wing Huffington Post—amused, as he put it, to show that there was little difference in outlook between an openly liberal website and supposedly objective media institutions like the *New York Times*.

But Andrew had bigger goals. He was not content with commentary and punditry. He wanted to change the way news was written, to talk about subjects the media preferred to ignore, and to give an army of "citizen journalists" the means to tell their stories.

In 2009, Andrew began launching the "Bigs," a series of blogs that aimed to expose the left-wing bias at the core of America's most powerful institutions. Big Hollywood was the first, followed by Big Government, which burst onto the scene with a series of undercover videos by the youthful investigative journalist James O'Keefe. Big Journalism and Big Peace followed. Then, in 2012, Andrew planned the consolidation of the Bigs into a single, twenty-four-hour news service: Breitbart.com.

Three days before the planned launch, Andrew died suddenly. He was 43. He left a wife, four children, and hundreds of thousands of fans behind.

Fighting through tears, the rest of the Breitbart News staff managed to launch the new website. I had been named editor-in-chief six months before, adding that to my original title of in-house counsel. For the eighteen months after Andrew's death, I worked harder than I ever had before. We could not replace Andrew, but we could fulfill his mission.

In September 2013, I traded places with Alex Marlow, who had been Andrew's first hire straight out of the University of California, Berkeley and has a better understanding of the media landscape than almost anyone else in the news business. As Alex took the reins in DC, I became senior editor-at-large, a title that gave me less responsibility and more freedom.

Liberated from the administrative challenge of overseeing the daily operations of the website, I could focus on journalism. I put together a small team of reporters to cover California—blue-state correspondents for our red-state readership.

During the 2016 presidential campaign, that meant covering the protracted battle between Sanders and former secretary of state Hillary Clinton, much of which took place on the West Coast. It was a bitter and bizarre fight for the ambivalent legacy of Barack Obama, torn between the left-wing utopianism of his "community organizing" youth and the Beltway establishment he had embraced in office.

Later in the campaign, I was assigned to cover Donald Trump as he carried out what many—including me—believed was a doomed presidential campaign.

Amazingly—shockingly—Trump won, and I coauthored a book about it: *How Trump Won: The Inside Story of a Revolution.*[17]

In approaching the 2020 election, I was more open to the potential of insurgent political campaigns and paid close attention to the radical takeover of the Democratic Party. Perhaps I was particularly sensitive to it, given my left-wing background: I understood the roots of the new "Resistance" to Trump and the passions animating it.

What I knew was that to cover that movement properly, I needed to be on the campaign trail.

Not everyone wanted "the guy from Breitbart" there. The very name "Breitbart" was a warning sign, to many, fairly or not. As you will read—or have heard—I had more than one run-in with presidential candidates who would have preferred not to have me there. But I got the story anyway.

And it is the story Andrew Breitbart anticipated a decade ago: that America would increasingly face a clear choice between Tea Party and Occupy[18]—between the restoration of its founding ideals or a democratic socialist revolution in the style of the rivals America had defeated.

—————

TWO

THE RESISTANCE

"The authors of this guide are former congressional staffers who witnessed the rise of the Tea Party.... We believe that protecting our values, our neighbors, and ourselves will require mounting a similar resistance to the Trump agenda—but a resistance built on the values of inclusion, tolerance, and fairness."
—Indivisible, "Introduction to the Guide"[19]

PRIMAL SCREAM

The campaign against President Donald Trump began the moment he took office—if not the moment he was elected.

In a celebrated—and widely mocked—video that became the subject of endless Internet memes, a bespectacled woman in a fluorescent green jacket reacted to Trump's inauguration with a primal scream: "Noooooooo!"[20]

Many Democrats never quite recovered from the shock of Trump's surprise victory in the wee hours of November 9, 2016. But some snapped into action.

They called themselves the "Resistance."

The Resistance—named both for the underground that fought the

Nazis in occupied Europe in World War II and for the rebel army in the *Star Wars* sequels—began just a few days after Donald Trump was elected president. But it had deeper roots.

It drew from the radical left-wing activism of the Occupy Wall Street movement, which President Barack Obama's administration had cultivated as a counterweight to the conservative Tea Party movement after Republicans won the U.S. House in a landslide in 2010. And the Occupy movement, in turn, had connections to the antiwar movement of the George W. Bush era, the antiglobalization protests that began in Seattle in 1999, and other past left-wing efforts.

Some enraged left-wingers actually rioted in the hours and days after Trump's election. Chanting "Not my president," protesters "smashed windows and set garbage bins on fire" in Oakland, California, and blocked traffic in downtown Portland, Oregon. Similar protests erupted in Seattle and Philadelphia.[21]

New demonstrations erupted the following weekend after President-elect Trump's announcement that Stephen K. Bannon would be his senior White House adviser.

Bannon, the former executive chairman of Breitbart News, had become a prime target of the Clinton campaign in August 2016, after he joined the Trump campaign as its CEO. Clinton had delivered a special address in Reno, Nevada, to mark Bannon's appointment. "The de facto merger between Breitbart and the Trump Campaign represents a landmark achievement for the 'Alt-Right.' A fringe element has effectively taken over the Republican Party. This is part of a broader story—the rising tide of hardline, right-wing nationalism around the world."[22]

Few of those present even knew what the "alt-right" was, as I had discovered by asking them.[23] (I barely knew, myself.) But millions of Clinton voters were soon informed that Trump, through Bannon, was *literally* Hitler.

To be sure, Bannon was the campaign's most important adviser at a crucial moment, steering Trump from a post-convention slump to victory on the home stretch. Before that, through Breitbart—especially the *Breitbart News Daily* morning show on Sirius XM, which he personally hosted—Bannon helped shape the audience that Trump's message would later reach.

It was to be expected that Bannon would play a leading role in the new administration. But he was not a racist, or a "white nationalist," or an anti-Semite, or a member of the alt-right. That was an idea planted into the public imagination by the Clinton campaign and a compliant media—an idea that later germinated into public hysteria.[24]

The emotions that exploded after Bannon's appointment were intense. I covered a rally against Bannon on the steps of the Los Angeles City Hall, a week after the election. Roughly five hundred people stood outside on a chilly autumn night, holding signs like "Bannon is a racist MANIAC" and worse. They chanted "No Bannon, no KKK, no fascist USA." A few recognized me from Breitbart or from television and surrounded me to intimidate me; I needed police to walk me to my car.[25]

The opposition to Trump soon evolved beyond screaming into the night. That was partly because the far left, disillusioned by Bernie Sanders's exit, had already begun looking beyond the election itself to bigger issues.

Throughout the fall, for example, protesters had been gathering in North Dakota to oppose the Dakota Access Pipeline, which ran near the Standing Rock Sioux Reservation. The protests continued through the winter and rallied many anti-Trump activists—including a young political neophyte named Alexandria Ocasio-Cortez, later recruited to run for Congress.[26]

Others began targeting Republican politicians. A new group, called Indivisible, was formed by former Capitol Hill staffers in the weeks after the election. They distributed information to activists across the country, unabashedly modeling their efforts on the Tea Party movement that sprang up after Barack Obama's election in 2008. Indivisible encouraged activists to attend town hall meetings held by Republican members of Congress and to ask them challenging questions.

Many Republicans were taken aback by the sudden flood of activists. The confrontations generated intense local media coverage, and suddenly long-term Republican incumbents began to look, and feel, vulnerable.

Indivisible and the Resistance laid the foundations for a successful 2018 midterm election campaign and attracted many young, left-wing activists to the Democratic Party's cause.

THE DEEP STATE REVOLT

While left-wing activists were organizing to oppose the new administration, civil servants and Obama "holdovers" were working *within* the government to frustrate Trump's policies—and, many hoped, to push him out of office.

Trump had hoped for a presidential "honeymoon," the traditional period of roughly several weeks in which critics and opponents lie low, deferring to the prerogatives of the new administration and the will of the electorate. He suggested that he could work with Democrats on funding new infrastructure projects, and he courted organized labor by fulfilling his promise to withdraw the U.S. from the Trans-Pacific Partnership (TPP).

One union leader gushed after an Oval Office meeting January 23: "We just had, probably, the most incredible meeting of our careers...[Trump] took the time to take everyone into the Oval Office and show them the seat of power."[27]

Though Trump had taken on the political "establishment" in his inaugural address, he had also appealed to Americans to "heal our divisions."[28]

It was not to be.

Already, before President Trump had been sworn in, members of the federal law enforcement and intelligence agencies—known colloquially as the "deep state"—began leaking damaging information about the president-elect to the press. The leaks supported allegations of "collusion" between the Trump campaign and the Russian government—allegations that were later found meritless. A so-called dossier alleging that Trump had corrupt ties to Russia, and had committed salacious acts with prostitutes there, was reported by Buzzfeed and CNN after circulating in Washington circles for months. Then FBI director James Comey allegedly used the pretext of a briefing with the president-elect to facilitate the leaking of the dossier to these outlets.[29] The *New York Times* reported on Inauguration Day[30]—on the top of the front page, in bold type—that the outgoing Obama administration had "wiretapped" key Trump aides.[31]

More broadly, the outgoing Obama administration had loosened the rules on the sharing of classified information within the federal government, making leaks more likely. Obama officials with high security clearance then began requesting the "unmasking" of American citizens whose conversations with foreign, especially Russian, officials had been wiretapped.[32] One conversation was leaked to columnist David Ignatius of the *Washington Post*, who reported that incoming National Security Advisor Michael Flynn had spoken to then Russian ambassador Sergey Kislyak.[33]

These cloak-and-dagger tactics continued after Trump was inaugurated.

On January 27, 2017, merely a week after taking office, President Trump issued an executive order banning immigration and travel from "terror-prone countries."[34] The ban affected seven Arab or Muslim countries, all either terror-prone or known sponsors of terror (and earlier identified as such by the Obama administration).

Almost immediately, left-wing protesters crowded the nation's airports. They chanted, they carried signs ("Fuck Donald Trump" among them[35]), and they demanded that travelers who had been apprehended by customs and immigration officials be allowed to enter the country. Democratic politicians began joining in—even when doing so meant delaying travelers to and from their own cities and states. In California, Lt. Governor Gavin Newsom, Los Angeles mayor Eric Garcetti, and others joined the protests—even though they were illegal, blocking traffic and causing many outbound passengers to miss their flights.[36] The American Civil Liberties Union (ACLU) recruited lawyers to represent detained travelers; lawyers signed up by the hundreds.

The left called the executive order a "Muslim ban." Trump had, in fact, proposed such a ban in the wake of the terror attacks in and around Paris in November 2015, when radical Islamic terrorists—including some who had posed as Syrian refugees—attacked a soccer game, restaurants, and the Bataclan theater, where the California band Eagles of Death Metal had been performing. The terrorists killed 130 people and wounded hundreds more. Trump later backed off the "Muslim ban" proposal, however, and his executive order said nothing in particular about religion.

That did not stop critics of the order from declaring that it was unconstitutional (though it is not clear that even an immigration ban based on religion would be unconstitutional, given that the people to whom it would apply would not, in fact, be in the United States). The order triggered another form of resistance—this time from within the government itself.

Acting U.S. Attorney General Sally Yates refused to enforce Trump's "travel ban," saying that it was unconstitutional and could not be defended in court. It was an extraordinary claim, one based on Yates's own personal views of Trump's political statements during the campaign. And it would later be defeated at the Supreme Court, which upheld a traditional view of presidential prerogatives in immigration policy.[37] But it was praised in the media[38] and inspired others in government.

Yates herself was fêted by the left—she was invited to deliver the Class Day lecture at Harvard Law School, for example.[39] It later emerged that she had played a role in investigating Flynn (on the dubious suspicion that he was violating the Logan Act of 1799, which prevents private citizens from conducting diplomacy but is almost never prosecuted).

She was just the first visible face of a quiet rebellion among civil servants, Obama administration holdovers, and—most alarmingly—establishment-friendly Trump appointees to bring down Trump, or at least bring the new administration to heel. *Politico* reported in February 2017: "Federal employees worried that President Donald Trump will gut their agencies are creating new email addresses, signing up for encrypted messaging apps and looking for other, protected ways to push back against the new administration's agenda."[40]

The urgency of the "Resistance" only grew as Trump notched up a string of successes—launching an air strike on the Syrian regime for using chemical weapons against civilians, withdrawing from the Paris Climate Accords, and reforming the U.S. Department of Veterans Affairs, to name a few.

The deep state would continue its rebellion, leaking classified or otherwise embarrassing information incessantly to friendly media and to

Democratic politicians. Such efforts eventually brought about Trump's impeachment and attempted removal from office.

THE NEW "TEA PARTY"

The most visible face of the Resistance was an organization called the Women's March, named for protests held in cities across the country on January 21, 2017, the day after Trump's inauguration. The flagship event was in Washington, DC, itself, where thousands marched through the streets. Some of the participants had booked hotel rooms in anticipation of Hillary Clinton's victory; when she lost, they kept their travel plans and signed up for the protest.

Some of the rhetoric at the demonstrations was whimsical, some militant. Madonna talked about blowing up the White House, for instance.[41] The trademark pink "Pussyhats"—pink woolen knit hats with ears, named for Trump's infamous *Access Hollywood* open-mic comment ("Grab them by the pussy")[42]—became ubiquitous. (A year later, women were urged to abandon the Pussyhats in deference to transgender women, who might not have actual vaginas.)[43]

Other radical protests began to arise, loosely aligned with the Resistance. Left-wing Jews formed a group called the Jewish Resistance, recalling underground fighters in the Second World War. (This meant Trump supporters were, by definition, Nazis.) Those who formed the group appear to have had little idea that the name "Jewish Resistance Movement" had been used before: it was a violent movement that began at the end of World War II in opposition to British rule in Palestine and was associated with the political right.[44]

But the sudden rise—and radical actions—of the Resistance also had the effect of solidifying Trump's core support behind him and of shocking at least some of the public. Michael Wolff, author of the controversial 2018 exposé *Fire and Fury: Inside the Trump White House* (Henry Holt and Company), reported that Bannon intended to provoke the left so that it would show its worst face to the public. Let the "snowflakes...show up at the airports and riot," he reportedly said.[45] He apparently knew that the movement would push the Democratic Party to the left and thus push moderate Americans to side—reluctantly, perhaps—with Trump.

Indeed, the more Americans learned about the Resistance—despite glowing media portrayals—the less they liked it. The Women's March, in particular, ran into controversy. One of its most prominent leaders, Linda Sarsour, a hijab-wearing Palestinian American, was articulate and photogenic—but also had a penchant for extreme anti-Israel rhetoric.[46] She attempted to exclude pro-Israel Jews from participation, saying that feminists could not be Zionists and vice versa.[47] Another Women's March leader, Tamika Mallory, openly supported the racist, anti-Semitic Nation of Islam leader Louis Farrakhan. The movement struggled to dissociate itself from Farrakhan and began losing support among Jewish leftists. (Sarsour and Mallory were dropped from the Women's March board in mid-2019; however, another Farrakhan supporter, Carmen Perez,[48] remained.)

Soon, the Resistance attracted major financial support from wealthy Democrats. The *New York Times* reported in October 2017: "It started as a scrappy grass-roots protest movement against President Trump, but now the so-called resistance is attracting six- and seven-figure checks from major liberal donors, posing an insurgent challenge to some of the left's most venerable institutions—and the Democratic Party itself."[49] The *Times* added: "While the new groups gained early traction mostly on the strength of grass-roots volunteers and small donations—and with relatively meager overall budgets—they are beginning to attract attention from the left's most generous benefactors."

Among the beneficiaries was Indivisible, which had forty employees and multimillion-dollar budgets less than a year after its founding. The Resistance boosted fundraising for many left-wing organizations. The *Times* noted that the left-wing Center for American Progress (CAP), by now part of the Democratic Party establishment, raised money by selling forty-dollar T-shirts emblazoned with the word "resist"—drawing the ire of activists who resented the implication that CAP was leading the movement.

The Resistance aimed at nothing less than ousting the new president. In 2017, the conservative Washington Free Beacon published a memorandum from David Brock, the conservative-turned-liberal founder of left-wing groups like Media Matters and the American Bridge super PAC, in which he proposed using an array of organizations to remove Trump through impeachment.[50]

The Resistance also attempted to silence its opponents. A new left-wing group called Sleeping Giants emerged and began organizing boycotts of conservative media, including Breitbart. (None of the mainstream media outlets that reported on the group showed any interest in exposing who its leaders were.[51] That task later fell to the Daily Caller, a conservative news website.[52])

Democrats also began pressuring Facebook, Google, and other Silicon Valley giants to police their content. They blamed the tech companies for allegedly allowing "fake news" to circulate, on the theory that only a misinformed public could possibly have elected Trump to the White House. By September 2019, Facebook CEO Mark Zuckerberg had admitted that some of the fact-checking organizations it used turned out to have been staffed by left-wing activists.[53]

NEW LEADERS EMERGE

The Resistance, like the Tea Party of 2010, began to attract new activists to the political process. And unlike the Tea Party, new Resistance figures enjoyed positive attention from the media, which they parlayed into political success.

The political math in 2018 did not favor a Democratic takeover of the Senate in 2018, where the party had to defend twenty-three seats (twenty-five including independents), including ten in states that Trump had won in 2016. By contrast, Republicans were defending only eight seats.

But the House was a different story. On the one hand, the congressional map favored the Republicans. State legislatures that shifted to the GOP during the Tea Party wave of 2010, a census year, had generally redrawn the districts to favor Republicans.

On the other hand, the 2016 election had demonstrated—and accelerated—a trend in which once-conservative suburbs were becoming more liberal, thanks to immigration and cultural shifts among elites. In 2016, Orange County, California, voted for Hillary Clinton—making her the first Democratic presidential candidate to win the Republican stronghold in decades.

Wealthy districts in liberal, "blue" states were particularly vulnerable. President Trump signed tax reforms in 2017 that lowered income and corporate tax rates—but also capped the state and local tax (SALT) deduction at $10,000. That hit wealthy homeowners, who had little hope of persuading Democratic state and local governments to lower taxes. In California, New York, and New Jersey, that created the basis for a backlash.

Democrats were also motivated by other grievances. They were horrified by President Trump's support for the Keystone XL pipeline, which would bring oil from Canada's tar sands to the United States, and which Obama had blocked. They were frightened by Trump's rollback of federal regulations, aided by the Congressional Review Act, a hitherto-obscure law that allowed Congress to repeal new rules that the executive had failed to report to the legislature. The Obama administration had ignored that law—and so Republicans set about dismantling as many of his regulations as they could.

Democrats also capitalized on public outrage at the scourge of mass shootings. Though mass shootings were not, in fact, growing more common,[54] they were horrific—and easily politicized.

A mass shooting at the Route 91 Harvest country music festival in Las Vegas, Nevada, on October 1, 2017, was the largest in American history, claiming 58 innocent lives. In another, at the Marjorie Stoneman Douglas High School in Parkland, Florida, 19 people, mostly students, were killed. And on October 27, 2018, a right-wing extremist—who hated Donald Trump[55] for being too pro-Jewish—killed 11 Jews at the Tree of Life Synagogue in Pittsburgh. It was the worst mass murder of Jews in American history.

Though it was not the top issue for voters, six in ten participants in the midterm election favored gun control.[56]

Other Democrats were motivated by the fight to block the confirmation of Brett Kavanaugh to the U.S. Supreme Court. As Kavanaugh's nomination moved through the Senate in the fall of 2018, Democrats began touting uncorroborated claims of sexual misconduct against him that had been leaked to, or uncovered by, the mainstream media. The allegations concerned episodes in high school and college, decades ago, which had never been reported before and could not be confirmed.

Republican voters rallied around Kavanaugh. But Democrats, fearing the Court's newly invigorated 5–4 conservative majority, attacked the Trump administration with greater urgency than before.

Ultimately, Republicans would net two additional seats in the Senate. But Democrats won a "wave" election in the House, flipping 41 seats and taking control with a 17-seat majority.[57]

Even before the midterm election in November 2018, however, there were the primary races. As occurred with the Tea Party in 2010, it was there that the effects of the Resistance were first felt.

The first and most important shock came in June 2018, when a 28-year-old Puerto Rican bartender-turned-political activist, Alexandria Ocasio-Cortez, challenged incumbent veteran congressman Joe Crowley, a trusted lieutenant of would-be Speaker of the House Nancy Pelosi (D-CA) in New York's Fourteenth Congressional District.

Ocasio-Cortez—or AOC, a nickname she later adopted—ran on a simple, radical promise: she pledged to abolish U.S. Immigration and Customs Enforcement (ICE), the agency within the Department of Homeland Security responsible for enforcing the country's immigration laws. She took Crowley to task in a televised debate in which he agreed that ICE was fascist, but not that it should be eliminated.[58]

Crowley, who had not faced a primary challenge in 14 years, struggled to keep up with AOC's spirited campaign. And on primary night, AOC's victory shook the political world.

Her successful insurgency inspired others. In September 2018, in Massachusetts, the previously unknown Ayanna Pressley challenged long-term incumbent Mike Capuano, who had represented Boston's northern suburbs for two decades in the same district once held by former Speaker of the House Tip O'Neill. Former Somali refugee Ilhan Omar won the Democratic nomination in Minnesota's Fifth Congressional District. Palestinian American Rashida Tlaib won her primary in Michigan's thirteenth district. Both would run against minimal or no

Republican opposition in the general election, becoming the first two Muslim women elected to Congress.

The insurgents changed everything. Most were radicals. There had been far-left Democrats before, usually from gerrymandered districts, chosen by the party machine, negotiating for seats at the table and pork at the trough.

These young leaders were different. They had defied the party hierarchy and owed it nothing. More than that, they had mastered social media and new methods of organizing through technology; they had an audience they did not need mainstream media to reach.

AOC was the unquestioned star of the Resistance class of 2018. While she seemed to know little about policy[59]—despite Boston University degrees in international relations and economics—she was an exceptionally gifted communicator.

The *Dilbert* cartoonist Scott Adams, who had famously predicted in August 2015 that Donald Trump would win the Republican nomination—and perhaps the presidency—noted frequently that AOC had many of the same skills. Like Trump, she was a "master persuader" who was good not only at taking apart her critics on Twitter but also at using social media to generate public support for her ideas.[60] She drew large audiences for her Instagram live streams as she held forth on politics while chopping vegetables or sipping wine. Other Democrats tried imitating her, not always successfully: Elizabeth Warren, for example, drew ridicule for streaming video of herself drinking beer in her kitchen with her reluctant husband.[61]

AOC was a formidable critic of the party's centrists and moderates. She repeatedly attacked the Problem Solvers Caucus, a bipartisan group of moderates that tried to set aside politics to solve common national problems. And through a group called the Justice Democrats, who sought unabashedly to replace white Democrats with progressive minorities, Ocasio-Cortez threatened moderate Democratic incumbents. (The group's official goal was to target "Democratic incumbents who are demographically and ideologically out-of-touch with their districts.")[62]

AOC and her cohort—derided by Speaker of the House Nancy Pelosi as the "Squad,"[63] a pejorative nickname later taken up by Trump—allowed the radical left to make the leap from the college campus, the streets, and social media directly into the halls of power. In the 2020 race, Ocasio-Cortez was openly disdainful of former vice president Joe Biden without dismissing him entirely. Though she initially declined to endorse a candidate, it was clear that without her, the Democratic primary field would not have been as far left as it turned out to be.

Through AOC and the Squad, the Resistance set the Democratic Party, and the country, on a course for Red November,[64] with no turning back.

THREE

DEMOCRATIC SOCIALISM

"Barack Obama's name appears on a large list of names and addresses in a folder labeled 'Socialist Scholars Conference,' in the Records of the Democratic Socialists of America (DSA)."
—Stanley Kurtz, *Radical-in-Chief: Barack Obama and the Untold Story of American Socialism*[65]

DEEP ROOTS

Democratic socialism did not simply spring upon the American political scene. It blossomed only after decades of quiet cultivation in the American academy and "community organizing" within the grassroots organizations loosely aligned with the Democratic Party.

Socialism itself enjoyed its heyday in the United States in the 1930s, when the country was in the throes of the Great Depression and the horrors of life in the Soviet Union—the pioneering "socialist" republic— were not yet widely known or had been obscured by sympathetic journalists like Walter Duranty of the *New York Times*.

Eugene V. Debs, the iconic American socialist, ran for president five times on the Socialist Party ticket from 1900 to 1920 but remained a marginal figure. In 1934, left-wing journalist Upton Sinclair ran for and won the Democratic Party nomination for governor of California on a social-ist platform. Though he lost in the general election, many of his ideas arguably shaped the New Deal policies of President Franklin Delano Roosevelt.[66]

World War II rehabilitated the image of the Soviet Union in the United States, and many intellectuals and artists—particularly in Hollywood—were attracted to socialist ideals. Some even joined the Communist Party, until the Cold War and the McCarthy era made doing so unpalatable.

The civil rights struggles of the 1950s and 1960s reshaped the Dem-ocratic Party. It had once been the party of segregation across the South. But a postwar generation of reformers, inspired by Dr. Martin Luther King Jr., led the party to embrace ideals of racial equality. By the end of the 1960s, activists had turned their attention to opposing the Vietnam War and to broader issues of socioeconomic inequality.

The advent of radical politics, associated with upheaval in the streets, sent many American voters running in the opposite direction. But a hard core of activists remained devoted to the cause, finding shelter on college campuses and within a constellation of left-wing organizations inspired by the lessons of Saul Alinsky, the iconic community organizer and polit-ical theorist.

Alinsky, who inspired a young former "Goldwater Girl" named Hil-lary Clinton (née Rodham) to write her senior thesis at Wellesley College about him, is known for his manual, *Rules for Radicals*. While Alinsky urged readers to disrupt the existing social order, he also instructed them to do so from within the existing system. "If the real radical finds that having long hair sets up psychological barriers to communication and organization," Alinsky wrote, "he cuts his hair."[67]

Democratic socialism emerged from the post-1960s world as the idea of achieving socialist ideals through democratic means. Unlike commu-nism, in which the state controlled the means of production and a sin-gle party organization directed political life, democratic socialism was to achieve radical socioeconomic equality through the consent of the governed.

Exactly how that was to be achieved was never quite clear. F. A. Hayek, the Austrian-British economist whose free-market philosophy inspired the revolutions of Ronald Reagan and Margaret Thatcher, cautioned in *The Road to Serfdom* in 1944 that even the softer idea of "social democracy" was an oxymoron. Once the state attempted to plan economic life, it had to do so through arbitrary power, sacrificing individual liberty and democracy itself: "a socialist government must not allow itself to be too much fettered by democratic procedure," Hayek wrote.[68]

The idea of democratic socialism could persist as a pleasant utopia only where it was never actually tested by governing, in a prosperous society where activists could depend on altruistic contributions from the surplus wealth of successful, perhaps guilt-ridden, capitalists. But from the safety of the academy, democratic socialism had a profound influence on successive generations of young politically minded Americans.

One of them was Barack Obama, who became a community organizer in Chicago after graduating from Columbia University where he was exposed to radical politics in New York. Obama did not join the Democratic Socialists of America, as some other Democrats did, but he did seek the endorsement of the socialist New Party in 1996 when he ran for the Illinois State Senate, and he may actually have joined the party organization itself, a fact his presidential campaign later obscured.[69]

There was good reason for Obama to conceal his socialist ties. Democratic socialism remained a marginal movement—until 2019, when the emerging Democratic presidential field looked like a casting call for a Politburo pantomime. If Debs had been able to travel forward in time, he would have been delighted.

To borrow a phrase coined by columnist George F. Will to explain the election of Ronald Reagan,[70] after conservative Barry Goldwater's resounding defeat to President Lyndon B. Johnson in 1964, Debs had actually won the 1912 presidential election—it just took 108 years to count all of the votes.

By November 2020, either Democrats would regret lurching so far to the left that they reelected Donald Trump—or Republicans would be aghast at the first openly socialist U.S. government.

THE ROAD TO SOCIALISM

How did we arrive at this point?

Anyone old enough to remember voting in the 1990s may also remember that the common complaint was that the two major parties had converged. President Bill Clinton had run for the White House in 1992 as a pro-business Democrat. His liberal policies—such as "Hillarycare"—had cost his party control of Congress in 1994, but he moved back to the middle—so much so that Republicans grumbled that he had stolen their core policy positions.

The holy grail of American politics at the time was the "soccer mom"—the suburban, middle-class, female voter, sensitive to social issues but primarily concerned about economic issues and nervous about crime. The old Democratic Party—with its loyalty to Big Labor and the failed policies of Lyndon Johnson's Great Society—was too left-wing for these voters.

In the aftermath of Ronald Reagan's victories in the 1980s, the "New Democrats" emerged to pull the party to the center. Led by the Democratic Leadership Council (DLC), the New Democrats combined enthusiasm for free markets and free trade with support for a stable safety net and liberal social policies.

Even as late as 2004, with the antiwar movement newly resurgent in response to President George W. Bush's policies in the Middle East, Democrats turned to Senator John Kerry (D-MA), a Vietnam War veteran who was supposedly more moderate than liberal contenders like Vermont governor Howard Dean. (As one campaign button put it: "Dated Dean—Married Kerry.")[71]

But after Kerry lost to incumbent President George W. Bush, a new group of left-wing activists—the "netroots"—made use of new technological tools, such as blogs and online fundraising, to take over the party. They made Dean chair of the Democratic National Committee (DNC) and fueled the party's 2006 midterm election win.

It was Obama who finally broke the mold. Obama took on not only the Clinton machine but also the conventional model of American politics. Rather than running to the center of the political spectrum, Obama presented Americans with unabashedly left-wing policies and radical perspectives on American society—which, he said, needed to be "fundamentally transform[ed]."[72]

Obama was skillful at cloaking his ideas in moderate rhetoric and the gauzy language of "hope and change." But his core supporters knew his true views—on gay marriage, on gun control, on government-run health care, and on other issues. Arguably, Obama's quiet, unwavering conviction to a set of left-wing principles allowed him to project an image of stability throughout the 2008 financial crisis that eventually ushered him into office.

Crucially, when Democrats lost the House of Representatives to the Tea Party–fueled GOP in the 2010 midterm elections, Obama did not triangulate, as Clinton had done. Rather, Obama doubled down on left-wing policies. He picked up the class warfare themes of the Occupy Wall Street movement, which cast American politics as a struggle between the "99 percent and the 1 percent." He urged Americans to vote against an alternative that represented the "privileged few."[73]

In so doing, Obama was applying the lessons he had learned during his years as a community organizer, in Alinsky style. He was also putting into practice the conclusions he had drawn from watching Chicago's mayor Harold Washington, who had become the city's first black mayor in 1983.[74] Washington had been stymied in his first term by white "ethnic" Democrats, many of whom were from the old Chicago machine and resented the rise of a black newcomer. So he made only incremental changes, using his executive powers where he could.

After several years of "Council Wars," the fever broke, and Washington won a narrow majority among the aldermen. In 1987, he was reelected to a second term—but promptly died of a heart attack, his progressive potential unfulfilled.

Obama was determined not to repeat that mistake. Like Washington, he would use executive powers to circumvent an opposition that he (mistakenly, in Obama's case) saw as racist. But unlike Washington, he would make big changes, lest he miss the opportunity.

Obama pushed the American system past its limit—though few within the mainstream media would acknowledge that he had done so. So many journalists agreed with Obama's policy goals that they failed to notice or protest when he exceeded his executive powers to help illegal aliens, evaded the Constitution to push through the Iran nuclear deal, or failed to cultivate consensus in favor of major new entitlements like Obamacare.[75] And when things went wrong, they rarely held him accountable.

It did not matter. In his election, and reelection, Obama taught Democrats that if the party was prepared to fight for its true values, it could win. He showed that governing was less important—at least, to a Democrat—than having the right beliefs. Obama's brand of politics was a secular faith: the important thing was to believe hard enough.

THE SHELL-SHOCKED CENTER

The party had not believed hard enough in Hillary Clinton. And perhaps she had not believed hard enough in the party or what its activist base wanted to achieve.

On paper, as her most earnest supporters often noted, she was among the most qualified people ever to have sought the presidency. She had made the leap from the ceremonial post of first lady to U.S. senator from New York and won reelection. She had nearly been her party's nominee in 2008 before settling into the new administration as secretary of state.

But her past support for the Iraq War haunted her in the 2008 primary and continued to do so in 2016. Worse, the party alienated some of its own voters by mishandling the entire nomination process. Clinton probably could have defeated Bernie Sanders in a fair fight, yet her backers in the DNC rigged the primary anyway. They leaked debate questions to her,[76] suppressed dissent at the Democratic National Convention in Philadelphia,[77] and even used anti-Semitic rhetoric in a dubious ploy to stir hostility to Sanders among the supposedly bigoted voters of Appalachia.[78]

At one point during the convention, as the roll call to nominate Clinton was complete, hundreds of Sanders supporters staged a walkout, barricading themselves inside the media center across from the plenary arena. I had been tipped off to the protest, called #Demexit (in homage to Brexit, which voters in the United Kingdom had passed just weeks before). Some Sanders delegates chanted, "This is what democracy looks like!"; others were silent, standing with tape over their mouths. Some held signs reading "Stolen election," "DNC lost most of us for good," and "The Democratic Party just elected Donald Trump."[79]

When Trump won on November 9, it was a surprise to much of the nation and a deep shock to the Democratic Party and the media who had confidently predicted a Clinton victory. But it was less of a shock to many Sanders supporters. Some Sanders voters—especially in the Upper Midwest, where both Sanders and Trump had stressed their opposition to free trade deals—had quietly crossed over and voted for the GOP ticket.[80]

The progressive base of the Democratic Party may have hated Trump just as much as members of the more moderate, establishment wing did. But the left understood that Trump was using many of their issues and their grievances against Washington and Wall Street.

Left-wing filmmaker Michael Moore saw it coming in his home town of Flint, Michigan. "Trump's election is going to be the biggest 'fuck you' ever recorded in human history—and it will feel good," he predicted.[81]

The Sanders wing of the party also believed that Clinton lacked the authenticity to connect to voters. And she had neglected Obama's example: though she tried to move left, she was not providing revolutionary new policies. She promised to break the "glass ceiling" that had held back female candidates—and that was good, especially when faced with a domineering male like Trump—but while identity politics thrilled pundits, voters wanted more.

The Democratic Party hierarchy, for its part, was shell-shocked. Everything party insiders thought they knew about the world was upended by Trump's win. Unlike the progressive base—the establishment had no way to explain what had happened, it was particularly susceptible to conspiracy theories about why Trump had won the election—from the influence of "fake news" in social media to the supposed influence of Russian "collusion" with the Trump campaign.

As the Brookings Institution's Shadi Hamid wrote of the "moderates" in the *Wall Street Journal*, "Democracy dies when one side loses respect for electoral outcomes. . . . Disrespect for democratic outcomes has become particularly acute on the center-left. . . . Many Democrats are unwilling to accept that Mrs. Clinton actually lost to Donald Trump. Those who find her standard center-left technocratic worldview congenial are disinclined to accept ideological explanations, so they look for scapegoats."[82]

The deep state, inclined to prefer the status quo, did Democrats no favors by unleashing the surveillance powers of the state against the Trump campaign and transition team. And the party establishment was no better served by the sympathetic mainstream media. CNN, the *Washington Post*, the *New York Times*, National Public Radio, and others served up a constant diet of stories presaging Trump's seemingly inevitable impeachment.

The world that the Clintons had built over more than two decades—their family foundation, the nonprofit groups, the academic network, the liberal policy think tanks, and the extensive web of personal and financial ties—was shattered by the election.

Instead of regrouping, many Democrats became preoccupied with what had happened in 2016. Many also believed some version of the nightmare that Hillary Clinton's campaign had been spinning for months—namely, that Trump's election represented the arrival of fascist dictatorship in the United States.

Meanwhile, the Sanders camp got organized. Again.

FREE-FOR-ALL

The 2020 Democratic Party presidential primary was to be defined by debate over a set of unabashedly socialist policies: free health care ("Medicare for All"), free college, free passage across the border, free jobs, free abortion on demand, and an environment free of fossil fuels (the Green New Deal).

Free everything, in return for nothing—paid for by taxing the rich. Some—notably, Bernie Sanders—admitted that they would tax the middle class, too, but claimed the savings those taxpayers would receive would more than make up for the burden they would be made to bear.

It was an extraordinary response to the defeat of 2016, in which large portions of the American electorate, particularly in the Upper Midwest, appeared to have shifted to the right. Counties that Barack Obama had won twice in the Rust Belt chose Trump instead. The Republican nominee—once a Democrat himself—won states like Michigan, Wisconsin, and Pennsylvania, which had eluded the GOP since the era of Democrat-turned-Republican Ronald Reagan.

That ought to have spurred reflection among Democrats as to whether their party's increasingly "progressive" policies had alienated the middle-class voters they claimed to represent.

Instead, the opposite happened: the 2020 candidates stampeded to the left.

Even Joe Biden rejected the "moderate" label, telling reporters that he was still a "liberal" in a changing party: "For my whole career, I wish had been labeled in Delaware, for the seven times I ran, as a 'moderate'." He lamented the shift, noting sardonically: "The definition of 'progressive' now seems to be changing. That is, 'Are you a socialist? Well, that's a real progressive.'"[83] He rejected the conventional labels, calling himself "an Obama-Biden Democrat" instead.[84]

Of course, Obama was partly responsible for the party's ideological shifts. And there were also other factors.

One was simply that the Cold War had faded too far from the memory of many Americans—particularly younger ones—to make them fear socialism or even understand it. Contemporary examples of failure like Venezuela or struggling South Africa (where communists sat in government) notwithstanding, young Americans polled in 2014 said they did not trust government but wanted more of it.[85] By 2019, one poll found that 61 percent of Americans ages 18 to 24 had a positive reaction to "socialism" while just 58 percent had a positive reaction to the word "capitalism"; the difference was barely within the poll's 3.5 percent margin of error (among 2,777 adults).[86]

College campuses became increasingly dominated by the left, as the radical protesters from the 1960s had returned by the 1990s to teach and to lead, shaping new generations in their image. Many young Americans yearned for a larger cause like the civil rights struggle or the Vietnam War had been for their parents, a cause that they could make their own.

Other cultural changes also pulled Democrats to the left. The gay rights movement, having won the right to marriage nationwide, pressed further. Gender could no longer be driven by biology. No lesbian, gay, bisexual, transgender, queer (LGBTQ) person could be free, it seemed, until the old norms were overthrown. Tolerance was no longer the goal: society itself had to be transformed.

Two catalytic events had also shaped the views of young Americans. One was the Iraq War, which the majority of Americans had originally supported but which many came to oppose as the rebuilding effort failed and fighting bogged down in counterinsurgency. Because there was no draft, the war did not have the same sweeping social effects as the Vietnam War had, but it eroded the trust that many Americans had in the traditional leaders and institutions that had originally made the case for intervention.

The other major event was the Great Recession of 2007–2009. When the housing bubble burst, it took with it the American dream of homeownership for many people. The policies of the Obama administration, which emphasized regulation and redistribution, slowed the economic recovery. Many young people, weighed down by student loans, came of age in an era when the free market seemed far less attractive than the proffered ideal of a society well managed by intelligent bureaucrats. Others, conversely, living—under Trump—through what proved to be the longest economic recovery in the history of the country, became convinced that the country could afford to do more to help the poor. To many young Americans, socialism seemed both necessary—and affordable, given the political will.

Another factor tempting Democrats to the left was Trump himself. The fact that he had won against all expectations and that he continued to defy rhetorical conventions (even though, more quietly, he was arguably more scrupulous than his predecessor about observing constitutional limits)[87] unleashed the dreams of the left.

Democrats had watched the other side win an astonishing victory. More amazing, Trump—defying opposition, as Obama had done—had fulfilled his campaign promises to his conservative base. In so doing, he had liberated the left to think about what might be possible when they regained power.

Why not campaign openly on the radical agenda at which Obama had only hinted?

FOUR

PRELUDE

"Back when the Democratic primary still had more candidates than a shot of the debate stage could comfortably hold—including Julián Castro, Cory Booker, Kamala Harris, Andrew Yang, Jay Inslee, Eric Swalwell, Kirsten Gillibrand, Pete Buttigieg, Amy Klobuchar, John Delaney, Michael Bennet, and even Marianne Williamson and Tulsi Gabbard—I remember thinking that whatever else might happen, this much at least was true: The Democratic Party had a deep bench of competent contenders. That seemed like good news, and so did this: The agendas most of these folks offered were considerably to the left of any I'd heard before."
—Writer Lili Loofbourow, *Slate*, March 4, 2020[88]

AN ENORMOUS FIELD

The field of contenders for the Democratic Party nomination to challenge President Donald Trump in 2020 was the largest and most diverse ever presented to the American public. Over two dozen candidates had thrown their proverbial hats into the ring by mid-2019. Two more candidates—both serious contenders, largely by virtue of their vast wealth—would join the fray by year's end.

They came from an astonishing variety of backgrounds. African American and Latino, Jewish and Hindu, male and female, gay and straight: almost every conceivable category was represented. The youngest was 37; the oldest was 77. There were governors and mayors, senators and representatives, businessmen and veterans—even a spiritual guru.

By the end, the choice proved to be shockingly conventional: former vice president Joe Biden versus Senator Bernie Sanders, two aging white men, representing the clash between the party establishment and the insurgent grass roots. Between them, they had spent nearly a century in public office.

All that was still far into the future at the start of a race that attracted a multitude of participants for two reasons: if Donald Trump could do it, anyone could; and if any president could be beaten, he could.

There was early favorite Senator Kamala Harris (D-CA), the country's only female African American senator, who had begun campaigning for the nomination almost from the moment she arrived in Washington. There was Senator Elizabeth Warren (D-MA), a former Republican and Harvard Law School professor who had built a national reputation by taking on Wall Street in the aftermath of the financial crisis. There was South Bend, Indiana, mayor Pete Buttigieg, making history as the first openly gay candidate for president. And there was Senator Amy Klobuchar (D-MN), who was less well known but managed to stay in the hunt much longer than anyone expected.

As for the others: some were often more amusing than amazing.

There was Representative Eric Swalwell (D-CA), known for his enthusiastic pursuit of claims of "Russian collusion" against the president, declaring at one point that Trump was a Russian "agent."[89]

Senator Kirsten Gillibrand (D-NY) attempted to mount a campaign by appealing to disaffected female voters still furious over Hillary Clinton's defeat. Joining her from New York was New York City mayor Bill de Blasio. Like Sanders, he was a socialist—one who had honeymooned in Cuba before eventually finding himself in Gracie Mansion—the mayor's expansive house on Manhattan's Upper East Side—after the implosion of former representative Anthony Weiner's comeback mayoral campaign in 2013. Senator Cory Booker (D-NJ), from nearby New Jersey, had built an unlikely profile as mayor of Newark, but struggled to gain national traction.

Former Housing and Urban Development secretary Julián Castro launched a campaign pitched directly at Latino voters. He made an early trip to Puerto Rico to show solidarity with the hurricane-ravaged island— whose residents, while U.S. citizens, could only vote in the primary, not the general election.

Businessman Andrew Yang developed a cult following that saw him qualify for most of the debates through the New Hampshire primary. His core campaign promise was a socialist fad called universal basic income—a promise to pay each American citizen $1,000 per month— that had caught on among the guilt-ridden hyper-billionaires of Silicon Valley.

Former representative Beto O'Rourke (D-TX) had thrilled Democrats nationwide when he challenged conservative Senator Ted Cruz (R-TX) in the 2018 midterm election, losing narrowly. He had the odd habit of live-streaming deeply personal events, such as haircuts, flu shots, and dental cleanings. Even left-leaning journalists found that too hard *not* to mock.[90]

And then there was Marianne Williamson, a best-selling author who had befriended Hollywood's A-list en route to a political career. She led crowds of supporters in chants about love and told Americans they owed $500 billion in reparations for slavery.

There were a few self-described moderates, but they fared poorly. When former representative John Delaney (D-MD) criticized government-provided health care—Medicare for All—and Colorado governor John Hickenlooper declared "socialism is not the answer" at the California Democratic Party's 2019 convention, they were booed off the stage.[91]

It was difficult not to be entertained—and one almost wished for the carnival to last through the entire election.

Most seemed to share the conviction that Trump's election had been, at best, a fluke—and, at worst, the result of a nefarious Russian conspiracy. "I believe history will look back on four years of this president and all he embraces as an aberrant moment in time," Biden said,[92] promising a return to the status quo ante.

Many, nonetheless, saw it as an opportunity. In 2008, then president-elect Barack Obama's incoming chief of staff, Rahm Emanuel, famously declared: "You never want a serious crisis to go to waste."[93] Likewise, several Democratic candidates saw the 2020 election as a moment ripe with revolutionary potential.

Regardless, all were united by a common purpose: getting rid of Donald Trump.

THE RESISTANCE ARRIVES IN WASHINGTON

"We're gonna impeach the motherfucker!"

So declared newly sworn-in Representative Rashida Tlaib, on her first day in office, to the lusty cheers of a crowd of supporters at a party hosted by the left-wing activist group MoveOn.org.[94]

The new Democratic Party majority in the House of Representatives owed much to the election of candidates in suburban districts who were moderate in their temperament, if not in their views.

But the party's effort had undoubtedly been motivated by the Resistance and the emergence of charismatic new leaders.

Representatives Alexandria Ocasio-Cortez, Ayanna Pressley, Tlaib, and others had replaced old party stalwarts with their new brand of uncompromising left-wing politics. Many identified openly as democratic socialists. They were unabashed in their insistence that Trump be impeached and that the country adopt urgent, progressive policies.

Speaker of the House Nancy Pelosi (D-CA), newly restored to that position after losing the gavel in the Tea Party wave of 2010, had clung to power within her diminished party for several successive elections in the hopes of regaining control of the chamber. During the midterm election, she had done all she could to discourage talk of impeachment, for fear of alarming the public. She let it be known publicly that she disapproved of the efforts of billionaire left-wing donor Tom Steyer,[95] for example, who backed pro-impeachment candidates and spent more than $100 million on his Need to Impeach campaign.[96]

But hope of undoing the 2016 election, one way or another, was the motivating force behind Democrats' campaign. "Moderate" candidates like Katie Hill, challenging incumbent Representative Steve Knight (R-CA) in suburban Ventura County, let it be known that she was a gun owner. But she also turned up at the U.S. Supreme Court to join left-wing and pro-choice activists in demonstrations against the confirmation of Justice Brett Kavanaugh.[97]

Even "moderate" incumbents had been moved by the new spirit of total, unrelenting opposition. Representative Ted Lieu (D-CA), a mild-mannered U.S. Air Force Reserve colonel first elected in 2014, had once shown an independent streak. In 2015, he was one of the few Democrats to oppose President Obama's ill-fated nuclear deal with Iran. Lieu even published a thoughtful twenty-three-page policy paper explaining in meticulous detail the reasons for his decision to oppose the agreement.[98]

But Trump's election turned the moderate Lieu into a fire-breathing radical. He posted a "Cloud of Illegitimacy Clock" on his congressional website in January 2017, arguing that President Trump was illegitimate, partly because of allegations that Russia had colluded in his election.[99] Lieu also criticized the president incessantly on Twitter, earning praise— and donations—from fellow Democrats, though managing to shock even his own mother.

"Lieu's mother," the Associated Press reported, "said he never showed such aggressiveness earlier in life, describing her son as a quiet man who never talked back to his parents and never mistreated his younger brother."

All it took was Donald Trump.[100]

Though the new arrivals on Capitol Hill often deferred to Pelosi, they extracted a price for their political support. One such arrangement, apparently, was the appointment of Representative Ilhan Omar (D-MN) to the House Foreign Affairs Committee.

Omar had a long history of radical anti-Israel rhetoric. She had called

Israel an "apartheid regime,"[101] and during Israel's war in 2014 against Hamas terrorists in Gaza, she tweeted: "Israel has hypnotized the world, may Allah awaken the people and help them see the evil doings of Israel."[102]

The Jewish community in Minneapolis—the largest outside Chicago—was so concerned about Omar's possible arrival in Washington that they staged an intervention in an attempt to learn more about her views and discourage her from using vitriolic anti-Israel language.

"Most of us came out of that conversation very troubled by the answers we received," said state legislator Ron Latz, a Democrat.[103] "I was not convinced she was going to give a balanced approach to policy in the Middle East, and I was not convinced…where her heart is on these things."

Omar initially toned down some of her anti-Israel policies. She told voters that she would oppose the anti-Israel "boycott, divestment, sanctions" (BDS) movement because it was "not helpful in getting that two-state solution." But after the November 2018 election, she came out in support of BDS, in what the left-wing *Forward* reported "seemed like a bait-and-switch to many Jewish Minnesotans."[104]

Pelosi and other Democratic leaders openly opposed BDS. Moreover, given Omar's past extreme anti-Israel rhetoric, she arguably had no place on the Foreign Affairs Committee.

But the Resistance had to be appeased. It was an appointment Democrat leaders seemed to regret[105] but not one they were willing to reject or reverse.

THE GREEN NEW DEAL

Perhaps the most significant impact of the Resistance on the new Congress, and the Democratic primary, came from Ocasio-Cortez in the form of the Green New Deal.

The representative-elect began talking about her proposed Green New Deal even before taking office. She tweeted in December 2018: "People are going to die if we don't start addressing climate change ASAP.

It's not enough to think it's 'important.' We must make it urgent. That's why we need a Select Committee on a Green New Deal."[106]

In February 2019, days after taking office, AOC released her Green New Deal legislation, coauthored with Senator Ed Markey (D-MA).[107] Its goal was to shift the United States from fossil fuels to 100 percent renewable energy sources by 2030—an absurdly ambitious and expensive goal. No cost was provided, but one study estimated it at between $51 trillion and $93 trillion over ten years—four times the existing national debt.[108]

The Green New Deal did not stop at the environment. The fight against climate change, the legislation declared, was "a historic opportunity—(1) to create millions of good, high-wage jobs in the United States; (2) to provide unprecedented levels of prosperity and economic security for all people of the United States; and (3) to counteract systemic injustices." It also promised "high-quality health care"; "affordable, safe, and adequate housing"; and "healthy and affordable food."[109]

The plan was built around the belief that climate change would be irreversible within twelve years—or, as AOC later put it, somewhat facetiously, "The world is going to end in 12 years if we don't address climate change."[110] Despite the urgency of the problem, she seemed to rule out a shift to nuclear or hydroelectric energy: the entire U.S. economy was to depend on solar and wind energy.

AOC, as the public face of the plan, became a lightning rod for criticism. As savvy as she was about branding, she was almost proudly ignorant of the commonsense details of life. In one Instagram live-stream video, for example, she professed wonder at her new apartment's garbage disposal; she, like many New Yorkers, had never seen one before.[111] (This was the woman who wanted to regulate the country's waste.) She also constantly hyped ordinary weather events—blaming climate change for a tornado warning in Washington, for example.[112]

Bizarrely, the Green New Deal echoed classic socialist, even communist, themes: the legislation mentioned "worker cooperatives," for example. An accompanying "frequently asked questions" document proposed eliminating "farting cows and airplanes"[113] and providing "economic security to all those who are unable or *unwilling* to work" (emphasis added).[114]

In one sense, AOC's plan was nothing new. The Obama administration had a plan for "green jobs," under "czar" Van Jones, who proposed working-class activists use environmental policy as a way to effect the "visible and dramatic transformation of the entire economy."[115] (That policy, once implemented, brought spectacular "green" failures as Solyndra, which manufactured solar cells; Fisker, which built electric cars; and A123, which supplied Fisker's batteries.[116]) But AOC's version was more attractive, with its allusion to FDR's popular Depression-era programs.

Almost immediately, AOC's Green New Deal won wide support among Democrats. Kamala Harris signed on as a Senate cosponsor. So, too, did Elizabeth Warren. "If we want to live in a world with clean air and water, we have to take real action to combat climate change now," Warren tweeted, conflating several unrelated issues.[117]

There were a few critics. Former New York City mayor Michael Bloomberg, who was considering a run for president at the time, panned it: "I'm a little bit tired of listening to things that are pie in the sky, that we never are going to pass or never are going to afford," he said.[118] Yet when he promised a supposedly more practical alternative, Bloomberg, too, used the phrase "Green New Deal." AOC's brand had stuck, even if the substance was shaky.

Democrats no longer felt ashamed to endorse a policy that called for the elimination of entire industries in the country's heartland, or to back the idea of government-backed jobs, or even to support the idea that people who were unwilling to work were still entitled to a guaranteed income. The idealism and the brand came first, the details later.

No one who wrote or supported the Green New Deal seemed to have any idea of how to implement it: they simply asserted that it was necessary and assumed that with enough political will—hadn't we put a man on the moon?—we would find a way to move in the right direction.

At one point, AOC's chief of staff, Saikat Chakrabarti, let the mask fall, disclosing to a fellow Democrat that the Green New Deal "wasn't originally a climate thing at all," adding that "we really think of it as a how-do-you-change-the-entire-economy thing."[119]

Democratic socialism was the true goal.

THE PRIMARY PROCESS

Thus the stage was set for the Democratic Party presidential primary—the long and often confusing process through which Democrats chose their nominee for the presidential election. (Republicans, too, had a primary in 2020, though it was contested only by a pair of marginal anti-Trump gadflies.)

In many other countries, particularly in parliamentary democracies, the parties simply hold internal elections. The leaders who emerge from that process—usually a one-time event—are presented to the public as candidates to lead the government.

The United States takes a different approach—largely because the election of the president stands on its own as a separate political event.

The nomination process is not a democratic one, though it has fundamentally democratic elements.

The two parties hold conventions at which delegates choose the respective nominees. But the process is more complicated than that.

Once upon a time, the conventions decided everything. They were occasions for close political combat, as delegates were courted by rival candidates in literal smoke-filled rooms. Nomination fights typically extended through several rounds of voting.

But over time, the process in each party was reformed—somewhat—to give more power directly to voters and to make the conventions themselves less consequential.

The essence of the presidential primary is a race for *delegates* to the conventions. Each candidate seeks to amass a majority of delegates who are "pledged" to vote for them. The delegates are allocated to the various candidates based on how many votes they win in primary elections in each state, though the rules in each state can be quite different. Some states use a rather typical voting process, where a voter enters a booth and casts a ballot (or mails it in).

Other states use a "caucus," where voters in a particular district meet and hear presentations from each of the different campaigns before consulting with one another and then casting their votes—sometimes by a show of hands.

The delegates are awarded to particular candidates according to methods that vary by party and even by state. Generally speaking, Republicans prefer a "winner-takes-all" approach, while Democrats use proportional representation (usually above a 15 percent threshold).

On the Republican side, there are 2,550 total delegates to the 2020 party convention, meaning the nominee needs to secure 1,276 delegates—a straightforward task for incumbent presidents with approval ratings within their own party that consistently exceed 90 percent.[120]

On the Democratic side, things are more complicated in 2020. There are 3,979 "pledged" delegates, meaning the candidates are chasing a majority of 1,991 delegates to win the nomination outright.[121]

But Democrats also have a system of "unpledged" delegates, known as "superdelegates." These are typically elected officials and high-ranking members of the party. The system was developed after the 1980 primary, when Senator Ted Kennedy (D-MA) challenged President Jimmy Carter, the incumbent of his own party, taking the fight to the floor of the convention in New York City.[122] The internal fight was thought to have weakened Carter, who went on to lose the general election.

The superdelegate system was meant to prevent any future insurgencies. But it faced a hard test in 2008, when then senator Barack Obama (D-IL) challenged then senator Hillary Clinton (D-NY). The Clinton machine had locked in many of the superdelegate votes. But the potential spectacle of insiders denying the first viable African American candidate a fair chance at the nomination was unacceptable. Civil rights icon Representative John Lewis (D-GA) switched his vote; others followed.

In 2016, Clinton again had the early support of the superdelegates. Bernie Sanders took aim at the whole superdelegate system, deriding it—correctly—as an undemocratic mechanism that allowed the party establishment to preserve itself. Clinton eventually won without it, but Sanders pushed for new rules for 2020. Superdelegates would vote on a second ballot, only if no one secured a majority on the first—an increasingly likely possibility as the 2020 primary unfolded.

Traditionally, the first states to vote are Iowa—which uses a caucus system—and New Hampshire. Nevada, the first in the West, and South Carolina, the first in the South, are next. Because of the outsized role these early states play in determining the course of the race, presidential candidates spend months—years, even—shaking hands and kissing babies in every rural hamlet and every diner, as their campaigns recruit volunteers and buy air time.

Along the way, dozens of televised town halls and several key debates among the candidates give voters in these early states and nationwide a chance to hear about their policies and watch them compete.

It is those interactions—on the campaign trail and the debate stage—that are the substance of the primary, playing out against the background of national politics, where our journey begins.

FIVE

THE MAJORS

"We are here because the American Dream and our American democracy
are under attack and on the line like never before. We are here at this
moment in time because we must answer a fundamental question.
Who are we? Who are we as Americans? So, let's answer that question.
To the world. And each other. Right here. And, right now. America,
we are better than this."
—Senator Kamala Harris, January 27, 2019[123]

"When government works only for the wealthy and well-connected, that is
corruption—plain and simple. It's time to fight back. Corruption is a cancer
on our democracy. And we will get rid of it only with strong medicine—with
real, structural reform."
—Senator Elizabeth Warren, February 9, 2019[124]

"Thank you for being part of a campaign which is not only going to win the
Democratic nomination, which is not only going to defeat Donald Trump,
the most dangerous president in modern American history, but with your
help is going to transform this country and, finally, create an economy and
government which works for all Americans, and not just the 1 percent."
—Senator Bernie Sanders, March 2, 2019[125]

"We are in the battle for the soul of this nation. I believe history
will look back on four years of this president and all he embraces
as an aberrant moment in time. But if we give Donald Trump eight
years in the White House, he will forever and fundamentally alter
the character of this nation—who we are—and I cannot stand by
and watch that happen."
—Former Vice President Joe Biden, April 25, 2019[126]

KAMALA HARRIS

Kamala Harris began running for president almost the moment that she
was elected to the U.S. Senate in 2016.

Donors to Hillary Clinton's campaign were already "buzzing" about
Harris by the summer of 2017, *The Hill* reported, when she courted them
in the Hamptons, the elite New York retreat. "She's running for president.
Take it to the bank," one reportedly said.[127] An early poll in July 2017
showed her narrowly defeating President Donald Trump.[128]

It marked a remarkable ascent for the first-term senator from California, who had yet to achieve much legislatively in Washington but had
built a formidable fundraising machine.

Harris specialized in turning confrontations with male colleagues
and witnesses before her committees into viral videos she would then use
to raise campaign cash.

In several hearings, Harris badgered witnesses such as Attorney General Jeff Sessions, interrupting him repeatedly during a June 2017 hearing
in which she asked him about possible communications with Russians
during the 2016 presidential campaign.

Sessions attempted to answer, mindful that Democrats had already
accused him of perjury.[129] But Harris continued to interject. Senator John
McCain (R-AZ) chimed in: "Chairman, the witness should be allowed
to answer the question." The chairman, Senator Richard Burr (R-MO),
added: "Senator Harris, let him answer the question."[130]

CNN described the exchange: "Once again, senators cut off Harris
as she rails on Sessions."[131] And Harris, in a fundraising message, claimed
she had been "silenced" by Republican men: "Too often women are

silenced in society and in the Senate. Make a contribution to defend the women of the Senate and fight back."[132]

Harris made several similar pitches after clashes she had instigated.[133] Those pitches were misleading but demonstrated her fundraising ability—and that she had powerful media allies to carry her message.

In a crowded field, Harris checked many of her party's boxes. She is African American, female, and the daughter of immigrants, born in Oakland, California, to graduate students from Jamaica and India. She grew up in Canada but studied at Howard University, immersing herself in the rich heritage of America's foremost historically black college (HBC)—referred to by author Ta-Nehisi Coates as "Mecca."[134]

Harris would face questions about whether she was authentically African American—just as Barack Obama had. For example, Don Lemon of CNN insisted: "All she had to do was say, 'I am black, but I'm not African American.'"[135] Harris pushed back: "They are trying to do what has been happening over the last two years, which is powerful voices trying to sow hate and division," she told a radio interviewer, adding: "I'm black, and I'm proud of being black."[136] And she campaigned that way, mobilizing the alumnae of her black sorority, Alpha Kappa Alpha, to canvas for support throughout the black community, especially in the South.[137]

Harris returned to the Bay Area to study law at UC Hastings College of the Law and served as a local prosecutor. She entered public office through her controversial romantic relationship with then speaker of the California State Assembly and San Francisco mayor Willie Brown.[138] Brown, who was married at the time, dated Harris and appointed her to two state jobs, salary included.[139]

She was elected San Francisco's district attorney and then California's attorney general—winning the latter thanks to late ballots in a close race that, on Election Day, she appeared to have lost. In the era before the Black Lives Matter movement, serving as a prosecutor was a reliable path to higher office, even for a Democrat—and most of Harris's high-profile targets were conservatives anyway. She prosecuted undercover journalists who exposed alleged efforts by Planned Parenthood staff to sell fetal tissue from abortions[140] and tried to force a group funded by Charles and David Koch (the "Koch brothers") to reveal their donors.[141]

She easily won election to the Senate, defeating fellow Democrat Representative Loretta Sanchez (D-CA), fighting her to a near-draw among Latino voters[142] after California's "jungle primary" delivered a general election without Republican opposition.[143]

An early warning about Harris's ability to sustain a long campaign came when her well-funded Senate campaign seemed in danger of running out of cash.[144] Notably, she had a habit of spending campaign funds on first-class airfares and high-end hotels.[145]

But Harris seized the initiative early in the presidential cycle, announcing her campaign on ABC's *Good Morning America* in mid-January 2019 and then drawing tens of thousands to a rally in Oakland on a sunny winter's day.[146]

"My whole life, I've only had one client: the people," she said.[147] "Our economy today is not working for working people," she added, one of several "truths" she promised to defend, promising to provide "Medicare for All" and "the largest working and middle-class tax cut in a generation" at the same time.

It was an ambitious agenda. And it set the tone.

ELIZABETH WARREN

Warren was the second major candidate to launch her campaign, calling for "big, structural change."[148] Like Harris, she had made the most of confrontations. When she called Sessions a "racist," violating the rules of the Senate, Majority Leader Mitch McConnell (R-KY) cut her off, explaining: "She was warned. She was given an explanation. Nevertheless, she persisted."[149]

The phrase "Nevertheless, she persisted" became her rallying cry.

But Warren's career contradicted the bleak picture of America that she often painted: it was a testimony to the possibility of upward social mobility in America.

As she told it, her story began in Oklahoma, in a struggling middle-class household, with three older brothers who joined the military.[150]

After Warren's father suffered a heart attack, Warren's mother went to work at a Sears department store, earning the minimum wage—which, she often recalled on the campaign trail, was enough at the time to sustain a typical household of three.

Warren earned a scholarship to college. After marrying, leaving school, and having children, she became a public school teacher, working with special needs students. Family life called again. She became pregnant and left teaching.[151] But she eventually enrolled in law school. And after practicing law for "45 minutes," she said, she returned to teaching—eventually reaching Harvard Law School.[152]

Politics beckoned after Barack Obama won the presidency, and Warren was appointed to oversee the administration's disbursement of the Wall Street bailout funds. She developed a reputation across party lines for integrity and political independence as she admonished government officials for lax oversight.

But her bipartisan appeal dimmed when she backed the Obama administration's plan to create a Consumer Financial Protection Bureau to oversee lending to households. The agency was to have virtually unlimited resources and would not have to report to Congress, raising objections from Republicans. They blocked the formation of the agency for years, preventing Warren from taking an appointment as its leader.

So she ran for Senate instead.

Warren challenged Republican incumbent Scott Brown, who had won a surprise victory in 2010 in the special election to replace the late Ted Kennedy. During that campaign, Warren was filmed telling voters at a house party:

> There is nobody in this country who got rich on his own. Nobody.
> You built a factory out there? Good for you. But I want to be clear:
> you moved your goods to market on roads the rest of us paid for. You
> hired workers the rest of us paid to educate. You were safe in your
> factory because of police forces and fire forces that the rest of us paid
> for. You didn't have to worry that marauding bands would come and
> seize everything at your factory, and hire someone to protect against

this because of the work the rest of us did. Now, look, you built a factory and it turned into something terrific, or a great idea—God bless. Keep a big hunk of it. But part of the underlying social contract is you take a hunk of that and pay it forward for the next kid who comes along.[153]

The video went viral and made her a star. It remained at the heart of Warren's appeal.[154]

Something else, however, that survived her 2012 campaign was the controversy over her alleged Native American heritage.

It emerged that Warren—pale white and blonde—once claimed that she was of Cherokee descent. In particular, she claimed Native ancestry while applying to work at Harvard, during a time when protests over faculty diversity were rocking campuses across the nation.

The basis for Warren's claim—one she may have believed—was family lore: her grandfather, or "Papaw," had told her one of her ancestors had been Cherokee. But she had no other evidence. She was not enrolled as a member of the Cherokee tribe or any other.

In pushing back, Warren made a series of blunders, the most serious of which came in the fall of 2018, when she took a DNA test and announced that, in fact, she may have had some Native American ancestry. The proportion was so small as to be insignificant—as little as 1/1024. She was no more or less indigenous than many white people. Warren eventually apologized for her debunked claims of Native heritage to the leadership of the Cherokee Nation in February 2019.[155]

Conservative bloggers called Warren "Fauxahontas." President Trump simply preferred "Pocahontas," and when she demanded he apologize for using what Democrats said was a racial slur, he apologized—to the original Pocahontas.

The "Pocahontas" issue damaged Warren's presidential prospects severely. Not long after her apology, for example, her campaign lost its chief fundraiser—a very bad sign.

However, Warren remained in the race, doggedly continuing to campaign and producing policy papers that applied serious thinking to the issues. Out of the ashes of controversy, she emerged as the "woman with a plan for everything."

Nevertheless, she had persisted.

BERNIE SANDERS

He seemed the most unlikely "revolutionary": a near-octogenarian with a decades-old stoop and an accent from the middle of the last century, an aging hippie still clinging to long-debunked dogma, leading a youthful army to the political barricades.

Born and raised in Brooklyn, Sanders found his way to the University of Chicago, known then (and today) as an intellectual haven. But he did not cloister himself inside the ivory tower. He joined—and was arrested in—the civil rights movement, participating in the Congress of Racial Equality (CORE), the Student Nonviolent Coordinating Committee (SNCC), and the iconic March on Washington in 1963. He had, literally, "walked the walk."

Later, Sanders relocated to the mountains of Vermont, living an ascetic life in a maple shack with a dirt floor. He never held a steady full-time job. He separated from his first wife, and he fathered a child, Levi, with another woman. He remained on the political fringe, even as Vermont became more and more left-wing.[156]

And then, in 1981, Sanders was elected mayor of the town of Burlington. His margin of victory was a mere ten votes. But he was the first public official in decades to be elected as a socialist, and attracted nationwide media attention. Sanders ran and lost for governor but won election to the U.S. House and Senate as an independent, albeit one who caucused with the Democrats.

When he ran for president in 2016, Sanders understood he had no chance as an outsider; the American system is theoretically open to multiple parties but in practice controlled by two. But running as a Democrat did not diminish Sanders's appeal. Rather, it expanded his audience. He appealed to Obama's core left-wing supporters: Sanders's 2016 slogan, "A Future We Can Believe In," even echoed Obama's "Change We Can Believe In."

Sanders had none of Obama's charm and was not interested in reframing radical ideas in terms more palatable to the average Midwestern voter nor in appeasing the Beltway. He didn't just want utopia: he demanded it.

As a candidate, much of Sanders's repertoire consisted of railing against the rich, the "1 percent." He favored confiscatory taxes on the wealthy. He promised government jobs with a "living wage."

No Sanders policy quite grabbed the imagination of his supporters like "Medicare for All." The idea tapped into the same dream that had propelled Obamacare: namely, the goal of universal, government-provided health care.

Obamacare was a halfway measure: as some supporters suggested, the system of complicated "exchanges" for overpriced private health insurance was intended to be a stepping-stone to a system of socialized medicine.

Sanders did not prescribe a "Trojan horse" but a quantum leap. And the suggestion attracted support: Medicare remains one of the most popular government programs. Though there are problems with "waste, fraud, and abuse,"[157] it has lowered poverty among the elderly dramatically.

Sanders did not pretend Medicare for All would be free. Quite the contrary: he acknowledged it would cost more. He declared, unabashedly, that his policy would raise taxes on the wealthy. When pressed, he even acknowledged that it would raise taxes on the middle class. But he argued that Americans would experience a net benefit, as lower health care costs compensated for higher income taxes.

Never mind that Sanders's own home state of Vermont had attempted its own version of state-sponsored health insurance. After a sincere effort lasting three and a half years, Vermont governor Peter Shumlin, a Democrat, abandoned the plan entirely in 2014, calling it "the greatest disappointment of my political life so far."[158] The cost was simply too high. Providing a "guarantee" of heath care would have destroyed the local economy.

But to Sanders, the question of Medicare for All was a political problem, not an economic one. What justified the policy was not cost-benefit analysis but Sanders's belief that health care was a "fundamental human right."

It was a policy he pursued with remarkable energy. Born in 1941, he was the oldest candidate but had displayed more passion than candidates half his age. His supporters were also remarkably loyal. In some ways, he was a victim of his own success. In 2016, he had been a unique figure. By 2019, he was inspiring many imitators—and almost all of the other candidates had moved toward his positions. In addition to being younger, many of the other candidates offered "diversity" in terms of gender, race, and sexuality. As the *New York Times* noted in September 2019 about Sanders, "He is no longer an insurgent, nor is he the only anti-establishment candidate in the race."[159]

But Sanders alone showed that democratic socialism was no obstacle to broad support, that an insurgent—once again—could challenge the party establishment, that the grass roots and the online community could not be taken for granted.

He also had recent history on his side: the establishment's conventional choice had lost in 2016. The left, if not the country, wanted to be led by a true believer.

JOE BIDEN

Joe Biden stood for the status quo ante—assuming he could stand at all.

Biden was born in Scranton, Pennsylvania, to a middle-class family who moved soon after to Delaware. He was an average student who avoided the Vietnam War through college deferments. He managed on charm and good looks rather than academic prowess, athletic ability, or actual achievements.

He had a knack for tall tales. He claimed, for example, to have played on the University of Delaware football team—but he had quit the team.[160] He was, by his own admission,[161] a mediocre student at college—though he had initially claimed in 1987, falsely, to have been an outstanding one.[162] During law school, he was nearly expelled for plagiarizing, a recurring habit.[163]

In 1972, Biden challenged an incumbent U.S. senator—and won, becoming the youngest senator ever at age 30. But in December 1972, before he took office, his wife and daughter were tragically killed in a car accident.[164] He suffered through the terrible pain of those losses and came back, climbing the greasy pole of politics through alliances with conservative Democrats. It was a pattern that would define him.

His congressional legacy was rather dubious. He took credit for the 1994 crime bill, later reviled by Democrats for leading to the mass incarceration of black men.[165] Like Hillary Clinton, he voted for the Iraq War, wrongly thinking it would build his credibility.[166] He had a lasting—and negative—impact on judicial appointments, destroying the confirmation of Judge Robert Bork in 1987 for his conservative ideological views. Biden was also perceived as unduly harsh toward attorney Anita Hill, who accused Supreme Court nominee Clarence Thomas in 1991 of sexual harassment.[167]

Biden also had a habit of touching—and sniffing—women at public events. Several women had complained over the years,[168] including former Nevada Assemblywoman Lucy Flores, who recalled in March 2019 that Biden had touched her shoulders, smelled her hair, and kissed her head in public, at a political event in 2014. She wrote:

> I felt him get closer to me from behind. He leaned further in and inhaled my hair. I was mortified. I thought to myself, "I didn't wash my hair today and the vice-president of the United States is smelling it. And also, what in the actual fuck? Why is the vice-president of the United States smelling my hair?"[169]

In 2019, a former staffer named Tara Reade claimed that Biden had sexually assaulted her in a Senate hallway in 1993, forcibly penetrating her with his fingers. Biden vehemently denied the claim, and the media largely ignored it.[170] Ironically, when Supreme Court nominee Brett Kavanaugh faced uncorroborated allegations of sexual assault from decades before in 2018, Biden had declared that women "should be given the benefit of the doubt."[171]

Biden also had a history of bizarre racial rhetoric. In 2006, he quipped that "you cannot go to a 7-Eleven or a Dunkin' Donuts unless you have a slight Indian accent. I'm not joking."[172] In 2007, he welcomed then-Senator Barack Obama to the presidential race by describing him as "the first mainstream African American who is articulate and bright and clean and a nice-looking guy."[173]

Biden first ran for president in 1988. He was among the serious contenders, but his campaign was tripped up when he was found to have plagiarized a speech by UK Labour Party leader Neil Kinnock. That early exit stung, but in 2007 he saw a way back to relevance. He proposed giving up on the Iraq War, dividing the country into ethnic enclaves, and bringing the troops home. It went nowhere, like Biden's campaign.

Donald Trump was fond of saying Obama had plucked Biden off the trash heap;[174] that fifth-place finish in Iowa was damning. But Obama needed Biden to add gray hair and gravitas to the ticket in 2008.[175]

In almost every other way, Biden was a liability. He was so gaffe-prone that Obama kept him out of the spotlight for weeks in the fall of 2008.[176] He struggled against the underrated newcomer, Sarah Palin, in their vice presidential debate.

In office, Biden oversaw the 2009 stimulus, a near-trillion-dollar package that lavished funds on pet projects and state and local governments. Biden touted beneficiaries like Solyndra, a solar firm both he and Obama visited. Within months of receiving government help, Solyndra failed.

Obama also tasked Biden with leading negotiations with Iraq about the U.S. troop presence. It was a thankless job: Obama was looking for an opportunity to leave—and did.

The only skill Biden had—schmoozing with senators—was one the aloof Obama did not care to exploit often. Biden was notable more for his antics—calling the passage of Obamacare a "big fucking deal" on a live mic, for example[177]—than for anything he actually did.

That said, Biden was an asset in Obama's reelection—almost by accident. He blundered his way into backing gay marriage, forcing Obama to do so as well, risking a backlash but earning the support of gay donors. He told black voters in 2012 that Republican nominee Mitt Romney would "put y'all back in chains"[178]—racist but effective. In his debate against

Representative Paul Ryan (R-WI), he triumphed with clownish gestures and sheer charisma.

Biden was good at one other thing: helping his family grow wealthy. "Amtrak Joe" was one of the poorest members of Congress—and one of the stingiest, giving precious little to charity.[179] But during his tenure as vice president, his hapless son, Hunter Biden,[180] who was lacking any qualifications or experience in the energy industry, was given a lucrative board seat on Ukraine's largest gas company, Burisma, renowned for its corruption.[181]

His other son, Beau, an Iraq War veteran who served as attorney general of Delaware, died of brain cancer in 2015, soon after he urged his father to run for president again. But Biden deferred to Hillary Clinton.

By 2018, it had become clear that unless Biden ran, Sanders would be the presumptive front-runner. That scared the party establishment and its donors. A Biden effort seemed almost necessary. At least, "normal" as understood by an "Obama-Biden Democrat."

Biden rejected the "moderate" label. He told reporters irritably that he remained a "liberal." What had changed was that "progressive" had become "socialist." And that, he said, he was not.

He was, he said, an "Obama-Biden Democrat. And proud of it."[182]

He was the one man who could hold together the fractious pieces of the coalition that had elected Obama twice.

Biden would restore "normal."

SIX

THE MINORS

"Change is coming, ready or not. The question of our time is whether families and workers will be defeated by the changes beneath us or whether we will master them and make them work toward a better everyday life for us all. Such a moment calls for hopeful and audacious voices from communities like ours. And yes, it calls for a new generation of leadership."
—Mayor Pete Buttigieg, April 15, 2019[183]

"We are all tired of the shutdowns and the showdowns, the gridlock and the grandstanding. Today we say enough is enough. Our nation must be governed not from chaos but from opportunity. Not by wallowing over what's wrong, but by marching inexorably toward what's right. That's got to start with all of us."
—Senator Amy Klobuchar, February 10, 2019[184]

"Under my plan, every American adult will receive $1,000 a month, free and clear, paid for by a new tax on the companies that are benefiting most from automation. If we provide a universal basic income, Americans will be able to go back to school, move for a new opportunity, start their own business, and really have their head up as they plan for the future."
—Entrepreneur Andrew Yang, February 2, 2018[185]

"For too long in this country, the powerful have maintained their privilege at the expense of the powerless. They have used...fear and division in the same way that our current president uses fear and division. Based on the differences between us of race, of ethnicity, of geography or religion to keep us apart, to make us angry, to make us afraid of ourselves and of one another, unrestrained money and influence has warped the priorities of this country."

—Former Representative Beto O'Rourke, March 30, 2019[186]

PETE BUTTIGIEG

Pete Buttigieg was only 37 years old and virtually unknown when he sought the nation's highest office. But he came closer than most of his rivals to winning it.

The mayor of South Bend, Indiana—only the fifth-largest city in his state—had never held state or federal office. He had lost a bid for state treasurer in 2010 and for Democratic National Committee chair in 2017. But by the second quarter of 2019, he led all rivals in fundraising, with $24.8 million. And after Iowa and New Hampshire voted in 2020, he would briefly lead the delegate race.

Despite his youth, his résumé was impressive. He was a Harvard graduate and a Rhodes scholar who had worked at the elite McKinsey & Company consulting firm. He was also a U.S. Navy Reserve veteran,[187] with one tour of duty in Afghanistan as an intelligence officer. He had been elected mayor, and reelected. And—almost as an aside—he was the first openly gay candidate to seek the Oval Office.

President Trump, in his characteristic style, reduced Buttigieg to one remark: "Alfred E. Neuman cannot become president of the United States."[188] Buttigieg said, perhaps truthfully, that he had to Google the unfamiliar insult. He understood his age as an asset: his slogan promised "a fresh start."[189]

Buttigieg was also the first "millennial" candidate for president. He volunteered for Barack Obama's campaign in Iowa in 2008, and seemed to imitate Obama in many ways: his preference for shirtsleeves over jackets; his Iowa-first primary strategy; even the tone of his voice on the stump.

Buttigieg had youthful exposure to communist thought. Obama had been influenced by the communist writer Frank Marshall Davis; Buttigieg's father had been a global authority on Antonio Gramsci, the Italian "cultural" Marxist. In college, he was active in Democratic Party politics and wrote columns for the Harvard *Crimson*, revealing a predilection for the left wing of the "progressive" spectrum.[190]

Buttigieg, who had dated girls in high school, came out as gay when he was 33. He married Chasten Glezman, a teacher, and happily indulged in (tasteful) public displays of affection on the trail.

His marriage, like his candidacy, showed how far gay rights had progressed as well as how radical the LGBTQ movement had become. In May 2019, a professor of women's studies at Yale University complained about how Buttigieg and his husband were posing as a potential "first couple," offering "a vision of heterosexuality without straight people."[191] Gay activists in Iowa told *Politico* that "Buttigieg didn't put LGBTQ issues and challenges more at the center of his policy prescriptions."[192] The exasperated candidate eventually had enough: "I can't even read the LGBT media anymore," he said.[193]

In one respect, however, Buttigieg shared some of their radicalism: his attitude toward Christianity. Buttigieg, who was baptized as a Catholic but is an Episcopalian, wrote his Harvard thesis on what he saw as the theological foundations of American foreign policy.[194] He refused to accept the weight of tradition on questions such as abortion and gay marriage, and he developed a conviction that his version of Christianity— liberal on abortion, tolerant toward same-sex couples, and concerned with economic redistribution—was authoritative.

That led to an intolerance evident in his bizarre, one-sided public feud with Vice President Mike Pence, well known for his evangelical beliefs. As the *Wall Street Journal* recounted: "Mr. Buttigieg went after Mr. Pence unprompted at the LGBTQ Victory Fund's National Champagne Brunch April 7. Referring disparagingly to 'the Mike Pences of the world,' the South Bend, Ind., mayor told the audience that the former governor has a 'quarrel' with him because Mr. Buttigieg is gay. Mr.

Pence's response? 'I've known Mayor Pete for many years,' he told CNN. 'I considered him a friend. He knows I don't have a problem with him.'"[195]

Buttigieg also attacked Republicans who opposed raising the minimum wage as "so-called conservative Christian senators" who were ignoring that "Scripture says that whoever oppresses the poor taunts their maker."[196] And he mocked Trump's claims to be Christian.

Ironically, Buttigieg faced similar doubts—in the black community. In 2012, as mayor of South Bend, he had fired the city's first black police chief in a dispute over racism in the department.[197] Black residents voted for Buttigieg but seemed ambivalent. "I ain't ever seen the dude," local resident Shawn White told CNBC, adding that nothing had changed for his neighborhood.[198] His poll numbers among black voters were abysmal, hovering near zero in some surveys.[199]

He inspired a core of followers and high-end donors, especially from Silicon Valley and the gay community. But the party's "progressive" wing saw him as a threat, an emissary of the billionaire class. Time would tell if he was a real contender—or, as critics said, an empty suit.

AMY KLOBUCHAR

Senator Amy Klobuchar (D-MN) was a "sleeper" candidate who ran a disciplined campaign that kept her in the race long after other, better-funded, and more charismatic candidates had long since dropped out.

The most remarkable thing about Klobuchar was her sheer resilience. She launched her campaign in a driving mid-February blizzard, standing outdoors in Minneapolis, one of the coldest cities in the United States. She devoted part of her speech to warning about the threat of climate change, prompting mockery from conservatives.

President Trump joined in the fun: "Amy Klobuchar announced that she is running for President, talking proudly of fighting global warming while standing in a virtual blizzard of snow, ice and freezing temperatures," he tweeted. "Bad timing. By the end of her speech she looked like a Snowman(woman)!"[200]

She took the president's jab as a badge of honor. On the campaign trail, she would remind audiences she had begun her journey "in the middle of a blizzard with four inches of snow on my head."[201] It was a visual symbol of resilience.

Klobuchar was born and raised in Minnesota, the granddaughter—she liked to say—of an iron ore miner and daughter of a famous sports columnist—though she preferred, on the campaign trail, to refer to her father as a recovering alcoholic. She attended Yale University and graduated from the University of Chicago Law School, interning for then vice president Walter Mondale along the way. Mondale became Klobuchar's "long-time mentor," and she remained close to him throughout her legal and political career.[202] Their long association prompted talk of Klobuchar as a vice presidential candidate long before the first votes had been cast.

Klobuchar took up private practice in Minnesota, joining Mondale at the Dorsey & Whitney law firm and attending to the affairs of large utility companies. In 1998, she won election to the office of Hennepin County District Attorney, where she built a reputation for prosecuting white-collar crime.

But as Breitbart News contributor Pete Schweizer wrote in *Profiles in Corruption*, her efforts depended "on what sort of white-collar criminal you were, and what sort of political connections you might enjoy." Klobuchar, Schweizer wrote, "seemed in her prosecutorial record to punch down by throwing the book at smaller fish, while avoiding prosecutions of larger and more serious criminal operators."

One fish she let go was Tom Petters, who ran a giant Ponzi scheme, second only to that of Bernie Madoff. He was, Schweizer noted, "in business with the Mondales" and was one of Klobuchar's "largest financial backers." He contributed to her campaign for U.S. Senate in 2006, and his employees in Petters Group Worldwide "had contributed more than $120,000 toward her successful bid." Despite "early warning signs" of Petters's scheme, Klobuchar looked the other way. He was only raided by the FBI in 2008, when Klobuchar was already in Washington. She called him after the raid. He was later convicted and sentenced to 50 years in prison.[203]

Klobuchar arrived in the U.S. Senate at the crest of Democrats' antiwar wave. She compiled a reliably left-wing record while cultivating an image as a pragmatist. She worked on bipartisan immigration reform in the ill-fated Gang of Eight bill of 2013, which passed the Democrat-run Senate but died in the Republican-run House.

But she also developed a fundraising technique, Schweizer reported, of "using her legislative agenda as a means of extracting donations from powerful corporations who wanted work done on Capitol Hill." She sought earmarks for contributors and wrote legislation designed to attract donations from special interests.[204] She boasted about not being "owned" by the pharmaceutical industry but fought for the medical device industry and raked in donations from law firms and lobbyists. Her "pragmatism" fit well with the way Washington has worked since the Gilded Age.

As the 2020 campaign began, Klobuchar joined the leftward stampede toward the Green New Deal, cosponsoring the Senate version of the radical proposal by Alexandra Ocasio-Cortez. She even chose the color green for her 2020 presidential campaign logo—a tribute, she said, to Paul Wellstone (D-MN), the liberal senator who was killed in a plane crash in 2002.[205]

But Klobuchar departed from most of her early rivals on Medicare for All, preferring the "public option" that allowed Americans to choose to join Medicare if they wished. She also stressed her ability to work across the political aisle.

Klobuchar failed to inspire on the debate stage—until the end—and her stump speech seemed designed to bore her audience into submission. Her strategy: provide an alternative to the radical rhetoric on display and then wait for an opportune moment when voters were ready to look elsewhere.

The question would be: Could Klobuchar seize that moment when it came?

ANDREW YANG

Entrepreneur Andrew Yang was one of many odd candidates in the 2020 presidential field, but he emerged as one of the most impressive, even if few expected he had any chance of winning.

Yang was born to Taiwanese immigrants, studied at Brown University and Columbia Law School, briefly practiced law—"I was an unhappy attorney for five months," he joked[206]—and entered the dot-com world. He founded an education company, sold it and then founded a nonprofit organization, Venture for America, to support entrepreneurs in America's inner cities. "By helping entrepreneurs create jobs in cities like Baltimore, Detroit, Pittsburgh, and Cleveland, we could create strong economies throughout the country and give children a reason to stay," he wrote on his campaign website.[207]

It was that experience, he said, that opened his eyes to the challenge that automation posed to the American workforce. American cities, after all, had been engines of prosperity until economic change saw jobs leave for the suburbs and overseas. Eventually, the people followed, leaving troubled communities behind.

He wanted to change that and believed he could.

Yang launched his presidential campaign a year ahead of the rest of the field, in February 2018. His message was "Humanity First," and he focused on the problems that technological advances could pose for a human workforce.

"Technology has already wiped out four million manufacturing jobs in Ohio, Michigan, Pennsylvania, and other states," he said in his campaign launch video, "and it's about to do the same thing to people who work in retail; food service and food prep; customer service; transportation; as well as industries like insurance, accounting, medicine, and law."[208] Yang was "deeply concerned" about a future with "fewer and fewer opportunities," where a "handful of companies and individuals" reaped the gains "while the rest of us struggle to find opportunities and eventually lose our jobs."

The remedy, Yang proposed, would be to provide every American with a basic income grant of $1,000 per month, which he called the "Freedom Dividend." It was to be "paid for by a new tax on the companies benefiting most from automation"—such as Amazon, for example.[209]

Yang's idea was not new. In fact, it had become fashionable in Silicon Valley among the tech elite, perhaps apprehensive about the new world their "disruptive" companies might be creating as they uprooted established industries. Facebook cofounder and CEO Mark Zuckerberg backed the idea in a speech at Harvard's commencement in 2017: "We should explore ideas like universal basic income to give everyone a cushion to try new things," he told graduates.[210] The city of Stockton, California, experimented with a $500 per month basic income grant, funded privately through a project run by Facebook cofounder and Barack Obama campaign aide Chris Hughes.[211] The Associated Press noted that Republican policymakers had run similar experiments in the 1960s and 1970s.[212] The results, though mixed, were generally positive.

But there was more to Yang's campaign than one idea. His style also attracted admirers. As the first serious Asian American presidential candidate,[213] Yang played into stereotypes. Where Trump had adopted the acronym MAGA for "Make America Great Again," Yang embraced "MATH" for "Make America Think Harder." "If you heard anything about me, you heard this: There's an Asian man running for president who wants to give everyone $1,000 a month."

He attracted a wonkish online army, dubbed the "Yang Gang." He gave esoteric talks about the "fourth industrial revolution" and mastered obscure facts and intricate details of policy, some of which were memorized by his supporters, who repeated them in call-and-response refrains at his rallies:

> YANG: One state actually passed a dividend...where everyone in that
> state now gets between one and two thousand dollars a year, no questions asked. And what state is that?
> CROWD: Alaska!
> YANG: And how do they pay for it?
> CROWD: Oil!
> YANG: And what is the oil of the 21st century?
> CROWD: Technology![214]

For all his focus on technology and entrepreneurship, Yang was hardly a centrist. Some of his policies were almost socialist. In addition to his plans for a guaranteed income, for example, Yang also envisioned a future in which Americans were compelled to use electric cars,[215] which they would not own.[216]

He did, however, adopt a more conservative approach to immigration than much of the rest of the Democratic field, limiting his $1,000 grant to U.S. citizens.[217] He also was one of the only candidates willing to support nuclear energy to fight climate change—even if he did offer one of the most alarmist predictions ever made about global warming, urging Americans to move to higher ground: "We are ten years too late."[218]

Yang did just enough to qualify for many of the early debates. It was a tribute to the power of his ideas—and the hunger for an alternative to the field.

BETO O'ROURKE

Beto O'Rourke's campaign would barely survive the summer of 2019. But he is included among the minor contenders—rather than among the also-rans—because he was an early favorite and helped define the field as a whole.

At the outset, O'Rourke was seen by many on the left as the potential heir to Barack Obama's "progressive" political legacy. The two shared the same aesthetic: breezy, high-minded rhetoric with a seasoned yet preppy look. In March 2019, *Vanity Fair* profiled O'Rourke for its cover story. In the photograph, O'Rourke stood outside a pickup truck on a dirt road, hands tucked into the back pockets of his jeans, his gray-streaked hair swept to the side. A pull quote proclaimed: "I want to be in it. Man, I'm just born to be in it."

The image seemed to allude to Robert F. Kennedy, whom O'Rourke resembled. Robert "Beto" Francis O'Rourke even shared the same Christian names as RFK; "Beto" was a nickname he had adopted as a boy growing up in the border town of El Paso, Texas. He attended Columbia University; dabbled in punk rock, bad poetry,[219] and computer hacking; and had brushes with the law, including an arrest for drunken driving at the age of 26. But he found his calling as a politician, serving on the local city council before winning a seat in Congress.

Beto married Amy Sanders, the daughter of a wealthy local real estate magnate, who funded O'Rourke's political ambitions. As the Associated Press noted: "O'Rourke, known as a down-to-earth champion of little-guy values, might never have made it on the national stage without the help of an intensely private tycoon who embodies the kind of figure top Democrats now rail against."[220]

Some admirers seemed to think Beto was Latino: there was some poetry in the idea that the country's first black president could be followed soon afterward by its first Hispanic president. But O'Rourke was Irish—as proudly documented by an Irish news website:

> Irish ghosts are powerful. They refuse to go away.
>
> It seems the ghost of Bobby Kennedy is now residing deep in the heart of Texas.
>
> . . .
>
> They are both liberal Democrats, they are both Irish, and they even look like each other. If someone told you that O'Rourke was Bobby Kennedy's son, on looks alone, you would not doubt it.
>
> But they also share a special gift. They can, like Abraham Lincoln at Gettysburg, speak off-the-cuff and make powerful statements to the American people.[221]

Much of the early coverage of O'Rourke was similarly glowing. *Vanity Fair* described his political "gift," the "near-mystical experience" of his power of extemporaneous speech.[222] O'Rourke agreed, describing himself as having been possessed "by some greater force" during an address in the course of his 2018 campaign to unseat Senator Ted Cruz (R-TX).

That race accounted for O'Rourke's national profile. The left hated Cruz, a hard-core Tea Party conservative—and loved the skateboard-riding O'Rourke. Moreover, Cruz had been weakened by the 2016 presidential campaign—less because he lost to Donald Trump, more because he declined to endorse Trump at the Republican National Convention, a decision seen by many Republicans as a betrayal.

Celebrities rallied to O'Rourke's cause. Hollywood raised money for him, and late-night comedian Jimmy Kimmel urged his audience to vote for him.[223] When O'Rourke defended National Football League players who knelt for the national anthem—"I can think of nothing more American," he said[224]—sports stars sympathetic to the Black Lives Matter movement showered him with praise. "Salute @BetoORourke for the candid thoughtful words!" tweeted National Basketball Association superstar LeBron James.[225] O'Rourke delighted fans—and provoked critics—by skateboarding onstage at political rallies; "BETO" T-shirts appeared in liberal enclaves from New York to Los Angeles.

In the end, O'Rourke fell short, but by less than 3 percent of the vote. Democrats imagined that, in a presidential election, O'Rourke might be able to flip Texas—finally!—into the blue column, virtually ensuring no Republican could win the White House for the foreseeable future.

O'Rourke launched his presidential campaign amid lofty rhetoric and great expectations. But his peculiar habit of gesticulating drew commentary from President Trump: "I've never seen so much hand movement. I said, 'Is he crazy or is that just how he acts?.' "[226] He also had the odd habit of sharing intimate personal moments on social media. O'Rourke once live-streamed a teeth cleaning on Instagram as he discussed health care policy awkwardly with a hygienist, his mouth full of dental instruments.[227]

Even friendly CNN noted that some voters saw O'Rourke as "light on substance."[228] What he lacked in position papers, however, he made up for in enthusiasm: no audience was too small, no venue too distant for O'Rourke, who would leap onto the nearest table and begin speaking.

In time, he would find his message—and his target.

===

SEVEN

THE ALSO-RANS

"Almost any major intractable problem, at the back of it, you see a big money interest for whom stopping progress, stopping justice is really important to their bottom line. All these issues go away when you take away the paid opposition from corporations who make trillions of extra dollars by controlling our political system."
—Investor Tom Steyer, July 9, 2019[229]

"Jobs creator. Leader. Problem solver. It's going to take all three to build back a country."
—Mike Bloomberg campaign video, November 24, 2019[230]

"Being a pragmatist doesn't mean saying 'no' to bold ideas; it means knowing how to make them happen."
—Governor John Hickenlooper, March 8, 2019[231]

"I came to believe that the ultimate revolution was love. I came to believe that the ultimate revolution was spiritual change."
—Marianne Williamson, January 28, 2019[232]

THE BILLIONAIRES: TOM STEYER AND MIKE BLOOMBERG

The 2020 Democratic Party presidential field, while arguably the most left-wing in history, also saw the arrival of self-funding billionaires as candidates. No longer content simply to donate to campaigns, super PACs, or left-wing organizations, these wealthy Democrats wanted to take on Donald Trump personally. If he had done it, they could, too.

At first, they backed away. Starbucks CEO Howard Schultz, who toyed with the idea of an independent run, later declined, partly for health reasons.[233] Billionaire left-wing donor Tom Steyer, the top individual contributor to Democrats in 2014 and 2016, announced in January 2019 that he would not be running "at this time."[234] Fellow billionaire Michael Bloomberg, who had served three terms as mayor of New York City, also bowed out, in March 2019: "I am clear-eyed about the difficulty of winning the Democratic nomination in such a crowded field," he said.[235]

There were two factors that dissuaded them. One was the fact that former vice president Joe Biden was about to enter the race and would do so as the clear front-runner. The other—particularly in Bloomberg's case—was that the Democratic electorate had simply moved too far to the left. "Some have told me that to win the Democratic nomination, I would need to change my views to match the polls," Bloomberg observed.[236]

Both would later change their minds.

Steyer, who made his fortune in fossil fuel investments through his Farallon Capital fund, later became a climate change crusader. At one point in 2014, he convinced Senate Democrats—then in the majority—to hold an all-night talkathon on climate change on the floor of the Senate. It went nowhere, legislatively, and Steyer's money could not save the Senate from Republican control. He began to consider his own political future, first turning down a run for U.S. Senate and then for governor of California.

Steyer, perhaps thinking bigger, funded two major national super PACs. One, NextGen America, was aimed at registering millennials to vote (presumably Democratic). The other, Need to Impeach, focused on encouraging Democrats to oust the president. Steyer spent upward of $100 million, hiring a thousand staff members and recruiting two thousand volunteers, to advance the cause.[237]

Steyer—who fell to third in the Democratic donor table in 2018—was a constant irritation for Nancy Pelosi, who worried that impeachment might cost her a chance at returning to the Speaker's chair. But he continued and announced in July 2019—after the first primary debate—that he would be joining the crowded field after all.

Bloomberg, a self-made billionaire whose media company dominates financial journalism, had run for mayor of New York City as a Republican in 2001. He replaced Rudy Giuliani, who reached the two-term maximum as he was guiding the city through the aftermath of the September 11, 2001, terrorist attacks.

Bloomberg was regarded as a capable administrator, willing to continue some of the law enforcement policies that had made Giuliani both successful and controversial. One of these was "stop-and-frisk," which allowed police to search people for weapons and drugs, right up to the Fourth Amendment constitutional limits established by *Terry v. Ohio*.[238] The black community hated it, but Bloomberg defended it as necessary to protect the city's achievements in the fight against violent crime.

He balanced that law-and-order conservatism with nanny-state liberalism, infamously trying to restrict the sale of large sodas and to encourage breastfeeding for new mothers by urging hospitals to deny them baby formula.[239] He also migrated to the left, politically, becoming an independent and then a Democrat. In 2009, he repealed term limits, on the argument that the city needed stable leadership through the financial crisis. He won a third term—narrowly—and then backed a return to the two-term maximum.[240]

After leaving the mayor's office, Bloomberg put his fortune behind left-wing causes. He backed gun control efforts and candidates nationwide—so much so that left-wing *Mother Jones* accused him of "buying" the gun control movement.[241] He also funded state-level prosecutors with the special task of pursuing crimes related to climate change—an effort even some Democrat-governed states prohibited because it placed public prosecutors at the behest of a private interest.[242]

Presidential politics soon beckoned, but as he considered a run, Bloomberg found his views were far to the right of the field. He greeted the idea of Medicare for All by declaring that "you could never afford it" and that it would cost the country "trillions."[243] And he panned the Green New Deal: "I'm a little bit tired of listening to things that are pie in the sky, that we never are going to pass or never are going to afford," he said.[244]

In declining to run, Bloomberg mocked Biden and O'Rourke: "It's just not going to happen on a national level for somebody like me starting where I am unless I was willing to change all my views and go on what CNN called an apology tour."[245]

But in late 2019, as Biden appeared to falter and as Sanders surged, Bloomberg's calculations began to change. By November, he was in.

THE PROGRESSIVES

There were nearly twenty other candidates for the Democratic nomination. Some never had a chance.

Few heard of Wayne Messam, the African American mayor of Miramar, Florida—though his city was about 20 percent larger than Pete Buttigieg's South Bend, Indiana. Former West Virginia state senator Richard Ojeda ran a perfunctory campaign, as did repeat candidate Mike Gravel, a former senator from Alaska, who achieved early YouTube fame in 2007 for throwing a rock into a pond.[246]

Others who stumbled out of the gate were more serious political figures. Representative Seth Moulton (D-MA), a retired Marine Corps combat veteran, upset long-term incumbent Representative John Tierney (D-MA) in 2014 but could not find the same magic in 2020 despite the assistance of former Obama administration spokesperson Marie Harf. Former Massachusetts governor Deval Patrick, a late entrant, fizzled quickly. Former representative Joe Sestak (D-PA), once at the heart of national political debate, barely registered.

The remaining dozen or so could be divided into "progressives" and "moderates."

Senator Cory Booker (D-NJ) had once been a top-tier contender. A Stanford football player and Rhodes Scholar, he had built his political career from the ground up, starting as mayor of Newark before running for Senate. He attracted attention and donations from Wall Street and Silicon Valley. But he had few actual achievements and betrayed pro-Israel donors by supporting the Iran deal in 2015.[247] His biggest flop came during the hearings for Brett Kavanaugh's confirmation to the Supreme Court, when Booker announced he was defying Senate rules and releasing confidential emails about the nominee. It was, he said, his "I am Spartacus" moment. However, those emails had already been cleared for publication.[248] Voters found it hard to take him seriously after that.

Former San Antonio mayor and Housing and Urban Development secretary Julián Castro had expected to be Hillary Clinton's running mate in 2016, only to be passed over in favor of Senator Tim Kaine (D-VA). In 2020, he made a bold pitch for Latino voters, though he was not fluent in Spanish himself.[249] Though he impressed some observers, he never graduated beyond a discussion of vice presidential candidates.

Some candidates were focused on a single issue above all others. Governor Jay Inslee of Washington state ran a campaign entirely focused on climate change, calling it "the most urgent challenge of our time."[250] No less than Ocasio-Cortez herself called his climate change policy the "gold standard."[251] He struggled to distinguish himself from the field, however, and to pitch himself to a party in search—at least at the outset— of more diverse voices: "I have a humility about being a straight white male," he acknowledged.[252]

Senator Kirsten Gillibrand (D-NY) ran a single-issue campaign focused on gender in the wake of the Me Too movement. She infamously declared that Bill Clinton should have resigned the presidency over his affair with Monica Lewinsky—after years of having sought the Clintons' favor and fundraising help.[253] Gillibrand also backed the creation of a third gender, "X," at the federal level[254] and promised she would be the best candidate to explain the concept of "white privilege" to suburban female voters.[255] Perhaps those voters knew about it already.

New York City mayor Bill de Blasio, a standard-bearer for the left, also jumped into the race, once the field was already bursting with candidates. De Blasio led a protest inside Trump Tower in Manhattan as a lead-up to his campaign launch but was drowned out by counterprotesters chanting, "Worst mayor ever!"[256] Police officers, outraged by De Blasio's support for the Black Lives Matter movement, followed him around the country to demonstrate against him. He would apologize to voters in Miami for shouting a Cuban communist slogan at a union protest at a local airport: "¡Hasta la Victoria, siempre!"[257]

Representative Eric Swalwell (D-CA) was a long-shot candidate who had pushed the "Russia collusion" conspiracy theory inside the House Intelligence Committee. He tried to raise money by posting a video of himself changing his infant daughter's diaper[258] and referred to his toddler son as "my little male feminist."[259] He soon focused on gun control, provoking strong opposition from conservatives but significant support from left-wing activists.

Perhaps the most entertaining of the also-rans was author and spiritual self-help guru Marianne Williamson. In 2014, she ran for Congress as an independent, denouncing political parties. In 2020, she took her campaign for "love" to the battle for the Democratic presidential nomination. She had a devoted following of New Age fans—and delighted conservatives, for whom she personified the ultimate liberal stereotype.

THE MODERATES

There was no shortage of moderate candidates in the Democratic presidential field. But most of them never seemed to go anywhere.

Former governor John Hickenlooper of Colorado agreed with the "progressive" candidates about most of the issues. He backed universal health care, which he saw as a "right," and also backed dramatic policies to fight climate change.[260] He had also taken on the National Rifle Association in a state that had seen two high-profile mass shootings—one in a movie theater in Aurora, in 2012; and the infamous Columbine High School shooting in Littleton in 1999.

What made Hickenlooper different was that he had fought for left-wing policies in a "purple" state, one that had only recently made the transition from a typical Western conservative state to a more urbane, diverse, liberal one. Colorado had been a swing state in several successive presidential elections and would be a battleground state again in 2020. Hickenlooper offered a "pragmatic" style as an alternative to the one projected by the more ideological candidates in the field. "Being a pragmatist doesn't mean saying 'no' to bold ideas; it means knowing how to make them happen," he said.[261]

But pragmatism and compromise were not on the minds of many Democratic primary voters. Hickenlooper also had an attractive Plan B. First-term Republican Senator Cory Gardner was up for reelection in 2020, and Hickenlooper's chances looked far more solid in a Senate race than in a presidential run.

Fellow Western governor Steve Bullock of Montana was more of a full-throated moderate than Hickenlooper. He had the added distinction of being a Democratic governor in a conservative state that had voted for Donald Trump and would likely do the same again. He boasted a strong record as governor and argued that he could appeal to the independent voters and working-class Democrats who had chosen Donald Trump in 2016.

Bullock broke with those Democrats who were pushing Medicare for All and backed the idea of a "public option"—once the left-wing position but now considered a conservative view within the party. And Bullock had a hidden advantage in the early caucus state of Iowa: he had campaigned there in the past on behalf of Democrats in down-ballot races. But he would struggle to build a national profile and to raise money; he, too, ran for Senate instead.

Representative Tim Ryan (D-OH) kicked off his campaign in his hometown of Youngstown, Ohio—the kind of Rust Belt city at the heart of Donald Trump's 2016 victory. Ryan's approach was to keep the best of Trump's policies without the divisive edge of his politics.

"We have politicians and leaders in America today that want to divide us," he said in his launch speech. "They want to put us in one box or the other. You know, you can't be for business and for labor. You can't be for border security and immigration reform. Right? You can't be for cities and rural America. You can't be for the north and south. You can't be for men and women. I am tired of having to choose. I want us to come together as a country."[262]

Ryan believed what he said—so much so that he challenged Speaker of the House Nancy Pelosi for leadership of the party's House caucus after 2016, saying Democrats had become a "coastal party."[263] He lost that fight but hoped he would do better on the national stage.

Senator Michael Bennet, also of Colorado, overcame prostate cancer to enter the race in the spring of 2019. He gained some notoriety in early 2019 after a fiery speech on the floor of the Senate, attacking Senator Ted Cruz (R-TX) over a Republican-led government shutdown over border wall funding. But, he added: "I don't think it defines my time in the Senate."[264]

Bennet pitched himself as a "pragmatic idealist" and took on the "progressive" candidates directly, calling Medicare for All a "lousy policy"[265] and declining to endorse the Green New Deal, backing what he called a "Real Deal" instead.[266]

Representative John Delaney (D-MD) likewise opposed those two signature "progressive" policies. Drawing on his blue-collar roots and successful business career, Delaney proposed policies for new infrastructure and education for a technology-dominated age. And he believed the private sector, not the state, should lead, prescribing a "future where responsible businesses work with our government to lead the world not only in growth and innovation but also in positive societal change."[267]

But few in the party were listening. As noted earlier, when Delaney and Hickenlooper addressed the California Democratic Party's 2019 convention, the former criticizing Medicare for All and the latter declaring "socialism is not the answer," they were both booed off the stage.[268] In the fight between left-wing "Berniecrats" and the Clinton-era establishment, moderates were an afterthought.

THE ROAD NOT TAKEN

In addition to Howard Schultz, there were several important figures in the Democratic Party who chose *not* to run for president, though they might well have done so.

Foremost was former candidate Hillary Clinton herself. She had, after all, won the popular vote in 2016, enjoyed universal name recognition, and had the most powerful motive of all, namely revenge. In late 2019, one poll even listed Clinton as the top choice among registered Democrats, ahead of Joe Biden (though within the margin of error).[269] She seemed an attractive alternative to the field as a whole, especially as it began to narrow. And she never quite seemed to rule it out.

But another Clinton run was never likely. She had been plagued by health problems toward the end of the 2016 campaign. Moreover, the left-wing grass roots resented her—both for displacing Bernie Sanders and for losing to Trump. She remained a polarizing figure in American politics and the subject of Republican demands for congressional investigation. Though Bloomberg was said to be considering her as a potential running mate, that was the closest she would come to the race.[270]

Another who opted out was Stacey Abrams, the Democrat who lost her race for governor of Georgia in 2018 but refused to concede for many months, blaming alleged voter suppression for her defeat. Abrams remained a rising star in the party and was considered on the short list for vice president—especially late in the primary, when the only remaining contenders were white.

When Abrams decided not to run for president—or for Senate, declining an invitation by Senate Minority Leader Chuck Schumer (D-NY)—it seemed she was preserving herself for that role. In the meantime, she joined an organization called Fair Fight 2020, which would aim to prevent election authorities from removing from the rolls those voters who Republicans believed were ineligible.[271]

There was speculation that Democrats might yet draft a celebrity to run, in the event no candidate could achieve a majority of delegates on the first ballot at the party convention or if the front-runner was somehow incapable of serving—or if there was a revolt by the party establishment against Sanders. Former first lady Michelle Obama was considered a likely stand-in or perhaps billionaire entertainer and entrepreneur Oprah Winfrey. At several points, former secretary of state John Kerry, who had lost to George W. Bush in 2004, was said to be considering a run.[272] But none of these scenarios panned out.

Perhaps the most telling decision not to run came from Senator Sherrod Brown (D-OH). Brown had represented the Buckeye State since 2006 and was broadly popular, especially among union voters. Republicans considered Ohio essential for victory, and Trump had won it by a wide margin in 2016; Brown could have helped Democrats fight to take it back.

Brown fueled speculation about his intentions in early 2019, when he launched what he called the Dignity of Work tour, a series of speeches in several early primary states. The theme of the campaign was economic inequality: Brown attacked Trump's "phony populism" and demanded that workers should share in the benefits of the strong economy.[273]

These were the familiar "progressive" themes that had become standard in the Democratic Party's rhetoric since the Occupy Wall Street movement of 2011–2012.

But Brown was not "progressive" enough. As *Politico* reported in February 2019, Brown declined to back Medicare for All or the Green New Deal, the two radical policies being embraced enthusiastically by the early entrants to the presidential race.[274] While Brown supported "a green new deal" in theory, he would not commit to the "specific legislation" introduced in Congress. And he said specifically that he preferred incremental changes to Medicare, such as lowering the eligibility age—not an overhaul of the system.

Once, Brown might have been thought of as too left-wing to be a serious candidate for president. In the new Democratic Party, he was too moderate. And by early March 2019, he had abandoned entirely the idea of running for president.[275]

He foresaw the dangers facing the party on its present course. As he told MSNBC's Chris Matthews: "Of course we play to a progressive base.... but we have to talk to workers.... I don't think that our candidates are thinking of the general election," he warned.

"I think that there is a bit of one bird flies off the telephone wire and five more birds fly off the wire. I just [think] there is a little bit of that. I just want candidates to think for themselves and to move the country forward and think about the general election."[276]

Few were listening to Brown's sage advice. And the stampede to the left continued, taking the whole field—"moderates" and front-runners, too—with it.

EIGHT

THE FIRST DEBATE

"Who wants to lose the election?
All major Dem candidates raise hand in favor of free health care
for illegal immigs"
—Front-Page Headline, *New York Post*, June 28, 2019

HOMESTEAD

June 26, 2019. The sunshine fell hard on Homestead, Florida, like a muggy rain of sweat in the 96-degree Fahrenheit mid-morning heat.

A dozen activists stood near a tent at the corner of 124th Avenue and 288th Street, carrying handmade signs: "Keep Families Together" and "Never Again"—the latter a reference to the Holocaust, in which Nazi Germany and its collaborators murdered six million Jews and millions of others.

Several of the activists lined the curb across from the Homestead Temporary Shelter for Unaccompanied Children, a facility for migrant teenagers who had crossed the U.S.-Mexico border illegally.

Reporters huddled in the meager shade behind the activists; those holding cameras sweated under the weight of their equipment.

I walked up to a young man holding a sign and posed the same question I always ask—at Trump rallies as well as left-wing protests:

"My name is Joel Pollak, from Breitbart News. Can I ask what brings you here?"

He had begun speaking to me when a gray-bearded man bellowed: "Nobody talk to him. He's from Breitbart. He's not on our side." The young demonstrator made a sheepish face and turned away.

Great, I thought.

Suddenly, there was a shout: "She's here!" A scrum of cameras quickly surrounded Senator Elizabeth Warren as she descended from a van and strolled toward the street and the front line of the protest.

The night before, she had promised an activist at a town hall meeting in Miami that she would visit the demonstrators, who gathered daily outside the shelter to demand it be closed. And here she was, just hours before the first presidential debate.

A year before, President Donald Trump ordered a zero-tolerance policy, under which migrants crossing the border illegally would no longer simply be released into the country after their arrest (a practice derided by immigration hawks as "catch and release"). Adults and children who had been detained together could not be held together because of the risk of child trafficking or other forms of abuse.

So as the adults were arrested, the government sent the kids to shelters. Critics called it the "family separation" policy—and it was, in a sense, a deterrent to would-be illegal aliens. But the alternative was to detain adults with children—or release them into the country and into the "shadows"—in which case more people would brave the long journey from Central America, paying the smugglers and risking their lives.

The public outcry against Trump's policy was intense—triggered, ironically, by a classic piece of bad information—that is, "fake news": a photograph of children lying on a concrete floor behind a chain-link fence inside a Border Patrol processing facility.[277] The photo had been taken during the Obama administration, when a surge of children flooded the border. (Breitbart News had broken that story in 2014.)[278]

Democrats decried the "kids in cages," blaming President Trump for the crisis.

On this particular day in Homestead, by sheer coincidence, a news wire photograph had just gone viral: two migrants, a father and his 23-month-old daughter from El Salvador, had just drowned while trying to cross the Rio Grande from Mexico.[279] Breitbart News had done twenty similar stories over the years. This time, the media paid attention.

Someone produced a bullhorn; Warren took the microphone, in street activist style.

"This isn't what we should be doing," she declared, a tremor in her voice. "We will fight it with everything we have."

Shaking with emotion, Warren seemed to be channeling not just the outrage of the protesters but all the resentment her party felt toward Trump—all the lingering grief of the 2016 presidential election.

Reporters jostled for position. Two activists tried to prevent me from filming, holding a hat and a large orange sign, reading "FREE THE CHILDREN," in my way.

From somewhere—it was not clear where—a child was produced, a girl, wearing a sad expression. She approached Warren and embraced her. The cameras clicked and whirred.

Other children appeared, seeking the same consolation. One presented the senator with a handwritten note that she later read aloud on a Twitter video. ("Dear Senator Warren…I live with the constant fear of losing my parents to deportation. Please fight for comprehensive immigration reform so I can finally feel safe. And also, please shut down the detention centers.")[280]

Warren's visit lit up the news. Though she had not been the first candidate to visit the protest outside the shelter—that had been Rep. Eric Swalwell, widely thought to have no chance at the nomination—she had been surging in the polls for two weeks.

One candidate after another announced that he or she, too, would add Homestead to their schedule before leaving town.

One exception: the front-runner, former vice president Joe Biden, could not make it. He would try another time, his campaign said.

THE DEBATE STAGE

Back in Miami, the crowds arrived in the sweltering heat for the first primary debate, which was to be spread out over two nights to accommodate
twenty of the twenty-four candidates. Only those candidates who had
achieved 1 percent or higher in approved polls or had raised money from
at least 65,000 donors qualified.[281] The candidates had been assigned to
different nights through what organizers said was a random drawing.

On one side of the street was the opera house, where the debate
would take place. The media would be based on the other side of the street,
in the theater whose stage would serve as the "spin room"—the arena where
candidates or their surrogates would emerge after the debate to tell journalists how well they had done.

Trump supporters stood on the corner opposite, beneath a sign that
read "*Miami: No socialismo, no comunismo, somos capitalista.*"

Onstage, ten candidates stood at ten podiums. Several of the men
looked like carbon copies of each other—besuited, well-manicured figures from central casting. Elizabeth Warren stood out in a purple outfit;
Bill de Blasio towered over his lectern (appropriately, on the far left).

President Donald Trump, watching from Air Force One en route
to the G-20 summit in Japan, responded on Twitter with a single word:
"BORING!"[282]

And it was—because almost everyone agreed that what the country needed was more government, free health care, amnesty for illegal
aliens, and drastic intervention to stop climate change.

There were few fireworks. One rare, interesting moment came when
Tulsi Gabbard, a major in the U.S. Army National Guard Reserve, took
on Tim Ryan over Afghanistan, urging total withdrawal. John Delaney
offered a lonely, albeit passionate, defense of private health insurance.

Others struggled. Midway through an answer about whether a boom-
ing economy needed fixing, O'Rourke burst into Spanish. Senator Cory
Booker (D-NJ) looked stunned by the sudden shift in languages.[283] He
soon tried some Spanish of his own, but his accent was so bad that some
journalists burst into laughter. Julián Castro promised abortion coverage

for "trans female" patients—that is, those born without a uterus.[284] At one point, NBC was forced to suspend the broadcast and go to an unplanned commercial, after sound from the tech crew began bleeding over the main speakers.

Trump taunted the network from abroad, tweeting that NBC and MSNBC "should be ashamed of themselves for having such a horrible technical breakdown."[285]

Warren emerged as the winner of that first night. Partly that was because the moderators kept steering policy questions in her direction, and they never asked her about her false claims of Native American ancestry. But it was also because she channeled all the passion of the progressive left, bringing the energy of the crowd in Homestead onstage.

With Warren's rise, the pundits had a new question to ponder: Was the Democratic Party moving too far left to win in the general election?

The *New York Times* led its coverage with a front-page article: "Democrats Split on How Far Left to Nudge Nation."[286] The article noted: "The strength of the party's progressive wing was on vivid display in South Florida…Ms. Warren, the highest-polling candidate onstage, called for the government to bring to heel oil companies and pharmaceutical companies, and embraced the replacement of private health insurance with single-payer care."

The *Los Angeles Times*'s Janet Hook, similarly, wrote an article titled "This Is Not Your Father's Democratic Party: Debate Shows How Leftward It Has Moved."[287] She noted that the party had gone even further left than Barack Obama, who had been the most left-wing president since Franklin Delano Roosevelt, if not ever: "Candidates took positions to the left of those embraced by either of the last two Democratic presidents, Bill Clinton and Barack Obama, who was barely mentioned by any of the candidates."

Likewise, *Politico*'s John F. Harris, in an article titled "Democrats Lead with Their Left," added a subhead: "It's not an illusion: The party is presenting its most liberal face since the 1970s."[288] Trump was not even the focus, he noted: "This is a party eager to go on the ideological

offensive not just against Donald Trump (whose name did not dominate the evening even as he was invoked plenty) but against an economic and political power structure that candidates argued is deeply
corrupt."

"What Night One did was pick up the entire party and put it down
outside the mainstream and apart from the center," wrote columnist
Peggy Noonan in the *Wall Street Journal*. "Every party plays to its base
in the primaries and attempts to soften its stands in the general. But I'm
wondering how the ultimate nominee thinks he or she will walk this all
back."[289]

Simply put: the Democrats' 2020 candidates were the most left-wing
the country had seen in decades.

HOMESTEAD, REVISITED

The next morning, there were more candidates in Homestead.

Bernie Sanders arrived in a white van and stepped out into a media
scrum. A crowd of supporters, several dozen strong, greeted him. One
young man wore a hat featuring the outline of Bernie's famous hairline,
above the slogan "Hindsight 20/20." This election was a chance to make
up for the mistakes of 2016 by nominating Sanders—or, if not him, someone in touch with the "progressive" base.

Sanders ran through a list of condemnations and criticisms. No, we
should not be doing this to children in the United States of America. No,
these are not criminals; these are not terrorists.

He moved away from the van, around the corner, to a small patch
of ground on the shoulder of the road, in the coarse grass, squeezed
between the asphalt and a line of trees. The activists had set up a small
ladder there, atop which it was possible to peer over the fence on the
other side of the street and to see within the facility—and, occasionally, to
be seen by the teenagers inside, as they moved from one tent to another
or as they took their daily exercise.

Sanders walked toward it—quickly. The oldest candidate in the race,
it turned out, was also the sprightliest.

The media, carrying their heavy equipment, walked with him, a crush of cameras, a moving nest of elbows. Someone stumbled and fell, and Bernie stopped to allow him to regain his feet, a look of admonishment and annoyance on his face. Some journalists shouted questions: he answered a few but ignored my question about how he would propose to secure the border, given that he wanted to shut down shelters like this one.

He reached the ladder, climbed it, scowled appropriately, gestured across the street, and listened to one of the activist leaders as he surveyed the scene. He dismounted and walked back the way had come—to the gates of the facility, where he made a symbolic attempt to enter. He accepted a letter from a young girl—one of the same girls who had greeted Warren the day before. She was American-born, I learned after a few inquiries—not like the children in the shelter—but worried that her mother would be deported, thanks to Trump's policies. Bernie embraced her and left.

Half an hour later, Beto O'Rourke arrived. Tall, lanky, his hair flecked with dusky gray, he was coming off what was widely considered to have been a poor performance on the debate stage the night before.

In Homestead, though, he showed something of his strength as a candidate, asking the activists to explain everything, interjecting with intelligent questions. He took the media scrum back with him toward the ladder. For Sanders, it had been a perch, a vista: for Beto, the ladder became a soapbox, as he launched into an impassioned political speech.

We are, he said, quoting Robert Kennedy, a nation with a mission, a nation of exiles. We dare not—here, his tone became biblical—turn away the stranger.

He denounced the evils of the Trump administration's policy; he repeated his exhortations in Spanish. He took a few questions from the press—and more from the activists, who wanted his advice, wanted him to lead them.

"What will you commit to do right now?" someone shouted.

Well, he said, we will stand with them. They cheered.

He told the small crowd of a couple dozen activists to turn to face the migrant shelter with him, and wave in unison to the teenagers. "¡Somos *con ustedes!"* they cried ("We are with you!"). Whenever one of the teen-agers waved back or doffed a bright orange cap, the activists cheered.

Beto kept going: climate change had caused the border crisis by mak-ing it too hot to grow food down south, he told them.

He would not stop; he was in his element. It was too much for some activists, who retreated into what little shade was left at the roadside.

Journalists trickled away, too, but Beto was not eager to leave. This was a moment to imagine crowds of supporters, a moment to make up for what seemed to be lacking in his campaign.

The next day, more politicians would come—a large group of pres-idential candidates, to climb the same ladder, greet the same activists, perhaps accept the same letter from the same little girl.

A sign at the roadside identified the place as "Trump Tower Chil-dren's Prison: Homestead Branch." But it, like many of the other shel-ters, had been opened by Obama, who at least had felt compelled to show some perfunctory concern for border security, even if his rhetoric spoke of transforming the country and a "pathway to citizenship" and the "long arc of history."

Obama, at least, had feigned an interest in governing. Not these can-didates, not this time. Things had changed.

"WHO WANTS TO LOSE THE ELECTION?"

The second night of the debate——"more raucous but similarly extreme," Noonan would write[290]—featured Joe Biden, who was the front-runner for several very good reasons.

First of all, there was the simple factor of name recognition: after eight years as vice president, more people simply knew who Biden was.

Second, Biden was one of the few remnants of the Obama legacy: though Obama had not endorsed him—yet—in 2020, Obama had cer-tainly put him on the ticket in 2008.

There was also another factor: Biden was the supposed "moderate," the one who would be a counterweight to the runaway socialism of the rest of the pack.

Earlier in the year, as I watched Bernie Sanders address an audience of about a thousand students and workers at a labor strike on a street corner near the University of California, Los Angeles, I imagined that the party's remaining pro-business, high-dollar donors had to be beating down Biden's door, virtually begging him to run in 2020.

They did, and Biden declared his candidacy in April 2019, instantly surging to a wide lead in the polls. He entered Miami as if he were the presumptive nominee, the indispensable man in a field that had moved so far left that the media had almost begun to panic, lest Democrats lose.

Biden was, moreover, playing what football fans know as the "prevent defense," wherein the team shifts players from the line of scrimmage to the backfield. The goal is not to stop the other team entirely but to prevent them from making any big plays; not to score points but to protect a lead.

Biden was not granting interviews; he was not showing up at public events; his campaign let it be known that he would not be going to the spin room after the debate to talk to journalists.

Why? Were they afraid he would sink to the level of his competitors? Would he be prone to make gaffes, turning a successful debate into a bad story that lasted for several days?

Something seemed eerily off about the Biden campaign, not quite right—whether it was the strategy or Biden's age (at 76, a year younger than Sanders) or the odd silence of the Obama camp about Biden's prospects.

Just how wrong things were became apparent as the former vice president attempted to answer the first question posed to him in the debate. He seemed weak or tired, almost slurring his words, running one too quickly into the next.

The first to pounce was Swalwell, daring Biden to "pass the torch" to a new generation of politicians.[291] Sanders attacked, too, challenging Biden on his vote for the Iraq War and reminding voters that he, Sanders, had led the opposition to it.

But Sanders himself was on his back foot, forced to admit that Medicare for All would, in fact, mean raising taxes on the middle class. He argued that people would save more in premiums than they would lose to the tax man—but it was an important admission, perhaps a consequential one.

The real blow to Biden came from Kamala Harris, who went straight for Biden's record on race and his record of having worked with segregationist senators during his early career. ("At least there was some civility. We got things done. We didn't agree on much of anything. We got things done," he had said earlier that month.[292])

"It was hurtful to hear you talk about the reputations of two United States senators who built their reputations and career on the segregation of race in this country. And it was not only that, but you also worked with them to oppose busing," Harris said, addressing Biden directly.

"And, you know, there was a little girl in California who was part of the second class to integrate her public schools, and she was bused to school every day. And that little girl was me."

Biden seemed wounded—perhaps badly. His surrogates, notably the redoubtable Symone Sanders, struggled to repair the damage in the spin room.

But if Biden dropped out of the race, who would stop the march to socialism?

"Bernie Sanders Won the Debate," the *Wall Street Journal* editorial page declared: "Typically a re-election campaign is a referendum on the incumbent, and Mr. Trump is losing that race. But the Democrats are moving left so rapidly that they may let him turn 2020 into a choice between his policy record and the most extreme liberal agenda since 1972 (which may be unfair to [Democratic nominee] George McGovern)."[293]

Sanders's ideas had come to dominate the party, the *Journal* noted, such that, while "[n]ot all of the candidates on stage in Miami endorse[d] all of these positions... most do favor most of them."

All ten candidates that night—Biden included—raised their hands when asked if they would pay for the health care of illegal aliens, a stance the *New York Post* mocked on the next day's cover, with the headline: "Who wants to lose the election?"

And what awaited the country if they won?

NINE

PROSECUTING THE PRESIDENT

"I'm not talking about the neo-Nazis and the white nationalists, because they should be condemned totally."
—President Donald Trump, August 15, 2017 [294]

"And that's when we heard the words of the President of the United States that stunned the world and shocked the conscience of this nation. He said there were, quote, some 'very fine people on both sides.' "
—Former Vice President Joe Biden, April 25, 2019 [295]

"What voters are going to want is...someone who has the proven ability to prosecute the case against this administration and this president."[296]
—Senator Kamala Harris, March 19, 2019

THE "VERY FINE PEOPLE" HOAX

Kamala Harris pounced. Minutes after uttering the words "That little girl was me" onstage in Miami, her campaign launched a full media blitz and fundraising effort around the phrase, even selling T-shirts: "That Little Girl Was Me."[297]

Harris would raise $2 million in the next twenty-four hours.[298] An

NBC poll after the debate showed the two in a statistical tie for first place, with Harris's support more than doubling among black voters.[299]

It was ironic that Biden would have suffered from the accusation that he was tone deaf on bigotry. He had launched his campaign with the same kind of accusation—against Trump.

Biden claimed he had been motivated to run for president—after sitting out 2016—by his alarm at riots in Charlottesville, Virginia, in August 2017.

On that occasion, white supremacist and neo-Nazi groups descended on the town, hijacking a protest against the removal from a public park of a statue of Confederate General Robert E. Lee. In response, left-wing groups organized counterdemonstrations. Some groups were peaceful, but some—especially from the black-clad "Antifa" (short for "anti-fascist") group—came armed for violent confrontation.

On August 11, a torchlight procession of right-wing extremists marched through the town, chanting "Jews will not replace us!" and the like. The next day, armed neo-Nazis and Antifa thugs clashed. One counterprotester, Heather Heyer, was murdered by a white supremacist.

Trump reacted swiftly: "We condemn in the strongest possible terms this egregious display of hatred, bigotry and violence on many sides," he said in a statement.[300]

To most Trump supporters, keenly aware of the threat groups like Antifa had posed, that was not controversial: there had indeed been violence "on many sides." But to the media, who presumed Trump was associated with the white supremacists and therefore had a special duty to condemn them, it was not enough and amounted to condoning their hatred.

So on August 14, Trump issued a second statement—on live television, from the White House—specifically condemning the far-right extremists. "Racism is evil," he said. "And those who cause violence in its name are criminals and thugs, including the KKK, neo-Nazis, white supremacists, and other hate groups that are repugnant to everything we hold dear as Americans."[301]

But the media could not stop. At a press conference in Trump Tower the following day, a reporter asked: "Mr. President, are you putting what you're calling the alt-left and white supremacists on the same moral plane?"

Trump denied that he was, and he repeated that there had been violence from both sides. "But you also had people that were very fine people on both sides," he added, specifically referring to nonviolent protesters on either side of the statue controversy.[302]

CNN reported—accurately—at the time that Trump was talking about the statue issue. He went on to specify: "I'm not talking about the neo-Nazis and the white nationalists, because they should be condemned totally."[303]

Nevertheless, in subsequent weeks and months, Trump's words were distorted by political opponents—and CNN—who claimed that he had called neo-Nazis and white supremacists "very fine people," condoning their views and violence.

Conservatives called it the "very fine people" hoax. For Biden, it was the perfect pretext for his campaign launch.

In a video announcing his candidacy, Biden said: "Charlottesville is also home to a defining moment for this nation in the last few years." The video showed the neo-Nazi procession, as Biden said that they were "chanting the same antisemitic bile heard in the '30s." He continued:

> And that's when we heard the words of the President of the United States that stunned the world and shocked the conscience of this nation. He said there were, quote, some "very fine people on both sides." Very fine people on both sides? With those words, the president of the United States assigned a moral equivalence between those spreading hate, and those with the courage to stand against it. And in that moment, I knew that the threat to this nation was unlike any I had ever seen in my lifetime.

It was a blatant lie, whose refutations had already been widely circulated.[304] Biden would later fall back on the claim that there could not possibly have been "very fine people" in a crowd that included white supremacists and neo-Nazis. But there were; even the *New York Times* had found them, legitimate protesters who had been swamped by the extremists.[305]

Shortly after launching her campaign, Kamala Harris also used the "very fine people" hoax. In a town hall on CNN, Harris claimed: "We have seen when Charlottesville and a woman was killed, that we've had a president who basically said, well, there were equal sides to this."

Yet Trump specifically condemned Heyer's murder as "terrorism."[306]

THE "RUSSIA COLLUSION" HOAX

Harris, a former district attorney and state attorney general, said she "has the proven ability to prosecute the case against this administration and this president."[307] She meant the *political* case, not a criminal case. But she went further in an interview with National Public Radio in June 2019, when she said that the Department of Justice under her administration "would have no choice" but to prosecute the (former) president for obstruction of justice.[308]

The president fired back, telling ABC News: "Oh, give me a break. She's running for president. She's doing horribly. She's way down in the polls." He added: "There was no crime. There was no Russia collusion." And he added that Special Counsel Robert Mueller had a conflict of interest.

Mueller had been appointed in May 2017 to investigate allegations of "collusion" between the Trump campaign and the Russian government, after the president fired FBI Director James Comey. Democrats hated Comey, blaming him for Hillary Clinton's defeat after he reopened investigations into her illicit email server in late October 2016. But with Comey overseeing investigations into Russian interference in the election, Democrats claimed Trump was trying to obstruct justice, and they demanded an independent investigation. Comey leaked memos after he was fired with the specific intention of forcing a special counsel inquiry.[309]

Russian interference was real though limited. It had nothing to do with voting itself, though two-thirds of Democrats reportedly believed it was "definitely" or "probably" true that Russia had tampered with the vote.[310]

Russian hackers allegedly hacked and leaked emails from the Democratic National Committee that showed party officials pushing Clinton over Bernie Sanders. And Russian hackers were suspected of involvement in a Wikileaks trove of emails from Clinton campaign chair John Podesta.

But there was no evidence that the Trump campaign had been involved. When Trump joked at a July press conference, "Russia, if you're listening, I hope you're able to find the 30,000 emails that are missing," the Obama administration's intelligence apparatus apparently took that seriously. A Trump aide, George Papadopoulos, also suggested in a bar to an Australian diplomat that Russia had Clinton's emails. That diplomat went to U.S. officials, who launched a counterintelligence investigation.

Meanwhile, the Clinton campaign and the Democratic National Committee (DNC) had used an opposition research firm, Fusion GPS, to find dirt on Trump. Part of that research involved working with Christopher Steele, a former British spy who used sources inside Russia. Ironically, it was the Democrats who had "colluded" with foreigners, ironically, in an attempt to influence the 2016 election.

Steele produced the so-called Russian dossier (also called the "pee-pee dossier" because it contained a tale about Trump hiring Russian prostitutes to urinate on a bed where President Barack Obama had slept). The document was handed to the FBI and leaked to the Democrats, who dropped hints about its existence in the fall of 2016.

After Trump won, Clinton campaign officials blamed Russia directly. And the mainstream media fell into line, with the *New York Times* and *Washington Post* publishing exposés on Russia investigations, based on leaks from intelligence and law enforcement.[311]

Attorney General Jeff Sessions, newly confirmed and under pressure, recused himself from Russia investigations and appointed Mueller, a former FBI director who had worked closely with Comey in the past. Mueller hired over a dozen prosecutors, some of whom were donors to the Democrat Party or tied to the Clintons.[312]

Trump complained constantly about what he called Mueller's "witch hunt." Still, his White House provided every document and witness Mueller requested, though it submitted only written answers from the president to Mueller's questions.

When Barr took over from Sessions in February 2019, it was clear he expected Mueller to bring his investigation to a conclusion. And on March 24, he summarized what Mueller had found: "The investigation did not establish that members of the Trump Campaign conspired or coordinated with the Russian government in its election interference activities."

As to the question of obstruction, Mueller "did not draw a conclusion one way or the other," Barr said.[313] But he and Deputy Attorney General Rod Rosenstein decided there was insufficient evidence to prosecute.[314] When Trump criticized the investigation, Barr later said, he had non-corrupt motives, because he had faced an "unprecedented" political assault.[315]

Democrats cried foul. They accused Barr of distorting the report; Mueller himself even wrote a letter to Barr complaining that the attorney general's summary "did not fully capture the context, nature, and substance of this offices work and conclusions."[316] Once the full report was released in April—with some redactions—Democrats fixated on details that painted Trump in the worst possible light.

But neither they nor Mueller could dispute what Barr had said was the report's central conclusion: "no collusion."

It was a conclusion Democrats could not accept, and Harris sought to tap their frustration as she sought the nomination.

KAMALA IN NEVADA

In May 2019, I traveled to Las Vegas, Nevada, to cover Harris as she made her pitch to local minority groups pulling together a diverse coalition to win the state.

It would seem the strangest place to decide the Democratic presidential nomination.

Vegas is the place America goes to dream—and it is the place that dream sometimes goes hopelessly wrong and then picks itself up and tries again. It is a city of excess, of extremes.

There are other casinos in the world. There is nothing quite like Las Vegas.

Yet in Vegas, in Reno, and across this dry, sparse, and utterly bizarre state, voters could potentially decide the fate of the Democratic primary—and the general election.

Nevada, traditionally, is the fourth state in the Republican primary calendar—but for Democrats, it is third. That meant it could play a crucial role in tipping the balance after the traditional Iowa and New Hampshire contests.

Joe Biden held a solid lead in Nevada, at least through 2019. But Harris hoped to change that.

Harris's first stop was an Asian restaurant in the small Chinatown district west of the Las Vegas Strip, a collection of pagodas and strip malls along Spring Mountain Road—a much smaller version of the Chinatowns in other American cities but growing rapidly.

The Harris campaign had rented an Asian restaurant in a new two-story development, surrounded by boba tea shops, massage salons, and empty commercial spaces being hastily readied for their first tenants.

The event was organized by a new group called One APIA Nevada, a nonprofit that described itself as advocating "for policies empowering everyday Asian Pacific Islander Nevadans." The director did not seem to mind chatting with a conservative reporter—though the group was clearly left-wing. Of President Trump's immigration policies, for example, he told me: "We want the administration to work to bring communities together and not to divide communities. It looks as if the administration is pitting one versus another."

Harris arrived late, to a warm welcome, and pitched herself as the "first Asian American president," noting that in addition to having a Jamaican father, she also had an Indian mother.

"I intend to be very active, and very vocal, in fighting for every vote, in particular the Asian vote," she said.

She echoed their concerns about the administration's immigration policy, blasting Trump's proposal, made earlier that day, to switch American immigration to a merit-based system from one that gives precedence to relatives. Harris called the new policy "shortsighted," adding that the president was "creating hierarchies among immigrants."[317]

Later, I followed Harris to an event with a local Hispanic political organization in a Mexican restaurant on the Strip. The Doña Maria Tamales Restaurant is a humble, single-story Mexican diner, situated halfway between the Stratosphere Casino, Hotel & Tower—with its famous spire—and the downtown district, in a neighborhood filled with boarded-up buildings, tiny bungalows, and the world's most famous pawn shop.[318]

The room was packed. And though Harris's stump speech seemed to ramble, the audience hung on her every word.

"We have a president of the United States," she said to nods, "that has consistently vilified...immigrants."

She repeated her earlier criticism of Trump's merit-based system: "The idea that you're gonna start categorizing folks, that there's gonna be a hierarchy now?...This is a nation that was founded on a principle that we articulated in 1776—that we are all equal, and should be treated that way," she said.

The audience applauded; though certainly the Founders had not intended to erase all distinctions of skill or even of wealth. Harris was, indirectly, channeling precisely what conservatives feared about new waves of immigration—even legal immigration: that new arrivals would bring socialist ideas from abroad that would obscure America's principles.

Yet the audience was no less American than anyone else in Las Vegas. These were the people who served the food, cleaned the hotels, and started businesses in economically depressed areas, long abandoned by those who had moved to more upscale neighborhoods—west to Summerlin or east to Henderson.

This was the new, emerging constituency of the Democratic Party, in Nevada and nationwide. It was an audience Republicans were finding increasingly hard to reach.

And yet what Harris and other Democrats were offering Nevadans seemed to be at odds with the ethos of the place.

What makes Las Vegas special is not that it offers a steady existence or the guarantees of middle-class life. What makes the city tick is the opposite: the possibility of massive fortune, of excitement and success to those willing to risk it all.

That is why visitors travel to Nevada; that is why the boldest put down roots in Las Vegas. And in Nevada, only the boldest would win.

THE WORST CAMPAIGN IN RECENT MEMORY

But did Kamala Harris have what it took to make it that far?

By the end of June 2019, she would be the bookmakers' favorite to win the Democratic Party's presidential nomination.[319] But there was more than a year to go, still, and a campaign to run.

And despite her rapport with voters and her strong performance in the first debate, Kamala Harris had one glaring problem: she was not very good at campaigning.

In May 2019, I covered one of the early Harris rallies in Los Angeles, her first organizing rally. She gathered a crowd of about two thousand boisterous supporters, a relatively big draw, to a local community college gymnasium on a Sunday afternoon.

The bleachers were stacked with supporters; the stage had a giant American flag as the backdrop. But these two attractive tableaux were not on the same side of the room: they were adjacent, meaning that the candidate had to address most of her supporters from across the room.

The media risers were in the middle of the gymnasium floor, meaning the cameras were aimed at Harris and not the crowd. Most campaigns place supporters behind the candidate at rallies to make sure television audiences can see them. The Harris campaign had failed to set up the room properly.

There were other mistakes. Several warmup speakers urged supporters to send text messages with the word "fight" to a special campaign number. However, a placard on the podium told them to text the word "fearless."

Harris was preceded by several energetic warmup speakers, none better than Los Angeles City Council President Herb Wesson. But after his raucous introduction, there was an inexplicable pause, as Tina Turner's "What's Love Got to Do With It?" played over the PA system. It almost seemed that a saboteur had wanted to remind the audience of Harris's former relationship with Willie Brown, to which she owed her start in politics.

I glanced at a cameraman, who shook his head: this was not how it was done.

Harris had a good campaign slogan—"For the People"—and a populist message. "Let's speak truth: America's economy is not working for working people," she said.

The difficulty was that the economy was, in fact, working for "working people." By February 2020, President Trump could rightfully boast of a "blue-collar boom" in his annual State of the Union address: "Since my election, the net worth of the bottom half of wage earners has increased by 47 percent—three times faster than the increase for the top 1 percent," he said. "After decades of flat and falling incomes, wages are rising fast—and, wonderfully, they are rising fastest for low-income workers, who have seen a 16 percent pay increase since my election."[320]

These facts were true—at least until the coronavirus crisis—and they made Harris's message a tougher sell.

One area where Harris scored well was in endorsements. She stacked up an impressive tally,[321] particularly among California politicians. Governor Gavin Newsom, often seen as a potential future presidential prospect himself, gamely boosted his state's junior U.S. senator, saying in May that she had been "outperforming," though he did not offer an endorsement.[322] The Golden State was more important than usual, since its primary had been moved from June to Super Tuesday on March 3, making it—along with over a dozen other states—part of the fifth primary contest and the largest delegate haul by far.

Harris had home-field advantage—but she also had competition, and it seemed she was being outhustled in California by Pete Buttigieg, who was pulling in massive amounts of money from Silicon Valley. More than that, he was campaigning in the right places—even pitching his candidacy to Latino votes in the rural Central Valley, a relatively conservative constituency often overlooked by leading presidential candidates from both parties.[323]

In addition, Bernie Sanders still had a large network of supporters throughout California. "Berniecrats" had nearly taken over the state party in the wake of the 2016 election. Elizabeth Warren's campaign appealed to many of the same voters: she had some of the same policies, even though she did not call herself a socialist. But the example of Hillary Clinton in 2016 had shown that establishment candidates still had great pull in the Golden State, and Joe Biden jumped to an early lead. Harris had the support of California's political establishment but struggled to make her case to the voters.

Much of her campaign was being run by her sister, Maya—a brilliant woman with experience on Hillary Clinton's campaign and deep ties to the Obama administration.[324] Yet trusting family appeared to have its downside: when things went wrong, they could not be fired.

And things were about to go very wrong for Harris in the next debate.

TEN

THE DETROIT DEBATE

"The bottom line is, Senator Harris, when you were in a position to make a difference and an impact in these people's lives, you did not. And worse yet, in the case of those who were on death row, innocent people, you actually blocked evidence from being revealed that would have freed them until you were forced to do so."
—Representative Tulsi Gabbard, July 31, 2019

"My entire career I have been opposed—personally opposed to the death penalty and that has never changed. And I dare anybody who is in a position to make that decision, to face the people I have faced to say, 'I will not seek the death penalty.' That is my background, that is my work. I am proud of it. I think you can judge people by when they are under fire and it's not about some fancy opinion on a stage but when they're in the position to actually make a decision, what do they do."
—Senator Kamala Harris, July 31, 2019[325]

"Is it possible that the Democrats have an overflow of talent but no one who's precisely right?"
—Frank Bruni, *New York Times*, August 1, 2019[326]

THE "SQUAD"

On July 4, 2019, President Trump did something no president had done, remarkably, in the modern history of the country: he headlined a large outdoor Independence Day celebration on the National Mall, a "Salute to America," complete with military flyovers, fireworks, and patriotic music.

Critics derided the event as a giant campaign rally at taxpayer expense or suggested the president was behaving like a Third World dictator at a military parade. But Trump's speech evoked themes of national unity. At one point, he celebrated the heroes of the civil rights movement:

> In 1960, a thirst for justice led African American students to sit down at the Woolworth lunch counter in Greensboro, North Carolina. [Applause.]
>
> It was one of the very first civil rights sit-ins and it started a movement all across our nation.
>
> Clarence Henderson was 18 years old when he took his place in history. Almost six decades later, he is here tonight in a seat of honor. Clarence, thank you for making this country a much better place for all Americans. [Applause.][327]

Just a few days later, the president would find himself involved in one of the worst racial arguments of his entire contentious presidency.

Ironically, the argument began as an intramural dispute between Alexandria Ocasio-Cortez—AOC—and Speaker of the House Nancy Pelosi. As noted in chapter 2, AOC was the star of a radical new cohort that subscribed to democratic socialism and eagerly played the game of identity politics.

For Pelosi, securing the speaker's gavel once again meant appeasing AOC and her faction, and Pelosi offered just enough concessions to win their grudging support.

But over time, the tension between AOC's progressives and the party leadership began to emerge in a public way.

In June 2019, the Democrat-led House and Republican-led Senate feuded over funding for the humanitarian crisis at the U.S.-Mexico border (one that Democrats had denied for months was a "crisis" at all). The left forced Pelosi to include strict conditions for the spending; these were rejected by the Senate, which passed a straightforward $4.5 billion spending package with bipartisan support. Rather than risk being blamed for harsh conditions in migrant shelters, Pelosi ignored AOC's objections and passed the Senate bill.

In response, AOC's chief of staff, Saikat Chakrabarti, compared moderate Democrats who had supported the bill to the Southern Democrats who had upheld segregation in the Jim Crow era. Many Democrats fumed that AOC's chief of staff would take potshots at them.[328]

Pelosi herself told the *New York Times* that "the Squad, as Alexandria Ocasio-Cortez of New York, Ilhan Omar of Minnesota, Rashida Tlaib of Michigan, and Ayanna Pressley of Massachusetts" were known had marginalized themselves.[329] "All these people have their public whatever and their Twitter world," Pelosi told *Times* columnist Maureen Dowd. "But they didn't have any following. They're four people and that's how many votes they got."

After AOC responded by accusing Pelosi of racism,[330] the Congressional Black Caucus weighed in, criticizing AOC and Chakrabarti publicly: "It shows you how weak their argument is when they have to resort and direct racist accusations toward Speaker Pelosi."[331]

That is when President Trump joined the fray, apparently attempting to exploit the division by siding with Pelosi against her detractors. He tweeted that members of the Squad, "who originally came from countries whose governments are a complete and total catastrophe," should "go back and help fix the totally broken and crime infested places from which they came. Then come back and show us how it is done."[332]

Democrats condemned his tweet as racist: Pelosi charged that Trump wanted to "make America white again."[333] Trump called *her* remark "racist"[334] and gloated that he had forced Pelosi into line behind the Squad.

He tweeted: "The Dems were trying to distance themselves from the four 'progressives,' but now they are forced to embrace them. That means they are endorsing Socialism, hate of Israel and the USA! Not good for the Democrats!"[335]

The theme continued later in the month, when Trump responded to criticism of his border policies by House Oversight Committee Chair Representative Elijah Cummings (D-MD), tweeting, "Cumming [sic] District is a disgusting, rat and rodent infested mess…maybe he could help clean up this dangerous and filthy place."[336]

Democrats and the media claimed, once again, that Trump was being racist: the term "infested," it was said, was somehow a reference to black people.[337] But Trump's attack on Cummings's district, which includes part of Baltimore, rang true with some residents and with others nationwide—including some black Americans. Thanks to Trump the media were finally talking about the maladministration of big cities run as virtual one-party states. Not only was Baltimore rat-infested, but it had suffered a surge in crime since the Black Lives Matter movement had discouraged police from patrolling aggressively in poor areas.

And with that, the Democrats descended on Detroit.

"THE RENAISSANCE FEELS REAL"

The first headline to greet me at the airport newsstand in Detroit was: "Barry's Goodbye: Twenty years later, Sanders' sudden retirement still hangs over a team and torments its fan base."[338]

The legendary running back left the game one season shy of Walter Payton's all-time rushing record. As a Bears fan, I could hardly mourn. But Detroit not only mourned Barry Sanders's retirement; it still could not get over it, two decades later.

And that, I thought, was Detroit—a place consumed with the past and its enduring scars.

The decline of the auto industry had gutted the city's industrial core. The race riots of the 1960s—especially the "rebellion" of 1967, in which forty-three people were killed—accelerated white flight from the city to the suburbs, leaving behind an impoverished inner city.

When I was a child in the 1980s, Detroit was a frequent stop—on the way to somewhere else, such as Canada. My grandparents had befriended a songwriter named Harvey Glassman, who once took me out for lunch when I was in town for a Jewish youth group event. His old car literally stalled in the middle of intersections as he regaled me with complaints about how Motown promised to buy a new song he had written for Smokey Robinson but never came through. That, to me, was a perfect summary of Detroit.

In high school, I participated in a Habitat for Humanity project in Detroit. Instead of building a home, we demolished one, clearing an abandoned house in a blighted area. While I enjoyed the thrill of taking a sledgehammer to a brick wall—especially when we found back issues of *Playboy* in the rubble—I marveled at the desolation, at a city slowly returning to nature.

Detroit was always supposedly going through revivals. In the 1970s, there was the Renaissance Center, a set of gleaming cylindrical skyscrapers downtown. In the late 1980s and early 1990s, there was a brief surge of pride around the Detroit Pistons, who repeated as NBA champions. Later, the Detroit Red Wings, filled with a roster of former Soviet hockey stars, rocked the NHL.

But corruption and mismanagement continued to take their toll. In 2001, the city elected a promising young mayor, Kwame Kilpatrick. Detroit played host to the 2005 All-Star Game and the 2006 Super Bowl. But Kilpatrick became notorious for mismanagement and scandal. Even after that, he was reelected in 2005. He blamed racism for criticism of his administration; the FBI thought differently, and in 2013, he was convicted on corruption charges and sentenced to twenty-eight years.[339] The auto industry nearly collapsed during the financial crisis of 2008 and was bailed out by the federal government. Detroit's finances were so dire that it declared bankruptcy, emerging from it in December 2018.

Yet now, amid the nation's economic recovery, there was again talk of revival, as entrepreneurs like Dan Gilbert, founder and chairman of Quicken Loans, invested billions in property downtown.[340]

I took a morning jog through a city center alive with activity. Hipsters lined up for gourmet coffee and sandwiches. Office employees read newspapers in parks and cafés. Police directed traffic through the vibrant streets.

Detroit had a pulse.

"The renaissance feels real this time," Jean-Paul Stando, a tour guide who showed me around the area later that morning, told me. Buildings that had been vacant above the ground floor were now renovated and fully occupied. The art deco treasures of downtown, a mix of Chicago modernism and Old World nostalgia, were being excavated from grime and neglect.

We visited downtown Detroit's last synagogue, which had been on the verge of being sold just ten years ago, before two young Jewish investors stepped in and revived it. Now it holds regular weekly services and houses other Jewish organizations.

The blight outside the downtown remained; I noted a mural painted on a now-abandoned building in tribute to the late Aretha Franklin in her old, run-down neighborhood. But there was hope.

I ventured into Dearborn and the heart of Detroit's growing Muslim community. One of the candidates, Governor Jay Inslee, had arranged a press conference nearby with Muslim community leaders, ostensibly to answer what they called Trump's years of "attacks" on the community.

The event was held at the Islamic Center of Detroit, an old industrial building converted into a mosque and social hall, with a separate entrance for women for religious services. My colleague and I were welcomed with a handshake by a woman in a *hijab* manning a table at the entrance to a banquet hall.

I said hello and set myself up at the far end of a U-shaped table; a bank of TV cameras, including Fox and CNN, was at the back. I noted some of the attendees: the moderator, Dawud Walid, was already familiar to me as a leading voice of the Council on American-Islamic Relations, a group with a radical past.[341]

And yet while there were questions about the right to boycott Israel and about trouble helping community members who had been erroneously placed—so they claimed—on terrorist "no-fly" lists, most of the questions dealt with ordinary, bread-and-butter concerns.

One man, for example, asked what Democrats would do about the national debt. It was a question that might have been expected at any Tea Party event.

And Inslee stayed on message, delivering remarks similar to what he would have said anywhere else: while the Palestinians needed a "two-state solution" to the conflict with Israel, he told the Muslim leaders, what they really needed was also a "climate change solution," in common with the rest of the planet.

Why should Detroit be any different?

"DARK PSYCHIC FORCE"

After Dearborn, I headed downtown, to "The District," a revitalized area housing Detroit's major sporting arenas. CNN, the host of the second debate, had secured the Fox Theatre, an ornate architectural landmark that opened in 1928, for the occasion.[342]

A few left-wing protesters milled about. Among them: Squad member Representative Rashida Tlaib herself, whose congressional district included the debate venue. My Breitbart colleague Matt Perdie asked her about Trump's feud with Cummings over Democratic governance in American cites: "I don't live in Baltimore, I live here," she said dismissively.

More demonstrators arrived, including supporters of the various candidates. By far the largest contingent from any campaign was the group supporting spiritual guru Marianne Williamson, chanting slogans about peace and love and reparations for slavery.

As the journalists hunkered down over their laptops in the media filing room, I decided to join the Williamson crowd at their debate-watching party in the lobby of the Fillmore theater next door.

En route, I stopped to film hundreds of left-wing protesters who had appeared suddenly, marching down the street, carrying signs: "Green New Deal," "Capitalism Isn't Working," "Abolish ICE," "Reproductive Justice Is Climate Justice," and so on. Some tried to provoke the police, while others taunted them: "No justice, no peace, no racist police!" But they moved on, a mixed multitude of radicalism.

Inside the debate hall, Bernie Sanders and Elizabeth Warren, the two left-wing front-runners, were onstage together for the first time. Rather than pit them against one another, the CNN moderators prodded the few moderates—John Delaney, Tim Ryan, and newcomer Steve Bullock[343]—to challenge their "progressive" rivals.

If CNN had hoped to push the party back from the fringe, the effort failed.

Delaney took aim at Sanders over Medicare for All, stressing that while he agreed that access to health care was a fundamental right, Sanders's plan would require some 150 million Americans to give up their private health insurance. Ryan later noted union members stood to lose the "Cadillac" plans for which they had bargained.

But Sanders and Warren weren't having it. They accused the moderates of using "Republican talking points." At one stage, Warren put down Delaney brutally: "You know, I don't understand why anybody goes to all the trouble of running for president of the United States just to talk about what we really can't do and shouldn't fight for. I don't get it."[344] The crowd roared.

Bullock accused the left-wing candidates of "wish list economics" and pointed out, with regard to immigration, that the idea of decriminalizing illegal border crossings was one the Obama administration had opposed because it would drastically increase the number of migrants. Moreover, he and others noted, giving free health care to illegal aliens— as most of the candidates said they would do—would create further incentives to cross illegally.

Sanders responded merely by asserting that his policy would be able to afford granting health care as a human right, regardless of immigration status. Pete Buttigieg and Elizabeth Warren, meanwhile, dodged questions about whether their health care policies, which resembled Sanders's, would require taxes on the middle class.

Amid the policy melee, the star of the night was Williamson. She eschewed the wonky talk for moral, philosophical, and spiritual themes. She described Trump, for instance, as a "dark psychic force" that had to be fought with "love."[345]

"I want a politics that speaks to the heart," she declared. It was zany— but it cut through the clutter.

At the Fillmore, Williamson's supporters were thrilled. "When the 'forces' allow her to speak, she's slam-dunkin' it," one fan told me. The only question, she added, was "whether the country is ready for a Jewish female, speaking almost prophetic, Christ-like words."

Williamson was a sensation—especially among conservatives, who enjoyed the spectacle of a stereotypical liberal running circles around the actual Democratic front-runners.

A *New York Times* reporter accused Breitbart of "propping up" Williamson.[346] But that wasn't accurate: I had been covering her for years in Los Angeles and had covered her debate party simply because it was newsworthy. The *Times* got it right the next day:

> Mr. Pollak, the Breitbart editor, who has been covering Ms. Williamson since her unsuccessful independent congressional bid in California in 2014, said his interest in her campaign is more than a cynical ploy to muddle the Democratic nominating process.
>
> "The debate was wonky," he said. "She spoke differently. There's a kind of populism in what she's saying that has a genuine appeal to people who also like Trump. That part of the interest is real, especially when she goes after the party establishment. She is confirming the suspicion Trump supporters have of the political establishment."[347]

Williamson was destined to fade, but she made the most of her moment. She, like the other left-wing candidates onstage, dominated through sheer passion alone.

TULSI DESTROYS HARRIS

The second night of the debate featured a rematch of the two main antagonists from Miami: Joe Biden and Kamala Harris. But there seemed to be little public interest outside the theater, save for a dozen Tulsi Gabbard supporters and a few stragglers from the Andrew Yang and Biden campaigns. Not even the protesters showed up. It was, to borrow Trump's phrase, "low-energy."

I headed to the media filing center: this time, I decided, I'd watch the debate and file my stories from the front of the rope line in the spin room to be at the front of the press scrum when the candidates emerged. But like the empty plaza outside, the debate seemed to lack energy.

In the first round of questions, focusing on health care, Kamala Harris took incoming fire from all of the other candidates for her repeated reversals on whether to eliminate private health insurance.

Egged on by the moderators, the candidates continued pounding each other in exchanges that were more tiring than enlivening. Cory Booker scolded the moderators, and his rivals, for bickering—then laid into Biden for his stance on criminal justice reform, accusing him (accurately) of being a latecomer to the cause. Biden punched back, noting that Booker had himself pushed zero-tolerance crime policies as mayor of Newark.[348]

The line of the night went to Kirsten Gillibrand, who vowed to "Clorox the Oval Office," an oddly domestic promise as she criticized Biden for past comments on women in the workplace. Another consequential moment was when Inslee backed Biden into a corner on climate change and the former vice president agreed to "eliminate" coal, fracking, and fossil fuels. What would working-class voters in Pennsylvania and Ohio think about that next November?

Aside from the melee onstage, hecklers in the audience interrupted the candidates three times. The first two hecklers shouted, "Fire Pantaleo" at Bill de Blasio, referring to New York Police Department officer Daniel Pantaleo, whose chokehold allegedly led to the 2014 death of an African American man, Eric Garner, during arrest for the petty crime of selling loose cigarettes.[349] The third shouted at Biden about deportations.

Bizarrely, one after another of the candidates criticized Obama's record and legacy. At one point, Booker observed: "The person that's enjoying this debate most right now is Donald Trump."

The only dramatic moment came when Gabbard confronted Harris about her record as a prosecutor. She noted that Harris had put "over 1,500 people in jail for marijuana violations" but had laughed on the campaign trail about having used the drug herself.[350] Gabbard added—mostly accurately—that Harris "blocked evidence that would have freed an innocent man from death row until the courts forced her to do so." (Indeed, Harris had opposed new DNA tests but later reversed herself; the man had not yet been exonerated.)

Harris fired back: "As the elected attorney general of California, I did the work of significantly reforming the criminal justice system of a state of 40 million people, which became a national model for the work that needs to be done." She noted that she had done more than "give fancy speeches" but had been in a position of real-world responsibility.[351]

Gabbard wasn't having it. She replied that Harris owed the people who had "suffered" under her "reign" an "apology." Harris balked, noting that while she was personally opposed to the death penalty, she had to balance idealism with responsibility: "I think you can judge people by when they are under fire and it's not about some fancy opinion on a stage but when they're in the position to actually make a decision, what do they do."[352]

The crowd was clearly on Gabbard's side. The CNN pundits, commenting after the debate, agreed that Harris had had a bad night. And while Biden had survived, as former Obama strategist David Axelrod said, "the bad news is this may be the best he could do."

There was a frisson of fear: "Is it possible that the Democrats have an overflow of talent but no one who's precisely right?" wondered Frank Bruni of the *New York Times*.[353]

Filmmaker Michael Moore, in an extended rant on MSNBC, went further: if the party was not going to choose a true leftist like Bernie Sanders, he argued, it had to draft a new candidate—namely, Michelle Obama.

"Who can crush Trump? Who is the street fighter? . . . I think there's a person that could do this, if the election were held today, there is one person that would crush Trump. And she hasn't announced yet . . . Michelle Obama. Everybody watching this right now knows she is a beloved American and she would go in there and she would beat him."[354]

As for Harris: she began plummeting in the polls and would never recover.

ELEVEN

FROM IOWA TO NEW HAMPSHIRE, PART I

"It's time—and this is my concluding comment to you all—it's time to remember who, in God's name, we are. This is the United States of America. There's nothing we've ever decided to do we've been unable to do, period. That's not hyperbole! We have never, never, never failed when we're together. And, ladies and gentlemen, it's time to get up. Everybody knows who Donald Trump is. Even his supporters know who he is. We've got to let him know who we are. We choose unity over division! We choose science over fiction! We choose truth over facts!"
—Former Vice President Joe Biden, August 8, 2019[355]

"We have, it seems to me, two jobs in front of us. Number one, we have got to defeat Trump. But the second thing we have got to do—and what this campaign is absolutely about—is transforming the economy and the government of the United States, so that it works for all of us, and not just the 1 percent."
—Senator Bernie Sanders, August 13, 2019[356]

"When you've got a government, when you've got an economy that does great for those with money and isn't doing great for everyone else, that is corruption, pure and simple. And we need to make structural change in our government, in our economy, and in our country."
—Senator Elizabeth Warren, June 26, 2019[357]

SEEKING BIDEN IN IOWA

Iowa rolled by my window in the soft, golden glow of late summer morning. The sun shone on rolling green fields, as the corn stood high, glowing, in rows sweeping along the contours of the earth.

Come frigid February, the stubble of these harvested fields would huddle under a sheet of white as the 2020 presidential election began in earnest in the Iowa caucuses, in church halls and fire stations and high school gymnasiums across the state.

I drove through Iowa early in the morning of August 8, having taken the red-eye from Los Angeles to Minneapolis, saving $500 or so by landing over 200 miles away. The only vehicle the agency had was a pickup truck. I would fit right in, on my way to the Iowa State Fair, the ritual stop for aspiring presidential candidates, where they would shake hands and sample fried Oreos and other delicacies.[358]

There, in a quadrennial tradition, the *Des Moines Register* was staging its "Political Soapbox," where each of the candidates would stand behind bales of hay and make his or her pitch, in old-fashioned style, to the people who would have the first opportunity to vote in the presidential primary.

In recent years, it has become fashionable to downplay the significance of the Hawkeye State. "Iowa picks corn; New Hampshire picks presidents," the saying goes. And it is true that the state's socially conservative, predominantly white electorate was not exactly a representative sample of the electorate as a whole.

On the Republican side, Mike Huckabee had won in 2008; Rick Santorum had won in 2012; Ted Cruz had won in 2016. None of them won the nomination. Donald Trump famously lost to Cruz in Iowa after skipping the state's debate—a mistake Ronald Reagan also made in 1980. Yet both won the presidency.[359]

But one candidate who understood the potential of Iowa was Barack Obama. He had long trailed Hillary Clinton—who was almost the presumptive nominee in late 2007—even among black voters. But then Oprah Winfrey traveled to a rally in Iowa and endorsed Obama, telling voters that he "knows who we are and...knows who we can be."[360] And then the members of a lily-white electorate chose Obama over Clinton.

That showed black voters he could win.

The shift was dramatic; Obama never looked back. He would later call his victory in the Iowa caucuses the "favorite night of my entire political career."[361]

One candidate who had done extremely poorly in the state was Joe Biden. He came fifth in the Iowa caucus that year, with less than 1 percent of the vote, well behind Obama, Clinton, John Edwards, and even former New Mexico governor Bill Richardson. After that crushing loss, it was clear that Biden's presidential ambitions—at least in 2008—were going nowhere. He dropped out of the race and disappeared—only to be rescued as Obama's running mate.

Iowa had remained loyal to Obama in the 2008 general election and in 2012 as well but swung heavily to Donald Trump in 2016. He won the state by nearly ten points. Democrats faced the challenge of finding a nominee in 2020 who could win it back.

The candidate I wanted to see most was Biden. He was the frontrunner—perhaps not by double digits anymore, but the front-runner nonetheless. After two debates, Biden also had a sizable lead in almost every other early primary state. Kamala Harris had shaken him in the first debate, but she had been pummeled by Tulsi Gabbard. Biden was poised for redemption.

Montana governor Steve Bullock was the first to leap to the stage that day, greeted by a crowd that included several Iowans wearing Bullock 2020 T-shits. His pitch: he could win Iowa and other red states Trump had won.

The only other candidate who might do likewise was waiting in the wings.

When Biden came to the stage, he looked sharper than usual, in a blue golf shirt and beige chinos. His age had started to show; he seemed to speak slowly or slur his speech, for example. Yet the Iowa sunshine did him good as he vamped behind his aviator sunglasses.

He told a particularly vicious version of the Charlottesville story, suggesting that Trump had reacted to Heather Heyer's murder by calling the neo-Nazis there "very fine people."[362] That was the reason he was running, he told the Iowa crowd: to restore a sense of unity, to restore our values.

He made a few Biden-esque gaffes—promising the farmers of Iowa a "carbon-less environment," for example, and declaring that Democrats believed in "truth over facts" (he meant "truth over lies"). Yet he connected with the crowd and seemed pleased with his performance.

Until he went backstage.

SHOWDOWN WITH BIDEN

Biden arrived at the press gaggle, waiting in a tent behind the stage. By the time I found my way back there, after maneuvering through the crowd, the scrum around him was already three or four journalists deep, with cameras and boom microphones largely obscuring my view.

If I wanted to ask Biden anything, I was going to have to be creative.

I reasoned that, when he was done, he would have to walk back the way he had come. As luck would have it, he happened to turn around and walk directly toward me—by mistake. No bodyguards, no staffers, no entourage. Just him.

I could not miss the opportunity.

The following exchange ensued:

BREITBART NEWS: Mr. Vice President, are you aware that you're misquoting Donald Trump in Charlottesville, he never called neo-Nazis "very fine people"?

JOE BIDEN: No, he called all those folks who walked out of that— they were neo-Nazis, shouting hate, their veins bulging.

BREITBART NEWS: But he said specifically he was condemning them.

JOE BIDEN: No, he did not. He said he walked out and he said—let's get this straight—he said there are fine people in both groups. They're chanting antisemitic slogans, carrying flags.

And with that, he turned away. But I had gotten under his skin.

And Biden was wrong. Trump had, in fact, condemned the neo-Nazis.

As I hurried to upload my video and write my article, versions of the exchange began to appear on Twitter. There had, of course, been dozens of cameras present, snapping away and recording video of our confrontation over Charlottesville, at the time the most important argument against reelecting Trump.

The initial reports from mainstream media reporters cast me as a kind of heckler or troll; some did not realize that I was a credentialed reporter doing what I was supposed to do—fact-check a politician at a press gaggle.

In the subsequent articles about the exchange, not one mainstream media outlet—*not one*—bothered to include the transcript of Trump's remarks on Charlottesville, so that readers might be able to judge for themselves who was really in the right.

But the conservative media lit up.[363] Many were thrilled merely by the fact that someone had finally asked Biden a tough question—and not a perceived hit job, like Harris's, but a query about the facts. More than that, conservatives realized that the taboo around Charlottesville had been pierced. Whatever else might be said about the riots and the president's reaction, it was not what the media and Democrats wanted it to be, not a lever to divide the nation.

I looked around the fair. Most people seemed simply to be enjoying themselves—the warm weather, the odd delicacies, the curious agricultural exhibits of butter sculptures and the like. These were the voters who would decide the fate of America. They did not seem particularly upset about anything; they did not inhabit the world of fear and division that Biden and the other candidates painted. I remembered how many "Now

Hiring" signs I had seen along Iowa roads; I would see many more across the country.

What happened between me and Joe Biden would not keep him from the nomination—but it did seem to knock him off his game for a few hours. Later that day, he would tell a town hall of Latino voters in Des Moines that "poor kids are just as bright and talented as white kids."[364]

Now it was Biden's turn to be accused of racism.

That was the path he and the other Democrats had chosen: a path of finger-pointing and guilt by association, a road to hell that could ultimately swallow them, and everyone with them.

After a few days, impressions of Biden's potential in Iowa began to shift. Elizabeth Warren—the woman with "a plan for everything"—also addressed a crowd at the state fair and made a solid impression. She and her campaign, making the most of her roots in the heartland, began generating buzz among voters. So, too, did Pete Buttigieg, emphasizing his midwestern background and talking about his faith.

Kamala Harris, struggling to stay with the front of the pack, would soon pour all of her resources into the Hawkeye State. "I'm fucking moving to Iowa," she was overheard saying to a Senate colleague by the end of the summer.[365]

Biden would continue struggling: his team began lowering expectations for the Iowa caucuses, with one adviser telling *Politico*: "Do I think we have to win Iowa? No."[366]

The vice president still had his "firewall" in South Carolina, where he enjoyed strong African American support, and hope among the other early primary contests.

But the supposed motivation for his candidacy—a lie about Charlottesville, based on mainstream media distortions—had absorbed a heavy blow.

BARNSTORMING WITH BERNIE

The setting was idyllic; the message, radical.

Bernie Sanders was addressing a gathering of about two hundred supporters on a lawn overlooking placid Lake Winnipesaukee in the summer resort town of Wolfeboro, New Hampshire.

"It never occurred to me in my lifetime we would have a president who is an overt racist, sexist, xenophobic, religious bigot," he told the largely white audience.[367]

The president was "not running for reelection on his ideas," Sanders claimed, "but is simply running by dividing people up based on the color of their skin or where they were born or sexual orientation or whatever they may be."

Likewise, Sanders said, the Republican Party had no new policies to offer. His alternative: "Bringing people together around an agenda that works for all, not just for the 1 percent."

Sanders ticked off his policies: Medicare for All, drastic action to stop climate change, "commonsense" regulations to stop gun violence, free tuition at public colleges and universities, free day care, and so on— until the time came to race to the next campaign stop, along the Granite State's narrow but impeccable roads.

In a sweltering gymnasium in a community center in North Conway, at the foot of the White Mountains, he would do it all again. Here, despite the oppressive heat and humidity, the crowd packed the place, standing along the walls, spilling outside the door into the dusk.

The next morning, at a breakfast town hall in the mountain village of Berlin, Sanders went even further. The goal of his campaign, he said, was not just to defeat Donald Trump. It was "transforming the economy and the government of the United States, so that it works for all of us and not just the 1 percent."

Obama had said something similar, just five days before winning the presidency in 2008: "We are five days away from fundamentally transforming the United States of America," he told a thrilled crowd on the campus of the University of Missouri in Columbia.[368] They both shared the same vision; Sanders put it in more specific, and stark, terms. He meant to pick up the baton where Obama, swamped by Republicans in the Tea Party wave of 2010 and dragged down by Washington-as-usual, had dropped it.

Late in his first term, Obama had echoed the rhetoric of the Occupy Wall Street movement, which spoke of an America divided between the "1 percent" and the "99 percent."

Sanders likewise told the Berlin town hall: "We need to transform the economics of this country and the politics of the country.... In the end, they are the 1 percent, and we are the 99 percent, and 99 is a lot bigger than 1."

In Littleton, New Hampshire, he packed the opera house, a charming and ornate venue—holding exactly 327 people, the campaign informed me—just hours after new polling data came out showing that he had taken the lead in the state from Biden. In the mix were aging hippies, holiday-makers from out of state, and true local Yankees, all of them eager to see the candidate.

Sanders had won New Hampshire handily in 2016, defeating Hillary Clinton by a two-to-one margin. During that campaign, he had told voters that he had the best chance of defeating Trump.[369] And perhaps, to judge by the enthusiasm of the crowd, he did again.

Trump, Sanders told supporters, was "the most dangerous president" in American history. Yet beating him would require more than merely pointing that out. It would require fighting the "corporate power elite in America whose greed and corruption has destroyed the middle class of the country." It would require taking on the gun lobby—the National Rifle Association—to ban "assault weapons," the "gun show loophole," and something called the "straw man provision," whatever that was.[370]

"I cannot take them on alone," he added, urging his audience to join his effort to win the presidency. "That's what this campaign is about.... I am asking your help, the day after we are inaugurated, to work with me to stand up to the corporate elite and tell them that this country does not belong to a handful of billionaires. It belongs to all of us."

Though Sanders had a grim vision of a divided society, yearning for "political revolution," he still had a sense of humor. When a voter sporting a large blond Afro stood up to ask a question, Sanders told him, with perfect comedic timing: "My hair looked like yours a few years ago." He was an old, disheveled socialist, but he had charisma.

"He's gonna win. He has to," said one voter, who had driven to Littleton from neighboring Vermont to see him. "He's for the people."

"There's no other president that has been directly for the people like he has…I love Bernie."

A TOWN HALL IN FRANCONIA

The junior senator from Massachusetts made her entrance in frantic style, running across the bright grassy lawn, bounding down the slope overlooking the majestic valley of the Franconia Notch, waving enthusiastically to the hundreds of supporters who had gathered at a local farm for an outdoor town hall with the presidential candidate.

Elizabeth Warren, at 70, was out of breath but otherwise looked younger than her age—and seemed, quite literally, to have momentum.

Trailing slightly in New Hampshire, Warren had been surging nationwide, even catching Joe Biden in some surveys. In the Granite State, she had somewhat stiffer competition, especially from Sanders.

But she was quickly becoming a threat. If she were to win Iowa— which looked increasingly possible—and then go on to win New Hampshire, her path to nomination would be clear.

Warren took the microphone and turned to her supporters, seated on neatly arranged white chairs, with dozens more in the shade—an audience that would be reported,[371] erroneously in my view, as numbering seven hundred people.

The question, Warren explained, was "whose side government is on."

"Think of it this way: we have a government that works fabulously, works terrifically, works wonderfully, for giant drug companies. It's just not working for people trying to get a prescription filled. Can I get an Amen on that?"

"Amen!"

She continued: "So when you see a government that works great for those at the top, works fabulously for those who hire armies of lobbyists and lawyers, works terrifically for the wealthy and the well-connected, and is not working so much for everyone else—that is corruption, pure and simple, and we need to call it out for what it is."

In Franconia Notch, as elsewhere, Warren presented herself as the candidate with a plan for everything. Later that evening, after another town hall meeting, a woman would tell me, "I love that she has a plan to do it all."[372]

Warren and Sanders had the same diagnosis for what ailed America and the same prescription. They both saw the country as divided between haves and have-nots, requiring massive state intervention to correct the injustice. But while Sanders's vision was explicitly "revolutionary," Warren's was technocratic, making sure government "works for you."

In Iowa, she tweeted a photograph of herself in the campaign RV, seated at the table and working on her next policy plan. The media gushed over her wonkiness: "Elizabeth Warren Even Has a Selfie Plan," wrote *New York* magazine, explaining how she incorporated selfies into her campaign stops (by arranging a line for people who wanted to snap photos of themselves with the candidate).[373]

Warren's plans were a shield as well as a sword. When she was confronted by reporters about her claim that 18-year-old Michael Brown had been "murdered" in 2014 by police in Ferguson, Missouri—a false claim that led to unrest in cities across the country at the time—Warren declined to correct herself, merely asserting, "I have a more comprehensive plan coming out just a little bit later," as if that sufficed.

It did—but only so far.

Later that evening, in an expansive, luxuriant back yard in Wolfeboro, a woman asked Warren how she would unite the country.

Warren responded by bashing Trump:

Look, Trump has a message. He says if there's something that's bad in your life, something that's not working for you—you're not making much money, you can't cover your expenses, you're worried about your kids—blame them. Blame people who aren't the same color as you. Blame people who don't sound like you. Blame people who weren't born where you were born. Blame people who don't worship like you. Blame them. And that is his message. That is it, at heart. And he thinks if he can stir up people against people, keep people fighting each other enough, then nobody will notice who's actually picking their pockets. And that the folks at the top are just getting richer and richer and richer, just scraping more and more of the wealth for themselves.

She eventually answered the question, arguing she could peel off some Republicans and independent voters once they realized her plans would make government work for them.

She seemed to have missed, however, what the voter meant: finding empathy with those who disagree.

That response epitomized one of Warren's major weaknesses: a didactic style that she had retained, perhaps, from her years in education.

Some of her supporters loved it. A retired teacher who had moved to New Hampshire told me that he loved Warren's tone: "She's a damned good teacher," he told me.

But in Franconia, one woman quietly told me she worried that Warren would lose a general election even if she were to win the Democratic nomination.

It was a fear Warren's campaign would never quite shake.

TWELVE

SOUTH CAROLINA

"Given this particular Breitbart employee's previous hateful reporting and the sensitivity of the topics being discussed with students at an HBCU, a campaign staffer made the call to ask him to leave to ensure that the students attending the event felt comfortable and safe while sharing their experiences as young people of color."

—Statement by Beto O'Rourke's Campaign, August 28, 2019[374]

THE BULLY PULPIT

South Carolina. The Palmetto State's unique symbol was emblazoned on the state's blue flag in 1861, when the state seceded from the Union, starting the Civil War.

The birthplace of the Confederacy, ironically, has become the primary state where black voters hold the greatest sway, and it is therefore crucial to both parties, especially Democrats.

In 2008, Barack Obama secured a path to the nomination by winning here, defeating both Hillary Clinton—the early favorite—and then senator John Edwards despite Clinton's early lead and institutional support from black churches and labor unions[375] and despite the fact that Edwards hailed from neighboring North Carolina.[376]

It worked—and prompted speculation that the Clinton machine was weak and could be beaten—even among black voters, once loyal to the Clintons through thick and thin.

Clinton also faced accusations that her campaign was exploiting racism, after Bill Clinton called Obama's opposition to the Iraq War—from outside Congress—a "fairy tale."[377] Hillary added that, while a movement leader like Dr. Martin Luther King Jr. had led people into the streets, it was an experienced politician, President Lyndon Johnson, who had made the real gains for civil rights—the point being that experience should count for more than rhetoric.[378]

Sean Wilentz observed in the *New Republic*:

> A review of what actually happened shows that the charges that the Clintons played the "race card" were not simply false; they were deliberately manufactured by the Obama camp and trumpeted by a credulous and/or compliant press corps in order to strip away her once formidable majority among black voters.[379]

It worked,[380] and history changed as a result.

In 2008, Joe Biden had dropped out before South Carolina. In 2020, it was his firewall. While he had seemed vulnerable in other early voting states, he consolidated his support in South Carolina, taking 39 percent of the vote in one poll, more than three times the support enjoyed by Kamala Harris (12 percent), in second place. Most telling of all, Biden had the support of 51 percent of black voters, who would form roughly 60 percent of the Democratic primary electorate.[381]

The one thing Harris—or any of the other candidates—might hope for seemed to be a strong second-place finish.

I landed in Charleston in the humid heat of a late August afternoon and made my way downtown. There, in the lush, green historic district, sits the College of Charleston, a time capsule of the state's antebellum past.

Beto O'Rourke was the guest of honor at the college's "Bully Pulpit" lecture series, which dates to the 2008 campaign. Students and faculty sat in a small outdoor amphitheater, a wooden pallet two feet square on each side the only stage.[382]

O'Rourke arrived, late, taking lanky strides to the center of the gathering. He launched into his new stump speech, focusing on the mass shooting in El Paso, Texas, earlier in the month and ripping into President Trump as the cause of it all. The shooting had given O'Rourke new prominence, a new message, and a new sense of urgency.

The El Paso mass murderer, he told the audience, had used the term "invasion" to describe Hispanics coming to Texas. Trump used the same word to describe illegal immigration, O'Rourke said.[383] He then added: "And lest you think this is an isolated strain of his [Trump's] hatred— this is the same man who called Klansmen, and neo-Nazis, and white supremacists 'very fine people' days after they were marching in the streets of Charlottesville, Virginia, chanting, 'Jews will not replace us.'"

Later, in the question-and-answer session, a young man stood up and asked O'Rourke about his support for third-trimester abortion.

"I was born September 8th, 1989," he said, "and I want to know if you think on September 7th, 1989, my life had no value."

The crowd murmured; a woman near me booed. It was a question one was simply not supposed to ask on campus.

"Of course I don't think that," O'Rourke answered. "And of course I'm glad you're here. But you reference my answer in Ohio, and it remains the same. This is a decision that neither you, nor I, nor the United States government should be making. That's a decision for the woman to make."

Rousing cheers.

Later, I caught up with O'Rourke at a press gaggle following the event. He was asked a series of puff questions by the assembled reporters before I challenged him on the "fine people hoax." Could he lie about that and still live up to his professed commitment to heal the country?

Without missing a beat, he repeated the lie—then went on to list several other examples that, he said, proved the president was responsible for inspiring racist violence.

I filed my story and returned to my hotel, thinking nothing of it—except how pervasive the lie had become, virtually unchanged in the speeches of the various Democratic candidates.

BOOTED BY BETO

I woke up before dawn and drove to Folly Beach, twenty minutes away, and ran along the fine white sand, diving into the cool, wild waves. I visited the Kahal Kadosh Beth Elohim synagogue, founded by Portuguese Jews in the eighteenth century, now a Greek Revival masterpiece dating to 1849.

I stopped by the Mother Emanuel AME church, just off the main town square, the site of the horrific mass shooting in 2015, where a crazed racist gunman had prayed with congregants and then murdered nine of them in cold blood.

I drove out of the coastal Lowcountry to the Midlands, the heart of the state's black population, the midst of the famed Black Belt, to the capital city of Columbia. After stopping for a lunch of spicy salmon at Mrs. B's Southern Soul Food, I drove to the state capitol itself.

On one side, there is a bas-relief sculpture depicting the entire sweep of African American history. On the other, a Confederate war memorial, proclaiming the virtues of loyalty and courage, even in the service of a "Lost Cause."

These two histories, adjacent on the capitol grounds, seemed to coexist uneasily in South Carolina. The Confederate flag had come down, but history could never be erased.

A short drive away was Benedict College, a small liberal arts college and part of the South's constellation of historically black colleges and universities (HBCUs). O'Rourke was to speak there, and I thought it would be interesting to hear the concerns of young black voters.

I found my way onto campus and, with the help of some students, found the building and the lecture hall where O'Rourke, trailing badly among black voters, was to deliver his speech.

The room was nearly full. I took a position to the side of the lecture hall, readying my smartphone to livestream O'Rourke's speech on

Breitbart News' Facebook page, one of the top political destinations in social media.

Just then, a staffer wearing a black BETO T-shirt approached me and asked me what outlet I was from: "Breitbart," he said, reading my press credential. He put a hand on my shoulder in friendly fashion and said, cheerfully, "All right." He disappeared.

A few moments later, a campus police officer approached me from the rear of the room and told me he needed to see me. I followed him toward the back. "No, with your property," he said. I retrieved my back-pack and realized they were going to eject me.

A tall white man in a golf shirt who would give his name only as Steven told me I was being asked to leave because I had been "disrup-tive" at previous events. I could leave voluntarily or involuntarily—that is, arrested.

Realizing that "resistance is futile," I left, and the police officer fol-lowed me all the way to my rental car, watching me leave. I was furious—but also realized that the story was about to become massive, in a way that O'Rourke was unable to control.

The irony was that, during his Senate campaign, O'Rourke had styled himself as a defender of press freedom: "If we don't have a free press, if we cannot make informed decisions at the ballot box, if we can't hold people like me accountable, and make sure that we're held honest to the promises that we made, to the job that we're performing in these positions of public trust, we'll lose the essence of our democracy," he said. "We need to vigorously defend the freedom of the press," he added."We need to call out violations."[384]

I wrote up my account of events at Benedict, and we published it. It became a sensation, shared on social media by conservatives eager to mock O'Rourke's "press freedom" pretensions and "snowflake" persona.

The O'Rourke campaign responded with a statement:

Beto for America believes in the right to a free press and works hard to ensure the campaign reflects that. However...Breitbart News walks the line between being news and being a perpetrator of hate speech. Given this particular Breitbart employee's previous hateful reporting and the sensitivity of the topics being discussed with students at an HBCU, a campaign staffer made the call to ask him to leave to ensure that the students attending the event felt comfortable and safe while sharing their experiences as young people of color.[385]

I had no idea what "hateful reporting" they were talking about—nor did anyone else. Suddenly, O'Rourke had the whole media against him—and *defending Breitbart.*

"Numerous members of the news media, including some that object to Breitbart's far-right political advocacy, have also criticized the O'Rourke campaign," CNN reported.[386]

Eventually, the campaign relented and said I would be allowed into future events. But there were to be very few future events. Beto was finished.

UNCLE JOE AT THE FAMILY REUNION

Joe Biden kicked off his two-day swing the next day in an ornate field house in Spartanburg, South Carolina. The crowd was older than O'Rourke's and also diverse: there were significant numbers of blacks and whites present.

When the former vice president emerged, I was almost convinced he had no business running for president. He spoke slowly and softly. He struggled with the handheld microphone. He had trouble remembering things. He was trying too hard.

The former vice president had been criticized earlier in the summer for praising old segregationists, and he had apologized. But he came right out and told the audience about his close friendship with the late Senator Ernest "Fritz" Hollings. Hollings changed his views later in life but ran for governor in the 1950s on a segregationist platform and flew the Confederate flag at the capitol.

Biden's stump speech, ironically, relied again on the "very fine people" hoax, which he had used since the start of the campaign. I wondered if his staff had decided that it was still worth pounding the lie—even after it had been exposed at the Iowa State Fair—or whether Biden was simply unable to switch to a new script. Perhaps it had been hard enough for them to teach him the talking points the first time around.

This was not the old Joe Biden, I thought. There were flashes of that old character—especially in the question-and-answer session, when he seemed sharper, with facts, figures, and talking points at his fingertips. But he seemed to have lost a step. At times, he was just lost altogether. He stumbled on Obama's name: "President...my boss," he said. The media, formerly sympathetic, were primed to feast on every new gaffe. And Biden knew it.

There was one particularly bizarre, and almost sad, moment. Biden had wrapped up the question-and-answer session and said goodbye. The music played—Jackie Wilson's "Higher and Higher"—and people began filing out. Then Biden appeared to have realized that he had failed to offer whatever concluding remarks were in the script. He took back the microphone—"Just sixty more seconds, folks"—and began speaking again, as people continued leaving.

Later that afternoon, after a drive through the gentle hills of Cherokee County—so named in memory of the tribe that once lived there, before being driven out along the Trail of Tears by Andrew Jackson, the president whose portrait Trump had hung in the Oval Office—I arrived at the campus of Limestone College, a small, Christian liberal arts school. A few rows of chairs had been set up on a small quadrangle, but most people—including the media—had taken refuge from the blazing sun in the meager shade offered by nearby buildings or by trees surrounding the quad.

Biden came out in a blazer, far too hot for the weather. I wondered if he might faint from the heat. But he persevered with his stump speech, "very fine people" and all.

During the question-and-answer session, a young black man, the president of the Black Students' Union at the college, asked Biden forthrightly why he and other black voters should continue supporting the Democrats, as they had done for over seventy years, if the community was doing so poorly in terms of incarceration, wages, and so forth.

It was an excellent question—and one Biden failed, utterly, to answer.

Instead, he seized upon the word "incarceration" to talk about his criminal justice policies, the target of withering attack by Senator Cory Booker in the last debate.

Weirdly, Biden took the handheld microphone and walked around almost the entire audience—now spread out over a wide area—addressing each person in turn, struggling to step back over the rope line.

But the crowd hung onto his every word.[387]

Then came a dramatic moment. A female major in uniform stood up and tearfully told Biden she and her soldiers in Afghanistan had collected "challenge coins"—commemorative military tokens—to give him and Obama. She had waited six years to do so, she said. He also gave her a coin of his own, as is the custom, and they embraced, twice, to cheers.[388]

In that gesture, I felt, it was clear why black voters were not ready to give up on Biden. He was a proxy for Barack Obama. A woman in the crowd told me as such: she didn't follow politics much, but Biden was with Obama, so she was with him.

Afterward, people lined up to take selfies with Biden—and he indulged all of them. He wasn't afraid of their smartphones, either, and seemed to know what he was doing with them. He seemed to be taking it all in, enjoying himself.

COWPENS AND THE NEO-CONFEDERACY

The next morning was clear, bright, and mild. I drove through the Upstate region in the northwest corner of South Carolina to a small town on the border with North Carolina, to Clinton College, a small HBCU. The crowd was standing room only—mostly white and middle-aged, ironically, though it included a few students and children.

I caught a glimpse of Biden waiting behind a curtain to deliver his speech. He looked eager, as if he could not wait, as if he were savoring the moment.

And, indeed, Biden emerged buoyantly, looking more collected and capable than he had the day before. Perhaps it was the setting, the black institution: Biden knew he was playing before a home crowd. The very fine people hoax was now joined by a new attack line: President Trump was deporting "kids with cancer." These were the "worst instincts" that Biden had warned the country Trump would soon indulge.

There was only one problem: Biden's claim was not true. The U.S. Citizenship and Immigration Services (USCIS) had merely transferred authority over medically deferred deportations to Immigration and Customs Enforcement (ICE).[389] Biden also said Trump was canceling citizenship for children of troops overseas—another distortion.[390]

It was outrageous to claim, or to believe, that the president, any president, would deliberately harm military families or children. Yet Biden hearkened back to the "kids in cages" controversy—the policy of zero tolerance toward illegal border crossings that Trump had adopted, then dropped, in 2018. Ironically, the first time children were put in "cages"— temporary chain-link partitions at Border Patrol processing facilities— was under Obama/Biden, to keep children safe from predatory adults.

I found myself reeling from the sheer weight of Biden's accusations and their seeming imperviousness to truth. These were the sort of outlandish claims that would have driven an entire news cycle, had Trump made them. I eventually pieced together a story by focusing not on Biden's accusations but on a joke he made at British Prime Minister Boris Johnson's expense. He did not know Johnson, Biden quipped, but he "looks like Donald Trump."

I found it odd that someone who was promising to restore America's alliances would begin by mocking the leader of Great Britain.

I drove back to Greenfield, taking a slight detour to stop at the Cowpens National Battlefield. The story of Cowpens fascinated me. In 1781, an arrogant British general, certain of victory, marched his tired troops up a hill to engage a mixed force of American regulars and irregular militia. The Americans fell back, as if retreating—then executed a brilliant pincer movement around the entrapped British soldiers, wiping out almost the entire British force.

I thought there might be a metaphor there. Democrats seemed so confident of victory, so certain that Trump was going to be a one-term president, that they were making wild claims and radical promises.

Trump appeared to be in retreat—but perhaps Democrats might soon learn that his apparent weakness was actually a strength.

It all depended on Trump. Could he pull himself together? Could he project competence and confidence?

I took a wrong turn and had to use a dirt road between a field and a forest to return to the main road. Suddenly, in a small clearing, I saw two obelisks marking a gravesite.

There, almost hidden from view, was the grave of a Confederate veteran who died in 1921; the grave was marked with a cross and a Confederate flag, evidently carefully attended and maintained.

Trump and his supporters were sometimes mocked as "neo-Confederates." Would that be their fate after 2020?

Soon after, I arrived back in Greenville for the final town hall of Biden's two-day swing. In the interim, the *Washington Post* had reported that a story about an encounter with a war hero that Biden had told at earlier stops on the campaign trail was almost entirely fabricated. It appeared to combine bits and pieces of other, real stories, but almost every detail of the story as told by the former vice president was inaccurate. They had ignored his other hoaxes; they chased that one.[391]

But Biden was in fine form, now. He felt the love in the room—the yearning for Obama, whom he represented, though the "boss" had not endorsed him (yet). One man told me, more pragmatically, that Biden was the only Democrat moderate enough to support.

For others, Biden was not just a default but a revival—and, what's more, he was running against the devil. "Sinful" was the word Biden used for Trump's policies.

More cheers, more selfies; more ducked questions; and he was gone, his firewall intact.

Time would tell if that firewall would hold—and if Biden were to win, how he would govern: as the "moderate" he denied he was but whom the party establishment quietly hoped he would be?

Or as the left-wing candidate he was becoming and whom the party base demanded?

THIRTEEN

FROM SOCIALISM TO IMPEACHMENT

"Hegel remarks somewhere that all facts and personages of great
importance in world history occur, as it were, twice. He forgot to add: the first
time as tragedy, the second as farce."

—Karl Marx, *The Eighteenth Brumaire of Napoleon Bonaparte*[392]

THE ORIGINS

The single-engine airplane buzzed high overhead, through the parting
rain clouds, over the campus of Texas Southern University. It was late
afternoon on September 12, 2019, and a line of overdressed people had
formed in the sticky late summer heat, waiting to enter the auditorium
where the third debate of the Democratic Party presidential primary
would take place.

The plane towed a large blue-and-white banner: "Socialism Will Kill
Houston's Economy. Vote Trump 2020."

Socialism—three decades after the fall of the Berlin Wall.
Unthinkable—yet here we were: socialism was on the ballot.

Just outside the campus gates, at the corner of Wheeler Street and
Ennis Street, dozens of protesters gathered. A group of black women held
up banners in favor of charter schools; antiabortion activists stood behind

giant photos of aborted children. The police milled about, ushering candidates through the campus gate.

Soon, however, a new group of protesters arrived, chanting against President Donald Trump. Some taunted the cops: "Fuck the police!"[393]

The Houston debate was to be the third—and the first confined to one night only, after the Democratic National Committee tightened the criteria.[394] Only ten candidates qualified for the debate on the HBCU campus, leading to the first wave of dropouts.

Colorado governor John Hickenlooper had pulled out, after months of speculation that he would run for Senate instead, which he duly did.[395] Washington governor Jay Inslee withdrew next, winning effusive praise from his rivals for raising the issue of climate change.[396] Representative Seth Moulton (D-MA) also dropped out; his lasting impact on the race was to have declared President Trump a "domestic enemy."[397]

Senator Kirsten Gillibrand dropped out a week later, earning a juicy tweet from the president: "I'm glad they never found out that she was the one I was really afraid of!"[398] Others, like New York City mayor Bill de Blasio, failed to qualify in Houston but deferred the inevitable.[399]

Inside, seasoned Democrats were fretting openly about the party's leftward drift. Not one of the moderate candidates had qualified; Joe Biden, Pete Buttigieg, and Amy Klobuchar were "moderate" only relative to Sanders and Warren.

I caught up with former Chicago mayor Rahm Emanuel, who had masterminded the Democrats' 2006 wave election by recruiting moderates to run in Republican districts. He panned the idea of Medicare for All or giving free health care to illegal aliens.

"People have enough anxiety in their lives, and you shouldn't start with trying to take something away from them, when they have a very low opinion of government, and then pledge to give it to people who just got here," he said.

"We did the Obamacare! Now let's build off of it—not take it down and rebuild it. I think that's a really risky strategy. The whole goal is about winning. I mean, I'm fine with all the candidates. It's about, how do we win?"

Andrew Yang had given some thought to that question and opened the debate with a gimmick: giving away $1,000 per month to ten families, chosen at random, as a pilot project to demonstrate his core campaign idea.

That generated some media buzz, but the focus was on the front-runners.

Elizabeth Warren declined to answer clearly whether her version of Medicare for All would require raising taxes on the middle class; she merely asserted that "costs" would go down. Beto O'Rourke continued his strident attack on the Second Amendment: "Hell yes, we're going to take your AR-15, your AK-47," he thundered.[400] Joe Biden took heat from the diminutive Julián Castro, standing—somewhat hilariously—on a box. He attacked Biden's memory—the first rival to focus on the front-runner's mental acuity. "Are you forgetting what you said two minutes ago?" he asked, to gasps and boos.[401]

Cory Booker, speaking to CNN after the debate, said it was a legitimate question.[402] Biden did not help himself by urging poor children to "play the radio, make sure the television—excuse me—make sure you have the record player on at night"—two devices almost certainly unfamiliar to anyone under 40.

The moderator posed a question to Bernie Sanders the likes of which had probably never been heard before in an American presidential debate: "What are the main differences between your kind of socialism and the one being imposed in Venezuela, Cuba, and Nicaragua?"

Sanders called the question "extremely unfair," saying he preferred the democratic socialism of Canada and Scandinavia, "guaranteeing health care to all people as a human right."

"Democratic socialism," Sanders added, meant "creating an economy that works for all of us, not 1 percent."

The audience applauded.

Meanwhile, on television, viewers saw an advertisement placed by a Republican political action committee showing a portrait of democratic socialist Alexandria Ocasio-Cortez, which was soon engulfed in flames, burning away to reveal a photo of skulls, victims of the Khmer Rouge killing fields.[403]

"That's socialism. Forced obedience. Starvation," the voiceover said.[404]

Thirty years after the end of the Cold War, socialism had become the key issue in the 2020 presidential election.[405]

How had it become so dominant among Democrats? And what did it mean for America's future?

TENACIOUS TULSI

In part, the popularity of left-wing policies like Medicare for All and the Green New Deal within the Democratic Party had begun with the return of the antiwar movement. And while foreign policy faded as an issue, one candidate was still carrying the torch for the antiwar cause: Representative Tulsi Gabbard (D-HI).

Gabbard, born in the territory of American Samoa, was a major in the Army National Guard Reserve from Hawaii and had served two tours of duty in Iraq. That made her an unusual, but uniquely legitimate, voice for those within the party for whom opposition to foreign intervention was still a powerful motivating force.

Young, media-savvy, and forthright, Gabbard became the first Hindu in Congress when she was elected in 2012. She also represented the millennial idealists who had supported Sanders for president in 2016, partly because he had opposed the Iraq War while Hillary Clinton had not. She resigned from her position as vice chair of the Democratic National Committee (DNC) to support Sanders openly.

"As a veteran and as a soldier I've seen firsthand the true cost of war," she explained, adding that Sanders was a candidate who would make sure "we don't continue to find ourselves in these failures that have resulted in chaos in the Middle East and so much loss of life.[406]

She continued to defy the party establishment, speaking about the fear in Washington of "going against the so-called Clinton machine"[407] and holding out against endorsing the party's front-runner.[408] After Clinton lost, former DNC chair Howard Dean called Gabbard "extremely ambitious with flexible principles."[409]

What was "flexible" were Gabbard's tactics, not her ideals. Unlike many on the left, Gabbard was willing to speak with center-right Fox News and met with President-elect Donald Trump. She found common ground with an antiwar constituency on the right for whom Trump's "America First" principles meant bringing troops home from the Middle East.

In early 2017, Gabbard took that cause seriously enough to embark on a highly controversial trip to Syria, where she met with dictator Bashar al-Assad in Damascus. Democrats had done so before, after winning the House in 2007, when they wanted to highlight diplomacy as an alternative to President George W. Bush's "neoconservatism."[410]

By 2017, Assad's butchery in the Syrian civil war was well known. But Gabbard defended her visit as a statement about ending "regime change wars": "I think we should be ready to meet with anyone if there's a chance it can help bring about an end to this war," she said.[411]

Gabbard subscribed to most of the left's views, including Medicare for All, the Green New Deal, and gun control. She also joined the far left in voting to protect boycotts of Israel.[412] But she was also willing to criticize her party from the right. In January 2019, for example, she wrote an op-ed in *The Hill* criticizing pro-choice Democrats for grilling a nominee for the federal bench over his Catholic faith and his affiliation with the Knights of Columbus.[413]

She ran into opposition from the LGBTQ community over her own early social conservatism: she had once opposed same-sex marriage vigorously.[414] She walked back that position but remained opposed to late-term abortions.[415] "I agree with Hillary Clinton on one thing, disagree with her on many others, but when she said abortion should be safe, legal, and rare, I think she's correct," she said, adding that she would prohibit abortion during the third trimester "unless the life or severe health consequences of a woman are at risk."[416]

Gabbard also opposed the idea of "open borders," taking a conservative stance on immigration that had once been the norm in the party.[417] And, crucially, she was one of the few Democrats willing to criticize her party's newfound hostility to Russia, which many blamed for Trump's victory.

Gabbard generated intense online enthusiasm: after she clashed with Tim Ryan over Afghanistan in the first debate, visitors to the Drudge Report website voted overwhelmingly that she had won. In the spin room, she told Breitbart News that the secret of her appeal was simple: "I'm the one who is most qualified" to be commander in chief, she said.[418]

She was also a formidable debater, crushing Kamala Harris's presidential ambitions in that brutal exchange in the second debate. Harris's campaign would later claim that a "Russian propaganda machine" was behind Tulsi's efforts[419]—a charge that would recur.[420]

But her military role had a cost, too: Gabbard took two weeks off campaigning in August 2019 to drill with her Army National Guard Reserve unit. It was a crucial period: while she met the DNC's donor threshold, she did not reach 2 percent in enough qualifying polls to make the stage for the Houston debate.

Tenacious as ever, Gabbard turned her exclusion into a rallying cry against the party establishment. At an event in downtown Los Angeles, she proclaimed that "debate or no debate," her campaign would move on—"because we know that it is 'We, the People' who decide who gets to lead our country." She would, eventually, return to the stage.

THE WARREN BOOMLET

The Houston debate confirmed that the Democratic field remained dominated by the left. It also accelerated a surge in support for Elizabeth Warren.

Warren's rise began at that town hall in Franconia Notch, New Hampshire. The Drudge Report—once reliably conservative but adopting a tone more critical of Trump over time—blared the headline: "WARREN PACKS CROWDS IN NH." It added: "*TRUMPGRET?*"[421] Warren enjoyed favorable media coverage, with journalists repeating the campaign's somewhat fanciful estimates of its own crowd sizes.[422]

Even the president seemed to realize what was going on. As the

Democrats were campaigning across New Hampshire, Trump held a rally in Manchester,[423] noting Warren's rise: "It's like Elizabeth Warren. I did the Pocahontas thing. I hit her really hard, and it looked like she was down and out, but that was too long ago. I should have waited."[424]

Warren's poll numbers rose even more dramatically after the Houston debate. The RealClearPolitics poll average showed Warren's numbers climbing sharply in mid-September and then peaking after the first week in October.[425]

The secret to Warren's sudden new appeal was no great mystery. In a field that was lurching to the left, she was a more palatable option than Bernie Sanders.

She had the same policies but did not call herself a socialist. She was also in her 70s, but on the early side. If elected, she would be the first woman president—and though Sanders belatedly embraced the idea that he could be the "first Jewish president," that label did not have quite the same appeal.[426]

Some of Sanders's supporters understood fully that Warren had copied policies like Medicare for All—and resented it. At a rally in California in July 2019, former Ohio state senator Nina Turner, a Sanders surrogate, took aim at Warren (among others): "For some of these folks—I'm trying to understand: did they believe all along, or do they believe just because they're running for president?"[427]

There was another, somewhat macabre, factor. In the spin room after the Houston debate, Warren held court long after the other candidates had gone home. Buttigieg almost ran past my Breitbart News colleague Kristina Wong, as she attempted to ask a question about Afghanistan.[428] Sanders made an appearance and spoke to me for several minutes. But he looked red-faced and sounded hoarse.

Less than three weeks later, while campaigning in Las Vegas, Nevada, Sanders suffered a heart attack. He was rushed to a hospital for emergency surgery and had two stents installed in a major artery.[429] He recovered quickly and returned to the campaign trail just days later. But the question of his health would linger throughout the campaign.

There was every reason to believe Warren could take over the race.

For a very brief window of time, in early October 2019, she surpassed Biden in the polls. But with that new status came renewed scrutiny.

Warren had particular trouble with the question of how she would pay for Medicare for All and her other plans for "structural change." Like Sanders, she focused on taxing the rich. Warren also proposed a confiscatory 2 percent tax on the wealth—not the income—of the richest Americans, calling it, somewhat disingenuously, a "two cent" tax, meaning the government would claim two cents of every dollar they owned over $50 million.[430]

But unlike Sanders, Warren was not willing to say that she would raise taxes on the middle class, though there seemed to be no alternative. The Warren campaign itself estimated that her version of Medicare for All would cost $52 trillion over ten years,[431] more than the $38 trillion that Sanders's plan might cost.[432] Not even the rich had enough money to pay for that.

In any other race, Warren might have been able to whistle past the question of middle-class taxes. Yet she was being compared to a candidate who was forthright about it—even if he claimed the net benefit would be positive.

Her position fell apart on—of all places—CBS's *The Late Show* with comedian Stephen Colbert:

> COLBERT: You keep being asked in the debates: "How are you going to pay for it? Are you going to raise the middle-class taxes?"
> WARREN: Right.
> COLBERT: How are you going to pay for it? Are you going to raise the middle-class taxes?
> WARREN: So, here's how we're going to do this: Costs are going to go up for the wealthiest Americans, for big corporations.
> COLBERT: "Taxes" is what you mean by costs?
> WARREN: Yeah.
> COLBERT: Okay.
> WARREN: Yeah, and hardworking middle-class families are going to see their costs go down.
> COLBERT: But will their taxes go up?

WARREN: Well—but here's the thing—

COLBERT: But, here's the thing. I've listened to these answers a few times before.[433]

Eventually, Warren's evasions became a subject of mockery on *Saturday Night Live*.[434] They reinforced the central idea of the "Pocahontas" narrative—namely, that she could not be trusted.

The decline was slow, but it was irreversible.

THE WHISTLEBLOWER

Yet the race was about to be upstaged by the drama on Capitol Hill.

A bizarre story had begun percolating in Washington: that President Trump had tried to pressure Ukraine, America's ally against Russia, to investigate Joe Biden, the Democratic front-runner.

On August 29, two weeks before the debate, *Politico* reported that the United States had withheld aid meant to help Ukraine defend itself against Russian aggression. "Trump holds up Ukraine military aid meant to confront Russia," the headline declared.[435]

A week later, on September 5, the *Washington Post*, citing an anonymous source—"we're reliably told"—claimed the president was "attempting to force [Ukrainian President Volodymyr] Zelensky to intervene in the 2020 U.S. presidential election by launching an investigation of the leading Democratic candidate, Joe Biden."[436]

Three days before the Houston debate, the *Wall Street Journal* reported: "Three House committees said they are investigating whether President Trump and his lawyer sought to pressure the Ukrainian government to pursue probes in an effort to benefit Mr. Trump's re-election bid."[437]

Several days later, a new story emerged—a tale of a "whistleblower" who had filed a complaint with the Intelligence Community Inspector General (ICIG) about a conversation between the president and a foreign leader. The House Intelligence Committee, chaired by Representative Adam Schiff (D-CA), issued a subpoena to Acting National Director of Intelligence Joseph Maguire to force the release of the complaint.

"Little is known about the person who made the complaint," the *Journal* reported.[438] Schiff claimed that he and his committee were in the dark: "We have not spoken directly with the whistleblower," Schiff told MSNBC. "We would like to."[439]

That claim, like many others, would unravel—but not before causing havoc.

The U.S. Constitution states, in Article II, Section 4: "The President, the Vice President, and all officers of the United States, shall be removed from office on impeachment for, and conviction of, treason, bribery, or other high crimes and misdemeanors."[440]

It is a last resort, meant to be used only in extreme circumstances, not as a political weapon for political parties to use against the president over ideological differences, much less personal disputes or arguments over style.

And yet to Democrats, and even some Republicans, impeachment was a first resort, an urgent option to be deployed against President Donald Trump[441] to reverse the results of an election that they still could not accept.[442]

In fact, some Democrats—and "Never Trump" Republicans, who refused to accept his ascent toward the party nomination—had begun discussing the possibility of impeaching Trump many months before he won the election. *Politico* magazine published an essay in April 2016 titled "Could Trump Be Impeached Shortly after He Takes Office?"[443] The argument was that Trump was so extraordinary, so extreme in his rhetoric and so unpredictable in his deeds, that it was possible to imagine scenarios in which he drove the country into the ground and violated the Constitution at will.

Enthusiasm for impeachment became urgent after Trump won. Harvard Law School professor Laurence Tribe argued in December 2016, for example, that President-elect Trump should be impeached upon taking office for allegedly violating the Constitution's Emoluments Clause, based on the fact that his businesses earned income from foreigners.[444]

The first elected Democrat to urge impeachment openly was Representative Maxine Waters (D-CA). She refused, along with many

Resistance Democrats, even to say Trump's name—as if he were Volde-mort, the *Harry Potter* villain—and referred to Trump as "45," leading "Impeach 45!" chants at rallies. Other left-wing members of Congress, especially the Squad, began taking up the cause.

Speaker Pelosi was walking a difficult tightrope. She told the country Democrats would follow where the facts led. They wanted to give time, she said, to Special Counsel Robert Mueller's investigation and would take their cues from him. In the meantime, she backed Democrat-led inquiries into every aspect of Trump's life.

There was only one problem: the investigations kept coming up empty. Lawsuits were tossed; probes came up empty.[445] Mueller's report was the most dramatic failure. When Attorney General William Barr refused to turn over the underlying evidence, citing federal law, Demo-crats accused him of aiding a cover-up and voted to hold him in criminal contempt of Congress.

Barr's refusal provided a pretext for most of the Democratic pres-idential field to back impeachment, in one form or another. Several senators—including Kamala Harris, Elizabeth Warren, and Bernie Sanders—pushed for an impeachment vote in the House. Others, like Pete Buttigieg and Joe Biden, were more careful, but only Tulsi Gabbard opposed impeachment outright, arguing that it would divide the country.

Pelosi relented in July 2019, after the Mueller report fizzled, and let the House vote on impeachment. It failed, with 95 votes in favor and 322 against. Too late: almost the entire Democratic field had committed to a lost, reckless political cause.

But the "whistleblower" had reset the game.

FOURTEEN

ADAM SCHIFF'S BASEMENT

"If a foreign power possessed compromising information on a
U.S. government official in a position of influence, that is a counterintelligence
risk. If a foreign power possessed leverage, or the perception of it, over the
president, that is a counterintelligence nightmare."
—Representative Adam Schiff, April 2020[446]

PELOSI MOVES—A DAY EARLY

On Tuesday, September 24, 2019, Speaker of the House Nancy Pelosi
emerged from an evening meeting on Capitol Hill with her caucus,
faced the cameras, and declared: "Today, I'm announcing the House
of Representatives moving forward with an official impeachment
inquiry."[447] She cited "press reports...of a phone call by the President
of the United States, calling upon a foreign power to intervene in his
election." She declared, gravely: "This is a breach of his constitutional
responsibilities."

The president had said, earlier that afternoon, that he had declas-
sified the transcript of the call, and it would be released the following
morning. But Pelosi would not wait.

It was a fateful decision.

The next day, President Trump released the official record of his telephone conversation with Ukrainian president Volodymyr Zelensky. Trump had never mentioned the 2020 election, nor did he mention security assistance, much less threaten to withhold it.

It was Zelensky who raised the issue of corruption, promising to "drain the swamp" in Ukraine. Trump asked Zelensky to "do us a favor"— in the context of talking about the "country"—by looking into the origins of the claims of Russian interference in the 2016 U.S. election and to "look into" allegations of corruption by Hunter Biden, the son of former vice president Joe Biden.[448]

Biden had boasted to the Council of Foreign Relations in 2018, in a lecture recorded on video that later went viral, that he had forced Ukraine to fire a prosecutor by threatening to withhold $1 billion in U.S. loan guarantees.[449] He neglected to tell his audience that the prosecutor had jurisdiction over the investigation into a Ukrainian fossil fuel company called Burisma Holdings, on whose board Hunter Biden sat, collecting a handsome salary of $83,000 per month.[450] It was just one of Hunter Biden's many overseas exploits: he also secured $1.5 billion in investment for his private hedge fund days after accompanying then vice president Biden to China on Air Force Two.[451]

Trump did have a personal and political interest in these allegations, dating back to Special Counsel Robert Mueller's investigation. Former New York City mayor Rudy Giuliani, representing the president as his personal attorney, had planned a trip to Ukraine in May 2019 to follow up on reports about Biden as well as on suspicions that Ukrainians may have been involved in Russia's alleged election interference.

As the *New York Times* reported, Giuliani was hardly shy about his intentions:

> Mr. Giuliani said he plans to travel to Kiev, the Ukrainian capital, in the coming days and wants to meet with the nation's president-elect to urge him to pursue inquiries that allies of the White House contend could yield new information about two matters of intense interest to Mr. Trump.

One is the origin of the special counsel's investigation into Russia's interference in the 2016 election. The other is the involvement of former Vice President Joseph R. Biden Jr.'s son in a gas company owned by a Ukrainian oligarch.[452]

Giuliani's task was to build a case for the president's defense. He canceled that trip but remained unabashed about his role, which he said was not "foreign policy" but legal work.

But in the "whistleblower" complaint, Giuliani's efforts took on a different guise: they were, the complaint alleged, an attempt to invite foreign interference in the 2020 election.

Pelosi noted Trump had "admitted to asking the president of Ukraine to take actions which would benefit him politically."

Yet Trump had an independent, legitimate purpose for his request: the question of whether a former vice president had obstructed justice in a foreign country, while his son exploited his father's position to enrich himself, was arguably a matter of public concern. Schiff and the Democrats had argued for years that the Obama administration had been justified in snooping on Trump's campaign in 2016 because of the risk he might have been "compromised" by Russia.

Trump's release of the transcript caught Pelosi and other Democrats by surprise. They had relied on the whistleblower complaint—which the administration had withheld, though Democrats clearly knew what was in it.[453]

The whistleblower—who acknowledged having no firsthand information—had claimed: "I have received information from multiple Government officials that the President of the United States is using the power of his office to solicit interference from a foreign country in the 2020 U.S. election."

There was nothing in the transcript about that: that was simply an interpretation. The whistleblower had never actually heard the call, which no one else seemed concerned about—least of all the Ukrainian president, who told reporters on September 25 that Trump had not pressured him about anything and that the call had been "normal."[454]

Under the circumstances, impeachment seemed far-fetched at best. Trump called it "THE GREATEST SCAM IN THE HISTORY OF AMERICAN POLITICS!" on Twitter.[455]

But Democrats had set the wheels in motion.

THE OHIO DEBATE

Impeachment hung over the fourth Democratic debate, cohosted by CNN and the *New York Times* at Otterbein University in Westerville, Ohio.

The debate featured the Democrats' return to a state that Trump had won by a wide margin in 2016, on the way to building a new working-class coalition in the Upper Midwest.

It also marked the return of Tulsi Gabbard to the stage—and the knives were out.

The *Times* warmed up for the debate by publishing a lengthy attack on Gabbard—as news—in which the paper of record suggested that Gabbard was attracting support from the far-right white supremacist fringe as well as potential Russian assistance.

The *Times* reported:

> On podcasts and online videos, in interviews and Twitter feeds, alt-right internet stars, white nationalists, libertarian activists and some of the biggest boosters of Mr. Trump heap praise on Ms. Gabbard. They like the Hawaiian congresswoman's isolationist foreign policy views. They like her support for drug decriminalization. They like what she sees as censorship by big technology platforms.
>
> Then there is 4chan, the notoriously toxic online message board, where some right-wing trolls and anti-Semites fawn over Ms. Gabbard, calling her "Mommy" and praising her willingness to criticize Israel. In April, the Daily Stormer, a neo-Nazi website, took credit for Ms. Gabbard's qualification for the first two Democratic primary debates.[456]

The article continued in that vein, suggesting that Gabbard had served Russian interests by threatening to boycott the debate. In the days leading up to the event, Gabbard had warned that the "DNC and the corporate media are essentially trying to usurp" the election.[457]

Based on the *Times* article, she may have had a point.

Joining her among the twelve candidates onstage was left-wing billionaire Tom Steyer, the Democrat mega-donor and climate change activist who had funded the Need to Impeach campaign. He had jumped into the race in July, sensing the weakness of the field and promising to wrest politics away from "corporate control."[458]

Steyer had qualified, in September, for his first debate —too late for the Houston debate but well ahead of the Ohio contest in October, thanks to strong poll numbers in Nevada.[459] He could hardly have expected that events would turn so favorably in his direction. His timing was perfect.

Impeachment dominated the debate from the start. Steyer was triumphant, and almost all of the other candidates also supported the decision: even Biden, who had been somewhat reticent, had come on board.

"This president—and I agree with Bernie, Senator Sanders—is the most corrupt president in modern history and I think all of our history," Biden said.[460]

CNN's Anderson Cooper raised a few prescient questions. He asked Cory Booker, for example, whether he could fulfill his constitutional duty to do impartial justice in a potential Senate trial of the president, given that he had said Trump's "moral vandalism" was disqualifying. He challenged Pete Buttigieg to defend an impeachment process pushed by Democrats after insisting for months that any impeachment be bipartisan.

None took the bait: all supported impeachment.

Except Gabbard.

"If impeachment is driven by these hyperpartisan interests, it will only further divide an already terribly divided country," she said. While she supported investigating Trump, she said, impeachment had potential to backfire.

"If the House votes to impeach, the Senate does not vote to remove Donald Trump, he walks out and he feels exonerated, further deepening the divides in this country that we cannot afford," she warned.

When Cooper asked Biden about his son Hunter, the pushback was firm.

"My question is, if it's not okay for a president's family to be involved in foreign businesses, why was it okay for your son when you were vice president? Vice President Biden?" Cooper asked.

"Look, my son did nothing wrong. I did nothing wrong. I carried out the policy of the United States government in rooting out corruption in Ukraine," Biden said.

He denied that he had ever spoken to Hunter Biden about his business interests and said he was "proud" of his son, though the younger Biden had admitted that serving on Burisma's board had been a mistake.

"What we have to do now is focus on Donald Trump. He doesn't want me to be the candidate. He's going after me because he knows, if I get the nomination, I will beat him like a drum."[461]

Later, Booker accused CNN of "elevating a lie and attacking a statesman" merely by raising the issue of Hunter Biden in asking about impeachment.

"And the only person sitting at home that was enjoying that was Donald Trump seeing that we're distracting from his malfeasance and selling out of his office," Booker admonished.

These questions were about to be hashed out, in secret, in the basement of the U.S. Capitol.

THE HEARINGS

Traditionally, impeachment investigations are handled by the Judiciary Committee, after the full House votes to authorize an inquiry.

Instead, Democrats began their investigation quietly, in Schiff's[462] House Intelligence Committee,[463] which could hold meetings behind closed doors, in a special room in the basement of the Capitol called the Special Compartmentalized Information Facility (SCIF). Nothing would leak except what Democrats wanted to be known.

Later, if and when public hearings were held, witnesses—called exclusively by Democrats—had already been auditioned. Those who were less than helpful could be omitted.

The hearings began in October, in what Republicans derided as "Adam Schiff's basement." The first witness was Ambassador Kurt Volker, the former U.S. representative for Ukraine negotiations, who resigned his post after being mentioned in connection with the controversy. Another promising witness was former National Security Council (NSC) senior official Tim Morrison, who had also left his post.

Ultimately, however, both of these witnesses proved more useful to the president's case than to Democrats. Volker testified that the president never withheld anything—neither aid nor a White House meeting—to pressure Ukraine and that senior Ukrainian officials were not even aware of the hold on U.S. aid until *Politico* reported it.

Morrison—who had left the NSC for unrelated reasons—testified that he had seen nothing wrong with the president's phone call with Zelensky. He also denied claims that the "transcript" of the Ukraine call had been hidden on a highly secure server as part of a cover-up.

Catherine Croft, a State Department official, provided testimony that would also prove crucial to the president's defense. She noted that President Trump had withheld military aid to Ukraine before, in 2017, for reasons having nothing to do with politics. His concern: corruption.

In fact, Trump had given Zelensky's predecessor a public dressing-down: "When this was discussed, including in front of the Ukrainian delegation, in front of President [Petro] Poroshenko, he described his concerns being that Ukraine was corrupt, that it was capable of being a very rich country, and that the United States shouldn't pay for it, but instead, we should be providing aid through loans," Croft said.[464]

Other witnesses were more helpful to the Democrats' cause. One was former U.S. ambassador Marie Yovanovitch, whom Trump had dismissed after she was accused in media reports of putting down the president and pressuring Ukraine not to prosecute certain Americans—allegations she vigorously denied. Another was Lt. Col. Alexander Vindman, a Ukraine expert at the NSC who was awarded a Purple Heart for wounds sustained in Iraq and who had raised concerns about the Ukraine call with the NSC counsel.

There was also U.S. Ambassador to the European Union Gordon Sondland, a political appointee who seemed to be at the center of discussions about pressuring Ukraine, though he testified that Trump had told him there was "no quid pro quo."

One witness who never appeared was the whistleblower. Schiff had originally insisted the whistleblower—a Central Intelligence Agency officer—be allowed to testify but abruptly reversed himself when the *New York Times* revealed his committee had been in touch with the whistleblower after all.[465]

Schiff "learned about the outlines of a C.I.A. officer's concerns that President Trump had abused his power days before the officer filed a whistle-blower complaint," the *Times* reported. "The early account... explains how Mr. Schiff knew to press for the complaint when the Trump administration initially blocked lawmakers from seeing it."

Schiff, determined to obscure his committee's coordination with the whistleblower, blocked every Republican question that might lead to exposing his identity. He and other Democrats claimed the whistleblower had the right to anonymity—a complete fabrication.[466]

By the end of October, investigative journalist Paul Sperry had reported that the whistleblower was likely Eric Ciaramella, a former NSC staffer who had "previously worked with former Vice President Joe Biden and former CIA Director John Brennan, a vocal critic of Trump who helped initiate the Russia 'collusion' investigation." Ciaramella stayed at the NSC after Trump took office but was sent back to the CIA "amid concerns about negative leaks to the media."[467] The situation reeked of conflicts of interest. But the media suppressed his name; Facebook even took down articles that mentioned it.

As the lengthy transcripts of testimony were slowly released, Democrats claimed they had proven their case; Republicans claimed Trump was exonerated. After Republicans, led by Representative Matt Gaetz (R-FL), staged a protest inside the SCIF against the closed-door hearings, Democrats relented and held a vote to authorize the impeachment inquiry.

The lopsided resolution broke with precedent by denying the

president legal representation during most of the inquiry and by removing the power of the minority party to veto witnesses, but it did provide for at least one public hearing.[468]

And as the drama unfolded, the Trump administration enjoyed one of its most successful months yet. A jobs report released October 4 showed that unemployment had fallen to 3.5%, the lowest level since 1969.[469] And on October 27, President Trump confirmed that U.S. forces had killed Islamic State leader Abu Bakr al-Baghdadi in a daring raid.

"He died like a dog. He died like a coward. The world is now a much safer place," the victorious president told his country, as Democrats attempted to remove him from office.[470]

"TOWN HALL" RADICALISM

Meanwhile, on the campaign trail, the candidates participated in a series of "town hall" meetings. The cable news networks specialized in these events, which followed one of two formats.

Traditional town hall meetings focus on one particular candidate, allowing each to make a case directly to a national audience—and be grilled by a live studio audience.

One of the most famous town hall questions in American political history came during President Bill Clinton's town hall on MTV in 1994: "Mr. President, the world's dying to know: Is it boxers or briefs?" He replied: "Briefs—can't believe she did that."[471]

The alternative town hall format focused on one particular issue, inviting all of the candidates to explain their policies. That allows for more in-depth discussion than in a general debate. The disadvantage is that candidates may tailor their responses to win the support of the audience most interested in that particular topic.

The result, especially before a live studio audience, is often a rush toward extreme positions, the better to win the most applause.

The archetypal example was a town hall meeting staged by CNN in Sunrise, Florida, in February 2018, barely a week after the mass shooting at the Marjorie Stoneman Douglas High School in nearby Parkland. The televised program, hosted by Jake Tapper—who worked briefly for a gun control organization[472]—was ostensibly open-ended and even included National Rifle Association (NRA) spokesperson Dana Loesch.

But given the raw emotions in the community and the area's strong Democratic political leaning, the discussion could head in only one direction. Speaker after speaker berated the NRA, which many held directly responsible for the nineteen deaths at the school. The event launched the national political careers of student activists David Hogg and Emma Gonzalez, who attacked Loesch as a mother: "I want you to know that we will support your two children in a way that you will not."[473]

CNN, which won the Walter Cronkite Award for Excellence in Journalism for that town hall,[474] decided to stage many such town halls during the 2020 election cycle. Arguably, these events reinforced the leftward shift of the entire presidential field.

In September 2019, for example, CNN held a town hall on the topic of climate change. Governor Jay Inslee had pressed the DNC for a climate change–centered debate; he dropped out of the race in August, but CNN picked up his idea.

For seven hours, displacing regular afternoon and evening news programming, CNN hosted the candidates in its New York studio, where they seemed to compete with one another to propose the most outrageous idea. Andrew Yang talked about forcing Americans to drive electric cars. Kamala Harris talked about banning plastic straws—a topic that had nothing to do with climate change. Several supported a "carbon tax"; most wanted to ban fracking, which has actually *reduced* carbon emissions;[475] and only Yang and Booker defended nuclear energy.[476] The most radical proposals earned the most applause; there was no room for moderation. Joe Biden drew attention for a burst blood vessel in his left eye that turned it a frightening dark red.[477]

At a similar event in October, just days before the Ohio debate, CNN held a town hall in Los Angeles devoted to LGBTQ issues.[478] The answers from the candidates were radical enough: Elizabeth Warren, for example, applauded a 9-year-old who claimed to be transgender.[479]

But the audience was even more ambitious. Anderson Cooper was busy interviewing Pete Buttigieg when activists interrupted from the audience: "Trans people are dying! Do something!"[480] Some members of the audience applauded, chanting, "Trans lives matter!"

During Beto O'Rourke's turn, a black transgender woman, Blossom C. Brown, seized the microphone from a female audience member who was attempting to ask a question. "Black trans women are being killed in this country, and, CNN, you have erased black trans women for the last time!" Brown said.

Moderator Don Lemon had to coax the microphone carefully back from her: "The reason that we are here is to validate people like you," he said. For his trouble, Lemon earned a racist rebuke: "That's how anti-blackness works among black people of color," she told him.

Alexandria Ocasio-Cortez preferred the single-issue format: "Honestly, there should be themed debates," she tweeted in February 2020. "Doing so educates the public far more on issues & actually serves the purpose of distinguishing who knows what they're talking about + who doesn't."

"Climate debate. Foreign policy debate. Healthcare. Racial justice. Labor&Econ. Can't hide."[481]

But the runaway radicalism of these forums made the entire party look unhinged. Impeachment was to be a similar stampede—a town hall on one issue, and one man, lasting several months—with severe consequences for the party, the election, and the country.

FIFTEEN

IMPEACHMENT AS PARODY

"While the Chairman was speaking, I actually had someone text me, 'Is he just making this up?' And yes he was, because sometimes fiction is better than the actual words or the texts, but luckily the American public are smart and they have the transcript."
— Representative Mike Turner, September 26, 2019[482]

THE CURTAIN RISES

The sun rose brightly over Washington, DC, on November 13—but the air outside was frigid. An arctic cold front had passed through the night before, bringing winter's chill, several weeks early.

The mood inside the hearing room at the U.S. House of Representatives was just as icy—enlivened only by the presence of Pissi Myles, a drag queen who crashed the event in a floor-length red evening gown.[483]

Adam Schiff, the chair of the House Intelligence Committee, was prepared to open the first public hearing in the impeachment inquiry.

The first two witnesses were at their table, ready. Acting Ambassador William Taylor, chargé d'affairs at the U.S. Embassy in Ukraine, was wearing a crisp charcoal-gray business suit and a teal-colored tie, his dark eyes confident behind wire-rim glasses. Next to him sat senior State Department official George Kent, deputy assistant secretary in the European and Eurasian Bureau at the State Department, a career bureaucrat in a snappy gray three-piece suit, with a beige patterned bow tie and matching pocket handkerchief.[484]

There could be no better picture of officialdom—the "deep state."

There was an urgent tension as millions tuned in to see what the Democrats had found, what the Resistance had produced, nearly three years to the day after Trump's election.

Schiff, a former aspiring screenwriter, had crafted the scene and cast the players. Now it was his turn: to open with a prologue, to draw the audience into the drama.

He had already tried once before.

In September, the day after Trump released the transcript of his call with President Volodymyr Zelensky, Schiff tried to explain the president's alleged wrongdoing by acting out his own version of events.

> And so what happened on that call?...Well, it reads like a classic organized crime shakedown.... "We've been very good to your country. Very good. No other country has done as much as we have. But you know what? I don't see much reciprocity here. I hear what you want. I have a favor I want from you, though. And I'm going to say this only seven times, so you better listen good. I want you to make up dirt on my political opponent. Understand?...And so, I'm only going to say this a few more times in a few more ways. And by the way, don't call me again. I'll call you when you've done what I asked."[485]

Republicans were outraged. Rep. Mike Turner (R-OH) said later in the hearing:

> While the chairman was speaking, I actually had someone text me, "Is he just making this up?" And yes, he was, because sometimes

fiction is better than the actual words or the texts, but luckily the American public are smart and they have the transcript.[486]

Schiff later tried to excuse his fakery by claiming it was a "parody."[487] He might have gotten away with it, had Trump not surprised Democrats by releasing the actual transcript. So when the public hearings began, Schiff had to try a different tack.

He began: "In 2014, Russia invaded the United States' ally Ukraine to reverse that Nation's embrace of the West and to fulfill Vladimir Putin's desire to rebuild a Russian empire."

He continued to meander through the details of his case, without explaining clearly what Trump had done.[488]

Ranking Member Representative Devin Nunes (R-CA) responded by calling Democrats' claims a "carefully orchestrated media smear campaign." He called the proceeding a "low-rent Ukrainian sequel" to the "Russia collusion" hoax—one, he noted, Schiff had pursued even to the point of seeking nude photos of the president from Russian pranksters.

More than any barbs from the opposition, what hurt Schiff's case the most was the fact that the hearing was simply boring. Democrats had built up public expectations of blatant wrongdoing, but in the full light of day their accusations seemed to be about minor points of foreign policy— where the president has broadest discretion—rather than "high crimes and misdemeanors."

Taylor and Kent exuded contempt for the president's approach to foreign policy, with Taylor adding that it would be "crazy" for the president to withhold aid in exchange for political help. Yet he had to admit the only knowledge he had about that accusation was what he read in the *New York Times*. Neither "witness" had any firsthand knowledge about what Trump was alleged to have done, in fact.

But Kent did have firsthand knowledge of something else: namely, Joe Biden's conflict of interest in Ukraine. He testified that he had specifically raised it with the vice president's office in 2015 but was told that Biden was grieving the death of his other son, Beau, and could not deal with the issue—which was never addressed.

At best, the first public impeachment hearing left Americans' minds largely unchanged. At worst—for Democrats—it strengthened the president's defense.

In mid-November, I was invited to debate impeachment in a national satellite broadcast on Sirius XM, hosted by legal analyst Dan Abrams. My opponent was former Watergate prosecutor Nick Ackerman.

I took time out from campaign coverage to hit the law books and study every available transcript of every "basement" deposition. We clashed in the "fishbowl" at SiriusXM's Manhattan studio—the first political debate held in the arena.

It was a lively, informative exchange—the best presentation, we agreed, for either side.

Curiously, Ackerman accused Trump of "bribery"—a high crime specifically mentioned in the Constitution.[489]

Democrats, too, would hint at that allegation. But they would never quite make it.

ADRIFT IN IOWA (OR OHIO?)

As impeachment began to suck up airtime and attention, the Democratic presidential candidates attempted to campaign as best they could.

Beto O'Rourke, once a front-runner, dropped out at the start of November, unable to raise cash.[490] But Elizabeth Warren was still in the hunt. A *New York Times* poll released November 1 had shown her leading Iowa, ahead of Biden—albeit narrowly.[491] But she continued to struggle to explain how she would pay for Medicare for All without raising taxes on the middle class. She released her formal plan, calling for over $20 trillion in new spending—and still claimed she would not raise middle-class taxes.

The Biden campaign reacted: "The mathematical gymnastics in this plan are all geared towards hiding a simple truth from voters: it's impossible to pay for Medicare for All without middle class tax increases," it said in a statement.[492]

Warren retorted that Biden was "running in the wrong presidential primary." To oppose Medicare for All was to oppose the party itself.[493]

Biden's campaign manager fired back by noting that Warren had been a Republican well into her 40s.[494] "Joe Biden has spent his life helping elect Democrats across the country and served with honor in the Senate and with Pres Obama," he tweeted.

But perhaps the wear and tear of that long career were showing: Biden appeared to confuse Ohio and Iowa at an event in Cedar Rapids the next day.[495] Though he earned an endorsement from Tim Ryan, who had dropped out in late October, and continued to hold a sizable lead in South Carolina, his weaknesses were glaring.

Biden's decline tempted other candidates to jump into the race. Michael Bloomberg, the former New York City mayor and self-made billionaire, changed his mind about sitting out the 2020 contest. His strategy was to skip the early primary states that vote in February, which were already saturated by the other campaigns, and to focus on states that were to vote on Super Tuesday in March. He filed first in Alabama, that hotbed of New York liberalism.

Joining Bloomberg as a late entrant was Massachusetts governor Deval Patrick, the Bay State's first black governor. "I admire and respect the candidates in the Democratic field. They bring a richness of ideas and experiences and depth of character that makes me proud to be a Democrat," he said in his announcement. But evidently, he did not think they could win.[496]

Meanwhile, Steyer's campaign hit a snag as a top aide in Iowa resigned over allegations that he had offered to pay local politicians to support the candidate.[497]

Another candidate with high hopes—which was also the title of his campaign's theme song—was Pete Buttigieg. With just weeks to go before voting began, Buttigieg was putting his campaign's vast war chest to good use. He made a large ad buy in South Carolina, hoping to build his black support, which was virtually nil.[498]

He did not help himself, however, by circulating an email claiming he had support from four hundred black leaders in the state, some of whom were supporting other candidates and some of whom were not even black.[499] His campaign also used a stock photo of a Kenyan woman in an ad highlighting his "Douglass Plan" for black America.[500]

Despite those struggles, Buttigieg gained steadily in the polls, such that he began to challenge Warren in Iowa and Sanders in New Hampshire.

Kamala Harris was less fortunate: though she had focused most of her energy on Iowa, even spending Thanksgiving there, she could not seem to gain traction. By the end of November, the *New York Times* would report that her campaign had "unraveled."[501] Once a threat to Biden, she was sliding out of contention.

Bernie Sanders kept plugging away, hitting the trail with vigor as he recovered from his heart attack. Representative Ilhan Omar, endorsing Sanders at a rally in Minneapolis, declared proudly that he would "fight against Western imperialism."[502]

He also campaigned with Alexandria Ocasio-Cortez in Iowa, bringing her star power to the trail. Both criticized Bloomberg's imminent candidacy: "I don't think billionaires should be president right now," Ocasio-Cortez said.[503]

The rise of the left within the party, and the prospect of Warren or Sanders emerging as the nominee, frightened the Democratic establishment. Even former president Barack Obama, who had prided himself on being a community organizer in the White House, began to drop hints about his displeasure with the field. The average American, Obama told Democratic Party donors, "doesn't think we have to completely tear down the system and remake it. And I think it's important for us not to lose sight of that."[504]

Sanders denied he was "tearing down the system"—he was merely demanding "human rights" as part of a "political revolution."[505]

With Biden floundering and the far left flourishing, impeachment was more urgent than ever.

THE COLONEL AND THE AMBASSADOR

Enter the Democrats' star witness: Lt. Col. Alexander Vindman, of the National Security Council. He arrived at the hearing room in full dress uniform; colleagues grumbled privately that he wore civilian clothes at the office.

Vindman was the NSC's director of Russia, Ukraine, Moldova, the Caucuses, and Belarus. He was everything Democrats could have hoped for: a soldier, an immigrant, a patriot—and a member of the bureaucracy clearly frustrated with the way Donald Trump was running the presidency.

According to the transcript of his closed-door testimony, Vindman shared the fears of the whistleblower that Trump had placed his own interest above the country's in asking Ukraine's president to investigate Biden. He didn't know whether the president had done anything illegal; he just felt it was "wrong."

But what also emerged in that testimony was the deep resentment he felt that Trump seemed determined to run foreign policy on his own, outside what Vindman called the "interagency consensus."[506] He particularly resented Giuliani's role—a sentiment shared by many of the foreign policy experts (though not all, as some saw him as a useful conduit to the president).

Vindman had also, oddly, been offered the position of defense minister in the incoming Ukrainian government. He had declined, but the offer added to the intrigue: just whom, exactly, did Vindman believe he was representing?

The public hearing retraced his closed-door testimony—but there was one moment of high drama. Vindman admitted, under questioning by Nunes, that he had discussed the Zelensky call with two people who did not work in the White House. One, he said, was George Kent; the other was "an individual in the intelligence community." Vindman would not name who that "individual" was.

Schiff, who had blocked any Republican questions that might have led to the identification of the whistleblower in the closed-door hearings,[507] did so again during Vindman's open testimony and struck down the question.

Republicans objected that if Schiff—and Vindman—claimed not to know the identity of the whistleblower, then asking Vindman whom he had spoken with about the Ukraine call could not possibly reveal the whistleblower.

"Per the advice of my counsel, I've been advised not to answer specific questions about members of the intelligence community," Vindman said.

"This is—are you aware that this is the Intelligence Committee that's conducting an impeachment hearing?" Nunes asked.[508]

It looked like Democrats had something to hide. But they were not done yet.

The highlight of the impeachment hearings was yet to come. Gordon Sondland, the U.S. ambassador to the European Union,[509] had originally defended Trump in his closed-door testimony, telling Schiff's committee that the president had told him directly that he wanted "nothing" from Ukraine and that there was no "quid pro quo."

But after other witnesses testified that Sondland was the one who had described a potential quid pro quo arrangement, he filed an amendment. Sondland now claimed that, "by the beginning of September 2019, and in the absence of any credible explanation for the suspension of aid, I presumed that the aid suspension had become linked to the proposed anti-corruption statement" about investigating the Bidens and Burisma. He added that it "would have been natural for me to have voiced what I had presumed" to the other witnesses at the time.

It was just a *presumption*, but Sondland was beginning to crack.

By the time he arrived on Capitol Hill for his public testimony, Sondland had changed his story again. In a lengthy opening statement that leaked to the *Washington Post*, Sondland claimed that there had been, in fact, a quid pro quo—not for military aid, but for a White House meeting.

"I know that members of this committee have frequently framed these complicated issues in the form of a simple question: Was there a 'quid pro quo?'" Sondland testified. "With regard to the requested White House call and White House meeting, the answer is yes."[510]

He did not confirm Democrats' central claim—that the president withheld aid in return for investigations—but he testified that it was the "only logical conclusion."[511]

Sondland's new stance fell apart quickly under cross-examination from Republicans. He admitted that the quid pro quo was his presumption, not something he could prove. Representative Jim Jordan (R-OH) asked Sondland to confirm the president had told him there was "no quid pro quo" and then asked, with evident frustration, why Sondland had not put that into his twenty-three-page opening statement.

Representative Mike Turner pinned Sondland down: "No one on this planet told you that President Trump was tying aid to investigations, yes or no?"

"Yes," Sondland replied.

But Democrats did not care. They had what they wanted: a witness who had said the magic words—"quid pro quo."

THE ATLANTA DEBATE

That drama unfolded in Washington as the candidates prepared to take the debate stage in Atlanta, Georgia—the unofficial capital city of black America.

The debate was being held on November 20 at the Tyler Perry Studios, a 300-acre compound created on a former Army base by the legendary African American filmmaker. Several buildings were named for famous black artists, such as Denzel Washington and Halle Berry.

And the African American electorate was, for the first time, at the center of the debate, thanks partly to Trump's efforts to reach out to the community.

Ironically, the focus of attention onstage was to be Pete Buttigieg, who had struggled to appeal to African American voters since the start of his campaign.

In the spin room, Pissi Myles made another splash, having obtained press credentials. Outside, dozens of Buttigieg supporters gathered on a traffic island. There were other campaigns there, too: Joe Biden had a small group, as did Andrew Yang, whose fans mounted an impressive LED light display spelling "MATH."

But the largest, with several dozen supporters, was the Buttigieg contingent, waving blue-and-yellow PETE signs mounted on long wooden poles.

I decided to wander into the crowd and ask them why they supported him.

"What do you think is his biggest achievement in South Bend?" I asked one man.

"You got me on that one!" he laughed. "Let me think about that one, okay?"

Others gave similar answers.

"He's been mayor, I think, for eight years," a middle-aged white woman told me. "He's had hits and misses, but he's learned from that and he's trying to do better."[512]

He was certainly trying.

In seeking to build bridges to the black community, Mayor Pete had tried the usual remedies—courting the support of Al Sharpton, for example, who despite a long history of racist and antisemitic rhetoric had become something of a kingmaker in the party.[513]

But in June 2019, a police officer shot and killed a 53-year-old black resident, Eric Jack Logan, in the parking lot of an apartment complex in South Bend where there had been reports of burglaries of cars.[514] Residents were outraged that the officer's body camera had not been turned on.

Buttigieg dashed home to deal with the crisis. Unfortunately, almost everything he did seemed to backfire.

At a town hall in South Bend, Buttigieg faced an angry audience of black residents, some of whom accused him of neglecting the city to pursue his presidential ambitions. "You gotta get back to South Carolina like you was yesterday?" one man shouted.[515]

In an attempt to appease the anger, Buttigieg began speaking about "racial injustice" among the police: "Even if a perfect human being were to put on that uniform, that would mean taking on that burden."[516] The police were furious, and there were reports of declining morale.[517]

As he rose in the polls in Iowa and New Hampshire, Buttigieg's record in South Bend became a target.

"I don't think you are in any position to be president," said Bernie Sanders surrogate Nina Turner at a fundraiser in Atlanta the night before the debate. She referred explicitly to the shooting in South Bend.[518]

Onstage, the attacks continued. At one point, the moderator invited

Kamala Harris to attack the mayor's "outreach to African American voters." Noting that Buttigieg "has made apologies" for the South Bend shooting, she chastised Democrats for taking black voters for granted. "They show up when it's...close to election time and show up in a black church and want to get the vote, but just haven't been there before."

He did not even try to push back. "I welcome the challenge of connecting with black voters in America who don't yet know me," he said.

But then Buttigieg argued that he could identify with African Americans because of the discrimination he felt as a gay man: "While I do not have the experience of ever having been discriminated against because of the color of my skin, I do have the experience of sometimes feeling like a stranger in my own country."[519]

The comparison fell flat. Harris described it the next day, somewhat charitably, as "a bit naïve."[520]

The one consolation: Biden did even worse.

"I come out of a black community, in terms of my support," the former vice president claimed.

He added that he had the support of "the only African American woman that's ever been elected to the United States Senate"—meaning former senator Carol Moseley-Braun of Illinois.

"The other one is here," Harris said, drawing laughter from the audience.

There were also questions about impeachment. They all supported it; Elizabeth Warren was ready to convict.

Buttigieg noted that when the dust settled, America would have to "address big issues that didn't take a vacation for the impeachment process."

He was right—though when the "big issue" arose, Democrats would be too busy to notice.

SIXTEEN

ABUSE OF POWER

"Is this a permanent inquisition against the president?"
—Representative Jerrold Nadler, October 29,1998[521]

JERRY NADLER'S GAVEL

This was Jerry Nadler's moment.

For months—ever since the 2018 elections—he had pushed for impeachment. As chair of the House Judiciary Committee, it was his responsibility to draft and approve the articles of impeachment, which would live on in history.

He had been through one impeachment before. In 1998, he protested vehemently against the impeachment of President Bill Clinton, arguing there should never be "an impeachment supported by one of our major political parties and opposed by the other." In a speech on the floor of the House, he declared:

> The American people have heard the allegations against the president, and they overwhelmingly oppose impeaching him. They elected President Clinton. They still support him. We have no right to overturn the considered judgment of the American people. Mr.

Speaker, the case against the president has not been made. There is far from sufficient evidence to support the allegations. And the allegations, even if proven true, do not rise to the level of impeachable offenses.[522]

Nadler told a protest against impeachment on the Capitol steps: "They are ripping from us, they are ripping asunder our votes! They are telling us that our votes don't count!"[523]

Nadler had initially applied the same standard to the idea of impeaching President Donald Trump. In November 2018, as he prepared to take the gavel of the Judiciary Committee, Nadler told MSNBC that impeachment had to be bipartisan because "you don't want to tear the country apart."[524]

Perhaps Nadler imagined the Mueller report would turn out differently. At any rate, things had not gone quite the way he imagined. Pelosi had given Schiff and his Intelligence Committee the starring role; Nadler would function, in effect, as a rubber stamp.

No matter: he was in charge. He had warned the day before his hearings began: "I'm not going to take any shit."[525]

The Intelligence Committee published its report that day, with almost no time for anyone to study its nearly three hundred pages.[526] Curiously, the report omitted any reference to "bribery," a charge that Schiff and Pelosi had brandished for days.[527]

In contrast to the Watergate hearings, which lasted for months, Nadler would preside over just two days of hearings. The first was a gathering of legal experts, who would offer their opinions on the constitutional grounds for impeachment. He denied Republicans a day to call their own witnesses, in violation of House rules.[528]

In the expert hearing, Nadler granted Democrats the right to call three witnesses and Republicans only one. The Democrats invited law school professors Pam Karlan of Stanford University, Michael Gerhardt of the University of North Carolina, and Noah Feldman of Harvard.

Republicans chose to call Jonathan Turley of George Washington

University, a liberal Democrat whose classical views on the separation of powers had brought him into alliance with the GOP, representing the Republican-run House against the Obama administration's overreach in modifying Obamacare without legislative approval.[529]

Feldman played along eagerly. When Democratic counsel Norm Eisen played a deceptively edited video in which Trump was seen saying, "I have the right to do whatever I want as president," Feldman said that, "as someone who cares about the Constitution," the president's words "struck a kind of horror in me." He, and Eisen, neglected to note the context: Trump had been speaking about his authority to fire and hire executive officials, not about his power in general.[530]

The others did likewise, confident that the facts were on their side. Karlan even claimed that when the president had asked Zelensky to "do us a favor, though, because our country has been through a lot,"[531] he was using the "royal 'We'"—referring to himself.

Karlan hurt the cause when she picked on the president's family: "While the president can name his son Barron, he can't make him a baron," she said. That earned a rebuke in real time from first lady Melania Trump, and Karlan apologized, sort of: she said the president should also apologize for things he had said in the past.[532]

Turley somberly testified that while he believed "abuse of power" was a valid reason to impeach a president, Democrats would be doing so with "the shortest proceeding, with the thinnest evidentiary record, and the narrowest grounds ever used to impeach a president."[533]

As to impeaching Trump for "obstruction of Congress," merely for resisting subpoenas in court, Turley warned: "If you impeach a president, if you make a 'high crime and misdemeanor' out of going to the courts, it *is* an abuse of power. It's *your* abuse of power."[534] Turley also agreed with Republicans that by the Democrats' standard, every president—including George Washington—would have had to be impeached for "abuse of power."

Against three-to-one odds, and a chairman who had already concluded the president was guilty, Turley had more than held his own.

"YOU HAVE MADE JOE McCARTHY LOOK LIKE A PIKER"

Pelosi had seen enough. The next day, she directed the Judiciary Committee to draft articles of impeachment.[535] There had not been one fact witness before the committee—nor would there be. It would not be necessary.

The next—and final—witness hearing considered the Intelligence Committee's report. Schiff did not even bother to show up to defend it. Instead, he sent committee counsel Daniel Goldman, a "Russia collusion" hoaxster and former MSNBC pundit who squirmed uncomfortably as he evaded questions about who had approved the request to snoop on Nunes's phone records.[536]

Representative James Sensenbrenner (R-WI) scolded Goldman, calling Schiff's tactics "the beginning of a surveillance state":

> Now, had Chairman Schiff decided to "man up" and come here and talk rather than hiding behind Mr. Goldman, his chief investigator, as his surrogate or legate, if you will, I think we could have gotten to the bottom of this and taken action to make sure that this never happens again. You know, I do not want to see members of Congress, through their subpoena power, being able to subpoena the telephone records of private citizens, willy-nilly.... That, I think, is an abuse of power. We're talking a lot about abuses of power here in the White House and in the executive branch. Here we see a clear abuse of power on the part of the people who are prosecuting this impeachment against the President of the United States. They should be ashamed of themselves. Now, I come from the state where Joe McCarthy came from. I met Joe McCarthy twice when I was first getting into politics as a teenager. Folks, you have made Joe McCarthy look like a piker, with what you've done with the electronic surveillance involved.[537]

Even more awkward were the antics of committee counsel Barry Berke, a lawyer who had donated thousands to Democratic candidates[538] and suddenly made an appearance on the committee panel, among the members of Congress.

Berke delivered an opening argument that was largely a partisan diatribe against the president. Chairman Nadler declined to swear him in—or his Republican counterpart—as a witness.

When Republicans asked why he had not done so, Nadler tried to explain that they were staff members, who are not typically placed under oath. Republicans replied that Berke had impugned the motives of the president, which House rules prohibited staff from doing. Nadler's defense: Berke had been a witness.

Bizarrely, Berke also appeared on the dais, among members of Congress, to grill Stephen Castor, the Republican counsel on the House Intelligence Committee. Representative Louie Gohmert (R-TX), a former judge, complained: "This is not appropriate to have a witness be a questioner... it's just wrong." He quipped: "How much money do you have to give to get to do that?"[539]

Nadler, who had vowed to run a tight ship, looked incompetent. But he brought the hearing to its prescribed conclusion: "The facts are clear. The danger to our democracy is clear. And our duty is clear," he pronounced.[540]

Three days later, the committee reconvened to consider the two articles of impeachment against Trump—without the participation of the White House, which opted not to legitimize the proceeding; without a single fact witness appearing before the committee; and without Republicans being allowed to call witnesses.

Nadler recited a Kafkaesque explanation of why he had not allowed Republicans to call their own witnesses: "The House rule does not require me to schedule a hearing on a particular day," he said, "nor does it require me to schedule the hearing as a condition precedent to taking any specific legislative action."

In other words, he was allowing himself to schedule a hearing after the president had already been impeached, at which point it would not matter.

Sensenbrenner, the elder statesman, condemned the whole affair:

Now, let's look at these two articles. Unlike the Nixon and Clinton impeachment, there is no crime that is alleged to have been committed by the President of the United States. There are policy differences, but I would submit that given the definition of treason, and bribery, and other high crimes and misdemeanors, that does not mean that the policy differences should be enough to remove a president from office. There is no allegation of bribery in these articles. There is no allegation of extortion. They have defined for themselves what a high crime and misdemeanor will be. This bar is so low that what is happening is that a future president can be impeached for any disagreement when the presidency and the House of Representatives are controlled by different parties. And that goes back to establishing a parliamentary system, which the Framers explicitly rejected at the time of the Constitutional Convention.[541]

His words failed to stir Nadler or his party, and the articles passed December 13 along partisan lines, as expected.[542]

"IMPEACH THE MOTHERFUCKER!"

Trump's fate was now set in stone. Though he was highly unlikely to be removed from office by the Senate, he would soon become only the third president in American history to be impeached.

Ironically, he scored one of his most important achievements at the same time. Speaker Pelosi finally relented and allowed a vote on the U.S.-Mexico-Canada Agreement (USMCA), the new and improved trade deal that was to replace the North American Free Trade Agreement (NAFTA), which Trump had promised to undo.

Pelosi had stalled the vote for more than a year, claiming that she wanted to improve provisions to protect American workers. But the changes to the treaty were small. The real reason for the delay was that Democrats wanted to deny the president a win. Impeachment had changed their incentives: they wanted to be able to show they could still govern while trying to oust the president. Allowing him to claim victory was a small price to pay if he were to be impeached at the same time.

The night before the impeachment vote, Democrats held rallies across the country. Five hundred gathered in front of City Hall in Los Angeles, for example, holding signs that said, "Impeach and Remove," "Impeach 45," and "Trump Is Not Above the Law." Some were vulgar: "Fuck Cheeto Voldemort," "Make the Asshole Go Away" [MAGA—a parody of the president's "Make America Great Again" slogan]. One man simply carried a rubber model of Trump's head on a pike.

Former representative Katie Hill spoke to the crowd, standing atop a large truck on which an LED light display flashing pro-impeachment slogans had been mounted. Once a promising member of the first-year class, defeating an incumbent Republican in a suburban district, she had quit over a sex scandal—after first voting to open the impeachment inquiry.[543] And now, she was liberated.

"Impeach the motherfucker!" she shouted into the microphone from the top of the truck, to loud cheers.

Her rally cry echoed that of Representative Rashida Tlaib, months before. Though Pelosi had admonished her caucus not to celebrate the impeachment, Tlaib posted a giddy video of herself walking through the halls of Congress on the way to vote.[544]

Pelosi opted for a more sensible black dress as she addressed the House. "As Speaker of the House, I solemnly and sadly open the debate on the impeachment of the President of the United States." She used the word "solemn," or "solemnly," three times; "sad" or "sadly" four times. And she described the task of impeachment as an urgent one: "If we do not act now, we would be derelict in our duty. It is tragic that the President's reckless actions make impeachment necessary. He gave us no choice."[545]

One by one, members stood up to deliver their own addresses. Schiff, in his speech, invoked the "Russia collusion" theory once again:

He tried to cheat, and he got caught.

Now, this wasn't the first time. As a candidate in 2016, Donald Trump invited Russian interference in his presidential campaign....

This Russian effort to interfere in our elections didn't deter Donald
Trump; it empowered him.

Schiff attacked the motivations of Republicans who would vote against
impeachment:

Many of my colleagues appear to have made their choice—to protect the president, to enable him to be above the law, to empower
this president to cheat again, as long as it is in the service of their
party and their power.

And he concluded:

In America, no one is above the law. Donald J. Trump sacrificed
our national security in an effort to cheat in the next election. And
for that, and his continued efforts to seek foreign interference in our
elections, he must be impeached.

There were some ugly scenes. Gohmert defended the president:

You said it was about this terrible Russia collusion. When that fell
through, it was about emoluments, it's about bribery, it's about
extortion. It's changed, but one thing hasn't changed and that's the
intent to impeach this president. It's always been there.

Nadler, who was leading the Democrats' presentation at that point,
responded by accusing Gohmert of "spouting Russian propaganda on
the House floor." The Texan was so incensed that he walked back to the
podium, shouting at Nadler to take back his words.[546]

Finally, the vote was taken. Article I, "abuse of power," passed
230–197; Article II, "obstruction of Congress," passed 229–198.[547]

Representative Jared Golden (D-ME) voted for the first but not the
second; Representative Collin Peterson (D-MN) opposed both; Representative Jeff Van Drew (D-NJ) voted against both and then switched

parties. Tulsi Gabbard, the presidential candidate, voted "present" on both.

When Pelosi announced that the first article had passed, a cheer broke out from Democrats on the floor.

She silenced it with an icy glare and a backhanded wave. But it was too late.

THE LOS ANGELES DEBATE

The next day, Democrats descended on Los Angeles, California, for the sixth presidential debate.

It had not been clear, until just days before, whether the debate would take place. Originally, it was to have been held at UCLA.[548] But the party moved it, in deference to a long-simmering union dispute with the university.[549]

The secondary venue was Loyola Marymount University, near Los Angeles International Airport. But there was another labor dispute there, and the union asked the candidates not to cross the picket lines. They all stood with the union and refused to participate. With two days left to go, the union agreed to a collective bargaining agreement, and the debate went forward.[550]

Outside, demonstrators gathered along Lincoln Boulevard, roughly a dozen from each campaign. Suddenly, marching from a distance, came some nine hundred charter school advocates—parents, children, and activists, most of them African American or Hispanic. Some held signs: "Stop Prepping Black Kids for Prison!" was one. They completely swamped the campaigns outside; they had even brought a marching band.

They held a particular grudge against Elizabeth Warren, who once supported school reform but had, like the other Democrats, bowed to the teachers' unions. One man told me he wanted to support a Democrat, but none supported charter schools. The goal was to make enough noise outside to attract the candidates' attention.

Would anyone listen?

The candidates seemed tired, after a long year on the campaign trail and weeks and weeks of impeachment coverage. The highlight was a fight between Warren and Pete Buttigieg over a high-dollar fundraiser he had held the previous Sunday in a chandelier-encrusted cave at the HALL winery in Napa Valley where $900 bottles of wine had been served.[551]

Online trolls had called it "Pete's Wine Cave." The Sanders campaign even set up a website, peteswinecave.com, which redirected to a Bernie donation page; surrogate Nina Turner showed up in the spin room wearing a Pete's Wine Cave T-shirt.

The group onstage was also the least diverse that the party had fielded thus far: as the DNC had tightened the debate criteria over time, more of the lower-tier candidates were excluded—and most of them happened to be minorities.

Earlier in the month, Kamala Harris had finally ended the long, miserable decline of her campaign. "I'm not a billionaire. I can't fund my own campaign," she had said, in a dig both at Trump and at the latecomers to the Democratic primary.[552] California was meant to be her Super Tuesday stronghold; she should have been onstage. Now, she would watch the debate on television.

Cory Booker had quipped: "If the debate stage stays what it is right now, it will have more billionaires than black people."[553] So much for the most diverse field in the party's history.

The only "diverse" candidate was Andrew Yang. And, breaking with his rivals, he offered a surprising perspective when the first question, inevitably, addressed impeachment:

It's clear why Americans can't agree on impeachment. We're getting our news from different sources, and it's making it hard for us even to agree on basic facts. Congressional approval rating, last I checked, it was something like 17 percent, and Americans don't trust the media networks to tell them the truth. The media networks didn't do us any favors by missing a reason why Donald Trump became our president in the first place. If you turn on cable network news today, you would think he's our president because of some combination of Russia, racism, Facebook, Hillary Clinton, and e-mails all mixed together.

But Americans around the country know different. We blasted away four million manufacturing jobs that were primarily based in Ohio, Michigan, Pennsylvania, Wisconsin, Missouri. I just left Iowa. We blasted 40,000 manufacturing jobs there. The more we act like Donald Trump is the cause of all of our problems, the more Americans lose trust that we can actually see what's going on in our communities and solve those problems. What we have to do is we have to stop being obsessed over impeachment, which unfortunately strikes many Americans like a ballgame where you know what the score is going to be, and start actually digging in and solving the problems that got Donald Trump elected in the first place. We have to take every opportunity to present a new positive vision for the country, a new way forward to help beat him in 2020, because make no mistake, he'll be there at the ballot box for us to defeat.

My Breitbart colleagues were stunned. Someone in the Democratic Party actually "got it."[554]

The rest of what Yang said sounded zanier than ever. He described his climate change plan: "move people to higher ground."

But on this night, he seemed the only one onstage with a clear idea of what Americans were feeling.

He would not qualify for the next debate.

SEVENTEEN

RED DAWN

> **Brutus:** Stoop, Romans, stoop;
> And let us bathe our hands in Caesar's blood
> Up to the elbows, and besmear our swords.
> Then walk we forth, even to the market-place,
> And, waving our red weapons o'er our heads,
> Let's all cry "Peace, freedom, and liberty!"
>
> **Cassius:** Stoop, then, and wash. How many ages hence
> Shall this our lofty scene be acted over
> In states unborn and accents yet unknown!
> —*Julius Caesar*, Act 3, Scene 1[555]

THE WORLD ENTERING 2020

President Donald Trump and First Lady Melania Trump strolled into a New Year's Eve party at Mar-a-Lago, looking glamorous. He was wearing the traditional black tie and tuxedo; she glittered in her gold-sequin sleeveless black Givenchy gown.[556]

They paused to speak to the press. Trump held forth, answering question after question, in his usual confident, bombastic style. He did not look like a president who had just been impeached; he looked like a president who expected to be reelected and was looking forward to the challenges ahead.

"I don't really care. It doesn't matter," he said, when asked about a possible impeachment trial in the Senate. "As far as I'm concerned I'd be very happy with a trial because we did nothing wrong."[557]

Melania offered a New Year's resolution: "Peace on the world."[558]

They turned and entered the party. The entire Trump world seemed to be there. The Trump children: Don Jr., Eric, Tiffany, and Ivanka, with husband Jared Kushner, Trump's trusted aide. Trump attorney Rudy Giuliani was also there; so, too, was a small army of conservative activists and social media influencers.

The band played; the lights flashed; the guests danced.[559] Dr. Gina Loudon, co-chair of Women for Trump 2020 and broadcasting on a Facebook livestream, briefly showed Trump and his friends before wishing her followers "a wonderful, happy new year. It's going to be the best ever, because we have the best president ever.…We know that you're going to win in 2020."

They had every reason to be happy.

The country was largely at peace. The troops would soon withdraw from Afghanistan. A few days hence, the president would score a remarkable victory with a precision strike on Iranian general Qasem Soleimani, the leader of the Iranian Revolutionary Guard Corps, responsible for terrorism across the Middle East and for a violent assault on the U.S. Embassy in Baghdad, Iraq. When Iran retaliated, firing missiles at bases in Iraq housing U.S. troops, no Americans died. Trump felt no need to respond; America had won a round without being drawn into a war. Even critics would call it a win for the president.[560]

The president had kept North Korea at bay with the opening of historic direct talks with leader Kim Jong-un. Even if the Korean peninsula was not yet denuclearized, few Americans feared a nuclear strike from the rogue regime anymore.

The economy was, arguably, the strongest it had ever been. A slow recovery that began under President Barack Obama with the Wall Street bailout and the Federal Reserve's "quantitative easing" had accelerated under President Trump. Tax cuts in December 2017 had boosted economic growth over 4 percent by the second quarter of 2018.[561] Though the Fed had slowed that growth with a controversial series of rate hikes over the following year, the central bank had since eased off, and growth hovered around a healthy 2 percent. The stock market had soared over the past year; the Dow Jones Industrial Average hovered near 30,000 points, hitting record highs.

Most important of all, the recovery had finally come to Main Street. Unemployment had dropped to 3.5 percent, the lowest level in fifty years. Minority unemployment was also at record lows, and black Americans enjoyed the lowest level of poverty ever, with fewer than one-fifth of African Americans living below the poverty line.[562] The president's tariffs, his trade war with China, and his tough enforcement at the border had led to a revival of American manufacturing and a revival of working-class wages. The bottom 25 percent of American wage-earners had seen the largest wage increases compared to all other income groups.[563] This was, truly, a "blue collar recovery."

The ongoing trade war with China, which had created uncertainty in the markets, looked set to wind down. On New Year's Eve, the president had promised that he would be "signing our very large and comprehensive Phase One Trade Deal with China on January 15. The ceremony will take place at the White House."[564] And a new free trade deal beckoned with a post-Brexit United Kingdom.

While Americans still held sharply divided opinions about Trump, his approval rating was solid at roughly 45 percent, and it would reach a high of 46.3 percent by the end of February.[565] Satisfaction with the state of race relations was still low, at 36 percent, but it had jumped sharply from 22 percent.[566] The president could list a string of accomplishments for his conservative base—nearly two hundred federal judges, a wall going up on the U.S.-Mexico border—and even some policies his "progressive" detractors could love, such as criminal justice reform.

The media hated him; the tech giants were suppressing him;

Hollywood had demonized him. But impeachment had not hurt him; it had made him stronger.

Trump was exactly where he wanted to be.

JUSTICE DELAYED

On Capitol Hill, Speaker of the House Nancy Pelosi had a new plan.

The first signs emerged two days before the impeachment vote, when Harvard Law School professor Laurence Tribe wrote an op-ed in the *Washington Post* suggesting that Democrats withhold the articles of impeachment from the Senate.

Tribe, who had coauthored a book about impeachment,[567] had been pushing for Trump to be impeached since before he took office. He was also reported to be advising Democrats on their legal strategy during the impeachment process.[568]

In his op-ed, he argued:

> Now that President Trump's impeachment is inevitable, and now that failing to formally impeach him would invite foreign intervention in the 2020 election and set a dangerous precedent, another option seems vital to consider: voting for articles of impeachment but holding off for the time being on transmitting them to the Senate.[569]

Tribe added that delaying the articles of impeachment "could strengthen" the bargaining position of Senate Minority Leader Chuck Schumer (D-NY) in determining Senate procedures for the trial. And he argued that the public was entitled to a "meaningful" trial—one, presumably, that would include more evidence against the president than was then available.

It was an odd argument, one that appeared to concede that Democrats lacked enough evidence to convict the president. It ignored the Constitution's explicit provision in Article I, Section 3: "The Senate shall have the sole Power to try all Impeachments."[570] It also ignored Alexander

Hamilton's argument in *Federalist No. 65*—widely, if selectively, quoted by Democrats as they attempted to justify Trump's impeachment—that a trial following impeachment should not be delayed.[571]

On the day of the impeachment vote, House Majority Leader Steny Hoyer (D-MD) suggested that Democrats would be open to a delay.[572] In a press conference after the impeachment vote, Pelosi declined to say when, exactly, she would deliver the articles of impeachment to the Senate, allowing the trial of the president to begin.

"We'll make that decision as a group, as we always have, as we go along," she said.[573]

Reporters were puzzled. Evidently the Democrats' plan was to withhold the articles of impeachment, the better to deny any kind of exoneration to President Trump—or until the Republican-run Senate could promise terms more favorable to Democrats' purposes.

But Pelosi had—*earlier that day*—argued that impeaching and removing the president was an urgent priority. "If we do not act now, we would be derelict in our duty," she said in her floor speech.[574] Other Democrats had done the same, partly to explain why they could not wait for the courts to resolve issues of executive privilege before impeaching Trump for "obstruction."

Republicans were livid.

Senate Majority Leader Mitch McConnell accused Pelosi of being "too afraid" to send the articles to the Senate.[575] He had already hinted, in a Senate floor speech the day before the House impeachment vote, that he would push for a vote to dismiss the charges. The Senate had no responsibility, he said, to make "Chairman Schiff's sloppy work more persuasive" by calling more witnesses.[576] And the day after the vote, he mocked Democrats for trying to delay:

> The prosecutors are getting cold feet in front of the entire country and second-guessing whether they even want to go to trial.
>
> They said impeachment was so urgent that it could not even wait for due process but now they're content to sit on their hands. It is comical.

Democrats' own actions concede that their allegations are unproven.

But the articles aren't just unproven. They're also constitutionally incoherent. Frankly, if either of these articles is blessed by the Senate, we could easily see the impeachment of every future president of either party.[577]

McConnell later added: "'Some House Democrats imply they are withholding the articles for some kind of 'leverage' so they can dictate the Senate process to senators. I admit, I'm not sure what 'leverage' there is in refraining from sending us something we do not want!"[578]

For his part, Minority Leader Schumer argued that the country was entitled to a "fair trial," which required new witnesses and documents.

Schumer, who had voted *against* hearing from new witnesses during President Bill Clinton's impeachment trial in 1999, argued: "To conduct a trial without relevant witnesses who haven't been heard from—to just rehash the evidence presented in the House—just doesn't make any sense. If Leader McConnell doesn't hold a full and fair trial, the American people will rightly ask: what are you, Leader McConnell, and what is President Trump hiding?"[579]

What Schumer overlooked is that the right to a "fair trial" applies primarily to the accused, not the prosecution, and has done so since the Magna Carta was drawn up in 1215.

But Democrats were determined to deny the president a speedy, inevitable acquittal.

THE INVISIBLE ENEMY

On December 31, 2019, as the president wished the country a happy new year, authorities in the city of Wuhan, China, confirmed they had been treating dozens of patients who had been suffering from a strange form of pneumonia.[580]

"Mr. Li is one of 59 people in the central city of Wuhan who have been sickened by a pneumonia-like illness, the cause of which is unclear. The cases have alarmed Chinese officials, who are racing to unravel the mystery," the *New York Times* reported on January 6.[581] "Symptoms of the new illness include high fever, difficulty breathing and lung lesions, the Wuhan health commission has said. No deaths have been reported but seven people are critically ill." Other causes had been ruled out, and authorities shut down the local Huanan Seafood Wholesale Market in Wuhan, out of fear that an illness might have crossed over from animals to humans.

A few days later, Chinese scientists said there was little reason to worry. They had identified a new virus—a coronavirus, similar in structure to those that cause the common cold—as the cause of the illnesses, but they did not think it was easily spread. "There is no evidence that the new virus is readily spread by humans, which would make it particularly dangerous, and it has not been tied to any deaths," the *Times* reported.[582]

By January 11, the first death had occurred. The *Times* reported, "There is no evidence that the virus can be spread between humans," citing Chinese authorities, who appeared to link it to contact with animals at the Huanan Seafood Wholesale market.[583] "Researchers have been encouraged by the fact that patients' relatives and hospital workers have not been reported to have gotten sick, signaling that the virus may not spread easily among humans."

Three days later, on January 14, the World Health Organization (WHO) declared in a tweet: "Preliminary investigations conducted by the Chinese authorities have found no clear evidence of human-to-human transmission of the novel #coronavirus (2019-nCoV) identified in #Wuhan, #China."[584] Several Asian countries were already on high alert, having been caught flat-footed by the outbreak of severe acute respiratory syndrome (SARS), which spread from China in 2002, as Chinese authorities covered up the severity of the epidemic.

On January 13, Thailand reported the first case of coronavirus outside China; Japan followed on January 15; and South Korea followed on January 20.[585] It was not yet clear if the virus was spreading among human beings, but it was finding its way around the world—thanks in part to Wuhan's role as a major travel hub.

Millions of Chinese travelers were preparing to move about the country for the Lunar New Year on January 24. There were temperature checks for passengers boarding flights at Wuhan's Tianhe International Airport, but travel continued as usual. Reuters reported on January 17 that there was "little worry" at the "epicenter" of the new virus.[586]

Then, on January 23, the Chinese government moved suddenly to shut down Wuhan, canceling all travel and closing it off to the rest of the country and the world. "At this point, at least 17 people had died and more than 570 others had been infected," the *Times* later recalled.[587]

The Chinese government was already in damage-control mode. On January 20, China declared that there was "no need to panic." The *Global Times*, controlled by the Chinese Communist Party, advised: "There is no need to overreact. If you haven't been in contact with some-one with a fever or haven't been to Wuhan, there is little chance you will get infected."[588]

The first victim had already arrived in the United States.

According to a study published in March in the *New England Journal of Medicine*, he had arrived in the United States on January 15 from Wuhan, where he had been visiting relatives.[589] Four days later:

> On January 19, 2020, a 35-year-old man presented to an urgent care clinic in Snohomish County, Washington, with a 4-day history of cough and subjective fever. On checking into the clinic, the patient put on a mask in the waiting room. After waiting approximately 20 minutes, he was taken into an examination room and underwent evaluation. . . .
>
> Given the patient's travel history, the local and state health departments were immediately notified. Together with the urgent care clinician, the Washington Department of Health notified the CDC Emergency Operations Center. Although the patient reported that he had not spent time at the Huanan seafood market and reported no known contact with ill persons during his travel to China, CDC staff concurred with the need to test the patient.

He was confirmed on January 20 to have the new virus—COVID-19, identified as a coronavirus because its structure looks like a crown. He would recover by the end of the month.

But America—and the world—would never be the same.

THE GOLDEN PENS

On January 15, President Trump, Vice President Mike Pence, and senior members of the administration gathered in the East Room of the White House for the signing of the "Phase One" trade agreement between China and the United States.

Two years before, Trump had launched a trade war against Chinese imports, defying conventional economic wisdom to protect American manufacturing at home and the rights of American companies abroad. Though China retaliated, targeting American agriculture, the U.S. economy was relatively unscathed, and China blinked first. The new agreement would not resolve all of the differences between the two nations but would at least set a boundary around the conflict.

In attendance from China were Vice Premier Liu He, Ambassador Cui Tiankai, and other Chinese dignitaries.

"Today, we take a momentous step—one that has never been taken before with China—toward a future of fair and reciprocal trade, as we sign phase one of the historic trade deal between the United States and China," President Trump said. "Together, we are righting the wrongs of the past and delivering a future of economic justice and security for American workers, farmers, and families."[590] He added that he hoped to visit his "very, very good friend" President Xi Jinping "in the not-too-distant future."

Vice President Mike Pence also spoke:

> Mr. President, we gather here today, thanks to your leadership, at a time that the American economy is booming. With the strong support of members of Congress who are gathered here, we are now experiencing an economy that's created more than 7 million jobs. The unemployment rate is at a 50-year low. The average American's household income has risen by more than $5,000. That's all a result

of your commitment to cut taxes, roll back regulation, unleash American energy. But it also reflects your commitment to free, fair, and reciprocal trade.

Early in this administration, you made it clear that the era of economic surrender was over. And you took a strong stand for American jobs and American workers. You said to our friends in China that things had to change. And thanks to your leadership, today the change begins.[591]

Vice Premier Liu kept his remarks brief, conveying a greeting from President Xi, promising to "work through dialogue and consultation to properly handle and effectively resolve relevant issues," and offering greetings for the Chinese Lunar New Year.[592]

No one mentioned impeachment, except the president himself. "They have a hoax going on over there," he joked, drawing laughter at Congress's expense.

On Capitol Hill, Speaker Pelosi convened an "engrossment" ceremony in the Rayburn Reception Room. This was to be the formal certification of the impeachment vote from December, exactly four weeks before. Afterward, the articles would be walked over to the Senate.

In addition to the press, Pelosi was joined by the committee chairs who had investigated the president for many months, as well as her hand-picked team of House impeachment managers.

Led by Adam Schiff, the team included Judiciary Committee chair Jerry Nadler; Representative Hakeem Jeffries (D-NY), chair of the House Democratic Caucus; Representative Zoe Lofgren (D-CA), who had been a staffer during the impeachment inquiry into President Richard Nixon; and Representative Sylvia Garcia (D-TX), a former local judge in Texas. The managers represented the diverse spectrum of Democratic Party constituencies. They were joined by Representative Maxine Waters (D-CA), chair of the House Financial Services Committee, who had led chants of "Impeach 45!" early in the Trump presidency.

"So sad, so tragic for our country," Pelosi said, as she opened her remarks, noting the "difficult time in our country's history."

The engrossment and transfer of the articles of impeachment, she said, would "make it be very clear that this president will be held accountable, that no one is above the law and that no future president should ever entertain the idea that…Article II says that he can do whatever he wants."

It was the same misquote that Democrats had used repeatedly in the Judiciary Committee.

Before her, on a table, on silver trays, lay several dozen commemorative ballpoint pens, each emblazoned with Nancy Pelosi's personal signature in gold, with metallic golden tips.

Pelosi sat at the table and slowly, laboriously, placed her name on the articles, using one pen after another to fill in small parts of her signature. It was the sort of ceremony typically reserved for presidents signing landmark legislation and brought to mind Pelosi's claim upon taking the speaker's gavel a year before that the Constitution made her the president's equal.[593]

Afterward, she and the impeachment managers smiled at one another and posed for photographs, holding their pens aloft, like the senators in Shakespeare's *Julius Caesar*, brandishing the swords with which they had stabbed the would-be tyrant.

So much for the "solemn" and "sad" nature of the occasion.

The White House responded, sarcastically, through Press Secretary Stephanie Grisham: "Nancy Pelosi's souvenir pens served up on silver platters to sign the sham articles of impeachment.… She was so somber as she gave them away to people like prizes."[594]

On the other side of the country, the first coronavirus patient was arriving in the United States from China.[595]

The Iowa caucuses were less than three weeks away.

EIGHTEEN

===============

ELECTION INTERFERENCE

"Some of you are upset because you should be in Iowa right now. But instead, we are here, and they are not ready to go. And it's outrageous. It's outrageous. And the American people won't stand for it, I'll tell you that right now. [Democrats] are not here to steal one election. They are here to steal two elections."

—White House Counsel Pat Cipollone, January 21, 2020[596]

THE IOWA DEBATE

The presidential campaign continued, as best it could, overshadowed by the impeachment proceedings. Democrats were about to try the president for interfering with the election, but they were busy interfering with their own.

They had not been completely dormant, of course. Newcomer Mike Bloomberg was tossing money out his window as fast as it could fly. He hired the best talent, promising they would work through November regardless of the primary result. He bought tens of millions of dollars in online ads—more in one month than Trump had spent in a year.[597]

The other candidates could not compete with Bloomberg's billions, so they returned to their donors, shaking the money tree. Pete

Buttigieg continued his impressive fundraising, racking up $24.7 million in the fourth quarter of 2019.[598] Bernie Sanders raised even more, $34.5 million—the largest total in one quarter of any Democrat thus far.[599] Joe Biden, by contrast, raised only $22.7 million.[600]

Other candidates fared less well. Julián Castro dropped out of the race on January 2, having hung on just long enough to say he had made it into 2020. He would endorse Warren a few days later. Marianne Williamson laid off her staff, ending her campaign a week later. Cory Booker lasted a few days longer and then dropped out as well, blaming impeachment for his inability to campaign.[601] John Delaney, the long-forgotten moderate, quit by month's end.

Michael Bennet trekked doggedly across New Hampshire, pledging to hold fifty town halls before the primary. Tulsi Gabbard, whose campaign was running on fumes, at least took some time to have fun, surfing in the frigid Atlantic waters off the coast of New Hampshire on New Year's Day.[602]

The entire field seemed to be flagging, as if they had run out of new things to say. Almost all of the candidates criticized the Trump administration's stunning air strike on Iran's Qasem Soleimani, for example. But their attacks seemed hollow, almost formulaic. The common complaint was that Trump lacked a "strategy" or would start a war.[603]

Buttigieg accused Trump of "chest-thumping militarism." Sanders went further, cosponsoring legislation to block military action against Iran without congressional authorization.[604]

The campaigns trudged across the wintry Iowa landscape, with snow clinging to bare trees and clumped among the stiff brown stubble of harvested fields, once green and gold in the summertime.

In diners and church halls across the state, they made their case to small huddles of voters. When Jill Biden addressed a gathering at a public library in the town of Boone, there seemed to be more reporters than voters present. There were a few Tulsi billboards staring across empty fields and Sanders yard signs popping up in places—and not much else.

On January 14, when the candidates finally gathered at Drake

University in Des Moines on a subfreezing night for the last debate before the Iowa caucuses, they presented Democratic voters with an all-white lineup of half a dozen candidates.

Outside, standing ankle-deep in snow, a mariachi band played for a group of immigration activists pushing for an end to deportations and amnesty for those already in the country illegally. In Spanish and English, they told their tales of woe, focusing their criticisms on Joe Biden, whom they said they could not forgive for the immigration enforcement—such as it was—of the former Obama administration.[605] A tractor, festooned with giant Trump flags, circled around and around, trolling the entire scene, with a bold—and possibly crazy—farmer seated proudly atop the rig, braving the arctic air.

Inside, Warren—with the aid of CNN—had attempted to lay a trap for Sanders. She had claimed, two days before, that Sanders had told her in a private meeting in 2018 that a woman could not win. Sanders denied it, and her campaign doubled down. After Sanders repeated his denial onstage, the CNN moderator pressed forward, as if nothing had happened: "Senator Warren, what did you think when Senator Sanders told you a woman could not win the election?"[606]

The audience laughed—at CNN. And after the debate, Warren confronted Sanders onstage—with the microphones still live: "I think you called me a liar on national TV."[607]

The stunt had backfired: Warren's attack looked petty. Castro, appearing in the spin room, attempted to put the bravest face on her performance, noting that she had name-checked the "disability community," "trans women," and "black and brown communities" in her closing statement.[608]

It was a lackluster night, looking nothing like what Democrats had dreamed their field of candidates would be. Van Jones, the radical-turned-CNN commentator, summed up the feelings of many in his party, calling the debate "dispiriting" and a "drudgery."

"There was nothing I saw tonight that would be able to take Donald Trump out," he said.

THE IMPEACHMENT TRIAL OPENS

Two days later, the Senate passed the USMCA trade deal. Minutes later, it received the House impeachment managers and swore in Chief Justice John Roberts, who, in turn, swore in the senators present. All vowed to provide impartial justice—an oath many had already broken, having long since declared their opinions as to the president's guilt or innocence.

The following week, the trial began in earnest on the afternoon of January 21, as the president was representing the country at the World Economic Forum in Davos, Switzerland. The first day of the trial involved an extensive, wearying debate over rules and procedures to be followed, and whether witnesses would be allowed up front, or whether the question would be decided after opening arguments.

There was some late drama: the week before, Lev Parnas, an associate of Rudy Giuliani who had assisted with his investigations on Ukraine, gave documents and text messages to the House impeachment managers. Though he was facing federal indictment for campaign finance violations, Democrats wanted to call him as a witness.

Schiff told reporters in the Capitol that if Senate Republicans refused to allow new witnesses and documents to be produced, that would "merely prove the Senate guilty of working with the president to obstruct the truth from coming out" and further the Democrats' case "that what's going on here really is a cover-up."[609]

Inside the chamber, Schiff presented the strongest—or the most fanciful—version of his case against the president, even though the debate was on procedural matters. He told the senators that Trump had told Volodymyr Zelensky, "I have a favor to ask, though"—once again misquoting the president.[610]

Schiff also claimed, wrongly, that the president had never before shown interest in corruption in Ukraine—ignoring the testimony of Catherine Croft, one of the Democrats' own witnesses. She was one whom Schiff had left in the "basement," never summoning for public hearings—and for good reason: she undermined his case.

The White House legal team offered a strong rebuttal. Led by White

House counsel Pat Cipollone, they offered the Senate—and the public—the first formal defense of the president, after months of hearings, leaks, and innuendo. "They're not here to steal one election [2016]," he said, "they're here to steal two elections." They wanted to undo the 2016 results and remove Trump from the 2020 ballot.

Among the rising stars on Cipollone's team was Patrick Philbin, tall and lanky, looking every bit the Yale legal nerd as he patiently delivered powerful arguments on the Senate floor. They were joined by Harvard Law School professor emeritus Alan Dershowitz, a Democrat who opposed Trump politically but would object to impeachment on constitutional grounds.

Tensions ran high—especially when the short-tempered Nadler was at the podium. Nadler told senators that if they were to vote against a Democratic procedural amendment requiring former National Security adviser John Bolton to testify about what he had seen in the White House in the summer of 2019, they would be "voting against the United States." Cipollone retorted: "The only one who should be embarrassed, Mr. Nadler, is you, for the way you addressed this body. This is the United States Senate. You're not in charge here." He demanded that Nadler apologize to the president, the Senate, and the American people.

Senator Susan Collins (R-ME), the mild-mannered Maine moderate, had been so appalled by Nadler's accusation that she passed a note to the chief justice. Roberts said:

> I think it is appropriate at this point for me to admonish both the House managers and the president's counsel in equal terms to remember that they are addressing the world's greatest deliberative body. One reason it has earned that title is because its members avoid speaking in a manner, and using language, that it not conducive to civil discourse.[611]

The amendment failed, along party lines. Democrats went on well into the wee hours of the morning, offering amendments they knew would fail, the better to accuse Republicans of a "cover-up" later.

The senators were squirming silently in their seats—especially those who were running for president: Sanders, Warren, Bennett, and Klobuchar.

Sanders fumed at the schedule, which had forced him to cancel campaign events, and demanded that Senate Majority Leader Mitch McConnell "hold the trial at a time when the American people can observe it and not at two o'clock in the morning."[612]

The president tweaked Sanders on Twitter: "They are taking the Democrat Nomination away from Crazy Bernie, just like last time. Some things never change!"[613]

Meanwhile, Biden—at the center of the drama—was free to campaign as he pleased, as was Buttigieg, who tended to his organization across the state.

"Some of you are upset because you should be in Iowa right now," Cipollone said.

He was right.

THE DERSHOWITZ ARGUMENT

The next session began, as every day would, with the Pledge of Allegiance and a prayer led by the Senate chaplain, Rear Adm. Barry C. Black (Ret.).

The Democrats had three days to present opening arguments. They repeated much of what they had said on the first day, during the procedural debate.

Schiff, perhaps having taken into account the Chief Justice's scolding, gave a more sedate presentation. He made the case for the first article of impeachment, "abuse of power," by stitching together excerpts from documents provided to the House impeachment inquiry as well as snippets of testimony from the public hearings.

For a trial supposedly without witnesses or documents, there certainly seemed to be many of them, at least on the screens above the Senate chamber.

Anti-Trump pundits gushed over Schiff's performance. "This is the most brilliant legal presentation I have heard," tweeted the *Washington Post's* Jennifer Rubin, a member of the "Never Trump" faction.[614]

The House impeachment managers cycled through their roster, each presenting part of the case.[615]

The senators—who were not allowed to speak or to use their cell phones during the proceedings—grew restless as Schiff and the impeachment team began repeating themselves. At one point, a reporter caught Senator Lindsey Graham (R-SC) sneaking out to use the bathroom.

"I'll tell you what," he said, "if there's a bladder contest, I'm entering Schiff."[616]

On and on it went, through the second article of impeachment—"obstruction of Congress"—for three days. As Schiff himself acknowledged, they were retreading old ground.

But there was one unusual moment. On the second day, Representative Sylvia Garcia (D-TX) brought up the Bidens.[617]

Democrats had been saying that the Bidens were irrelevant to the president's defense. But Garcia brought them in, declaring: "Biden's son didn't do anything wrong in connection with Burisma."

That gave the White House a potential opening to call him as a witness, to prove there was a legitimate public interest in Trump's request for Ukrainian investigations. Even Jay Sekulow, the president's personal attorney and lead outside counsel for the White House during the impeachment trial, was puzzled: "What I don't understand is for the last five hours it's been a lot about Joe Biden and Burisma. They kind of opened the door."[618]

Finally, after the third day, the White House began its defense. For two hours, the president's lawyers gave an overview of their case. Deputy White House Counsel Michael Purpura outlined six "facts"—each of which, he argued, would sink the Democrats' case on its own:

1. There was never any connection made on the Ukraine call between investigations on the one hand, and U.S. aid, or a White House meeting, on the other;

2. There was never a "quid pro quo" and Ukraine felt no pressure to investigate the Bidens;

3. Ukraine did not even know there had been a temporary pause in "security assistance";

4. None of the witnesses could testify that Trump ever said anything about a link between aid and investigations;

5. Ukraine received the aid and a meeting anyway; and

6. Trump gave more support to Ukraine than Obama had done.[619]

Sekulow noted that Trump had been a victim of false accusations of "Russia collusion," which Democrats were now trying to revive long after they had been debunked. And Philbin pushed back against "obstruction": rather than "blanket defiance" of congressional subpoenas, he explained, the White House had a legal justification in every instance, including that Democrats had not authorized their own impeachment inquiry.

Cipollone summed up the first day of the president's rebuttal by taking on Democrats' claim that the facts were not in dispute. It was the Democrats who feared the facts—"facts that, they know, completely collapse their case."

The following evening—a Sunday—the *New York Times* broke the story that John Bolton's forthcoming memoir would say that Trump had told him "in August that he wanted to continue freezing $391 million in security assistance to Ukraine until officials there helped with investigations into Democrats including the Bidens."[620] Democrats were ecstatic.[621]

But the White House lawyers pressed on, regardless, as Dershowitz rose to present the constitutional case the next day.

"Nothing in the Bolton revelations, even if true, would rise to the level of an abuse of power or an impeachable offense," he argued.[622]

Impeachment, he said, requires "criminal-like conduct akin to treason and bribery." Democrats had not even alleged a crime.[623]

Furthermore, he said, a *"quid pro quo* alone is not a basis for abuse of power," absent criminal-like conduct. "If a president does something which he believes will help him get elected in the public interest, that cannot be the kind of quid pro quo that results in impeachment," he said.

Schiff and the Democrats—and the compliant media—would misquote Dershowitz for days, saying he had argued that a president could not be impeached for *any* "quid pro quo," no "matter how corrupt that quid pro quo is."[624]

But Senate Republicans heard correctly, and it was enough to convince many of them that they had heard enough.

LAST DASH IN IOWA

The moment there was a break in the trial, the senator-candidates raced for the airport (some taking private airplanes, climate change notwithstanding).

Sanders made it to Marshalltown, Iowa, for a rally with left-wing filmmaker Michael Moore and Alexandria Ocasio-Cortez herself,[625] who had earlier told an audience that the United States was a "nation in decline."[626] Warren won the *Des Moines Register* endorsement,[627] to add to her *New York Times* endorsement, shared with Klobuchar.[628]

Not to be outdone, Biden declared "transgender equality" to be the "civil rights issue of our time," adding there was "no room for compromise."[629] But he was floundering as his poll numbers sank. One poll even showed him losing to Sanders in his home state of Delaware.[630]

A desperate Biden floated Michelle Obama as a potential running mate[631] and suggested he should choose a younger woman because he might die in office: "I'm an old guy."[632]

Buttigieg, sensing a Sanders surge, sent a fundraising email telling supporters Sanders could be the party nominee—and that they should send money to stop him.[633] In his final Iowa ad, he told voters it was "time to turn the page" and follow the "next generation."[634] He began attacking both Sanders and Biden, by name, as too focused on the past.[635]

For the senators, it was back to Washington for the next stage of the trial: a question-and-answer session, in which senators could submit written queries to be read aloud by the chief justice and posed to either or both sides.

Over two days, and nearly two hundred questions, the process devolved into a war of attrition. Minority Leader Chuck Schumer (D-NY) asked a rhetorical question about how many documents or witnesses the White House had provided (answer: zero). Senator Ted Cruz (R-TX) responded with a question about the whistleblower.[636] And so on.[637]

One comic moment captured it all: as the last question was answered, Jerry Nadler, who had been silent for much of the proceedings, decided to have the last word. As he strode to the podium, Schiff tried to stop him, hissing: "Jerry. Jerry. Jerry."[638]

A triumphant Nadler denounced the White House lawyer's previous reply as "the usual nonsense," insulting the decorum of the Senate for the last time during the trial.[639]

The Senate responded the next day by voting down Democrats' request for new witnesses by a 51–49 majority.[640]

Meanwhile, Buttigieg, on the ground in Iowa, was onto something in attacking Sanders. Biden's poll numbers were not just slipping in Iowa; they were falling everywhere. The impeachment trial had aired never-heard stories of Biden's self-dealing. Former Florida attorney general Pam Bondi, added to the White House team, had laid out a devastating case against the Bidens.[641]

By early February, Sanders would be within just 5 points of Biden in South Carolina, the supposed "firewall."[642] Even Tom Steyer was beginning to catch up, after spending a fortune: he accounted for 91 percent of political television ad spending in the state (and 97 percent in Nevada).[643]

A panic was setting in among senior Democrats. NBC News reported that former secretary of state John Kerry, the party's nominee in 2004, was overheard on a telephone call at an Iowa hotel discussing the possibility of jumping into the presidential race himself, given "the possibility of Bernie Sanders taking down the Democratic Party—down whole."[644]

On January 31, the DNC suddenly changed the rules to qualify for the eighth debate, in Nevada: candidates would no longer have to reach a minimum number of donors. It was a change custom-made for Bloomberg.

Sanders campaign manager Faiz Shakir did not mince words: "DNC changing the rules to benefit a billionaire," he tweeted.[645] It was true, of course: the party needed Bloomberg's money. More than that, it needed an alternative to Sanders if Biden failed. And it was not going to be Steyer.

President Trump, meanwhile, was enjoying himself. He crashed the Democrats' party, holding a massive rally in Des Moines on January 30, trolling the opposition—"They want to kill our cows. That means you're next!" he joked.[646] *Politico*'s Ryan Lizza, who had not attended a Trump rally since 2016, wrote of the "unexpected joy" he witnessed among Trump supporters at the event.[647]

Earlier that week, the White House had formed the president's Coronavirus Task Force;[648] CNN's main concern was that it lacked racial and gender diversity.[649] Trump chaired the task force formally for the first time on January 29. Two days later, on January 31, against considerable internal dissent, the president banned travel to and from China.

The WHO criticized the China travel ban,[650] saying travel bans "unnecessarily interfere with international travel and trade." Biden accused the president of "hysterical xenophobia...and fearmongering."[651]

Trump told the rally in Iowa that he was working with China on the threat of coronavirus. "Hopefully it's all going to be great....but it's something that we have to be very, very careful with."[652]

NINETEEN

FROM IOWA TO NEW HAMPSHIRE, PART II

"Protecting Americans' health also means fighting infectious diseases. We are coordinating with the Chinese government and working closely together on the coronavirus outbreak in China. My administration will take all necessary steps to safeguard our citizens from this threat."

—President Donald Trump, State of the Union, February 4, 2020[653]

THE IOWA CAUCUSES

It was another bright, bitterly cold Iowa morning. The Iowa caucuses were just hours away.

All four of the senators running for president were still in Washington, watching closing arguments in the president's impeachment trial.

The arguments were, by now, familiar,[654] with few new points.[655]

Schiff ended as he had begun: with a rant. He called President Trump "a man without character or ethical compass," warning that, if senators did not vote to remove him, "your name will be tied to his with a cord of steel and for all of history."[656]

With that, the Senate was adjourned, the senators released.

The great tradition of the Iowa caucuses involves citizens from each community meeting together and working out, collectively, whom to support—more like rowdy Quaker meetings than quiet polling places.

I decided to observe the caucuses from Roosevelt High School in Des Moines.

In a typical election, primary or general, campaigns cannot interfere with voters within a certain distance of the entrance. That is not the case with caucuses, where campaigns speak directly to voters both outside and inside the venue, canvassing for support and marshaling supporters in various corners of the room.

In the big gym at Roosevelt High,[657] the Bernie Sanders supporters stood out: they tended to be lanky, male, and bearded. Pete Buttigieg's supporters were also notable: many were middle-aged moms. Elizabeth Warren's camp included women and young families, children in tow. The Joe Biden camp seemed to be a mix of senior citizens, seated in the bleachers, warily observing the scene.

A party official explained the rules. First, a representative of each campaign would make a short presentation. Then everyone would fill out a slip indicating their "first preference" and group themselves accordingly.

Once the "first preference" votes had been counted, all candidates with at least 15 percent—102 votes, at Roosevelt—would proceed to the second round. Those who had voted for candidates whose totals did not meet the threshold would have a chance to vote for a "second preference."[658]

It was a form of "ranked choice" voting, and it would prove disastrous.

There was a special guest in the building: Elizabeth Warren, who had flown in to make her pitch in person. She greeted voters in the hallway outside the gym, posing for the now-obligatory selfies, before taking the megaphone inside the gym. She urged voters to take a stand for those "left behind" in Trump's economy and argued that she had the leadership skills and the organization to unite the party.

Then it was time to vote—by a show of hands. Warren was first, followed by Sanders, Buttigieg, and Klobuchar.

Joe Biden, with seventy-two votes, was a distant fifth and failed to clear the threshold.

After that, it was time for the "second preference." Some of the Biden voters made their way from the bleachers to the Buttigieg or Klobuchar camps. The brash Sanders crowd had a tough time coaxing new voters to join their group.

But many voters simply left.

I dropped by the Biden victory party, where drinks were plentiful and faces nervous as donors and volunteers gathered around television screens. Somehow, there was a delay in the results.

I moved on to the Sanders party, at a Holiday Inn across from the airport. Parking was impossible; I had to find a distant spot and trudge across icy streets. Inside, the campaign had begun barring the door, even to credentialed journalists: there were simply too many people already in the ballroom.

But they, too, were waiting.

Something had gone wrong. The "ranked choice" system had been too confusing.

The state Democratic Party had also used an app that failed to count votes properly. Developed by a company called Shadow—one that had done work in the past for Buttigieg[659]—the program had crashed when used simultaneously by hundreds of people.

It was a complete humiliation.

Buttigieg, cleverly, took the stage at his own victory party, anyway—and declared himself the winner.

"We don't know all the results, but we know by the time it's all said and done, Iowa, you have shocked the nation," Buttigieg told a cheering crowd.[660]

Klobuchar had done likewise, using the delay in reporting results to launch into a speech that she knew would be picked up by all the news networks.

"We are feeling so good tonight," she said, adding: "We are bringing this ticket to New Hampshire."[661]

Sanders, clearly irritated, told supporters that he had "a good feeling we're going to be doing very, very well here in Iowa."

His supporters, who believed he had been cheated by Hillary Clinton in Iowa in 2016, knew whom to blame: "Pete the Cheat" began circulating on social media.

Trump was exultant: his supporters had turned out in record numbers, though he faced only perfunctory opposition.[662]

He tweeted: "The Democrat Caucus is an unmitigated disaster. Nothing works, just like they ran the Country.

"The only person that can claim a very big victory in Iowa last night is 'Trump.'"[663]

STATE OF DISUNION

In the wee hours of February 4, another quadrennial ritual unfolded as the candidates arrived in New Hampshire, greeted at the airport by small groups of supporters—a symbol of having earned a "ticket out" of Iowa.

Klobuchar arrived at roughly three o'clock in the morning; so, too, did Andrew Yang, though he had likely fared less well in the yet-to-be-counted caucus results.

Meanwhile, in Washington, preparations were under way for another ritual: the annual State of the Union address, to be delivered by President Trump—on the eve of the Senate's vote to remove him from office.

And Trump had, in his usual style, prepared a spectacular show.

His past addresses had moved audiences—and even critics, despite themselves—with special tributes, such as a moment in 2017 honoring the first soldier to die in combat under his administration, Senior Chief Petty Officer William "Ryan" Owens.

Owens's widow, Carryn Owens, wept and gazed heavenward as the chamber stood and applauded.[664]

In 2019, even after Republicans lost control of the House, Trump again managed to surprise his critics, congratulating the new Congress on having the most women ever. Even Alexandria Ocasio-Cortez, wearing suffragette white, high-fived her colleagues.[665]

But the 2020 address would surpass them all.

Trump not only celebrated the achievements of his administration—"seven million new jobs," unemployment at "the lowest in over half a century," black poverty at "the lowest rate ever recorded," the USMCA, and so on—but he also used the element of surprise to create an emotional crescendo.[666]

He introduced 13-year-old Iain Lanphier, for example, as a student who aspired to join the new Space Force—and then honored the boy's grandfather, 100-year-old Tuskegee Airman Charles McGee, in full uniform, promoting him on the spot to brigadier general.

Trump welcomed conservative radio host Rush Limbaugh, recently diagnosed with advanced lung cancer. That much was expected; people knew he was coming. But then Trump stunned Limbaugh and the nation by having first lady Melania Trump present him with the Presidential Medal of Freedom in the gallery.

The entire chamber—and the Capitol itself—became his instrument. He honored military spouses—and then welcomed Sgt. 1st Class Townsend Williams, who had been waiting in the hallway, into the gallery to join his wife Amy and his two children after seven months' deployment.

Trump acknowledged challenges—notably, the coronavirus spreading in China—but told the nation: "Our spirit is still young, the sun is still rising, God's grace is still shining, and, my fellow Americans, the best is yet to come."

It was a triumph.

Van Jones, reacting to the speech on CNN, warned Democrats: Trump was helping black people "in real life"—and they had better be prepared.[667]

And as Trump acknowledged the applause, Pelosi—knowing the cameras were still live—lifted her copy of his speech and tore it in half.

It was a potent symbol of the nation's divisions—and it was what people would remember about the speech, weeks later.[668]

In New Hampshire, the candidates attempted to move forward, though the results from Iowa were only trickling in. Buttigieg and Sanders both claimed to have won—Buttigieg on the basis of delegates,

Sanders on the popular vote.[669] Only two things were known: turn-out had been low, and Biden had done poorly, finishing fourth after Warren.

Mayor Pete's "victory" speech was premature but did the trick: he surged in New Hampshire, pulling within a point of Sanders in one poll.[670] Suddenly, Buttigieg looked like a potential national front-runner if he could win the Granite State or come close.

Also surging was Amy Klobuchar. She had been stuck in the Senate for weeks and only finished fifth in Iowa, but—like Buttigieg—had used an early speech to create an impression of momentum.

Then, at the New Hampshire debate, she stole the show.

When the moderator, George Stephanopoulos of ABC News, asked the seven candidates—including Yang, who had qualified again—if they were "concerned about having a democratic socialist on the top of this ticket," only Klobuchar raised her hand.[671] She also defended the state's two Democratic senators for voting for the USMCA.[672]

As she had in previous debates, Klobuchar clashed with Buttigieg. But this time, her attacks seemed to land.

Taking on Buttigieg's lack of experience, she noted that he had called the impeachment trial "exhaust[ing]." While it was easy to criticize those in Washington, she said, that was where the difficult decisions had to be made. Attacking "every single thing that people do," she said, "makes you look like a cool newcomer." However, she added, "We have a newcomer in the White House, and look where it got us. I think having some experience is a good thing."

She was the clear winner. And soon, her poll numbers soared.

FIVE CANDIDATES, ONE DAY

In the interim, President Donald Trump had been acquitted by a majority of the Senate, which voted 52–48 to reject the first article of impeachment ("abuse of power") and 53–47 to reject the second ("obstruction of Congress").

The only Republican to vote to remove him—on the first article—was Mitt Romney. Democrats praised his courage. However, Romney's

justification—which misquoted Dershowitz, as Schiff had done—
seemed, to critics, like a rationalization for revenge.

Trump—who had endorsed Romney for Senate in 2018—tweeted
that Utahns would never look at Romney again "with anything but contempt & disgust!"[673]

On the eve of the New Hampshire primary, the impeachment may
as well have never happened.

Amy Klobuchar was on a roll. Two new post-debate polls showed
her moving into third place.[674] She seemed to be attracting disappointed
Biden voters.

The former vice president had, the day before, called a voter a "lying,
dog-faced pony soldier" for asking whether he could win the election.[675]
And he actually said, during the debate: "I took a hit in Iowa, and I'll
probably take a hit here."

That was the signal for "moderate" voters to look elsewhere. "I mean,
who says that?" one voter told me, standing in line to see Klobuchar on a
snowy morning at a rural state college.

Inside, Klobuchar told an excited group of middle-aged Democrats
that this election would be a "decency check" on the president. Pointing
to her record of working across the aisle, she promised to end the "noise"
in Washington.

She continued—at monotonous length—to describe her policies.
One news crew began packing up its equipment.

But that was exactly her aim: focus on substance, never mind style.

Half an hour away, in a driving snowstorm at Franklin Pierce University, Bernie Sanders prepared to rile up students and activists for what he
hoped would be a repeat of his lopsided win in 2016.

I asked some student activists—many of whom would be voting for
the first time—why they supported the septuagenarian socialist.

One told me that his ideas—canceling student loan debt, Medicare for All, and other "free" policies—eased her "stress about the real
world."

In the town of Rochester, near the Maine border, Elizabeth Warren entertained a capacity crowd at the local opera house. Her pitch had barely changed since the summer—other than jabs at the "billionaires" joining the Democratic primary: it was too bad, she said, that Kamala Harris had to drop out of the race "on the same day that a billionaire bought his way onto the debate stage." Members of the audience held signs that read "Vote to End Corruption."

The question-and-answer session was a lottery: those whose names were drawn from a hat had to shout "Persist!"—a throwback to the heady, early days of her campaign—before asking their questions.

"Fight back!" she told the audience. "Fighting back is an act of patriotism!"

At St. George's Greek Orthodox Cathedral in Manchester, Joe Biden was running late. Supporter David Pecoraro, a retired public school teacher, told me he had driven all the way from New York to canvass for his candidate. He placed his hope in the more diverse electorates of Nevada and South Carolina, the early primary states to come.

"Of course he'll go forward," Pecoraro said. "Because, with all due respect to New Hampshire and Iowa, they don't look like the rest of America."

He said the party would come around to Biden—or lose.

"Mayor Pete's a nice guy. But this election's not a joke. I lived through George McGovern in 1972.

"If Sanders is the nominee, Kevin McCarthy will become speaker of the House and Mitch McConnell will have a filibuster-proof majority in the Senate.

"That might make you happy," he said, referring to me, "but to me, it means Vladimir Putin will be running our country."

Buttigieg, meanwhile, looked suddenly like a serious national candidate. He packed several hundred supporters into the atrium of Exeter High School for a late-night rally.

Oscar-winning actor Kevin Costner warmed up the crowd, in his deadpan yet sincere way.

"The person that I'm voting for... is also going to be someone who listens," Costner said. "I found Pete to be that way. He doesn't compete to be the loudest. His silences are those of someone who's thinking."[676]

Buttigieg, the great listener, had plenty to say about Bernie Sanders. The idea that "you're either for the revolution, or you're for the status quo," Mayor Pete said, left out more Americans.

A middle-aged woman, wearing a T-shirt emblazoned with Buttigieg's "core values" in colorful letters, told me that she admired him for his "moral compass."

Asked about his youth, she quipped: "He's the same age as the Founding Fathers were."

SANDERS TAKES THE LEAD

Trump put his stamp on the primary, returning to the Southern New Hampshire University (SNHU) Arena in Manchester the night before the vote—his first rally since surviving impeachment.[677]

He joked that his supporters should vote in the Democratic contest— "pick the weakest one," he said—and suggested, again, that the party would try to steal the nomination from Sanders.[678]

He mentioned coronavirus, briefly, praising China: "The virus, they're working hard. . . . Rough stuff, I tell you. Rough, rough stuff, but I think it's going to work out good. We only have 11 cases and they're all getting better."[679]

Early February 11, just after midnight, the tiny community of Dixville Notch, New Hampshire—population 12 in the 2010 census—cast the first primary votes. The winner—in both parties—was a write-in candidate: former New York City mayor Mike Bloomberg, who was not actually on either ballot.

Though Dixville Notch has long been a poor predictor of the statewide result, Bloomberg enjoyed several hours of good news coverage—a prelude to his imminent arrival on the next debate stage.[680]

Almost on cue, opposition research on Bloomberg began to drop. An audio recording was leaked in which then mayor Bloomberg, speaking to a wealthy audience at the 2015 Aspen Institute, defended his controversial "stop-and-frisk" policy.

The key, he explained at the time, was to "get guns out of [the]... hands" of those who were "male, minority, and between the ages of 15 and 25."[681] For good measure, Bloomberg added that "we put all the cops in minority neighborhoods...because that's where all the crime is."

Bloomberg scrambled to respond, releasing a statement disavowing his past comments and committing to "criminal justice reform and racial equity."[682] His campaign put together a meeting with over twenty black religious leaders, who declared in a press statement: "None of us believe that Mike Bloomberg is a racist."[683]

That was not enough for Sanders spokeswoman Nina Turner, who said, speaking "as a black woman in America" (though not for the campaign), that Bloomberg should drop out of the race. Other controversial Bloomberg comments were leaked, such as an apparent defense of Putin's seizure of Crimea from Ukraine.[684]

Across the state, which was blanketed in snow, fieldworkers for the various campaigns fanned out as they worked hard to get out the vote. Then, in the middle of voting, came the news that Joe Biden had decided to leave the state before his "victory" party. He would, instead, address supporters in South Carolina—his "firewall," where he would rely on African American voters to keep him in the race.

It was an audacious move—and roundly mocked. "Electile Dysfunction: Joe Biden Pulls Out Early from New Hampshire" was the headline at Breitbart News.[685]

The Sanders camp could feel the momentum of the race—finally!—shifting in their favor. A Quinnipiac poll the day before had shown Sanders leading the *national* race for the first time by 8 points—well outside the poll's 2.5-point margin of error.[686]

Toward evening, a long line of supporters formed outside the Southern New Hampshire University Field House in the subfreezing cold, ready to savor their win. Inside, organizers chanted and sang: "We! Are! Unstoppable! Another world is possible!"[687]

One volunteer, a self-declared, red-jacket-wearing member of the Democratic Socialists of America, told me democratic socialism was not something the candidate should avoid:

This isn't Soviet communism, this is policies that meet human needs, like "Medicare for All."...Bernie is so good at coming out, and saying he's a democratic socialist, but also talking about being the "organizer-in-chief," and "Not me. Us," and how he'll use the presidency to build a movement of ordinary people to change things for themselves, right—just like Eugene Debs did at the turn of the century.[688]

The mood became more tense as election results came in. Sanders had jumped to an early lead, but Buttigieg appeared to be closing the gap—especially as results came in from the southern counties, near the Massachusetts border.

Klobuchar was close behind Buttigieg—in third, as the last polls had predicted, a stunning result. "Hello America. I'm Amy Klobuchar, and I will beat Donald Trump," she declared, as supporters held "Win BIG" signs behind her.

Joe Biden spoke from a rally in South Carolina. "Iowa and Nevada have spoken," he said, mixing up states again.[689]

Buttigieg delivered his own speech—and was roundly booed at the Sanders victory rally, the scars of Iowa not yet forgotten.

Sanders finally emerged, as the networks began calling the race for him. He had won 26 percent of the vote—less than 2 points ahead of Buttigieg. It was a far cry from the 60 percent he won in 2016,[690] and with half the votes.[691]

Still, he was defiant. He had won *both* Iowa and New Hampshire, he declared, to cheers.

"Together, I have no doubt that we will beat Donald Trump."

TWENTY

FIGHT IN NEVADA

"I want to take him, I'm going to cut him, and see how he feels like.
I'm going to see if he's going to get up off the floor. I don't think he's got
the bottle, minerals, bollocks, whatever you want to call it. He ain't got it.
He's an on-top fighter. He's a bully fighter. And when a bully gets bullied,
he folds every single time."
—Heavyweight Boxer Tyson Fury, February 19, 2020[692]

TRUMP'S VICTORY LAP

"ACQUITTED."

President Donald Trump waved the front page of *USA Today* as he arrived onstage at the National Prayer Breakfast in Washington on February 6, the morning after the Senate had voted on removing him from office.

Also present: Speaker of the House Nancy Pelosi, his nemesis.

During the impeachment hearings, she had snapped at a reporter who asked her if she hated the president. "I don't hate anyone. I was raised in a way that is a heart full of love and always pray for the president," she claimed.[693]

That remark evidently had grated on the president for weeks. So, too, had Mitt Romney's declaration in the Senate, on February 5, that he was "a profoundly religious person," before voting to remove the president—the only Republican to do so.[694]

Trump spoke to the assembled faithful at the prayer breakfast: "We come together as one nation, blessed to live in freedom and grateful to worship in peace."

But he added a sharp—albeit indirect—rebuke as Pelosi sat silently on the dais.

"I don't like people who use their faith as justification for doing what they know is wrong. Nor do I like people who say, 'I pray for you,' when they know that that's not so."[695]

For three years, Trump had endured baseless charges of "Russia collusion." No sooner had he been exonerated than his foes found another reason—a *phone call*, no less—to pursue him.

He won the presidency in stunning fashion but was denied a "honeymoon"—or even a sense of legitimacy.

He and his family had been under investigation from Day One, as the government he was elected to lead joined the Resistance and its efforts to oust him.

Now, finally, he had tasted victory—and he would savor it.

In a televised gathering later that day in the East Room of the White House, the president thanked his close friends, advisers, attorneys, and congressional allies.[696]

Holding aloft the front page of the hated *Washington Post*—which read "Trump Acquitted"—Trump thanked the "incredible warriors" who had stood by him against an "evil" inquisition.

For over an hour, he offered his candid assessment of those who had risen to the occasion—and those who had sought to destroy him.

He even apologized to the people of Utah: "Sorry for Mitt Romney."[697]

The president had much else to celebrate.

On the day Democrats gathered to debate in New Hampshire, the January jobs report came out: 225,000 jobs, smashing expectations of 158,000. The *New York Times* acknowledged that black workers' wages were rising, after a "decade of stagnation."[698]

Former representative Joe Walsh (R-IL), a Never Trump advocate and political chameleon who had been fêted by cable news when he declared a primary challenge to the president, gave up after Iowa, saying Trump "can't be beat."[699]

The Associated Press declared it could not call a winner among Democrats in the Iowa caucuses, thanks to the party's vote-counting debacle. Trump mocked his opponents: "I think they should blame RUS-SIA, RUSSIA, RUSSIA again! If they can't count votes properly, how are they going to run U.S. HealthCare?"[700]

The DC Circuit Court of Appeals—which Trump's predecessor had stacked with liberal judges—ruled unanimously in Trump's favor in tossing out a lawsuit by Democrats seeking to disqualify him from office for allegedly violating the Emoluments Clause.[701]

And all that was on just one day.[702]

In the New Hampshire primary, President Trump had earned 123,629 votes, smashing the record for the most votes earned there by an incumbent president, more than doubling Barack Obama's 2012 total.[703] The next day, the Dow Jones Industrial Average hit an all-time high, just short of 30,000 points.

The following weekend, Trump took Air Force One to the Daytona 500. Other presidents had visited the race, but Trump did something new: he took the presidential limousine, the "Beast," on a lap around the track, pacing the other drivers. Former champion Jeff Gordon, offering commentary on television, said the spectacle made him wish he had not retired.[704]

A victory lap, indeed.

But at the finish line, driver Ryan Newman suffered a spectacular crash. He spun out, struck the wall, flipped over, and went flying.

He finished fourth and would later recover from his injuries, but it was a shock.

And perhaps a bad omen.

On January 20, Chinese officials told the world there was "no need to panic" as the first isolated cases of coronavirus began appearing abroad.[705]

Much of the American media seemed to agree.

A health and medicine reporter for the *Washington Post* advised:

"Clearly, the flu poses the bigger and more pressing peril; a handful of cases of the new respiratory illness have been reported in the United States, none of them fatal or apparently even life-threatening."[706] National Public Radio, among others, agreed."[707]

But some were sounding a warning.

Senator Tom Cotton (R-AR) sent a letter to the administration on January 22, urging a travel ban on China to stop the spread of coronavirus.[708]

After Trump imposed that ban, critics argued it would not work but would "scapegoat already-marginalized populations."[709] Meanwhile, Hong Kong doctors urged the world to take "draconian" measures, as Chinese scientists announced that a victim could spread the illness for days before showing symptoms.[710]

Quietly, some American consumers were buying masks. But aside from the president, few of America's leaders did anything.

Democrats in the House convened the first subcommittee meeting to discuss coronavirus—on February 5, the day impeachment ended.[711]

LATE NIGHT IN VEGAS

The field of candidates descended on Nevada, fewer in number than they had been just days before. Deval Patrick dropped out after a dismal finish in New Hampshire. So, too, did Michael Bennet. Andrew Yang's quirky campaign also came to an end, though he would return to the trail as a CNN commentator.

Amy Klobuchar, however, remained hopeful. Voters were beginning to see her not only as an alternative to Joe Biden but also as a safe pair of hands to lead the country.

Her problem was time. Klobuchar's campaign announced that it had raised $2.5 million in the hours since the polls closed in New Hampshire.[712] That was good news, but Klobuchar would be starting from scratch in Nevada. She opened two field offices and hired fifty staffers in the state.[713] But others had been there for months, and Bloomberg and Steyer had bought up most of the available airtime.

So Klobuchar tried a novel approach. The midwestern mom would hold a "late-night" town hall meeting—Las Vegas style.

The event was held at 9 p.m. above a theater in downtown Las Vegas. About two hundred supporters and curious voters gathered to hear the jet-lagged senator, who had just flown in from Washington.

One voter told Breitbart News that he had supported Biden but was switching to Klobuchar because "it doesn't look like Biden will make it."

A retiree from Michigan was more certain.

"She's got common sense," she told me. "She'll end the chaos and calm things down."

One thing Klobuchar would *not* end was her speech. She began strong, but—as in New Hampshire—she insisted on hitting every point on her list, in detail.

After more than half an hour, people began heading for the exits.

Earlier that day, Klobuchar had joined Tom Steyer and Pete Buttigieg at a Latino voters' forum at a local college; Sanders joined by video.[714] Though immigration came up several times, the most frequent question was: How will you counter President Trump's message on the economy?

Few seemed to have an answer.

Most were stumped again after the event, when each was led into an interview with Telemundo, the Spanish-language NBC subsidiary, and asked to name the president of Mexico.

Klobuchar could not; Steyer could not. Only Buttigieg found the right answer—after some nervous hesitation: "López Obrador...I hope," he said.[715]

If Iowa had been a debacle, Nevada was shaping up to be a gamble.

Biden had led there throughout the primary. But Sanders surged, following his win in New Hampshire, and took the lead.[716] The others were close enough that it seemed anyone could do well—or crap out.[717]

The most powerful vote, among Democrats, was the union vote. And no endorsement was more coveted than that of the UNITE HERE! Culinary Workers Union Local 226—the union representing casino and hotel workers.

But the union had begun clashing openly with Sanders over his Medicare for All plan, which it feared could end the generous private health insurance plans it had won in collective bargaining agreements.

The press gathered eagerly on a warm Las Vegas winter afternoon to hear whom—if not Sanders—the union would choose.

Secretary-Treasurer Geoconda Argüello-Kline approached the microphone.

"We're not going to endorse a political candidate," she said.[718]

The campaign became even zanier. Steyer hired a mariachi band and gave away tacos, hoping to reach Latino voters.[719] Sanders was interrupted onstage at a rally in Carson City by topless women protesting against dairy products.[720] Biden rallied Asian American voters in a Chinese restaurant—the only venue, it seemed, he could pack. He told them the idea of limits on immigration was "absolutely bizarre." Campaigning elsewhere in Nevada, he referred to the state as "California."[721]

Buttigieg, hoping to show he could win a minority-heavy state, ran a campaign right out of a McKinsey PowerPoint presentation. He hit every demographic, every media market—even flying to far-flung Elko, a day's drive from anywhere else in the state.

But it was Sanders who found a groove.

Addressing a crowd at the University of Nevada in Reno, he compared his campaign to the freedom struggles of the past.

"You know, I think back now, and I think, in fact, some of you may be familiar with Nelson Mandela—remember that, and his fight for freedom in South Africa?—and people marching to the polls," he said.

"I'm thinking about the civil rights movement, and people marching to the polls. Well, we're fighting to change America."[722]

And with that, he led them on a march to the nearest polling station for early voting.

Sanders was offering aging hippies a chance to relive their youth—and young voters a chance to reenact the past.

Across the state, they were marching with him.

FIGHT NIGHT IN VEGAS

The rivals glowered at each other onstage. They thumped their chests. They hurled abuse at one another. They vowed to deliver victory.

No—not at the Democrat debate.

This was earlier in the day, at the press conference before the heavy-weight boxing championship, at the next hotel down the Strip.

Tyson Fury and Deontay Wilder, two of the greatest champions box-ing had produced in decades, were previewing their fight.

Both were undefeated. Their last meeting, in December 2018, had ended in a draw, with Fury dominating the entire fight—until the twelfth round.

That was when Wilder, with a right hand nicknamed "The Eraser," knocked Fury to the canvas. Wilder made a throat-slashing gesture: it looked like an improbable comeback.

But what happened next was more improbable still.

Fury, regaining his senses, beat the count. He stood up and finished the round, going the distance.

On Saturday, February 22, they would have their rematch—right after the results of the Democratic caucus.

The presidential campaign was an undercard bout. But it was to be no less fierce.

Billionaire Mike Bloomberg had been spending hundreds of mil-lions of dollars on his campaign, without once appearing on a ballot or participating in a debate.

And the others—Sanders and Warren, especially—were eager to take him on.

Bloomberg seemed to be the last hope of the establishment, given Biden's struggles. The media elite—of which he was part, through his own news company—seemed convinced that he would sweep away all other contenders, including Trump.

Sam Donaldson, the retired ABC News legend, emerged to endorse Bloomberg for president days before the debate—the first time he had ever endorsed a candidate. He called Trump a "threat" to the country and said Bloomberg could defeat him.[723]

The former New York City mayor had skipped the early primary states—even writing an op-ed trashing Iowa and New Hampshire as "homogenous"[724]—and spent $124 million on advertising in Super Tues-day states.[725]

He had qualified for the Nevada debate, thanks to a change in the rules. And his rival billionaire, Steyer, had not.[726]

Even though Bloomberg would not be competing in the Nevada caucuses, he would be onstage: it would be his first introduction to the national electorate.

It was to be a memorable one. To quote another great boxer, Mike Tyson: "Everybody has a plan until they get punched in the mouth."[727]

And Warren was the one who delivered the fateful jab.

"So I'd like to talk about who we're running against, a billionaire who calls women 'fat broads' and 'horse-faced lesbians,'" she said. "And, no, I'm not talking about Donald Trump. I'm talking about Mayor Bloomberg."[728]

Bloomberg tried to sidestep those quotations,[729] but it did not matter. The comparison to Trump was a knockout blow.

Warren continued:

> Democrats are not going to win if we have a nominee who has a history of hiding his tax returns, of harassing women, and of supporting racist polls like redlining and "stop-and-frisk."
>
> Look, I'll support whoever the Democratic nominee is. But understand this: Democrats take a huge risk if we just substitute one arrogant billionaire for another.

Klobuchar got a few shots in as well, noting that Bloomberg had asked the other candidates to drop out so he could have a clear shot at the nomination, and at Trump.

"I have been told as a woman . . . many times to wait my turn and to step aside. And I'm not going to do that now."

Bloomberg did land a few counterpunches. Asked about Sanders's plan to give employees a 20 percent stake in their companies, Bloomberg said: "It's ridiculous. We're not going to throw out capitalism. We tried. Other countries tried that. It was called communism, and it just didn't work."

The audience booed.

Later, he tried again, with greater success: "What a wonderful country we have. The best-known socialist in the country happens to be a millionaire with three houses. What did I miss here?"

This time, there was laughter. But he never recovered.

Buttigieg tried moving the focus back to Trump. "We could wake up two weeks from today, the day after Super Tuesday, and the only candidates left standing will be Bernie Sanders and Mike Bloomberg, the two most polarizing figures on this stage," he said.

But Warren would not be deterred. She clearly relished the fight.

The winner—almost by default—was Sanders. His most dangerous foe, Bloomberg, had been dispatched. And with Biden fading, Sanders seemed to have found himself on a path to the nomination.

In the spin room, reporters began asking the Sanders team about Cabinet picks.

I asked Sanders aide Jeff Weaver what the campaign would do if the party tried to take the nomination away from him at the convention.

"You know how we're gonna beat them? We're gonna win."

THE MAIN EVENT

The debate drew an audience of nearly twenty million, a record for a Democratic primary debate.[730] Those high ratings were matched by heavy turnout in early voting.[731]

Bloomberg had been the big draw on television. But Sanders was motivating Democrats on the ground.

Buttigieg stuck to his perfect-on-paper campaign schedule; Warren held town hall meetings; Biden posed for as many selfies as he could; Klobuchar did her best to keep up.

President Trump flew in, regaling supporters with an impromptu speech in the lobby of the Trump Hotel on the day of the debate and addressing thousands more at a rally the day before the caucuses. Dozens camped out overnight to see him.

No one could evoke that kind of enthusiasm among Democrats— except Sanders. Polls showed his lead growing to double digits.[732]

The party establishment began to worry.

A bombshell story broke in the *Washington Post*: "U.S. officials have told Senator Bernie Sanders that Russia is attempting to help his presidential campaign," it reported.[733]

Buried deep within the story: Sanders said the briefing happened "about a month ago." Yet suddenly, it had surfaced, with twenty-four hours to go before Nevadans voted.

There were other attacks. After a Bloomberg campaign office was vandalized in Knoxville, Tennessee, Bloomberg blamed Sanders, saying that the violence "echoes language from the Sanders campaign and its supporters."[734]

All to no avail.

Sanders not only won Nevada, he hit the jackpot, winning nearly 50 percent of the vote—more than twice as many votes as Biden, his closest rival, who barely broke 20 percent.

Borrowing a tactic from Biden, Sanders addressed supporters from San Antonio, Texas—painting a target on the Lone Star State.

"In Nevada, we have just put together a multigenerational multiracial coalition, which is going to not only win in Nevada, it's going to sweep this country," Sanders told ecstatic fans.[735]

Sanders had won union members despite his fight with union leaders. He had won half the Latino vote and 28 percent of the black vote— just 10 points behind Biden.[736]

The Sanders movement could taste victory.

Representative Pramila Jayapal (D-WA), an early Sanders supporter, tweeted: "I am tearing up just thinking about what it would mean to Americans everywhere—and to the world—to have @BernieSanders as President, fighting for US. I am so ready for that."[737]

Biden trumpeted his second-place finish, however distant. A member of the audience at his victory party shouted that he was the "Comeback Kid," a name Bill Clinton had bestowed upon himself after finishing second in New Hampshire in 1992.[738]

Buttigieg, in third with just over 14 percent, delivered an extraordinary "victory" speech that sounded a warning.

After congratulating Sanders, he said:

Senator Sanders believes in an inflexible ideological revolution that leaves out most Democrats, not to mention most Americans. I believe we can defeat Trump and deliver for the American people by empowering the American people to make their own health care choices with Medicare for all who want it. Senator Sanders believes in taking away that choice, removing people from having the option of a private plan and replacing it with a public plan, whether you want it or not.

I believe that we can bring an end to corporate recklessness and rebalance our economy by empowering workers, raising wages, and insisting that those who gained the most must contribute the most in order to keep the American dream going forward. But that is different from Senator Sanders's vision of capitalism as the root of all evil, that would go beyond reform and reorder the economy in ways that most Democrats, not to mention most Americans, don't support.

Buttigieg had to know he was unofficially ending his campaign with that speech. He would need the help of Sanders's supporters to win, and they would never vote for him after that.

Warren, who once had the largest organization in Nevada, finished fourth. She delivered a speech from Seattle, which would not vote for weeks. Her message was that she intended to fight beyond Super Tuesday. But aside from attacking Bloomberg—which she continued to do—her race was run.

Fifth-place Klobuchar's hopes, like those of so many Vegas newbies, had gone bust.

A 78-year-old socialist was on the verge of seizing the Democratic nomination.

Over at the MGM Grand Las Vegas Hotel & Casino, another unlikely champion had emerged.

Tyson Fury stunned the boxing world, dropping Deontay Wilder twice before Wilder's corner threw in the towel in the seventh.

In the past, Fury had tried to out-box Wilder. This time, he was ruthless. At one point, Fury even licked the blood off Wilder's neck.

"I'm never going to be body beautiful," Fury said afterward, patting his soft belly.

"It's not about aesthetics. It's about what's in here [tapping his heart], and what's in here [tapping his head]."

He told the post-fight press conference: "I can't wait for the next fight. The rematch, if he wants it."

In South Carolina, another rematch was on the cards.

TWENTY-ONE

THE SOUTH (CAROLINA) RISES AGAIN

"South Carolina should be voting for Joe Biden, and here's why.... Making
the greatness of this country accessible and affordable for all. We don't need
to make this country great again—this country is great, that's not what our
challenge is.... I know his heart. I know who he is. I know what he is."
—Representative James Clyburn, February 26, 2020[739]

FIREWALL IN FLAMES

Joe Biden's South Carolina firewall was in flames.

His poll numbers were declining steadily in the Palmetto State,
where he had dominated since entering the race. New polls showed Bernie Sanders climbing within single digits of the former vice president.[740]
At least one poll showed them tied.[741]

Sanders was on a roll—and after his stunning win in Nevada, he
seemed unstoppable.

No candidate for president in either party had ever won the popular
vote in all three of the first primary contests.[742]

Former rival Marianne Williamson endorsed him: "What happened
in Nevada on Saturday was extraordinary, and the energy is unquestionably with Bernie," she said in a statement released on social media.[743]

"A 40-yr-old trend of capitalism without conscience—corporate elites and their errand boys in government—have created the inevitable blowback in the form of a political revolution."

Former rival Bill de Blasio, who had pointedly endorsed Sanders over Bloomberg, his predecessor as mayor, taunted Pete Buttigieg for his speech attacking the senator from Vermont.

"Try to not be so smug when you just got your ass kicked," de Blasio tweeted.[744]

Far from pivoting toward the center, Sanders seemed determined to win in the same radical style in which he had campaigned.

In an interview with Anderson Cooper on CBS News' *60 Minutes*, Sanders defended his past support for communist regimes, including Cuba's.

"We're very opposed to the authoritarian nature of Cuba but you know, it's unfair to simply say everything is bad. You know?" he said. "When Fidel Castro came into office, you know what he did? He had a massive literacy program. Is that a bad thing? Even though Fidel Castro did it?"[745]

That evening, Sanders issued a strident statement adamantly refusing to attend the annual policy conference of the country's most influential pro-Israel group, the American Israel Public Affairs Committee (AIPAC). He declared: "I remain concerned about the platform AIPAC provides for leaders who express bigotry and oppose basic Palestinian rights. For that reason I will not attend their conference."[746]

It was not clear what "bigotry" Sanders meant. AIPAC, which strives (to a fault) to maintain an appearance of bipartisanship, responded with unusual anger:

Senator Sanders has never attended our conference....

By engaging in such an odious attack on this mainstream, bipartisan American political event, Senator Sanders is insulting his very own colleagues and the millions of Americans who stand with Israel. Truly shameful.[747]

The Democratic Party establishment was in a full-on panic. George Stephanopoulos—the host of ABC News' *This Week* but also a former Clinton operative—asked House Majority Whip Representative James Clyburn (D-SC) the day after Nevada: "If he's the nominee, do you think it could put the House majority in danger?"

Clyburn responded: "A lot of people think so. I do believe it will be an extra burden for us to have to carry."[748]

Joe Scarborough, the nominally conservative half of MSNBC's *Morning Joe* program, suggested that Klobuchar and Warren drop out of the race so that the party could unite behind a candidate who had a better chance of stopping Sanders.[749]

His colleague, Chris Matthews, compared Sanders's rise to the Nazi occupation of France.[750]

The media began reporting on so-called Bernie bros, online supporters of the Vermont senator who were supposedly abusive toward his opponents.[751]

On the ground in South Carolina, it did not look like the other contenders had much of a chance.

Pete Buttigieg, who had always struggled with the black voters who make up almost two-thirds of the Democratic Party primary electorate, did not even try to defend his record. Campaigning in North Charleston, he tried humbling himself: "I do not have that lived experience [of African Americans] and I recognize that I don't," he said, promising "to show up, to seek to understand, and to assure that those voices are elevated in our campaign, and will be elevated in our administration."[752]

At a march with McDonald's employees that day to demand a $15-per-hour minimum wage, Buttigieg was confronted by protesters from a group called Black Votes Matter, chanting, "Pete can't be our president, where was $15 in South Bend?"[753]

At the College of Charleston that evening, Joe Biden struggled to fill half a school gymnasium. A pitifully small crowd encircled the stage as he attempted to walk through his stump speech, often turning his back to the audience.

He invoked the "very fine people" hoax again, telling the half-empty room: "This guy is more George Wallace than he is George Washington."[754]

The alternatives to Sanders looked so weak that even Tom Steyer, who had qualified for the debate stage again, began to look competitive. He had spent millions on advertising and staff. He also spent a small fortune in the black community, leading to accusations that he was trying to "buy" the black vote.[755]

Sanders, and his "political revolution," loomed.

THE CAMPAIGN CATCHES CORONAVIRUS

As the candidates made their way across the countryside, some Americans were barred from moving at all.

Passengers aboard the Princess Cruises liner *Diamond Princess* had been quarantined, in archaic maritime fashion, at port in Yokohama, Japan, since February 3. A former passenger had tested positive for coronavirus.

By the time the ordeal was through, over 600 passengers and crew[756]—out of roughly 3,700—had tested positive for coronavirus and were taken to local hospitals.[757] Several passengers would die of the illness.[758]

The United States flew fourteen infected Americans back to the country aboard aircraft with other, healthy passengers[759] despite objections from the U.S. Centers for Disease Control and Prevention (CDC).[760]

Few understood coronavirus or its potential impact. A January 28 poll showed most Americans were concerned, but 72 percent were confident the health system could manage it.[761] Fed Chairman Jerome Powell told a press conference January 29 that the economic impact was "very uncertain."[762]

President Trump's January 31 travel ban on China was among the first in the world. At that time, the United States had several coronavirus cases—none fatal, yet.

Other countries had begun to take drastic action—especially Taiwan, South Korea, Hong Kong, and Singapore, which had recent experiences with outbreaks of respiratory illness. Israel—whose civilian army needs to be ready to mobilize at any given moment—followed suit. Northern Italy, with close business ties to China, saw a catastrophic spread of coronavirus. In Iran, coronavirus spread rapidly, infecting much of the country's leadership.

China continued to suppress information and to lash out at critics. The Communist Party's official newspaper called "racism, profile, hate and alienation" a scourge "worse" than coronavirus itself.[763] Dr. Li Wenliang, who had warned others about the coronavirus, was arrested; he died, authorities claimed, from the illness, though some critics of the regime suspected he was killed.[764]

Ron Klain, an adviser to Joe Biden who had managed the Obama administration's response to Ebola, told the *Pod Save America* podcast on February 12 that while he believed Trump had not done enough, there was "no reason to really panic."[765] But financial markets began to worry about the disruption to global trade and supply chains in China. American medical supplies and pharmaceuticals, many of which were made in China, were particularly vulnerable.[766]

Yields on U.S. Treasury bonds plummeted to record lows, as global investors sought a safe haven. The stock market began to wobble, falling nearly 1,000 points as markets opened on Monday, February 24.

Trump's focus was on keeping the country calm[767] and the economy healthy: "The Coronavirus is very much under control in the USA. We are in contact with everyone and all relevant countries. CDC & World Health have been working hard and very smart. Stock Market starting to look very good to me!" he tweeted on February 24. And, indeed, U.S. consumer confidence continued to rise.[768]

But on February 25—the day of the Democrats' debate in Charleston—Dr. Nancy Messonnier, a senior official at the CDC, told reporters: "It's not so much of a question of if this will happen in this country anymore but a question of when this will happen."[769]

That rang the alarm bell.

Most Democrats had not heard it yet. They had not even mentioned the word "coronavirus" in any debate.[770] No moderator had even asked the question.[771]

Outside the debate hall in central Charleston, a motley group of protesters—and pranksters—gathered to push their pet preoccupations. A group of climate change activists, one wearing a polar bear costume, handed out report cards on each of the candidates. Pro-life Democrats protested what they saw as the party's increasing enthusiasm for abortion.

There were also half a dozen mock protesters, calling themselves "Bernie bros." Young, bearded, and boisterous, they looked the part, holding signs like "Work Is Hard," "Trust Fund Low, Send Cash," and "Cuba Has Grate Litterasey." (They were organized by a pro-Trump super PAC.)[772]

Just a block away towered the steeple of Mother Emanuel AME Church. In this debate, cosponsored by the Congressional Black Caucus, the stage would, once again, be entirely white.

The candidates spent the first part of the debate trying to out-woke one another. "My entire career has been wrapped up in dealing with civil rights and civil liberties," said Biden.[773]

"I've apologized and asked for forgiveness," said Bloomberg. "I come at this with a great deal of humility," Buttigieg preened.

Finally, midway through, Bloomberg brought up coronavirus: "You read about the virus, what's really happening here is the president fired the pandemic specialist in this country two years ago. So there's nobody here to figure out what the hell we should be doing."

That claim was inaccurate,[774] but it was one of the few times any candidate had discussed the problem and the first time it had been tackled in the debates.[775]

The moderator later asked the candidates if they would close the country's borders to stop the spread of the pandemic, as President Trump had done.

No, was the answer.

THE CLYBURN ENDORSEMENT

The fight continued in the spin room. Steyer told me that the coronavirus crisis—suddenly a hot topic, now that candidates had finally addressed it—proved that Trump was "incompetent" on the economy. "He's unprepared . . . to deal with the real world when things go wrong."[776]

Surrogates for Sanders and Warren struggled to defend their radical views on Israel, which had come out during the debate. Sanders had called Israeli Prime Minister Benjamin Netanyahu a "reactionary racist"; Warren had waffled on the question of whether she would move the U.S. Embassy back from Jerusalem to Tel Aviv.[777]

The next morning, Biden told NBC's *TODAY* show that Sanders's promises of "revolution" would fail to motivate American voters to go to the polls.

"Americans aren't looking for revolution," Biden said. "They're looking for progress."[778]

But these were just mere skirmishes. The most important battle in South Carolina—the key to the primary—was the fight for the African American vote.

The morning after the debate, the candidates lined up to speak at a breakfast in North Charleston for local black religious leaders hosted by none other than Reverend Al Sharpton and his National Action Network (NAN).

Sharpton had already played an outsized role in the primary. His rise had been an unlikely one. In the 1980s and 1990s, he was viewed as a rabble-rouser, roiling New York with angry protests, his long hair combed back, his portly frame draped in velvet track suits. He was lampooned in *The Bonfire of the Vanities,* the famous satire by novelist Tom Wolfe, who based the character of Reverend Bacon on Sharpton.

Beyond the comedy, there was a grim—and deadly—history.[779] Sharpton had played a role in inciting riots, most notoriously in the Crown Heights neighborhood of Brooklyn, where Hasidic Jews and African Americans live side by side.[780]

In another infamous case, Sharpton backed Tawana Brawley, a 15-year-old black teenager who falsely claimed to have been gang-raped by a group of white men and smeared in feces with "KKK" written on her body.[781]

Sharpton later went on to run for president in 2004, in an ill-fated effort that ran into campaign finance violations.[782] He was so toxic that Barack Obama wanted nothing to do with him in 2008.[783] This was during a campaign when Obama *refused* to disavow his racist pastor, Jeremiah Wright—at least, for several weeks.

But once Obama entered office, he found Sharpton to be a useful ally.[784] At the same time, left-wing MSNBC found Sharpton to be a convenient hire for a prime-time news slot in its lily-white lineup.

In 2012, when a black teen named Trayvon Martin was shot in Florida by a neighborhood watch volunteer, Sharpton and NAN turned the local story into a national crisis. Obama weighed in, telling reporters that "if I had a son, he'd look like Trayvon."[785]

It was exactly the issue Obama needed to energize complacent black voters. But it was, arguably, terrible for America: it led race relations into a decline from which they have not yet recovered.[786] The Trayvon Martin crisis was followed by the Black Lives Matter movement, which critics alleged had inspired deadly attacks on police in Dallas, New York, and elsewhere.

Despite his disturbing record, Sharpton was accepted as a civil rights leader by the media and by the Democrats.[787] Few bothered to challenge his credentials.[788] They found it easier to submit: the breakfast in Charleston was partly sponsored by the Boeing Company, for example, a major local employer.[789]

One by one, the candidates made their pitches. Steyer promised "blacker" and "browner" leaders in government.[790] Buttigieg acknowledged he had made "mistakes" in South Bend and thanked Sharpton for his "leadership."

But as famous—or notorious—as Sharpton was nationwide, there was a more important kingmaker in South Carolina: Representative James Clyburn.

The House Majority Whip was the highest-ranking elected black Democrat. And for weeks, he had kept his endorsement a secret.

But that morning, Clyburn revealed that he would endorse Joe Biden.

At a press conference, Clyburn cited his own experiences in the civil rights struggle and explained:

> South Carolina should be voting for Joe Biden, and there's billboards around this county. On those billboards is my pledge... "Making the greatness of this country accessible and affordable for all."
>
> We don't need to make this country great again. This country *is* great..... Our challenge is making the greatness of this country accessible and affordable for all! If it's health care—is it accessible? Is it affordable? Education—is it accessible? Is it affordable? Housing, energy—making it accessible and affordable.
>
> And nobody with whom I've ever worked in public life is any more committed to that motto, that pledge, that I have for my constituents, than Joe Biden.[791]

Later, when asked why he had not endorsed Sanders, Clyburn noted: he had never asked.[792]

JOE BIDEN WINS—FINALLY

Clyburn's endorsement had changed the race. It was far too much to say, as columnist Peggy Noonan of the *Wall Street Journal* would later claim, that it had saved the Democratic Party.[793] But it had definitely saved Biden's campaign.

That was not clear right away, as the candidates continued to barnstorm the state. Just hours after Clyburn backed Biden, Sanders addressed a packed convention hall in North Charleston, reminding them that he was within "single digits" and could win the state.

The speakers who preceded him had been a kaleidoscope of "progressive" intersectionality: an antiwar veteran, an "undocumented" immigrant, and spokeswoman Nina Turner, who gave a rousing speech placing Sanders among the icons of the left.

"There is only one Senator Bernie Sanders carrying on the tradition of FDR; carrying on the tradition of that freedom fighter, Eugene Debs; carrying on the tradition of Mother Jones; carrying on the tradition of Fannie Lou Hamer...carrying on the tradition of the Reverend Dr. Martin Luther King Junior....carrying on the tradition of Cesar Chavez!" she declared.

"We're gonna show you what the people's revolution looks like!"

But "the people" had not yet spoken—at least, not in South Carolina.

Polls began to shift back in Biden's direction. The results were almost difficult to believe.

One poll, taken *before* the debate, showed Biden opening a twenty-point lead over Sanders in the Palmetto State.[794] Another poll, taken after the debate, showed Biden with a lead of nearly 30 points—with Sanders in a distant third, behind Steyer.[795]

Whether Clyburn's endorsement had led the trend or followed it, it had stamped Biden with a seal of approval for African American voters.

Politico ran a story under the headline "Joe Biden's campaign isn't dead yet"[796]—perhaps, in retrospect, the most understated claim in recent political history.

The article said Biden's once "flagging" campaign was optimistic once more:

A second-place finish in Nevada, a major endorsement in South Carolina, a strong debate Tuesday and a pair of polls showing him with a staggering lead here have given new hope to his campaign. Money is flowing anew into his war chest, as well as to a super PAC supporting him.

Armed with those data points, the campaign and super PAC are telling donors that Biden—given his strength among African American voters and momentum kicking in at the right time—is quickly emerging as the alternative to front-runner Bernie Sanders.

One factor was Bloomberg's poor performance in the debates. He was, arguably, much better than Biden onstage. But he showed real weaknesses—and he had made the risky decision to debate before two primaries where the best he could finish was at 0 percent. Moderates began turning back to the Biden—the familiar, if flawed, elder statesman.

Biden suddenly began to draw crowds. "Biden drew something rarely seen at his rally at Coastal Carolina University in Conway on Thursday: a long line of enthusiastic supporters," *Politico* reported. Senator Tim Kaine (D-VA), Hillary Clinton's running mate, added his endorsement the day before the primary.

The two main factions of the party—the white liberal gentry and the African American base—were beginning to come together.

On Election Day, exit polls told the story. Nearly half of all Democratic voters said that Clyburn's endorsement had been "the most important" (24 percent) or "one of several important" (23 percent) factors in their vote.[797] A majority (51 percent) wanted to return to Barack Obama's policies, while only three in ten wanted more radical policies.[798] And 55 percent of black voters said that Biden best understood the concerns of minorities. No other candidate was close.[799]

When the results came in, they proved the polls right. Biden won over 48 percent of the vote, and Sanders won just under 20 percent. Biden had taken the rematch—decisively. It was almost an exact reversal of the result from Nevada the week before—and with a much more populous state, it meant Biden overtook Sanders in the overall popular vote nationwide.

Steyer barely cleared 11 percent; the rest were in single digits.

The firewall had held. And for the first time in four decades of trying, Joe Biden had won a presidential primary contest.

"For all those of you who've been knocked down. Counted out. Left behind. This is your campaign," Biden told supporters in his victory speech.[800]

He took aim at Sanders: "Most Americans don't want the promise of revolution. They want more than promises, they want results.... Talk is cheap. False promises are deceptive, and talk about revolution ain't changing anyone's life. We need real changes, right now."

He thanked Clyburn: "You brought me back." And, for good measure, he added one more classic Biden gaffe, calling U.S. Senate candidate Jaime Harrison "the next president," before correcting himself.

What transpired next was unprecedented in the history of American politics.

TWENTY-TWO

SUPER TUESDAY

"This had been a year of great surprises, though many of them highly predictable, and perhaps the greatest surprise was the resurrection of Hubert Humphrey. One was surprised by how easily it was done, and how readily the party faithful moved toward a man who had never proven himself in any sort of national election.... In early 1968 no one had seemed a frailer politician than Humphrey."

—David Halberstam, *The Unfinished Odyssey of Robert Kennedy, 1968*[801]

SHOCK AND AWE

In the hours after the South Carolina primary, Tom Steyer dropped out of the presidential race. He had achieved a respectable third place in the state,[802] with over 11 percent of the vote. But it was not good enough.

"Honestly, I can't see a path where I can win the presidency," he said late Saturday night.[803]

The other candidates, meanwhile, struggled to dust themselves off for Super Tuesday.

Amy Klobuchar had looked to Super Tuesday for months as her best chance to pick up her first win. Her home state, Minnesota, was one of over a dozen states that would vote on March 3.

But Klobuchar's rally on Sunday in Minneapolis was disrupted by Black Lives Matter activists, who marched onto the stage demanding that she drop out of the race. They were angry about Klobuchar's role in prosecuting a black man named Myon Burrell for murder nearly two decades before. Many activists believed he had been wrongly convicted.[804]

Klobuchar's campaign tried to negotiate with the Black Lives Matter activists, to no avail. Her homecoming rally was canceled forty minutes before it began.[805]

Pete Buttigieg seemed contemplative. He and his husband, Chasten, had traveled to Georgia for breakfast with former president Jimmy Carter and his wife, former first lady Rosalynn Carter, on Sunday morning.

After meeting with Buttigieg, President Carter told reporters: "He doesn't know what he's going to do after South Carolina."[806]

Or perhaps Mayor Pete was simply playing his cards close to his chest.

Early Sunday evening, Buttigieg held a conference call with his staff to inform them that he was dropping out of the race.[807] And on Monday, a campaign adviser told Reuters that Buttigieg planned to endorse Joe Biden.[808]

Hours later, Klobuchar also dropped out and told aides that she would endorse Biden.

The reason: the party had to stop Sanders from becoming the nominee.

Politico reported:

> [Klobuchar] informed Biden's campaign Monday morning that she was quitting the race and endorsing him....
>
> Klobuchar told her aides that she wanted to get behind Biden quickly—"it all happened in a matter of a couple hours," she said—over fear that Sanders would lose badly to President Donald Trump if he won the Democratic nomination—something she raised in debates earlier this year.[809]

Other endorsements followed in rapid succession. Beto O'Rourke, quiet since November, came forward to endorse Biden.[810] So, too, did Susan Rice, President Obama's former UN ambassador and national security advisor.

In a tweet endorsing Biden, Rice posted a photograph showing him comforting her after her mother died.[811]

Nothing had changed about Biden. In a speech in Houston, Texas, that day, he forgot the words of the Declaration of Independence: "We hold these truths to be self-evident, all men and women created by, go, you know, you know—the thing."[812] But the party was uniting behind him, regardless, with sudden and unprecedented urgency.

Buttigieg, Klobuchar, and O'Rourke all flew to Dallas, Texas, to join Biden at what was billed as a "rally" but looked more like a hastily assembled meet and greet at a bar.

Ramshackle though it was, it was the epicenter of a political earthquake.

Buttigieg, in his customary shirtsleeves, explained that the man he had been trying to beat just forty-eight hours before was the best choice for president.

"We need a politics that's about decency, politics that brings back dignity. And that is what we sought to practice in my campaign. That's what Joe Biden has been practicing his entire life."[813]

O'Rourke went next.

"The man in the White House today poses an existential threat to this country, to our democracy, to free and fair elections, and we need somebody who can beat him. In Joe Biden, we have that man."

Klobuchar added: "If you feel tired of the noise and the nonsense and our politics, and if you are tired of the extremes, you have a home with me. And I think you know you have a home with Joe Biden."

The three former rivals repeated one idea, over and over: "empathy."

"He is somebody of such extraordinary grace and kindness and empathy," Buttigieg said, "from taking time to talk to somebody who struggles to speak, to taking time for a family that's struggling with loss."

Klobuchar echoed that sentiment: "We have a president that has no empathy, that cannot put himself in the shoes of the people of this country. Well, guess who can do that? And that is Joe Biden."

O'Rourke spoke about the pastor of Mother Emanuel in Charleston, who lost his wife in the 2015 shooting. "Joe Biden listened to him, in fact, with his eyes closed so that he could concentrate on every single word that that man said, and then he spoke back to him and to all of us from his heart filled with compassion and love and the power to heal."

"I felt Joe Biden healing us," he concluded.

Biden was so moved that he appointed O'Rourke to an administration post on the spot.

"You're going to take care of the gun problem with me. You're going to be the one who leads this effort," he said.

Super Tuesday was just hours away.

BERNIE SANDERS, PUBLIC ENEMY

Meanwhile, in downtown Los Angeles, thousands of people were gathering for that Bernie Sanders rally at the convention center.

The rally was billed as "Fight the Power: Bernie Sanders + Public Enemy." The poster for the event featured a silhouette of Sanders with his fist raised, clenched around a microphone. Sanders volunteers wore T-shirts emblazoned with the same logo.

It was a defiant image, symbolizing the synthesis of democratic socialism with pop culture. It was also a signal that Sanders had no intention of pivoting back toward the center as he moved closer to the nomination.

Outside, Sanders supporters stood patiently in seemingly endless lines. It was the closest thing to a Trump-sized crowd I had seen in months of covering the Democratic candidates.

Three Sanders fans showed up wearing facemasks, the first sign of any awareness of coronavirus on the campaign trail.

A group of pro-Sanders demonstrators held homemade signs: "Feel the Bern," "Go Democratic Party," and also "Fuck Trump: Trump Is Racist." One man waved a Trump flag—with "Bernie" replacing "Trump" in the center of the logo.

Another man, dressed in an olive-green military cap and jacket, held a "Million to Milwaukee: Let's Have Bernie's Back" sign. He told me he wanted Sanders supporters to stage a mass demonstration at the Democratic National Convention in July against any attempt to use superdelegates to deny Sanders the nomination.

I asked him what he thought of Buttigieg dropping out, since the news had just popped up on my smartphone. He was so excited that he gave me a high-five.

Inside the convention center, the lines continued, as the crowd waited patiently to pass through metal detectors. If they were aware of coronavirus, they did not seem concerned. Aside from the three people wearing masks, everyone else had seemed content to pack the arena. At one point, the fire marshal closed the doors; the hall had reached capacity.

Onstage, Sanders was preceded by the venerable Dick van Dyke, a legend of Hollywood musicals and the golden age of television. At 94 years old, he joked about his age—and Sanders's relative youth.

"I would like to say a word about age. I'm 15 years older than Bernie," he said, to cheers and laughter.[814] At one point, the crowd chanted: "We love Dick!"[815]

When Sanders emerged, to wild cheers, he returned the favor, promising to nominate the "youthful, vigorous" Dick van Dyke for vice president.[816]

Promising also to "transform this country," Sanders said: "With your help on Tuesday, we're going to win the Democratic primary here in California. With your help, we're going to win the Democratic nomination. And with your help, we are going to defeat the most dangerous president in the modern history of America."

But privately, the Sanders campaign was stunned.

"The swiftness of the coalescence around Mr. Biden caught the Sanders team off guard," the *New York Times* reported.[817]

There was some good news. Poll results released that morning showed Sanders ahead of Biden in Texas by a staggering 15 points, 34 percent to 19 percent.[818] A poll released the next day would show Sanders with a similar lead in North Carolina, with 31 percent to Bloomberg's 18 percent. Biden was in third place at 14 percent.[819]

But all of those polls had been taken before Biden won South Carolina and before the cascade of endorsements. It was impossible to accept those polls at face value. The party establishment was determined to stretch Biden's lone victory—in a state he had always been *expected* to win—into a referendum on the entire Democratic field.

The primary had essentially collapsed into a two-man race, with the weight of the Democratic Party tipping the scale to Biden.

Elizabeth Warren continued to campaign—though no one quite understood why. Her only remaining potential path to victory was to be a spoiler, hoping to deny Sanders a majority on the first ballot at the convention and then sway the "superdelegates" to her side.

Mike Bloomberg was still trying to carry out his plan to sweep the Super Tuesday states, but his momentum had gone, and he faced new opposition at every turn. When he spoke from the pulpit at the historic Brown Chapel AME Church in Selma, Alabama, on the morning of its annual commemorative civil rights march, several worshippers stood up in their pews and turned their backs to him.[820]

On the surface, nothing had changed. Sanders held a large rally in Minneapolis on the eve of the big primary. Ilhan Omar, warming up the crowd, told the crowd of six thousand people[821] to hold hands— coronavirus be damned.[822]

Joe Biden, addressing supporters in Houston on Monday, had reminded them to vote the next day.

"Tomorrow is Super Thursday," he said, before correcting himself.[823]

A FAULTY TEST

On the morning of Super Tuesday, March 3, Vice President Mike Pence addressed reporters in the White House briefing room.

The fight against the coronavirus had suffered several serious setbacks.

"At this point, we are at 77 domestic cases of coronavirus," Pence said. "Sadly, Washington State confirmed three additional deaths today. Our condolences go to the families of those that were lost. That puts us at nine deaths, domestic."[824]

Most of the deaths had been concentrated in one location: the Life Care Center in Kirkland, Washington. About 25 percent of the nursing home's residents had tested positive for the coronavirus. Being elderly, residents were particularly vulnerable to the illness; many also had underlying health conditions.

And the outbreak was spreading.

"We are at 13 states, plus New York City—14 total jurisdictions at this point—where we have coronavirus cases currently operating," Pence said.

Worse still, the country's ability to develop a test for the illness had stalled. The CDC had a test, based on the genome sequence of the virus, as provided by Chinese scientists.

But something had gone wrong. The tests did not work, thanks to apparent contamination in their production. And the discovery was made in mid-February—weeks after the first coronavirus patient had arrived in the United States and only after hundreds of tests had already been sent to state laboratories.[825]

Critics sought to blame Trump for the problem. But Dr. Anthony Fauci, director of the National Institute of Allergy and Infectious Diseases and a rare figure respected on both sides of the political aisle, would later say that the mistake was no one's fault.

"It was a complicated series of multiple things that conflated that just, you know, went the wrong way," he told the *Hugh Hewitt Show*. "One of them was a technical glitch that slowed things down in the beginning. Nobody's fault. There wasn't any bad guys there. It just happened."[826]

Regardless, the country had lost weeks of valuable time. Pence and his team were scrambling to catch up.

"Today, we will issue new guidance from the CDC that will make it clear that any American can be tested with no restrictions, subject to doctor's orders," he said. He added that new, "CDC-approved tests are moving out," adding: "We should have 2,500 kits out before the end of this week, which represents about 1.5 million tests."

In addition, he said, the administration would push the private sector to help develop and process tests. Dr. Stephen Hahn, the commissioner of the Food and Drug Administration (FDA), stepped up to explain that the administration had cut through regulations, with an "emergency use authorization," to accelerate the process.

Meanwhile, President Trump was fighting the public relations battle.

He cited a poll March 1 showing that the public had more confidence in his administration than it had in the previous administration's handling of other outbreaks.[827]

But he was facing an unprecedented full-court press from the media and the opposition. Many had been fomenting panic since November 9, 2016. From "Russia collusion" in 2017 to faulty claims of an imminent recession in 2019, Trump's enemies had primed half the public to expect the worst.

Now that there was a real threat—albeit one that could be managed— they could finally wound Donald Trump.

At a rally in North Charleston, the day before the South Carolina primary, Trump accused Democrats of "politicizing the coronavirus," saying it was their new "hoax."[828] In context, Trump had used the word "hoax" to refer to past partisan attacks on his administration. But the word was destined to be weaponized by his critics.

The administration was moving fast—but the virus was moving faster.

On March 1, the day after the South Carolina primary, the State of New York confirmed its first case of the coronavirus.[829] The next day, Dr. Fauci warned that the United States would have to start "thinking about" closing schools and canceling public gatherings.[830]

Trump tried to do three things at once: assuage the markets, fight his critics, and solve the problem. He tweeted: "I was criticized by the Democrats when I closed the Country down to China many weeks ahead of what almost everyone recommended. Saved many lives. Dems were working the Impeachment Hoax. They didn't have a clue! Now they are fear mongering. Be calm & vigilant!"[831]

But things were spinning out of control. On March 3, the Fed announced that it was lowering interest rates by half a percentage point to boost the economy. Stocks dropped the next day, as investors wondered what the Fed knew that they did not.

On Super Tuesday, Surgeon General Vice Adm. Jerome M. Adams, MD, wrote an op-ed for CNN: "Be cautious, but not afraid of coronavirus."[832]

But fear had a mind of its own.

SUPER TUESDAY

As dawn broke March 3, the front page of *The New York Times* ran an article titled: "How the Democratic Establishment Stumbled as Sanders Surged."[833]

It called Sanders "a formidable front-runner," explaining:

> His agenda has galvanized liberal voters yearning for change....
>
> He holds significant financial and organizational advantages that he was able to accumulate over a long season of disarray among traditional Democrats. And he has begun to make an increasingly direct case to the rest of the party that his urgent message is the best match for a trying political moment, and that he is the candidate most prepared to do battle with President Trump.[834]

The Hill also reported that Sanders "is poised to win the most delegates," adding that Biden's "best-case scenario" involved winning the South, especially with Bloomberg on the ballot.[835]

For its part, the Biden campaign was optimistic. It made the bold prediction early Tuesday morning that Biden would win an upset over Sanders in Texas.[836]

Voters in fourteen states—plus the territory of American Samoa and Democrats overseas—cast their ballots. There were reports of irregularities in Los Angeles, where there was a power outage near the airport.[837] In Houston, voters waited for hours at Texas Southern University, amid reports of other problems in the state. Sanders supporters feared a "rigged" election.[838]

The Biden campaign chose a small community center in Baldwin Hills for its victory party. The neighborhood, a black middle-class community, had been the site of a memorable rally for Barack Obama in

2008; the community center was just off Rodeo Road, which had been renamed Obama Boulevard in 2019.[839] Though the former president had not endorsed his former running mate, the symbolism was impossible to miss.

Inside, Biden's staff and supporters barely filled half a basketball court. But as the sun set on the crisp, warm late winter evening, results began to filter in from across the country.

The exit polls showed that a huge proportion of Democratic primary voters—nearly 50 percent in several states—had made up their minds in the last few days before the election. Some 44 percent said they wanted a return to Obama's policies; 38 percent said they wanted more liberal policies. And minority voters said they preferred Biden—by staggering margins.

Mike Bloomberg, surprisingly, won American Samoa. (Tulsi Gabbard, who was born there, came in second.)[840] Sanders picked up a big win in his home state of Vermont—though not quite as big as he had in 2016—and won Colorado and Utah, continuing his string of wins in the West.

But the next victories were all for Biden.

The former vice president racked up a huge win in Virginia, winning over 50 percent of the vote and drawing a massive turnout—especially in Northern Virginia, the heart of the Trump-hating "deep state." He won Alabama with nearly two-thirds of the vote and picked up lopsided wins in Tennessee, Arkansas, and Oklahoma.

That much of the pattern matched expectations.

But Biden also won North Carolina—a state Sanders had led by double digits just days before.

Then Biden won Minnesota. Not only was it Klobuchar's home state, but it was also a win outside the South. It was also a state the Trump campaign was determined to flip in 2020, having come close in 2016.

This was not to be Sanders's night.

By the time the night was over, Biden had even won Massachusetts— a state Sanders had made a push to win—and relegated Warren to third place.

Sanders took the biggest prize, California—but Biden did well enough to take more than a quarter of its 415 delegates. And Biden—true to his campaign's upset predictions—took Texas as well. As votes came in later in the week, he would also be declared the winner in Maine.

Like Vice President Hubert Humphrey in 1968, Biden found himself the frontrunner, after his radical opponents had dominated the primary.

The tiny crowd on the basketball court was ecstatic as their candidate approached the podium flanked by his wife, Jill, and his sister, Valerie, to face the nation.

He smiled and reached for—his sister's hand.

"Oh no, they switched on me. This is my wife, this is my sister, they switched on me," he said.[841]

It was perfect—perfectly Joe.

"We are a decent, brave, resilient people," he concluded. "We can believe again, but we are better than this moment. We are better than this president. So, get back up and take back this country, the United States of America."

As Biden spoke, there was a sudden commotion. Two anti-dairy protesters—the same group that had interrupted Sanders in Nevada two weeks before—rushed the stage. Symone Sanders, Biden's redoubtable spokeswoman, hauled one off the stage herself.

She was celebrated all over social media: this was her night, too. For weeks, she had taken abuse in the spin room. On Super Tuesday, she made the tackle to save her candidate.

At least one Sanders had a better night than expected.

TWENTY-THREE

CORONAVIRUS

> "Advise the health authorities, the Ministry, that's the first thing to do, if it
> should turn out to be an epidemic, measures must be taken, But no one has
> ever heard of an epidemic of blindness, his wife insisted, anxious to hold on
> to this last shred of hope..."
> —José Saramago, *Blindness*, 1995[842]

STATE OF EMERGENCY

Joe Biden descended into a crowd of well-wishers, shaking hands and posing for selfies. It shocked me at the time because the coronavirus was already something people knew about, and I myself was beginning to measure my distance from other people.

A liberal blogger who had hounded me at every Democratic event in LA decided to apologize. He offered me a fist bump. I started at his clenched hand and decided making peace was worth the risk.

It was the last handshake I would have for months.

Biden's victory completely upended the primary race. On Super Tuesday morning, the *New York Times* could foresee no outcome other than a decisive Sanders sweep or a long war of attrition ending at the July convention.

By Super Tuesday evening, Democratic strategist James Carville was predicting on MSNBC that Democrats would ask Sanders to drop out, adding that James Clyburn had "literally saved the Democratic Party."[843]

The stock market rebounded nearly 1,200 points the next day, relieved that a President Sanders was no longer likely. Health care stocks rose nearly 6 percent, ahead of the market as a whole.[844]

Mike Bloomberg dropped out, having spent more than a billion dollars to win a handful of delegates.[845] He went on to endorse Joe Biden, whom he praised for his "decency."[846]

Trump taunted his New York City rival, saying he had been swindled by consultants, calling it the "worst, and most embarrassing, experience" of Bloomberg's life.[847]

Elizabeth Warren hung on, prompting bitter attacks from the Bernie Sanders camp. "Imagine if the progressives consolidated last night like the moderates consolidated, who would have won?" asked Ilhan Omar.[848] Trump poured fuel on the file, tweeting that Warren was a "SPOILER!"[849]

Warren dropped out the next day, in an emotional press conference in front of her home in Cambridge, Massachusetts—but she refused to endorse anyone.[850] In an interview that evening, she reserved particular bitterness for the army of Sanders supporters who had trolled her online.[851]

The campaigns reloaded for the next battle: "Mini Tuesday," half a dozen contests in the West and Midwest. The biggest prize was Michigan, which also carried immense symbolic importance: Sanders had won the state in a come-from-behind victory over Hillary Clinton in 2016, and Trump had won it in the general election.

Biden raked in more endorsements. John Delaney backed him,[852] as did Deval Patrick.[853] By the weekend, Kamala Harris was backing the man she had once attacked for his racial insensitivity.[854] John Kerry campaigned for Biden in Michigan,[855] as did Cory Booker, who endorsed Biden in Flint,[856] calling him a "lightworker,"[857] whatever that was. Booker's doubts about Biden's mental faculties were apparently no longer relevant.

One national poll just days after Super Tuesday showed Biden leading Sanders among Democrats by 16 points.[858] Other, similar polls followed.[859] The Democratic electorate had swung decisively against
Sanders. A plan for Biden's future administration leaked, stacked with
Obama alumni and former 2020 rivals.[860]

A desperate Sanders concentrated on Michigan, canceling rallies
elsewhere. Jesse Jackson—who had won Michigan in 1988—endorsed
him;[861] so did the "Justice Democrats," linked to Alexandria Ocasio-
Cortez.[862] Sanders also appealed to Muslim voters, hoping his anti-Israel
stances might help.[863]

But there were already recriminations: some accused AOC of not
helping enough before Super Tuesday.[864] There were also strange new
disruptions: a man appeared at a Sanders rally in Arizona and waved a
swastika.[865] The event received disproportionate media coverage.

And the money was swinging behind Biden. Priorities USA, the
super PAC funded by left-wing philanthropist George Soros, launched
ads for Biden.[866]

Elsewhere, politics continued as usual. Senate Minority Leader
Chuck Schumer headlined a pro-choice rally on the steps of the Supreme
Court. He offered an ominous threat to Trump's appointees Brett Kavanaugh and Neil Gorsuch: "You have released the whirlwind and you will
pay the price. You won't know what hit you, if you go forward with these
awful decisions."[867] That drew a rare rebuke from Chief Justice Roberts, who called Schumer's statements not only "inappropriate" but also
"dangerous."[868]

Yet politics was no longer the most important story.

On March 4, the day after Super Tuesday, Governor Gavin Newsom declared a state of emergency in California over the threat of
coronavirus[869]—the first outside Washington State to do so. Other states
began to do the same.[870]

Trump touted a poll from February showing three in four Americans
had confidence in the government's ability to handle the virus.[871] He
tried to reassure the public he was "working very hard."[872]

But the danger was rising. The U.S. Navy self-quarantined its ships in Europe.[873] And on March 7, the Conservative Political Action Conference (CPAC)—which the president, vice president, and senior officials had addressed in the last days of February—announced that one attendee had tested positive for coronavirus, sending a frisson of fear throughout the conservative world.[874]

BLACK MONDAY

It almost seemed unreal.

On Friday, March 6, the U.S. Bureau of Labor Statistics released one of the best monthly jobs reports in American history.

The media called it a "blockbuster."[875] The U.S. economy had created 273,000 new jobs in February, "smash[ing]" expectations of 175,000.[876] Numbers for December and January were also revised upward. Unemployment was at 3.5 percent, tying the lowest level in fifty years.[877]

And yet.

"This could be the last perfect employment report the market gets for some time," one economist told CNBC.[878]

Trump tried to calm fears. In a tweet he would later have cause to regret, he said: "So last year 37,000 Americans died from the common Flu. It averages between 27,000 and 70,000 per year. Nothing is shut down, life & the economy go on. At this moment there are 546 confirmed cases of CoronaVirus, with 22 deaths. Think about that!"[879]

But it took an unrelated shock to tank the economy.

Saudi Arabia—that most problematic of U.S. "allies"—had been urging fellow members of OPEC to tighten production as a buffer against reduced demand in the coronavirus outbreak. But when Russia refused to play along, Saudi Arabia retaliated by driving up its own production dramatically—thereby causing prices to drop.[880]

It was an attack aimed at Moscow. But it detonated on Wall Street.

What followed was chaos. The markets could barely contain one crisis. Two at once spelled disaster.

The Dow Jones Industrial Average dropped over 2,000 points— the worst day on Wall Street since the 2008 financial crisis.[881] Two days later, the Dow officially entered "bear market" territory, meaning it had dropped more than 20 percent from its high—tantalizingly close to 30,000—on February 12, just four weeks before.[882]

For millions of Americans watching, memories of those dark days suddenly resurfaced. Would all the gains of the past decade—and especially of the past three years—suddenly disappear?

Those—like myself—who had been optimistic about America's ability to manage the outbreak were forced to confront the fact that panic, justified or not, would make the economic damage inevitable.

The reality of coronavirus began to hit home as public figures began to announce that they had self-quarantined. Tom Hanks—a national icon, "Forrest Gump" himself—announced on social media that he and his wife, Rita Wilson, had tested positive for the virus in Australia.[883]

He urged fans to be positive: "There is no crying in baseball," he would later say, quoting one of his most famous lines from A League of Their Own.[884] His symptoms were mild; he and Wilson would soon recover.

But the panic had begun. And the effect on the presidential campaign was dramatic.

On the morning of "Mini Tuesday," Biden toured an auto plant under construction in Detroit. As he spoke with construction workers, one of them pinned him down over his position on gun control.

"You are actively trying to diminish our Second Amendment right to keep and bear arms," the worker, wearing his hard hat and safety vest, told the former vice president.

"You're full of shit!" Biden countered.[885]

It was a deeply damaging encounter for the candidate, on a par with Barack Obama's argument with "Joe the Plumber" in October 2008, when he told Joe Wuerzelbacher in Ohio that raising taxes on small business, mid-financial crisis, was justified because of the need to "spread the wealth around."[886]

It went "viral"—but then, so had the coronavirus. By the end of the day, both Biden and Sanders had canceled their planned victory rallies in Ohio.

The results were almost an afterthought.

Biden crushed Sanders in Michigan, winning nearly 53 percent of the vote to just over 36 percent for Sanders. The former vice president also swept all of the other primary states: Missouri, Mississippi, Idaho, and—once the mail-in votes were counted—Washington, as well.

Sanders took the lone caucus state, North Dakota. With just fourteen delegates, it was the smallest contest, a consolation prize.

Sanders declined to make any sort of public statement. Biden, appearing at the National Constitution Center in Philadelphia, took the stage with a small group of supporters a safe "social distance" away, at the edge of the room.

It was, perhaps, his best speech of the campaign thus far: "At this moment," he said, "when there's so much fear in the country and there's so much fear across the world, we need American leadership. We need presidential leadership that's honest, trusted, truthful, and steady, reassuring leadership."

At one point, Biden appeared to forget which office he was running for: "These are all people that have been working like the devil to try to get us elected as the, uh..." he said.[887]

But with Trump scrambling to catch up to the coronavirus, Biden suddenly looked like a viable alternative.

THE OVAL OFFICE ADDRESS

The next day, the World Health Organization—which had dallied in the early days of the crisis—declared coronavirus a "pandemic." A staffer for Senator Maria Cantwell (D-WA) tested positive for coronavirus, the first such case to be linked to Capitol Hill.[888] And after another day of steep losses on Wall Street, the White House understood it had to change its strategy.

"Plan A," so to speak, had been to contain the coronavirus and keep markets calm. But "Plan A" had failed—or, perhaps more charitably, had worked as long as it could.

"Plan B" was war.

Shortly after markets closed on Wednesday, the president tweeted: "I will be addressing the Nation this evening at 9:00 P.M. (Eastern) from the Oval Office."[889]

News began to leak about the substance of Trump's address: he would declare a thirty-day travel ban on Europe, which Dr. Anthony Fauci had pinpointed as the main incoming source of the virus.

But there was more: the nation would henceforth be on a war footing.

"This is the most aggressive and comprehensive effort to confront a foreign virus in modern history," he said. "I am confident that by counting and continuing to take these tough measures, we will significantly reduce the threat to our citizens, and we will ultimately and expeditiously defeat this virus."[890]

Trump announced $8.3 billion in spending directly on the coronavirus fight and promised "emergency" financial relief for the economy as a whole.

He said he had met with health insurance industry leaders, who had agreed "to waive all copayments for coronavirus treatments, extend insurance coverage to these treatments, and to prevent surprise medical billing."

In addition, he said, "We are cutting massive amounts of red tape to make antiviral therapies available in record time. These treatments will significantly reduce the impact and reach of the virus."

Trump also urged Americans to take stiff precautions. He advised nursing homes to limit "all medically unnecessary visits," for schools to consider closing, and for large gatherings to be avoided.

He urged: "For all Americans, it is essential that everyone take extra precautions and practice good hygiene. Each of us has a role to play in defeating this virus. Wash your hands, clean often-used surfaces, cover your face and mouth if you sneeze or cough, and most of all, if you are sick or not feeling well, stay home."

The president sought to reassure Americans that this was not a "financial crisis," like as 2008 had been: "Our banks and financial institutions are fully capitalized and incredibly strong. Our unemployment is at a historic low. This vast economic prosperity gives us flexibility, reserves, and resources to handle any threat that comes our way."

He announced low-interest loans for small businesses and said he would instruct the Treasury Department to delay the April 15 tax filing deadline.

He closed:

If we are vigilant—and we can reduce the chance of infection, which we will—we will significantly impede the transmission of the virus. The virus will not have a chance against us.

No nation is more prepared or more resilient than the United States. We have the best economy, the most advanced healthcare, and the most talented doctors, scientists, and researchers anywhere in the world.

We are all in this together. We must put politics aside, stop the partisanship, and unify together as one nation and one family.

As history has proven time and time again, Americans always rise to the challenge and overcome adversity.

Our future remains brighter than anyone can imagine. Acting with compassion and love, we will heal the sick, care for those in need, help our fellow citizens, and emerge from this challenge stronger and more unified than ever before.

God bless you, and God bless America. Thank you.

Across the nation, there was pandemonium. An NBA basketball game between the Utah Jazz and the Oklahoma City Thunder was abruptly postponed after one of the Jazz players tested positive, right before tipoff, for coronavirus.

In Dallas, Mavericks owner Mark Cuban, sitting courtside, reeled, open-mouthed, in shock, as he read the news on his smartphone and then walked over to the referees to let them know. Other leagues followed suit.

Never mind "no crying," as Hanks had said; there was to be no baseball, period—for many months, at least.

Stunned Americans overseas began making frantic plans to return home before the weekend deadline. They would crowd airports on their arrival, overwhelming Chicago's O'Hare International, standing next to each other in hours-long lines as each passenger waited to be screened for the disease.

The day after Trump's address, the Dow plunged nearly 2,400 points—its worst day since 1987[891] and the largest single-day point drop in its history, to that point, accounting for 10 percent of the market's value.

It would not be the last such drop—or the worst.

THE MOMENT OF TRUTH

For Joe Biden, and for Democrats in general, it was an unparalleled opportunity.

In 2008, as the financial markets were melting down, the Republican presidential nominee, Senator John McCain (R-AZ), had declared that the "fundamentals" of the economy were "strong."[892] Days later, he "suspended" his campaign, citing the crisis, and rushed to Washington to help President George W. Bush pass an unprecedented Wall Street bailout.

Obama voted for the bailout, too—but he had remained calm and steady throughout the crisis. The contrast between McCain's earnest but erratic response and Obama's "no-drama" reaction was impossible to ignore. The Obama campaign never looked back.

The day after Trump's Oval Office address, the Biden campaign decided it, too, needed to respond, as well. Biden, who had promised "steady, reassuring leadership" two days before, had the opportunity to demonstrate it.

The cable news networks tuned in: he had the nation's attention.

But instead of providing the "unity" he had promised, Biden, reading haltingly from a teleprompter—after a half-hour delay for microphone problems[893]—used the opportunity to bash the president:

The World Health Organization now has officially, officially declared COVID-19 a pandemic. Downplaying it, being overly dismissive, or spreading misinformation is only going to hurt us and further advantage the spread of the disease. But neither should we panic or fall back on xenophobia. Labeling COVID-19 a "foreign virus" does not displace accountability for the misjudgments that have been taken thus far by the Trump administration. . . .

Public fears are being compounded by a pervasive lack of trust in this president, fueled by [an] adversarial relationship with the truth that he continues to have. Our government's ability to respond effectively has been undermined by hollowing out our agencies and disparagement of science. And our ability to drive a global response is dramatically, dramatically undercut by the damage Trump has done to our credibility and our relationships around the world. We have to get to work immediately to dig ourselves out of this hole. And that's why, today, I'm releasing a plan to combat and overcome the coronavirus.[894]

Ironically, Biden's plan, posted on at his website,[895] seemed to repeat much of what Trump had said the night before or had done weeks earlier.[896] There were two glaring exceptions: Biden's plan called for action on "climate change" and made no mention of China.[897]

At no point had Biden ever offered the president his support.

Sanders's speech was even more extreme. Speaking from Burlington, Vermont, Sanders stopped just short of calling for Trump to be removed from office, insisting that he pass authority to a committee of "experts" and to Congress:

Because President Trump is unwilling and unable to lead selflessly, we must immediately convene an emergency bipartisan authority of experts to support and direct a response [to coronavirus] that is comprehensive, compassionate, and based first and foremost on science and fact. In other words, Congress in a bipartisan manner must take responsibility for addressing this unparalleled crisis.[898]

Sanders also claimed that the United States was at a particular disadvantage in the fight against coronavirus because, he said, "we do not guarantee health care to all people as a right."

He did not bother to explain why Italy, with its socialized medical system, had been hit hardest of all.

The Democrats' remarks were petty, partisan, and tone-deaf. And they were a missed opportunity.

In the same vein, Speaker of the House Nancy Pelosi gave her own televised address the following day. She did not mention the president once.[899]

Democrats refused to acknowledge his legitimacy, let alone his authority.

Meanwhile, as Pelosi spoke, President Trump was preparing another speech: a declaration, in the Rose Garden of the White House, that he was declaring a national emergency, and thereby releasing a torrent of federal funds.

But while the announcement was ominous, the tableau was cheerful.

The president was flanked not only by the members of his coronavirus task force but also by top executives in the American pharmaceutical industry, including representatives of Walmart, CVS, Target, and Walgreens.[900] One by one, they pledged their support to the president's effort to expand testing and to develop new products for the fight.

Liberals fumed on social media. Author Stephen King tweeted that "Trump's coronavirus team is all male, all old, and all white"—shortly before Dr. Deborah Birx stepped forward to explain the new testing system and Centers for Medicare and Medicaid Services administrator Seema Verma spoke about new regulations for nursing homes.[901]

It was a scene Americans had craved and deserved: the sight of leaders coming together around the president in a moment of crisis. And Democrats, inexplicably, had cropped themselves out of the picture.

The Dow rose nearly 2,000 points, its biggest single-day gain since 2008[902]—much of that gain as President Trump was speaking.

Hope was back, again.

TWENTY-FOUR

CONCLUSION

"Every generation has its central concern, whether to end war, erase racial injustice, or improve the condition of the working man. Today's young people appear to have chosen for their concern the dignity of the individual human being. They demand a limitation on excessive power. They demand a political system that preserves the sense of community among men. They demand a government that speaks directly and honestly to its citizens. We can win their commitment only by demonstrating that these goals are possible through personal effort."

—Robert F. Kennedy, "Youth," 1967[903]

THE END OF THE PRIMARY

The coronavirus marked the end of Trump.

So claimed his critics: "The Trump presidency is over," wrote Peter Wehner in *The Atlantic*, the day of the president's Rose Garden presentation.[904]

But perhaps the Trump presidency had simply arrived at a new beginning.

What *was* over was the Democratic primary.

The field had shrunk, effectively, to two: Joe Biden and Bernie Sanders.

Tulsi Gabbard hung on, having won two delegates in American Samoa. But the party changed the debate rules again, this time requiring a minimum of 20 percent of delegates to qualify, effectively excluding her.[905] She would finally quit and endorse Biden, her misgivings about the Iraq War and the Democrat establishment suddenly less important than party unity.[906]

Mike Bloomberg wound down his operations ignominiously, giving $18 million in campaign funds to the Democratic National Committee[907] and then refusing to pay his staff through November, as he had promised to do. (They promptly sued.)[908]

The party wanted the primary to end. "I think it is time for us to shut this primary down," Representative Clyburn told National Public Radio on "Mini Tuesday." He was afraid further attacks by Sanders could make Biden's task harder in the general election: "People will say things that you cannot overcome."[909]

Biden attempted to appease Sanders, adopting his pledge to provide "free" college to many students.[910] But Sanders mocked him: "It's great that Joe Biden is now supporting a position that was in the Democratic platform four years ago."[911]

The candidates met for their first—and last—one-on-one debate March 15. The debate was to have been held in Arizona on the Ides of March. But CNN, citing coronavirus fears, canceled the live audience, the media filing center, and the spin room. In the end, the entire event was moved to CNN's Washington, DC, studio—the candidates placed several feet apart, the moderators halfway across the room, all maintaining a "social distance." (Critics mocked the two opponents, both near 80 years old, as "Statler and Waldorf"—the crotchety old men sniping from a balcony in *The Muppet Show*.)

For the first time, the debate addressed the coronavirus head-on. Both candidates fumbled.

Biden declared: "We've been through this before with dealing with the viruses, the N1H1 [*sic*] virus as well as what happened with

Africa," that is, Ebola.[912] He also falsely claimed that Trump rejected testing kits from the World Health Organization: they had never been offered.[913]

Sanders suggested, as a first step, that "we have to shut this president up right now. Because he's undermining the doctors and the scientists who are trying to help the American people."[914] He touted universal health care. And he attacked the pharmaceutical industry, frantically working on a vaccine and life-saving drugs: "You got people in the pharmaceutical industry who are saying, 'Oh, wow, what an opportunity to make a fortune.'"[915]

Biden's leftward shift continued. He promised not to deport any illegal aliens—he used the term "alien," despite himself—in the first one hundred days of his administration, and thereafter to deport only those convicted of felonies.[916] He pledged to nominate a woman for vice president and a black woman for the Supreme Court, making race an explicit criterion: "It's required that they have representation now. It's long overdue."[917]

Biden went on to sweep the March 17 primaries in Illinois, Florida, and Arizona. But in the coronavirus crisis, voting was almost an afterthought for many.

Ohio postponed its primary, for fear of people crowding in polling places. Chicago officials slammed Illinois governor J. B. Pritzker for holding a primary at all.[918] Many poll workers simply failed to show up for duty. In the chaos, pro-choice crusader Marie Newman unseated incumbent pro-life Democrat Representative Dan Lipinski, the last of an endangered species.[919] Alexandria Ocasio-Cortez celebrated from afar.

Sanders was rumored—and even reported[920]—to be suspending his campaign. No: he angrily vowed to continue.

But it was no longer even clear what "campaigning" even meant.

The rallies were postponed. The fundraisers—at least in person—were over, the money wells dry.[921] Activists could no longer go door-to-door: "The Bernie Sanders Revolution Has Moved to Mom's Couch," the *New York Times* prodded.[922]

Both Biden and Sanders attempted to campaign via live stream. The tech-savvy Sanders campaign had ample experience with the medium, dating back to 2016.

But for the Biden campaign, it was a disaster. His first attempt, a "virtual" town hall in Illinois, was marred by failing audio, faulty cameras, and even a wailing baby.[923]

Biden disappeared from public view for several days while his campaign converted a room in his Wilmington, Delaware, home to a studio. But the result was hardly an improvement. Biden looked old and pained; he sometimes rambled, adrift. In one interview with CNN, he coughed directly into his hand, prompting a rebuke from anchor Jake Tapper.[924] "I'm alone in my home," Biden explained.

Sanders enjoyed one more victory: he trounced Biden among "Democrats Abroad," by a margin of nearly three to one.[925]

He declared himself ready for the next debate—whenever that would be.[926]

A WARTIME PRESIDENT

With his rivals sidelined, Trump was in front of the cameras every day—speaking, leading.

For two months, he had tried to manage a crisis. Now, he was leading a war.

At the outset, a majority of registered voters disapproved of his handling of the coronavirus.[927] But that would soon change.

The president began by declaring a National Day of Prayer on March 15. That evening, the Fed cut interest rates to zero, putting Trump and his "frenemy," Fed chair Jerome Powell, finally on the same page. Stocks plunged the next day by nearly 3,000 points—but surged the day after, causing trade to be suspended because the market was rising too *fast*.

Trump began the week feuding openly with New York governor Andrew Cuomo. The media had seized on Cuomo as a kind of alternative president, as he led New York's response. Cuomo seemed to relish the role.

But after a few Twitter rebukes from the president—"Andrew, keep politics out of it"[928]—Cuomo learned to play along.

Trump was "ready, willing, and able to help," Cuomo told reporters March 17. "His team is on it."[929]

Several milestones passed almost unnoticed. Canada ratified the USMCA on March 14. And with the Illinois primary, Trump formally won the Republican nomination. He largely ignored both achievements. He was focused on what he called the "war with an invisible enemy,"[930] reminding Americans daily: "WE WILL PREVAIL!"[931]

He made unusual alliances. When California governor Gavin Newsom praised the president for his assistance—"every single thing he [Trump] said, they followed through on"[932]—Trump set aside years of feuding. After Al Sharpton raised concerns about the risk to prisoners, Trump called him to discuss the issue.[933]

The one foe remained the "fake news." But Trump faced them directly, as he led daily briefings personally from the White House. Millions tuned in—as much to watch the confrontations as to hear the latest administration updates. Ratings rivaled those of *The Bachelor* and *Monday Night Football.*[934]

The most difficult task was to be the "stimulus" bill.[935] Senator Tom Cotton—a rock-ribbed conservative—floated a new idea: "Surge cash to Americans."[936] He proposed giving out Andrew Yang–style $1,000 "tax-rebate checks" to households facing sudden economic shock. As the White House embraced the idea, Yang offered Trump his support—the first Democratic leader to do so.[937]

The price tag quickly climbed over $2 trillion. Critics mocked Republicans for dropping all pretense of fiscal conservatism. Republicans countered: the government had shut down the economy, so the government had to make the American people whole.

Democrats were still reluctant to allow Trump a win. Speaker Pelosi returned to the Capitol and promptly tanked bipartisan negotiations in the Senate. She prepared her own legislation, loaded with left-wing priorities like nationwide same-day voter registration a grant to the John F. Kennedy Center for the Performing Arts in Washington, DC; and pork for the solar and wind energy lobbies.

Biden chirped from the sidelines, accusing Republicans of putting "corporate bailouts ahead of families."[938] Sanders raged on the Senate floor. Alexandria Ocasio-Cortez called the stimulus "shameful" for helping save American companies.[939]

It was a colossal blunder.

In the end, Pelosi and the Democrats acquiesced, claiming meekly that they had turned the bill "upside down from a Republican corporate focus to a Democratic workers-first focus."

The Senate—missing several members due to coronavirus, illness, and self-quarantine, passed it 96–0. The House passed it two days later by voice vote.

Trump's approval ratings soared. Polls showed that a majority now approved of his response to the crisis.[940]

But was he still the president he once was? Could a president who had just signed the biggest spending bill in American history still be called a "conservative"?

The answer came in an exchange in the White House Briefing room with a reporter who pressed Trump on why he had not yet used the Defense Production Act to order American companies to produce much-needed medical supplies.

Trump's reply was a classic defense of the free-market economy.

"Call a person over in Venezuela. Ask them: How did nationalization of their businesses work out? Not too well," Trump quipped, adding, "The concept of nationalizing our business is not a good concept."

He explained that while he *could* order companies to act—as he did a few days later, ordering General Motors to produce ventilators—the government was a poor judge of which companies would best do the job. And so many companies were stepping forward to volunteer, he said, that nationalization—which would have frightened the markets—was not necessary.

In 2008, then president George W. Bush declined to make a similar stand.

"I'm a market-oriented guy, but not when I'm faced with the prospect of a global meltdown," Bush had said.

Trump was willing to compromise—but not to cast aside the basic principles of the American system.[941]

THE SHAPE OF THE RACE

Had the coronavirus pandemic erupted in September instead of March, the 2020 presidential race would have come to a predictable conclusion.

As in 2008, the chaos would have ushered Democrats back into power—despite the party's radical shift to the left.

The early timing of the outbreak gave Trump a chance to recover. But his path to reelection remained an uphill climb.

Trump, like any Republican, faced the entrenched opposition of the media and the hostility of Silicon Valley.

The left blamed social media companies for having allowed Trump to win in 2016. Since then, left-wing groups had organized boycotts of conservative news outlets, urged the de-platforming of conservative leaders on social media, and suppressed the dissemination of facts helpful to the conservative cause.[942]

Now, the economy was also in free-fall. The first report on jobless claims after "Black Monday" showed a jump to 281,000, a rise of 70,000;[943] a week later, the number had risen to a staggering 3,283,000[944]—and it doubled the week after. Some 26 million Americans lost their jobs in the first month of the pandemic.

If Trump entered 2020 as, at best, a slight favorite, by the spring, he was the underdog.

Having governed, to the surprise of his Never Trump critics, as a conservative, Trump now presided over a government that was—out of necessity— sending checks to households, commandeering factories, and promising to reimburse hospitals for any care provided to the uninsured, at Medicare rates.[945]

What Democrats had campaigned on as policy, Trump had been forced to adopt on an emergency basis.[946]

And the risk, as in 2008, was that a new administration would exploit a temporary crisis to attempt ambitious, permanent change.

"We are five days away from fundamentally transforming the United States of America," then senator Barack Obama told a cheering crowd in Missouri on October 30, 2008.[947] Days after the election, Rahm Emanuel declared: "You never want a serious crisis to go to waste." He explained: "This crisis provides the opportunity for us to do things that you could not do before."[948]

Bernie Sanders, likewise, promised Democrats a "political revolution," declaring that his goal was "transforming the economy and the government of the United States."[949]

Biden had run against that "revolution." But James Clyburn, the man who had saved Biden's campaign, told Democrats during negotiations on the coronavirus relief bill: "This is a tremendous opportunity to restructure things to fit our vision."[950]

The candidate at the top of the ticket was the supposed "moderate"— though he rejected that label. The party beneath him was radical, "woke," slouching toward democratic socialism. And exit polls on Super Tuesday revealed that the same electorate that pushed Biden to victory also held favorable views of socialism.[951]

To win the nomination, Biden had to fight Sanders but accept most of his agenda. On almost every issue, Biden cast aside lifelong convictions in favor of the new radical fashion.

On abortion: Biden once prided himself on a "middle of the road" approach,[952] opposing federal funding for abortion and allowing states to overturn *Roe v. Wade*.[953] In 2019, he rejected the Hyde Amendment and condemned state efforts to limit abortion.[954]

On crime: Biden once championed a law-and-order approach, referring to a controversial Clinton-era law as the "1994 Biden Crime Bill" as late as 2015.[955] In 2019, he acknowledged "mistakes that were made" and supported criminal justice reform.[956]

On energy: Biden campaigned in West Virginia in 2008 by promising that he and Obama favored "clean coal."[957] In 2020, he backed a version of the "Green New Deal," vowing to end coal and "eliminate" fracking.[958]

On immigration: as recently as 2006, then senator Biden vowed to oppose "amnesty" for illegal aliens[959] and voted for a border fence.[960] In the first Democratic debate in 2019, he backed free health care for illegal aliens.

Biden also joined his rivals in promising to raise taxes[961] and opposing the successful air strike on Qasem Soleimani.[962]

The only issue on which Biden was a relative "moderate" was health care. Unlike Sanders, he rejected "Medicare for All," saying Americans should have the choice to join Medicare, the program for the elderly.

That position—the "public option"—was itself so radical in 2009 that Democrats had rejected it.

Moreover, Biden, who had built alliances with old segregationists and had a record of offensive racial rhetoric, reinvented himself as a paragon of political correctness, championing transgenderism as the civil rights cause of our time.[963]

To secure Sanders's support, Biden promised to lower the Medicare eligibility age to 60, and to forgive student loans for low- and middle-income Americans who had attended public universities or HBCUs. He did not say how he would pay for any of it.[964]

Instead of "pivoting" to the center after securing the nomination, the *Wall Street Journal* observed, Biden had pivoted to the left.[965]

When Sanders finally endorsed Biden on April 13, Biden thanked him by taking up Sanders's pledge to "transform this nation," promising "one of the most progressive administrations since Roosevelt."[966]

He did not clarify if he meant Theodore or Franklin.

Obama finally endorsed Biden the next day—when there was no one else left to endorse—saying Biden had "the most progressive platform of any major party nominee in history."[967]

Biden was no longer the opponent of "democratic socialism." He had become its emissary. A Biden presidency would be a regency, with Obama's staffers and Sanders's policies.

In May 2020, he told a "virtual" town hall on the coronavirus pandemic: "I truly think that if we do this right, we have an incredible opportunity to not just dig out of this crisis, but to fundamentally transform the country."

He had adopted Obama's—and Sanders's—vision as his own.[968]

If he won, Democrats would exploit the extraordinary new powers of the government, intended for emergency use, for a permanent, radical agenda.[969]

As the country fought the coronavirus pandemic, the future of freedom was also at stake.

THE FUTURE OF FREEDOM

Donald Trump stood on the dock at Naval Station Norfolk on March 28. Behind him, ready to launch, was the USNS *Comfort*—a "70,000-ton message of hope and solidarity" in his words—its white hull gleaming, its red crosses shining.

The hospital ship, originally scheduled to remain in Virginia for four weeks' maintenance, had been prepared in just four days to depart laden with relief aid to New York City, where hospitals were struggling with the surge of coronavirus patients.

Trump, acting as both commander- and comforter-in-chief, said:

> The battle in which we're now engaged has inflicted many hardships on our nation and our families—tremendous hardship on some families—and much death. Much death. But through it all, the world has witnessed the unyielding resolve of our incredible American people.[970]

Trump called the nation "one family, bound together by love and loyalty." And he concluded: "I cannot be more thankful to the American people. And I can say this from the bottom of my heart: I am very proud to be your president."

Win or lose in November, Trump has arguably sealed his place in history.

Not only had he won an extraordinary election in 2016, but he had governed with extraordinary success. He accelerated economic growth to 4.2 percent, while driving unemployment down to a 50-year low of 3.5 percent.

It was true that Trump had inherited an economy in recovery, but it was also true that his policies had expanded that recovery from Wall Street to Main Street. Trump dared to challenge Washington's free trade orthodoxy, leading to a revival in American manufacturing without a widely predicted rise in consumer prices. Under his leadership, the U.S. became the world's number-one oil producer—ahead of Russia and Saudi Arabia.

Minorities arguably fared better in Trump's presidency than they had under any other American president. He signed the First Step Act, which enacted criminal justice reforms long sought by African American leaders. And Trump was the first president to take seriously the opioid epidemic ravaging the American working class.

Long before the coronavirus pandemic, Trump loosened regulations to encourage medical innovation and lower the cost of health care. His Right to Try Act allowed terminally ill patients to use experimental drugs. He could not repeal Obamacare, but he slowed the rise of health insurance premiums and even lowered drug prices for the first time in nearly half a century.[971]

Trump reversed America's decline as a world power, expanding military spending while sparing the use of force. He launched the "Space Force," expanding America's reach to the final frontier. He destroyed the Islamic State's terrorist caliphate, and confronted China and Iran.

Yet he also opened negotiations with North Korea, even visiting the Demilitarized Zone (DMZ) in 2018, becoming the first sitting U.S. president to visit the Hermit Kingdom. He made overtures to Russia, but also sanctioned Russian officials and attacked Russian allies (Syria being just one example). And he replaced NAFTA with the USMCA—as promised.

Trump stood up for long-neglected national symbols like the flag and the anthem, defying protests by pampered athletes and celebrities, and delighting sports fans tired of seeing their favorite pastimes turned into agitprop spectacles. He defended Christianity from post-modernism and political correctness. And he dared to fight back against the mainstream media as no Republican had before.

Yet Trump also showed a surprising degree of flexibility. He opposed gun control, yet imposed a ban on "bump stocks"—which allow normal rifles to mimic automatic ones—after the Las Vegas mass shooting. He diverted defense funding—legally—to build his "wall" on the U.S.-Mexico border, and rescinded Obama's controversial Deferred Action for

Childhood Arrivals (DACA). Yet he also proposed compromises that would allow the so-called "Dreamers"—children brought to the U.S. illegally as minors—to stay in the country. He opposed abortion, but accepted same-sex marriage; he reversed transgender policies, while promoting gay officials.

In the coronavirus crisis, Trump led an unprecedented effort to save American lives—and did so by decentralizing and deregulating, rather than building up the power of the federal government. A second term would allow him to lead America's economic comeback—perhaps with the cooperation of a more cooperative Congress—and advance his populist vision of restoring political and economic power to the American people.

Regardless, he will be remembered for sacrificing his fortune and reputation for the opportunity to lead the country—and again for sacrificing the economy he built to save the lives of his countrymen, at the risk of his presidency.

He will be remembered for pulling the country together, in its darkest moments. Whatever his other achievements, or failures, that is his legacy.

Impeachment will be remembered not as a stain on his record but as an abuse of power by Congress—and a grave mistake. When Nancy Pelosi decided opening an impeachment inquiry was more urgent than waiting half a day for the Ukraine transcript, she doomed that effort to failure.

She gave Trump voters something more than socialism to vote against: they were also fighting against their own disenfranchisement. But she also distracted the country's leaders at the very moment that a deadly enemy loomed.

Democrats compounded that error in that fateful forty-eight-hour period in mid-March, when instead of offering the president support, they offered their fervent wishes that he had never been elected.

Their refusal to accept the legitimacy of the last election hurt their effort to win the next.

Time will tell if those mistakes count in November.

On the day the *Comfort* arrived in New York City, Joe Biden was in his strongest position ever—and his weakest.

A poll of registered voters released that day showed Biden leading Trump 55 percent to 45 percent, thanks to deep economic pessimism.[972]

And that same day, Biden appeared to lose his train of thought in an interview on MSNBC: "We have to do at least several things: one, we have to, uh, depend on what the president's going to do right now."[973]

One can understand Bernie Sanders's refusal to yield: the lapses of "Sleepy Joe" were impossible to ignore. And as Tara Reade's allegation of sexual assault in 1993 drew new attention at the end of March,[974] some Democrats began to regret their party's choice.

The question of who Biden would choose as a running mate soon became all-important. He had promised to pick a woman, and the likeliest candidate seemed to be Kamala Harris. In May 2019, she had angrily dismissed the prospect of being Biden's number two, and suggested he should be her running mate instead: "Joe Biden would be a great running mate. As vice president, he's proven that he knows how to do the job," she snapped.[975]

But a year later, she had warmed to the prospect of running for vice president—and replacing him, if it came to that.

But regardless of who would go on to be the Democratic nominee, or who would win the general election, one thing remained certain: "socialism" would remain a force.

The movement that Bernie Sanders brought into the mainstream of American politics has shaped the thought of a young generation that has lived through not one, but two economic collapses.

Alexandria Ocasio-Cortez, the most influential young voice in the party, will reach her 35th birthday mere weeks before the 2024 election. She will be eligible for the presidency. Whether she runs then, or later, she will carry the torch Bernie Sanders has lit.

When they return to power, now or in the future, Democrats will be unrestrained. They will be able to abuse power the way they did by targeting Trump, Flynn, Kavanaugh, and others. They will feel tempted to wield power the way they believe Trump has done.

Informed by a press corps that has exaggerated Trump's sins while hiding Obama's constitutional violations, they will knock our wobbling republic even further off balance.

Biden called Trump's election, and his presidency, an "aberrant moment in time."[976] That ignores the voters for whom Trump is a messenger—the people whom he has called the "forgotten men and women of our country"—and denies the legitimacy of democracy itself.

This is a different Democratic Party than that of John F. Kennedy—and of his brother Robert, whose visionary campaign in 1968 was violently cut short.

Robert Kennedy spoke, bravely, in South Africa in 1966:

> We stand here in the name of freedom.
>
> At the heart of that Western freedom and democracy is the belief that the individual man, the child of God, is the touchstone of value, and all society, groups, the state, exist for his benefit. Therefore the enlargement of liberty for individual human beings must be the supreme goal and the abiding practice of any Western society.[977]

No Democrat today would dare to offer such a stirring defense of individual liberty. It may take defeat—perhaps several—for Democrats to return to that vision.

Because ultimately, the greatest and most worthwhile changes are not those the state enacts on our behalf, but those we, the people, make in our own lives.

In his State of the Union address in 2019, facing the members of the new Democratic majority in the House, "democratic socialists" and all, President Trump declared:

> Here, in the United States, we are alarmed by new calls to adopt socialism in our country. America was founded on liberty and independence—not government coercion, domination, and control. We are born free, and we will stay free. Tonight, we renew our resolve that America will never be a socialist country.[978]

That resolution is on the ballot in 2020. That choice—between the path of liberty, or the road to socialism—is in the hands of American voters.

APPENDIX A: TIMELINE OF SIGNIFICANT EVENTS

2016

November 9: Donald Trump elected President of the United States

2017

January 10: Russia "dossier" published as part of effort to discredit Trump

January 19: *New York Times* reports Trump was "wiretapped" in Russia investigation

January 20: President Trump inaugurated

January 21: Women's March, Washington, DC, and nationwide

January 23: Trump withdraws U.S. from Trans-Pacific Partnership (TPP) negotiations

January 24: Trump revives Keystone XL pipeline project blocked by Obama administration

January 27: Trump signs executive order on travel ban; "Resistance" protests

February 14: Trump repeals first of several regulations under Congressional Review Act

February 28: Trump delivers well-received first address to Congress

April 6: Trump launches air strikes against Syria over use of chemical weapons

April 7: Neil Gorsuch confirmed to U.S. Supreme Court

May 9: Trump fires FBI director James Comey

May 17: Robert Mueller appointed Special Counsel in Russia "collusion" investigation

June 1: Trump withdraws U.S. from Paris Climate Accords

June 30: Trump signs first of several laws reforming Department of Veterans Affairs

July 27: John McCain gives "thumbs down" to effort to repeal and replace Obamacare

August 11–12: Charlottesville riots

August 15: Trump condemns neo-Nazis, praises non-violent statue protesters (for and against) as "very fine people"

September 5: Trump administration rescinds Deferred Action for Childhood Arrivals (DACA) program

September 22: Trump criticizes National Football League players who kneel for national anthem

October 1: 58 killed in mass shooting in Las Vegas, worst in U.S. history

October 26: Trump declares national public health emergency on opioid addiction

December 12: Trump signs expansion of military spending

December 22: Trump signs Tax Cuts and Jobs Act of 2017; Obamacare mandate repealed

2018

January 30: Trump announces "four pillars" of immigration reform in State of the Union address

February 2: Andrew Yang launches presidential campaign

February 14: Parkland, Florida, shooting at Marjorie Stoneman Douglas High School

February 20: Trump announces ban on "bump stocks" in response to Las Vegas shooting

March 8: Trump announces tariffs of 25% on steel and 10% on aluminum

March 22: Trump begins process to apply tariffs to Chinese imports, launching trade war

April 6: Trump administration announces "zero tolerance" policy at border

May 8: Trump withdraws U.S. from Iran deal

May 15: U.S. formally opens embassy in Jerusalem, Israel

May 30: Trump signs Right to Try Act allowing terminally ill patients access to experimental medicines

June 12: Trump meets North Korean leader Kim Jong-un in Singapore

June 20: Trump signs executive order ending family separations at border

June 26: Supreme Court upholds Trump's travel ban; Alexandria Ocasio-Cortez wins upset victory in NY-14 primary

July 27: U.S. economic growth for second quarter announced as 4.1 percent, later revised up to 4.2 percent

September 12: U.S. becomes world's #1 oil producer, surpassing Saudi Arabia and Russia

October 6: Brett Kavanaugh confirmed to U.S. Supreme Court

October 27: Mass shooting at Tree of Life Synagogue in Pittsburgh, Pennsylvania

November 6: Midterm elections: Democrats win House; Republicans expand Senate majority

November 30: United States, Mexico, and Canada sign "USMCA" free trade agreement

December 21: Trump signs First Step Act for criminal justice reform

2019

January 21: Kamala Harris announces presidential campaign

February 5: Trump declares "America will never be a socialist country" in State of the Union address

February 7: Ocasio-Cortez releases "Green New Deal"

February 9: Elizabeth Warren launches presidential campaign

February 10: Amy Klobuchar launches presidential campaign

February 15: Trump declares national emergency on border, diverts military funding to build wall

February 19: Bernie Sanders launches presidential campaign

February 27: House Democrats introduce "Medicare for All" bill

March 5: Michael Bloomberg declines to run for president

March 14: Beto O'Rourke announces presidential campaign

March 24: Attorney General William Barr announces Special Counsel Robert Mueller's report found no "Russia collusion" and reached no decision on obstruction

April 18: Mueller report released with redactions as Democrats protest

April 25: Joe Biden launches presidential campaign

June 26–27: First Democratic Debate, Miami, Florida

June 30: Trump becomes first sitting U.S. president to visit North Korea in visit to DMZ

July 9: Tom Steyer joins presidential race

July 30–31: Second Democratic Debate, Detroit, Michigan

August 3: Mass shooting at Walmart in El Paso, Texas

August 8–18: Iowa State Fair

August 14: Warren town hall in Franconia, New Hampshire

August 27: Beto O'Rourke ejects Breitbart News from Benedict College event

August 29: *Politico* reports U.S. withholding military aid from Ukraine

September 1: Trump expands tariffs to Chinese goods, covering two-thirds of imports from China

September 4: CNN climate change town hall, New York, New York

September 12: Third Democratic Debate, Houston, Texas

September 24: Speaker Nancy Pelosi announces impeachment inquiry

September 25: White House releases Ukraine call transcript

October 3: First closed-door hearing in House Intelligence Committee impeachment inquiry

October 4: Unemployment rate falls to 3.5 percent, lowest rate in 50 years, in September jobs report

October 10: CNN's LGBTQ town hall, Los Angeles, California

October 13: Fourth Democratic Debate, Westerville, Ohio

October 27: Trump confirms U.S. killed ISIS leader Abu Bakr al-Baghdadi

October 31: House votes to approve impeachment inquiry, 232-196

November 1: O'Rourke drops out of presidential race

November 13: First public hearing in House Intelligence Committee impeachment inquiry

November 20: Fifth Democratic Debate, Atlanta, Georgia; Gordon Sondland testimony

November 24: Michael Bloomberg joins presidential race

December 4: House Judiciary Committee "expert witness" hearing

December 5: Pelosi orders House Judiciary Committee to draft articles of impeachment

December 9: House Judiciary Committee hearing on House Intelligence Committee report

December 13: House Judiciary Committee passes articles of impeachment against Trump

December 18: House debates, passes articles of impeachment, 230–197 and 229–198

December 19: Sixth Democratic Debate, Los Angeles, California

December 20: Trump signs law creating U.S. Space Force

December 31: China confirms new form of pneumonia, later known as coronavirus

2020

January 2: U.S. launches successful strike on Iranian general Qasem Soleimani

January 11: China reports first confirmed death from coronavirus

January 14: Seventh Democratic Debate, Des Moines, Iowa; WHO eases coronavirus fears

January 15: Pelosi "engrosses" articles of impeachment; first U.S. coronavirus case arrives; Trump signs "Phase One" trade deal with China

January 16: Senate approves USMCA; impeachment trial formally begins

January 21: Opening arguments in impeachment trial

January 27: First meeting of White House coronavirus task force

January 29: Trump signs USMCA into law

January 31: Trump announces travel ban on China; Senate votes against new witnesses

February 3: Iowa caucuses (Buttigieg wins delegates, Sanders wins popular vote)

February 4: State of the Union Address

February 5: Senate votes against removing Trump from office, 52–48 and 53–47; House holds first subcommittee hearing on coronavirus

February 7: Eighth Democratic Debate, Manchester, New Hampshire

February 11: New Hampshire primary (Sanders wins); Yang withdraws from presidential race

February 12: Dow Jones Industrial Average hits all-time high of 29,551.42

February 19: Ninth Democratic Debate, Las Vegas, Nevada

February 22: Nevada caucuses (Sanders wins)

February 25: Tenth Democratic Debate, Charleston, South Carolina

February 26: Rep. James Clyburn (D-SC) endorses Biden

February 29: South Carolina primary (Biden wins); Steyer withdraws from presidential race

March 1: Buttigieg drops out of presidential race

March 2: Klobuchar withdraws; Buttigieg, Klobuchar, O'Rourke endorse Biden

March 3: "Super Tuesday": Joe Biden sweeps to victory, including Texas, Massachusetts

March 4: Bloomberg drops out of presidential race; endorses Biden

March 5: Warren drops out of presidential race; declines to endorse

March 6: U.S. jobs report smashes expectations as unemployment again hits 50-year low of 3.5 percent

March 9: "Black Monday"; stock market drops on coronavirus, oil market fears

March 10: "Mini Tuesday": Joe Biden wins Michigan

March 11: Trump addresses nation on coronavirus from Oval Office

March 13: Trump declares national emergency on coronavirus from Rose Garden

March 15: Eleventh Democratic Debate, CNN studios, Washington, DC (relocated)

March 17: Illinois, Florida, Arizona primaries; North Dakota caucuses; Ohio postponed

April 1: U.S. coronavirus deaths surpass 1,000 per day for first time

April 8: Sanders suspends presidential campaign; Biden becomes presumptive nominee

April 13: Sanders endorses Biden; Biden promises to "transform this nation"

April 14: Former president Barack Obama endorses Biden, saying he had "the most progressive platform of any major party nominee in history"

May 4: Biden promises to use coronavirus crisis to "fundamentally transform the country"

ACKNOWLEDGMENTS

Thanks and praise are due, first and foremost, to the Holy One, Blessed be He, who has granted me the opportunity to pursue and complete this project and who has blessed my family and me with good health, love, sustenance, and happiness.

This book was made possible by the vision of my publishers and editors at Hachette, Kate Hartson and Sean McGowan, and the hard work of their team, including Thomas Watkins and Leslie Connor. It was also made possible by the patience of my agents, Keith Urbahn and Matt Latimer of Javelin. Thanks are due to all of my colleagues at Breitbart News, whose coverage fills these pages, and especially to Larry Solov, Alex Marlow, and Jon Kahn, Wendy Colbert, and Christian Gonzales. And thanks, again, to Andrew Breitbart—you are missed, and celebrated, every day.

Thanks, too, to Sirius XM, for granting me leave to chase candidates on the campaign trail, and to Scott Adams, who provides daily insight and inspiration. Thanks to Helmut Schulze of Rees Electronics, who serviced the typewriters (yes, typewriters) on which the rough drafts of this book were written: a Brother Charger 11 Portable (early 1980s), which he sold me; and an Imperial Good Companion 5 (late 1950s), which I brought to him from South Africa.

I am deeply grateful for the support of my family, and particularly my wife, Julia; my children, Maya and Alexander; and my mother-in-law, Rhoda Kadalie, who helped edit page proofs, entertain children, and cook delicious dinners. I traveled almost every week for nearly a year as I worked on this book—but I made sure I was home for Shabbat. Thanks, too, to my brother Nathan; my sister Beth; my parents, Naomi and Raymond; and my grandmother, Esther Perkel, a century young. I am also very lucky to enjoy the enduring friendship of Zachary and Abigail Shrier; Dan and Kelly Horowitz; Jessica Tardy; and Taya Weiss, who does not agree with me about anything.

I am grateful for the religious guidance, over several years, of Rabbi Baruch and Rebbitzin Rivka Rabinowitz; Rabbi Dovid and Rebbetzin Chana Shifra Rabinowitz; Rabbi Zushe and Rebbetzin Zisi Cunin; Rabbi Hirschy and Rebbetzin Elkie Zarchi; Rabbi Eli and Rebbitzin Zelda Fradkin; Rabbi Shlomo Yaffe; and Rabbi Eli Stefansky of the daily Daf Yomi program, a pillar of strength.

I would not have reached this point without the mentorship of Tony Leon and Alan Dershowitz, and the help of many more teachers and leaders. Throughout the writing process I have also drawn encouragement from the sermons of Joel Osteen and the leadership of Coach Matt Nagy, two relentlessly positive people. They don't know me, but I thank them.

I wish to acknowledge the influence of David Halberstam's *The Unfinished Odyssey of Robert Kennedy,* which I was lucky enough to find more than 20 years ago while browsing in a used bookstore, and which I have read and re-read countless times. It remains one of the most inspiring works in the genre of campaign journalism. My attempt to follow in Halberstam's footsteps is the fulfillment of a lifelong dream.

This book honors the memory of the late Emma Rishton, who helped me let go of what was no longer useful and gave me the courage to pursue what I really wanted to write. It also honors the memory of my colleague, Ana Barrera; my classmate, John Sheriff, who lived life to the fullest, defying cancer to leave a legacy of love; the great Orson Bean, without whom Breitbart News would never have been created; and the victims of the coronavirus pandemic, still raging at the time this book was completed.

Better days are ahead: "All this has come upon us, but yet we have not forgotten Thee" (Psalm 44).

NOTES

1. Barack Obama, tweet, April 14, 2020, https://twitter.com/BarackObama /status/1250088269502709762.

2. Joe Biden, remarks to virtual town hall (Wilmington, Delaware, May 4, 2019), https://www.youtube.com/watch?v=3zWNQn9KHWI.

3. Geoffrey Skelley, "What Happens If a Presidential Nominee Can No Longer Run for Office?," FiveThirtyEight, accessed April 15, 2020, https://fivethirtyeight.com /features/what-happens-if-a-presidential-nominee-can-no-longer-run-for-office/.

4. Elizabeth Bruenig, "Democrats, It's Time to Consider a Plan B," *New York Times*, May 3, 2020, https://www.nytimes.com/2020/05/03/opinion/joe-biden-tara -reade.html.

5. Norman Rush, *Mating: A Novel* (New York: Vintage, 1991), 80–81.

6. Bernie Sanders, speech (Los Angeles Convention Center, Los Angeles, California, March 1, 2020), https://www.rev.com/blog/transcripts/bernie-sanders -los-angeles-rally-transcript-before-super-tuesday.

7. Chuck D, quoted at Bernie Sanders, "Los Angeles Rally with Public Enemy Radio" (Los Angeles, CA, March 1, 2020), https://www.youtube.com /watch?v=Tz48E8hzUX4.

8. Lars Brandle, "Public Enemy Parts Ways with Flavor Flav," *Holly-wood Reporter*, March 1, 2020, https://www.hollywoodreporter.com/news/public -enemy-parts-ways-flavor-flav-1282021.

9. Flavor Flav, quoted in Alana Mastrangelo, "Rapper Flavor Flav Blasts Ber-nie Sanders for Using His Likeness for a 'Fake Revolution.'" Breitbart News, March 2, 2020, https://www.breitbart.com/entertainment/2020/03/02/flavor-flav-blasts -bernie-sanders-for-using-his-likeness-for-a-fake-revolution/. The group later claimed Flavor Flav's expulsion had been a "hoax." (Christie D'Zurilla, "On April Fools' Day, Public Enemy Reveals Flavor Flav's Firing Was a Hoax," *Los Angeles Times*, April 1, 2020, https://www.latimes.com/entertainment-arts/music/story/2020-04-01 /chuck-d-flavor-flav-firing-public-enemy-radio.)

10. Mike Bloomberg, quoted in "Full Transcript: Ninth Democratic Debate in Las Vegas," NBC News, February 19, 2020, https://www.nbcnews.com /politics/2020-election/full-transcript-ninth-democratic-debate-las-vegas-n1139546.

11. "1972 Presidential Election," 270toWin, accessed March 3, 2020, https:// www.270towin.com/1972_Election/.

12. "1984 Presidential Election," 270toWin, accessed March 3, 2020, https:// www.270towin.com/1984_Election/.

13. James Freeman, "Elizabeth Warren's Unconstitutional Wealth Tax," *Wall Street Journal*, January 25, 2019, https://www.wsj.com/articles/elizabeth-warrens -unconstitutional-wealth-tax-11548442306?mod=article_inline.

14. Tara Golshan, "Bernie Sanders Defines His Vision for Democratic Social- ism in the United States" (speech at George Washington University, Washing- ton, DC, June 12, 2019), https://www.vox.com/2019/6/12/18663217/bernie-sanders -democratic-socialism-speech-transcript.

15. Orson died tragically as this book was being written.

16. Andrew Breitbart, *Righteous Indignation: Excuse Me While I Save the World* (New York: Grand Central Publishing, 2011).

17. Joel B. Pollak and Larry Schweikart, *How Trump Won: The Inside Story of a Revolution* (Washington, DC: Regnery, 2017).

18. Andrew Breitbart, speech at Conservative Political Action Conference (CPAC) (Washington, DC, February 10, 2012), https://www.c-span.org/video /?c4486775/user-clip-andrew-breitbart.

19. Indivisible, "Introduction to the Guide," accessed September 19, 2019, https://indivisible.org/guide.

20. Martin Geissler, "Protester Who Screamed at Trump's Inauguration: 'This Is Not America,'" iTV, January 20, 2017, https://www.itv.com/news/2017-01-20 /protester-who-screamed-at-trumps-inauguration-this-is-not-america/.

21. "'Not My President': Leftists Riot over Donald Trump's Election Victory," Breitbart News, November 9, 2016, https://www.breitbart.com/live/2016-election -world-reacts-donald-trumps-stunning-upset-victory/leftists-riot-donald-trumps -election-victory/.

22. Hillary Clinton, "Tinfoil Hillary: 'Alt-Right,' Alex Jones, Brexit, Putin All Part of Global Conspiracy against Her" (remarks at Truckee Meadows Com- munity College in Reno, Nevada, August, 25, 2016), https://www.breitbart .com/politics/2016/08/25/tinfoil-hillary-alt-right-alex-jones-brexit-putin-global -conspiracy/.

23. Joel B. Pollak, "WATCH: Hillary Clinton Supporters at 'Alt-Right' Speech Don't Know What It Is," Breitbart News, August 25, 2016, https://www.breitbart .com/politics/2016/08/25/alt-right-hillary-clinton-supporters-struggle-explain/.

24. Bannon did himself no favors by boasting to *Mother Jones* that Breitbart News was "the platform for the alt-right." (Sarah Posner, "How Donald Trump's New Campaign Chief Created an Online Haven for White Nationalists," *Mother*

Jones, August 22, 2016, https://www.motherjones.com/politics/2016/08/stephen
-bannon-donald-trump-alt-right-breitbart-news/.) It was an inaccurate statement
when he made it, and it is inaccurate today. Then as now, I put Bannon's claim
down to braggadocio: he was promoting the website. (The author described Bannon
as boasting.) But Breitbart News was never a "haven for white nationalists."

25. Joel B. Pollak, "Feeling the Hate at the Los Angeles 'Stop Bannon'
Protest," Breitbart News, November 16, 2016, https://www.breitbart.com/local
/2016/11/16/stop-bannon-trump-feeling-the-hate-los-angeles-protest/.

26. Charlotte Alter, "'Change Is Closer Than We Think.' Inside Alexandria Ocasio-Cortez's Unlikely Rise," *Time*, March 21, 2019, https://time.com
/longform/alexandria-ocasio-cortez-profile/.

27. Sean McGarvey, president of North America's Building and Construction Trades, remarks, White House, January 23, 2017, https://www.c-span.org/video
/?422483-101/union-leader-white-house-meeting&event=422483.

28. President Donald Trump, "The Inaugural Address," White House, January
20, 2017, https://www.whitehouse.gov/briefings-statements/the-inaugural-address/.

29. Mollie Hemingway, "Comey's Memos Indicate Dossier Briefing of
Trump Was a Setup," The Federalist, April 20, 2018, https://thefederalist
.com/2018/04/20/comeys-memos-indicate-dossier-briefing-of-trump-was-a-setup/.

30. Michael S. Schmidt et al., "Intercepted Russian Communications Part
of Inquiry into Trump Associates," *New York Times*, January 19, 2017, https://www
.nytimes.com/2017/01/19/us/politics/trump-russia-associates-investigation.html.

31. P. J. Gladnick, "New York Times January Wiretapping Headline Goes
Viral," NewsBusters, March 7, 2020, https://www.newsbusters.org/blogs/nb/pj
-gladnick/2017/03/07/new-york-times-january-wiretapping-headline-goes-viral.

32. Joel Pollak, "Mark Levin to Congress: Investigate Obama's 'Silent
Coup' vs. Trump," Breitbart News, March 3, 2017, https://www.breitbart.com
/politics/2017/03/03/mark-levin-obama-used-police-state-tactics-undermine-trump/.

33. David Ignatius, "Why Did Obama Dawdle on Russia's Hacking?,"
Washington Post, January 12, 2017, https://www.washingtonpost.com/opinions
/why-did-obama-dawdle-on-russias-hacking/2017/01/12/75f878a0-d90c-11e6-9a36
-1d296534b31e_story.html.

34. President Donald Trump, "Executive Order Protecting the Nation from
Foreign Terrorist Entry into the United States," Order 13769, January 27, 2017,
https://www.whitehouse.gov/presidential-actions/executive-order-protecting-nation
-foreign-terrorist-entry-united-states/.

35. Joel B. Pollak, "Anti-Trump Protests Block Airports, Frustrate Travelers," Breitbart News, January 30, 2017, https://www.breitbart.com/politics/2017
/01/30/anti-trump-protests-block-airports-frustrate-travelers/.

36. Pollak, "Anti-Trump Protests Block Airports."

37. The version of the ban considered by the Supreme Court was the third,
not the original; the later versions of the ban included some non-Muslim countries.

38. For example: "The hero America needs right now is a 56-year-old lawyer from Georgia named Sally Yates." Liana Maeby, "Can We Get Back to Sally Yates for a Minute?," *New York Times*, May 12, 2017, https://www.nytimes.com/2017/05/12 /opinion/can-we-get-back-to-sally-yates-for-a-minute.html.

39. "Sally Yates to Harvard Law School Graduates: 'Be Bold. Take a Risk,'" *Time*, May 25, 2017, https://time.com/4793996/sally-yates-harvard-law-school-2017 -graduation-speech/.

40. Andrew Restuccia, Marianne Levine, and Nahal Toosi, "Federal Workers Turn to Encryption to Thwart Trump," *Politico*, February 2, 2017, https://www .politico.com/story/2017/02/federal-workers-signal-app-234510.

41. Jerome Hudson, "Madonna Drops F-Bombs at Anti-Trump Rally: 'I've Thought a Lot about Blowing Up the White House,'" Breitbart News, January 21, 2017, https://www.breitbart.com/live/womens-march-washington-live-updates/madonna -drops-f-bombs-anti-trump-rally-ive-thought-lot-blowing-white-house/.

42. David A. Fahrenthold, "Trump Recorded Having Extremely Lewd Conversation about Women in 2005," *Washington Post*, October 8, 2016, https://www .washingtonpost.com/politics/trump-recorded-having-extremely-lewd -conversation-about-women-in-2005/2016/10/07/3b9ce776-8cb4-11e6-bf8a -3d26847eeed4_story.html.

43. Dr. Susan Berry, "Women's Marchers Urged to Ditch 'Pussyhats': Offensive to Transgender People," Breitbart News, January 18, 2018, https://www.breitbart.com /politics/2018/01/18/womens-marchers-urged-ditch-pussyhats-offensive-transgender/.

44. "Jewish Defense Organizations: The Jewish Resistance Movement," Jewish Virtual Library, accessed September 19, 2019, https://www.jewishvirtuallibrary .org/the-jewish-resistance-movement-in-pre-state-israel.

45. Stephen K. Bannon, quoted by Michael Wolff, *Fire and Fury: Inside the Trump White House* (New York: Henry Holt and Company, 2018), https://books.google.com /books?id=E3M-DwAAQBAJ&q=snowflakes#v=snippet&q=snowflakes&f=false.

46. Linda Sarsour, quoted in Steven Emerson, "ISNA Convention Uses Shame, Fear to Stir Radical Agenda," *Algemeiner*, September 2, 2018, https://www .algemeiner.com/2018/09/04/isna-convention-uses-shame-fear-to-stir-radical -agenda/.

47. Collier Meyerson, "Can You Be a Zionist Feminist? Linda Sarsour Says No," *The Nation*, March 13, 2017, https://www.thenation.com/article/archive /can-you-be-a-zionist-feminist-linda-sarsour-says-no/.

48. Jonathan Greenblatt, "Louis Farrakhan...Again," Anti-Defamation League, March 1, 2018, https://www.adl.org/news/op-ed/louis-farrakhan-again.

49. Kenneth P. Vogel, "The 'Resistance,' Raising Big Money, Upends Liberal Politics," *New York Times*, October 7, 2017, A1, https://www.nytimes.com/2017/10/07 /us/politics/democrats-resistance-fundraising.html.

50. Joe Schoffstall, "Confidential David Brock Memo: Defeat Trump through Impeachment," Washington Free Beacon, January 21, 2017, https://freebeacon .com/uncategorized/confidential-david-brock-memo-defeat-trump-impeachment/.

51. These efforts would later come back to haunt the media. Boycotting Breitbart News and other conservative websites often involved tinkering with the algorithms behind Google ads to single out particular sites and topics, leading to a new practice called "keyword blacklisting." As Sleeping Giants later admitted, companies that learned to use keyword blacklisting against Breitbart soon found the technology could be used to avoid linking their brand to unpleasant topics on mainstream news websites. When the coronavirus pandemic struck, keyword blacklisting resulted in massive advertising losses to the news industry, leading to devastating layoffs. Sleeping Giants, in vain, tried to put the evil genie back in the bottle with a "whitelist" of approved news websites that would be safe from boycotts—to little avail. Nandini Jammi, "Good News: You Can Advertise on Bad News (It's Brand Safe)," Branded, April 1, 2020, https://branded.substack.com/p/good-news-you-can-advertise-on-bad.

52. "Sleeping Giants' Anonymous Founder Unmasked; Top Ad Writer behind Boycott Campaign Targeting Breitbart, Ingraham," Daily Caller News Foundation, July 16, 2018, https://dailycaller.com/2018/07/16/sleeping-giants-founder-rivitz/.

53. Allum Bokhari, "Report: Mark Zuckerberg Admits Facebook's 'Clear Bias,' Dependence on 'Activist' Fact Checkers," Breitbart News, September 19, 2019, https://www.breitbart.com/tech/2019/09/19/report-mark-zuckerberg-admits-facebooks-clear-bias-dependence-on-activist-fact-checkers/.

54. Christopher J. Ferguson, "Mass Shootings Aren't Growing More Common—and Evidence Contradicts Common Stereotypes About the Killers," Public Radio International, August 7, 2019, https://www.pri.org/stories/2019-08-07/mass-shootings-arent-growing-more-common-and-evidence-contradicts-common.

55. Kelly Weill, "Pittsburgh Synagogue Suspect Robert Bowers Hated Trump—for Not Hating Jews," Daily Beast, October 27, 2018, https://www.thedailybeast.com/robert-bowers-is-neo-nazi-who-posted-about-killing-jews-on-gab.

56. Jennifer de Pinto, "Election 2018: Voters Supported Stricter Gun policy, But It Wasn't Priority for Most," CBS News, November 9, 2018, https://www.cbsnews.com/news/election-2018-voters-supported-stricter-gun-policy-but-it-wasnt-priority-for-most/.

57. Ballotpedia. "United States Congress elections, 2018," accessed on May 5, 2020, https://ballotpedia.org/United_States_Congress_elections,_2018.

58. Shane Goldmacher and Jonathan Martin, "Alexandria Ocasio-Cortez Defeats Joseph Crowley in Major Democratic House Upset," New York Times, June 26, 2018, https://www.nytimes.com/2018/06/26/nyregion/joseph-crowley-ocasio-cortez-democratic-primary.html.

59. In July 2018, for example, she explained that she opposed the "occupation" of Palestine but could not explain exactly what that meant: "I am not the expert on geopolitics on this issue." Alexandria Ocasio-Cortez, quoted by Joshua Caplan, "Alexandria Ocasio-Cortez Can't Explain 'Occupation of Palestine' but Opposes It," Breitbart News, July 16, 2018, https://www.breitbart.com/politics/2018/07/16/alexandria-ocasio-cortez-cant-explain-occupation-of-palestine-but-opposes-it/.

60. Scott Adams, "Episode 124: Children in Cages (i.e. Democrats), New Master Persuader, Socialism, NK and More," podcast, June 30, 2018, https://www.scottadamssays.com/2018/06/30/episode-124-children-in-cages-i-e-democrats-new-master-persuader-socialism-nk-and-more/.

61. Joshua Caplan, "Elizabeth Warren Copies Ocasio-Cortez with Casual, Beer-Drinking Live Stream," Breitbart News, January, 1 2019, https://www.breitbart.com/politics/2019/01/01/elizabeth-warren-copies-ocasio-cortez-with-casual-beer-drinking-live-stream/.

62. Joel B. Pollak, "Alexandria Ocasio-Cortez Declares War on White, Moderate Democrats," Breitbart News, November 18, 2018, https://www.breitbart.com/politics/2018/11/18/alexandria-ocasio-cortez-declares-war-on-white-moderate-democrats/.

63. Nancy Pelosi, quoted in Maureen Dowd, "It's Nancy Pelosi's Parade," *New York Times*, July 6, 2019, https://www.nytimes.com/2019/07/06/opinion/sunday/nancy-pelosi-pride-parade.html?module=inline.

64. A note on the color red. It has long been associated with communism, socialism, and the left in general. It only became associated with Republicans through the presidential election of 2000, when the infamous deadlock produced familiar maps of a divided country: red for Republicans, blue for Democrats. The late Tim Russert of NBC News claimed credit for the color scheme; Democrats had sometimes been assigned red in previous elections. The British Labour Party still uses red, as opposed to blue for the Tories of the Conservative Party. Paul Farhi, "Elephants Are Red, Donkeys Are Blue," *Washington Post*, November 2, 2004, https://www.washingtonpost.com/wp-dyn/articles/A17079-2004Nov1.html.

65. Stanley Kurtz, *Radical-in-Chief: Barack Obama and the Untold Story of American Socialism* (New York: Threshold, 2010), 62.

66. Ben Christopher, "California Democrats Embrace a Socialist? We've Been Here Before," CalMatters.org, March 4, 2020, https://calmatters.org/blogs/california-election-2020/2020/03/california-democrats-bernie-sanders-socialism-upton-sinclair/.

67. Saul Alinsky, *Rules for Radicals: A Pragmatic Primer for Realistic Radicals* (New York: Random House, 1971), xix.

68. F. A. Hayek, *The Road to Serfdom* (Chicago: University of Chicago Press, 1944), 70.

69. "In 1995–96, Obama ran for the Illinois State Senate, with New Party support. As a condition of that support, Obama surely became an active member of this far-left, ACORN-controlled party.... [C]andidates endorsed by Chicago's New Party were required to sign a contract mandating 'a visible and active relationship' with the party. There is no good reason why Obama would have been exempted from this requirement." Kurtz, *Radical-in-Chief*, 256–57.

70. George F. Will, "'The Cheerful Malcontent,'" *Washington Post*, May 31, 1998, C07, https://www.washingtonpost.com/wp-srv/politics/daily/may98/will31.htm. Will joked that Barry Goldwater had really "won" the 1964 election, but "it just took 16 years to count the votes."

71. Philip Gourevitch, "The Shakeout," *New Yorker*, February 1, 2004, https://www.newyorker.com/magazine/2004/02/09/the-shakeout.

72. "We are five days away from fundamentally transforming the United States of America." Barack H. Obama, speech (University of Missouri, Columbia, Missouri, October 30, 2008, https://www.realclearpolitics.com/articles/2008/10/obama_rallies_columbia_missour.html.

73. Barack H. Obama, "Remarks by the President on the Economy in Osawatomie, Kansas," December 6, 2011, https://obamawhitehouse.archives.gov/the-press-office/2011/12/06/remarks-president-economy-osawatomie-kansas.

74. Joel B. Pollak, "Blue State Blues: Obama's Council Wars, from Chicago to Washington," Breitbart News, October 31, 2013, https://www.breitbart.com/politics/2013/10/31/blue-state-blues-obama-s-council-wars-from-chicago-to-washington/.

75. A rare exception was *Saturday Night Live*, which lampooned Obama's penchant for executive orders in a spoof of the *Schoolhouse Rock* videos shown to children in civics class: "How a Bill Does Not Become a Law." *Saturday Night Live*, NBC, November 22, 2014, https://www.nbc.com/saturday-night-live/video/how-a-bill-does-not-become-a-law/2830152.

76. Callum Borchers, "Donna Brazile Is Totally Not Sorry for Leaking CNN Debate Questions to Hillary Clinton," *Washington Post*, November 7, 2016, https://www.washingtonpost.com/news/the-fix/wp/2016/11/07/donna-brazile-is-totally-not-sorry-for-leaking-cnn-debate-questions-to-hillary-clinton/.

77. Joel B. Pollak, "WATCH: Delegates Protest, Walk Out of Hillary's DNC Speech," Breitbart News, July 28, 2016, https://www.breitbart.com/politics/2016/07/28/watch-delegates-protest-walk-hillarys-dnc-speech/.

78. John Hayward, "DNC Staffers Conspired against Sanders, Using His Religion, Leak Shows," Breitbart News, July 22, 2016, https://www.breitbart.com/politics/2016/07/22/leaked-dnc-memo-shows-staffers-conspiring-sanders-using-religion/.

79. Joel B. Pollak, "#Demexit: Sanders Delegates Walk Out of Convention in Protest," Breitbart News, July 26, 2016, https://www.breitbart.com/politics/2016/07/26/demexit-sanders-delegates-walk-convention-protest/.

80. "Fully 12 percent of people who voted for Sen. Bernie Sanders, I-Vt., in the 2016 Democratic presidential primaries voted for President Trump in the general election." Danielle Kurtzleben, "Here's How Many Bernie Sanders Supporters Ultimately Voted for Trump," National Public Radio, August 24, 2017, https://www.npr.org/2017/08/24/545812242/1-in-10-sanders-primary-voters-ended-up-supporting-trump-survey-finds.

81. Michael Moore, quoted by Mark Maynard, "Michael Moore on 'the Biggest "Fuck You" Ever Recorded in Human History' and the Righteous Anger of the Dispossessed American Trump Supporter," MarkMaynard.com, October 26, 2016, accessed September 4, 2019, http://markmaynard.com/2016/10/michael-moore-seems-to-have-a-better-handle-on-the-righteous-anger-of-the-former-american-middle-class-than-anyone/.

82. Shadi Hamid, "Why the Center-Left Became Immoderate," *Wall Street Journal*, February 12, 2018, https://www.wsj.com/articles/why-the-center-left -became-immoderate-1518479151.

83. Joel B. Pollak, "Joe Biden: I'm Not a 'Moderate,' It's Just That 'Progressive' Became 'Socialist,'" Breitbart News, April 5, 2019, https://www.breitbart.com /politics/2019/04/05/joe-biden-im-not-a-moderate-its-just-that-progressive-became -socialist/.

84. Pollak, "Joe Biden: I'm Not a 'Moderate.'"

85. "A Reason-Rupe survey of 2,000 Americans between the ages of 18 and 29 finds 66 percent of millennials believe government is inefficient and wasteful... However, millennials also support more government action and higher spending in a number of key areas...71 percent favor raising the federal minimum wage to $10.10 an hour...69 percent say it is government's responsibility to guarantee everyone access to health care and 51 percent have a favorable view of the Affordable Care Act." Reason Staff, "Millennials Think Government Is Inefficient, Abuses Its Power, and Supports Cronyism," Reason, July 10, 2014, https://reason .com/2014/07/10/reason-rupe-2014-millennial-survey/. Joel B. Pollak, "Millennials Believe Government Has Failed—and Yet They Want More of It," Breitbart News, July 10, 2014, https://www.breitbart.com/local/2014/07/10/millennials-believe -government-has-failed-and-they-want-more-of-it/.

86. Felix Salmon, "Gen Z Prefers 'Socialism' to 'Capitalism,'" Axios, January 27, 2019, https://www.axios.com/socialism-capitalism-poll-generation-z-preference -1ffb8800-0ce5-4368-8a6f-de3b82662347.html.

87. As I have argued elsewhere: "Journalists under-reported Obama's many constitutional violations, and therefore missed the degree to which 2016 was a constitutional reckoning by an electorate that had had enough. There are plenty of examples—far beyond Obama's unconstitutional usurpation of the power to declare the Senate in recess, for which he received a 9–0 smackdown from the Supreme Court. There was the individual mandate in Obamacare, which Chief Justice John Roberts essentially had to rewrite as a tax to find it constitutional. There was the contraceptive mandate, which violates religious freedom by forcing church institutions to fund abortifacients. There was also the Iran deal, in which Obama flouted the Constitution's Treaty Clause by refusing to let the Senate ratify the agreement (and, indeed, Senate Democrats filibustered even a weaker version of that oversight power). In addition, Obama enacted DACA and DAPA to grant amnesty to illegal aliens: both usurped Congress's legislative powers under the Constitution, and the latter was rejected by the courts because it ran afoul of administrative law. Obama refused to strike deals with Congress. Instead, he simply used—or, rather abused— the power of executive agencies to do what he wanted in stark defiance of the separation of powers. He used the Environmental Protection Agency to launch the Clean Power Plan—which even left-wing Harvard Law professor Larry Tribe said violated the Constitution—and the 'Waters of the United States' rule, both of which have since been rescinded by Trump....Not only did the media miss that story, but

when Trump took office and began implementing his agenda, the media falsely declared unconstitutional policies that were completely kosher. The best example is Trump's executive order on immigration, restricting travel from several terror-prone countries. The media fell in lockstep with the left and presumed the order was unconstitutional, cheering Acting Attorney General Sally Yates for refusing to enforce it. Earlier this month, when the Supreme Court struck down the latest challenge to Trump's executive orders by a 7–2 margin, the media largely ignored the story. And while hyperventilating about the threat Trump supposedly presents to the First Amendment, the media have overlooked the fact that Trump has, unlike the constitutional law lecturer who preceded him in the post, actually deferred to the courts rather than doing whatever he wanted to do anyway." Joel B. Pollak. "The Media Have Not Learned the Most Important Lesson of 2016: The Constitution Matters," Breitbart News, December 17, 2017, https://www.breitbart.com /politics/2017/12/17/constitution-media-not-learned-important-lesson-2016/.

88. Lili Loofbourow, "The Most Diverse Field in History Has Come Down to This," *Slate*, March 4, 2020, https://slate.com/news-and-politics/2020/03/democratic -primary-from-the-most-diverse-field-in-history-to-probably-joe-biden.html.

89. Eric Swalwell, interviewed by Chris Matthews, *Hardball*, MSNBC, January 18, 2019, https://www.breitbart.com/politics/2019/01/19/eric-swalwell-all -evidence-ive-seen-shows-trump-is-a-russian-agent/.

90. Joshua Caplan, "Reporters Mock Beto O'Rourke for Live-Streaming Dental Cleaning," Breitbart News, January 10, 2019, https://www.breitbart.com/politics /2019/01/10/reporters-mock-beto-orourke-for-live-streaming-dental-cleaning/.

91. John Hickenlooper, quoted by Joshua Caplan, "John Hickenlooper Booed at CA Democrat Convention for Denouncing Socialism," Breitbart News, June 1, 2019, https://www.breitbart.com/politics/2019/06/01/john-hickenlooper-booed-at-ca -democrat-convention-for-denouncing-socialism/.

92. Joe Biden, campaign launch video, YouTube, April 25, 2019, https://www .youtube.com/watch?v=VbOU2fTg6cI.

93. Rahm Emanuel, quoted in Gerald F. Seib, "In Crisis, Opportunity for Obama," *Wall Street Journal*, November 21, 2008, https://www.wsj.com/articles /SB122721278056345271.

94. Kyle Morris, "Rashida Tlaib's First Day in Congress: 'We're Gonna Impeach the Motherf**ker,'" Breitbart News, January 3, 2019, https://www.breitbart.com /politics/2019/01/03/rashida-tlaibs-first-day-in-congress-were-gonna-impeach-the -motherfker/.

95. Joel B. Pollak, "Nancy Pelosi vs. Tom Steyer over Trump Impeachment Ads," Breitbart News, November 2, 2017, https://www.breitbart.com/local/2017/11/02 /nancy-pelosi-vs-tom-steyer-trump-impeachment-talk/.

96. Joel B. Pollak, "Democrats' Impeachment Army: $110 Million, 1000 Staff, 2000 Volunteers," Breitbart News, July 31, 2018, https://www.breitbart.com /politics/2018/07/31/democrats-impeachment-army-110-million-1000-staff-2000 -volunteers/.

97. Katie Hill, tweet, July 9, 2018, https://twitter.com/KatieHill4CA/status /1016505439763161089.

98. Ted W. Lieu, "Statement of Representative Ted W. Lieu in Opposition to the Joint Comprehensive Plan of Action (JCPOA)," September 2015, https://lieu .house.gov/sites/lieu.house.gov/files/documents/Ted%20W.%20Lieu%20 JCPOA%20Statement.pdf.

99. Joel B. Pollak, "Should Rep. Ted Lieu (D-CA) Be Court-Martialed?," Breitbart News, January 26, 2017, https://www.breitbart.com/local/2017/01/26/rep -ted-lieu-d-ca-court-martialed/.

100. Associated Press, "California Immigrant Emerges as Congressional Trump Critic," *Santa Monica Daily Press*, August 16, 2019, https://www.smdp .com/california-immigrant-emerges-as-congressional-trump-critic/178633.

101. Ron Kampeas, "Ilhan Omar, Who Once Called Israel an 'Apartheid Regime,' Wins Congressional Primary in Minnesota," Jewish Telegraphic Agency, August 15, 2018, https://www.jta.org/2018/08/15/politics/ilhan-omar-called-israel -apartheid-regime-wins-congressional-primary-minnesota.

102. Ilhan Omar, quoted in Scott W. Johnson, "The Anti-Israel Seat," *Washington Examiner*, June 22, 2018, https://www.washingtonexaminer.com/weekly -standard/the-anti-israel-seat.

103. Ron Latz, quoted in Dave Orrick, "MN Jewish Leaders Talked with Ilhan Omar about Anti-Semitism Last Year. Why They Remain Frustrated," TwinCities. com, February 12, 2019, https://www.twincities.com/2019/02/12/mn-jewish-leaders -talked-with-ilhan-omar-about-anti-semitism-last-year-why-they-remain-frustrated/.

104. Aiden Pink, "Muslim Trailblazer Ilhan Omar Admits She Backs BDS— Now That Election Is Over," *Forward*, November 13, 2018, https://forward.com /news/national/414050/muslim-trailblazer-ilhan-omar-admits-she-backs-bds-now -that-election-is/.

105. Deanna Paul, "Top Democrat Demands Another Apology from Rep. Ilhan Omar, Accusing Her of 'a Vile Anti-Semitic Slur,'" *Washington Post*, March 4, 2019, https://www.washingtonpost.com/politics/2019/03/02/top-democrat-demands -another-apology-rep-omar-accusing-her-vile-anti-semitic-slur/.

106. Alexandria Ocasio-Cortez, tweet, November 23, 2018, https://twitter.com /AOC/status/1066067657278070785.

107. Joel B. Pollak, "Pollak: 'Green New Deal' Is a Republican Parody of the Democratic Platform," Breitbart News, February 7, 2019, https://www.breitbart.com /politics/2019/02/07/pollak-green-new-deal-is-a-republican-parody-of-the -democratic-platform/.

108. Sean Moran, "Study: Green New Deal Would Cost $93 Trillion, over Four Times the National Debt," Breitbart News, February 25, 2019, https://www .breitbart.com/politics/2019/02/25/study-green-new-deal-would-cost-93-trillion-over -four-times-the-national-debt/.

109. H. Res. 109, as presented by National Public Radio, https://apps.npr.org /documents/document.html?id=5729033-Green-New-Deal-FINAL&

fbclid=IwAR3zOWJhxCDq-QhG9tdwBVEm0nM8I2sgKJRYdKFlow-zjNB2kXX
GNIArYTg.

110. Matthew Boyle, "Alexandria Ocasio-Cortez: 'The World Is Going to End in
12 Years If We Don't Address Climate Change,'" Breitbart News, January 21, 2019,
https://www.breitbart.com/politics/2019/01/21/alexandria-ocasio-cortez-the-world-is
-going-to-end-in-12-years-if-we-dont-address-climate-change/. The twelve-year timeline
was drawn from a controversial United Nations scientific report that recommended the
world begin cutting emissions drastically before 2030 to limit global average surface
temperature increase to 1.5° C (Intergovernmental Panel on Climate Change, "Global
Warming of 1.5 °C," accessed September 5, 2019, https://www.ipcc.ch/sr15/).

111. Kyle Morris, "Alexandria Ocasio-Cortez Discovers a Garbage Disposal,
Asks If It Is 'Environmentally Sound,'" Breitbart News, May 7, 2019, https://www
.breitbart.com/politics/2019/05/07/alexandria-ocasio-cortez-discovers-a-garbage
-disposal-asks-if-it-is-environmentally-sound/.

112. Bob Fredericks, "Meteorologist Takes Alexandria Ocasio-Cortez to Task
about Climate Change Message," New York Post, May 24, 2019, https://nypost
.com/2019/05/24/alexandria-ocasio-cortez-chided-by-dc-meteorologist-about
-climate-change-message/.

113. Joshua Caplan, "Green New Deal Aims to 'Fully Get Rid of Farting
Cows and Airplanes'—Eventually," Breitbart News, February 7, 2019, https://www
.breitbart.com/politics/2019/02/07/green-new-deal-aims-to-fully-get-rid-of-farting
-cows-and-airplanes-eventually/.

114. John Hayward, "Hayward: Ocasio-Cortez Disavows the Green New Deal's
FAQ after It Becomes a Mockery," Breitbart News, February 11, 2019, https://www
.breitbart.com/politics/2019/02/11/hayward-ocasio-cortez-disavows-green-new
-deals-faq-after-becomes-mockery/. Ocasio-Cortez later disavowed that document,
scrubbing it from her congressional website.

115. Van Jones, The Green Collar Economy: How One Solution Can Fix Our
Two Biggest Problems (New York: HarperOne, 2008), 16.

116. Tony Lee, "Obama Vows to 'Bet On' Green Energy Loans That 'Will
Fail,'" Breitbart News, November 3, 2012, https://www.breitbart.com/politics/2012
/11/03/obama-i-will-continue-to-bet-on-green-energy-loans-that-will-fail/.

117. Elizabeth Warren, tweet, February 7, 2019, https://twitter.com/SenWarren
/status/1093539704622993408.

118. Michael Bloomberg, quoted by Al Weaver, "Bloomberg Calls for 'Achievable' 'Green New Deal,'" Washington Examiner, January 29, 2019, https://www
.washingtonexaminer.com/news/congress/bloomberg-calls-for-achievable-green
-new-deal.

119. David Montgomery, "AOC's Chief of Change," Washington Post, July 10,
2019, https://www.washingtonpost.com/news/magazine/wp/2019/07/10/feature/how
-saikat-chakrabarti-became-aocs-chief-of-change/.

120. Richard E. Berg-Andersson and Tony Roza, "The Green Papers," accessed
March 3, 2020, https://www.thegreenpapers.com/P20/R.

121. "2000 Primary Elections: Delegate Count," NBC News, accessed March 3, 2020, https://www.nbcnews.com/politics/2020-primary-elections/delegate-count.

122. Maria Cramer, "A Brokered Convention? Here's What's Happened Before," *New York Times*, February 27, 2020, https://www.nytimes.com/2020/02/27 /us/politics/brokered-democratic-convention.html.

123. Kamala Harris, campaign launch speech (Oakland, California, January 27, 2019), https://www.ktvu.com/news/transcript-kamala-harris-kicks-off-presidential -campaign-in-oakland.

124. Elizabeth Warren, campaign launch speech (Lawrence, Massachu-setts, February 9, 2019), https://www.masslive.com/politics/2019/02/read-elizabeth -warrens-2020-announcement-speech.html.

125. Bernie Sanders, campaign launch speech (Brooklyn, New York, March 2, 2019), https://vtdigger.org/2019/03/02/full-text-sen-bernie-sanders-2020-presidential -campaign-kickoff-speech/.

126. Joe Biden, campaign launch video, YouTube, April 25, 2019, https://www .youtube.com/watch?v=VbOU2fTg6cI.

127. Amie Parnes, "Dem Donors Buzzing about Kamala Harris," *The Hill*, July 18, 2017, https://thehill.com/homenews/campaign/342431-dem-donors-buzzing-ab out-kamala-harris.

128. Public Policy Polling, "Health Care a Mine Field for Republicans; Many Trump Voters in Denial on Russia," July 18, 2017, https://www.publicpolicypolling .com/wp-content/uploads/2017/09/PPP_Release_National_71817.pdf.

129. Democrats claimed Sessions had perjured himself because he neglected, in questioning by then senator Al Franken (D-MN), to mention two meetings with then ambassador Sergey Kislyak, one apparently a perfunctory greeting during a larger event. (Joel B. Pollak, "Fake News: Media, Democrats Distort Remarks to Target Jeff Sessions," Breitbart News, March 1, 2017, https:// www.breitbart.com/politics/2017/03/01/jeff-sessions-fake-news-washington-post -misquote-used-target/.)

130. "Attorney General Testimony on Russian Investigation," C-SPAN, June 13, 2017, video at 01:56:34, https://www.c-span.org/video/?429875-1/attorney-general -calls-collusion-accusations-detestable-lie.

131. Dylan Stafford and Tom LoBianco, "Once Again, Senators Cut Off Harris as She Rails on Sessions," CNN, June 14, 2017, https://www.cnn.com/2017 /06/13/politics/kamala-harris-jeff-sessions-hearing/index.html.

132. Kamala Harris, "Stand with Women Senators," ActBlue, accessed March 8, 2020, https://secure.actblue.com/donate/kh-slate.

133. Joel B. Pollak, "Kamala Harris Fundraises Off Senate Interruptions," Bre-itbart News, June 19, 2017, https://www.breitbart.com/politics/2017/06/19/kamala -harris-fundraises-off-senate-interruptions/.

134. Ta-Nehisi Coates, *Between the World and Me* (New York: Spiegel & Grau, 2015).

135. Don Lemon, quoted by Jessica Bennett, "Don Lemon & April Ryan Have Tense Debate over Sen. Kamala Harris," *Ebony*, February 12, 2019, https://www.ebony.com/news/don-lemon-april-ryan-have-tense-debate-over-sen-kamala-harris/.

136. Kamala Harris, appearance on *The Breakfast Club*, WWPR, February 11, 2019, https://thebreakfastclub.iheart.com/featured/breakfast-club/content/2019-02-11-kamala-harris-talks-2020-presidential-run-legalizing-marijuana-rumors/.

137. Ryan C. Harris, "Kamala Harris Has a Network of Black Sorority Sisters Mobilizing for Her in the South," Buzzfeed, June 12, 2019, https://www.buzzfeednews.com/article/ryancbrooks/kamala-harris-south-carolina-alpha-kappa-alpha.

138. Brown suggested shortly after Harris launched her campaign that neither she nor any of the other contenders had yet shown an ability to defeat Trump. "They all have impressive credentials, winning personalities and positive messages, but none displays the 'people personality' that our media-savvy president has mastered," he wrote. Willie Brown, "Democrats Have a 2020 Problem: Trump Is Good at Elections," *San Francisco Chronicle*, February 9, 2019, https://www.sfchronicle.com/bayarea/williesworld/article/Democrats-have-a-2020-problem-Trump-is-good-at-13603018.php.

139. Joel B. Pollak, "Willie Brown: So What If I Dated Kamala Harris and Gave Her State Jobs?," Breitbart News, January 27, 2009, https://www.breitbart.com/politics/2019/01/27/willie-brown-so-what-if-i-dated-kamala-harris-and-gave-her-state-jobs/.

140. Susan Berry, "Kamala Harris-Initiated Criminal Case against Planned Parenthood Video Journalists Heads to Trial," Breitbart News, December 6, 2019, https://www.breitbart.com/politics/2019/12/06/kamala-harris-initiated-criminal-case-planned-parenthood-video-journalists-heads-trial/.

141. Joel B. Pollak, "California Wins Appeal to Force Koch Brothers-Linked Group to Reveal Donors," Breitbart News, September 12, 2018, https://www.breitbart.com/local/2018/09/12/california-wins-appeal-to-force-koch-brothers-linked-group-to-reveal-donors/.

142. "Exit Polls," CNN, November 9, 2016, https://www.cnn.com/election/2016/results/exit-polls/california/senate.

143. The "jungle primary," also known as the "top two" system, pools all of the candidates into one common primary (except for presidential elections). All voters may choose among all candidates, and the top two vote-winners advance to the general election, regardless of party affiliation. As a result, voters are sometimes presented with two candidates from the same party on the November ballot.

144. Christopher Cadelago, "Kamala Harris Spending Big Chunk of Money Raised for Senate Race," *Sacramento Bee*, October 29, 2015, https://www.sacbee.com/news/politics-government/capitol-alert/article41873313.html.

145. Jonathan Swan and Amie Parnes, "Kamala Harris's Spending on Upscale Hotels, First-Class Airfare Draws Scrutiny," *The Hill*, September 12, 2015, https://thehill.com/homenews/campaign/262570-spending-under-scrutiny.

146. Stacey Solie, "Kamala Harris Kicks Off 2020 Campaign with Oakland Rally," *New York Times,* January 27, 2019, https://www.nytimes.com/2019/01/27/us /politics/kamala-harris-rally-2020.html.

147. Kamala Harris, presidential campaign launch (Oakland, California, January 27, 2019, https://www.ktvu.com/news/transcript-kamala-harris-kicks-off -presidential-campaign-in-oakland.

148. Elizabeth Warren, quoted by Tom McCarthy. "Senator Elizabeth Warren Officially Launches 2020 Presidential Campaign," *Guardian,* February 9, 2019, https://www.theguardian.com/us-news/2019/feb/09/senator-elizabeth-warren -democrat-2020-presidential-campaign.

149. Amy B. Wang, "'Nevertheless, She Persisted' Becomes New Battle Cry after McConnell Silences Elizabeth Warren," *Washington Post,* February 8, 2017, https://www.washingtonpost.com/news/the-fix/wp/2017/02/08/nevertheless-she -persisted-becomes-new-battle-cry-after-mcconnell-silences-elizabeth-warren/.

150. As Warren would later recount in her stump speech, only one of them grew up to be a Democrat. One brother, Don Reed, died in April 2020 after testing positive for coronavirus. Daniella Diaz, "Sen. Elizabeth Warren Says Her Older Brother Died of Coronavirus," CNN, April 23, 2020, https://www.cnn.com/2020/04/23 /politics/elizabeth-warren-coronavirus-donald-reed-herring-brother/index.html.

151. There is controversy about whether her contract was not renewed because she was pregnant or whether she left voluntarily.

152. I was a student at Harvard Law when Warren was a professor there. She specialized in teaching bankruptcy law and was well liked by students, even though she was notoriously strict. She was rumored to have turned off the wireless routers near her classroom, for example, so that students would not surf the Internet during class and would pay closer attention to her lectures.

153. "Elizabeth Warren on Debt Crisis, Fair Taxation," LiveSmartVideos, September 18, 2011, https://www.youtube.com/watch?v=htX2usfqMEs.

154. Warren's speech bore a striking resemblance to the "you didn't build that" line President Barack Obama would utter the following year—and which would reappear in Republican attack ads for months thereafter: "If you were successful, somebody along the line gave you some help. There was a great teacher somewhere in your life. Somebody helped to create this unbelievable American system that we have that allowed you to thrive. Somebody invested in roads and bridges. If you've got a business—you didn't build that. Somebody else made that happen." President Barack Obama, remarks (Roanoake, Virginia, July 13, 2012), https://obamawhite house.archives.gov/the-press-office/2012/07/13/remarks-president-campaign-event -roanoke-virginia.

155. Astead W. Herndon, "Elizabeth Warren Apologizes to Cherokee Nation for DNA Test," *New York Times,* February 1, 2019, https://www.nytimes .com/2019/02/01/us/politics/elizabeth-warren-cherokee-dna.html.

156. Michael Kruse, "Bernie Sanders Has a Secret," *Politico,* July 9, 2015, https://www.politico.com/magazine/story/2015/07/bernie-sanders-vermont-119927.

157. The refrain appeared frequently in Obama administration arguments for the Affordable Care Act. (See, for example, Stephanie Cutter, "Fighting Fraud and the Consequences of Defunding the Affordable Care Act," White House, September 20, 2010, https://obamawhitehouse.archives.gov/blog/2010/09/20/fighting-fraud-and-consequences-defunding-affordable-care-act.)

158. The *Washington Post* observed: "The choices Shumlin favored would essentially have doubled Vermont's budget, raising state income taxes by up to 9.5 percent and placing an 11.5 percent payroll tax on all employers—a burden Shumlin said would pose 'a risk of economic shock'—even though Vermonters would no longer pay for private health plans." Amy Goldstein, "Why Vermont's Single-Payer Effort Failed and What Democrats Can Learn from It," *Washington Post*, April 29, 2019, https://www.washingtonpost.com/national/health-science/why-vermonts-single-payer-effort-failed-and-what-democrats-can-learn-from-it/2019/04/29/c9789018-3ab8-11e9-a2cd-307b06d0257b_story.html.

159. Sydney Ember, "Young Voters Still 'Feel the Bern,' but Not Just for Bernie Sanders Anymore," *New York Times*, September 20, 2019, https://www.nytimes.com/2019/09/20/us/politics/bernie-sanders-young-voters.html.

160. Ron Dicker, "Vice President Joe Biden Caught in Lie about Playing Football? (UPDATE)," HuffPost, October 17, 2012, https://www.huffpost.com/entry/vice-president-biden-caug_n_1975371.

161. "In the first semester of my junior year I started to get a little worried. I was no longer sure, given the state of my academic transcript, that I could talk my way into a good law school." His performance later improved. Joe Biden, *Promises to Keep: On Life and Politics* (New York: Random House, 2007), 27.

162. The *New York Times* reported in 1987 that Biden had "relatively poor grades in college and law school." Biden's exaggerated claims about his academic prowess unraveled on the campaign trail during his failed 1988 presidential bid. E. J. Dionne Jr., "Biden Admits Plagiarism in School but Says It Was Not 'Malevolent,'" *New York Times*, September 18, 1987, https://www.nytimes.com/1987/09/18/us/biden-admits-plagiarism-in-school-but-says-it-was-not-malevolent.html.

163. Ibid.

164. For years, Biden claimed incorrectly that his wife and daughter had been killed by a drunk driver. She apparently drove into an intersection against a red light and collided with a truck. Investigators found the other driver had not been at fault. Jack Fowler, "The Most Disturbing Thing about Joe Biden," *National Review*, April 5, 2019, https://www.nationalreview.com/corner/joe-biden-most-disturbing-thing/.

165. As rival Senator Cory Booker (D-NJ) would point out, Biden had even called it the "Biden Crime Law."

166. Curiously, he had voted *against* the Gulf War, a conflict viewed by history as far more legitimate and successful.

167. Women flocked to the polls in 1992 in response, electing an unprecedented number of female candidates in what become known as the "Year of the Woman." Later, Biden sponsored the Violence Against Women Act (VAWA), aimed

at deterring domestic violence. More recently, Hill said that she would still vote for Biden, certainly if he was the alternative to Trump. (Anita Hill, interview with *NBC Nightly News*, June 13, 2019, https://www.breitbart.com/clips/2019/06/13/anita -hill-on-voting-for-joe-biden-of-course-i-could/.)

168. John Nolte, "Nolte: Tara Reade Is Joe Biden's Eighth Accuser," Breitbart News, May 1, 2020, https://www.breitbart.com/politics/2020/05/01/nolte-tara-reade -is-joe-bidens-eighth-accuser/.

169. Lucy Flores, "An Awkward Kiss Changed How I Saw Joe Biden," The Cut, March 29, 2019, https://www.thecut.com/2019/03/an-awkward-kiss-changed-how-i -saw-joe-biden.html.

170. Penny Starr, "AP Admits Not Reporting, Deleting Tara Reade 2019 Interview Detailing Charges Against Joe Biden," Breitbart News, May 2, 2020, https:// www.breitbart.com/politics/2020/05/02/ap-admits-not-reporting-deleting-tara-reade -2019-interview-detailing-charges-against-joe-biden/.

171. Joe Biden, quoted by Penny Starr, "Flashback–Biden on Blasey Ford: Women Should Be Given 'Benefit of the Doubt'," Breitbart News, May 2, 2020, https://www.breitbart.com/politics/2020/05/02/flashback-biden-on-blasey-ford -women-should-be-given-benefit-of-the-doubt/.

172. Joe Biden, quoted by CBS News, "Biden's Comments Ruffle Feathers," July 7, 2006, https://www.cbsnews.com/news/bidens-comments-ruffle-feathers/.

173. Joe Biden, "Biden's Description of Obama Draws Scrutiny," CNN.com, February 9, 2007, https://www.cnn.com/2007/POLITICS/01/31/biden.obama/.

174. President Donald Trump, quoted by Jordan Fabian, "Trump Unleashes on 'Failing' and 'Slower Than He Used to Be' Biden," *The Hill*, June 11, 2019, https://thehill.com/homenews/administration/447932-trump-insults-biden -obama-took-him-off-the-trash-heap.

175. The Obama campaign also saw Biden as a hedge against the so-called Bradley effect, named for Los Angeles mayor Tom Bradley, who was the favorite for governor until, supposedly, white voters entered the privacy of the voting booth.

176. Karen Tumulty, "Hidin' Biden: Reining in a Voluble No. 2," *Time*, October 29, 2008, http://content.time.com/time/subscriber/article/0,33009,1855355,00 .html.

177. Joe Biden, remark captured on open microphone (White House, Washington, DC, March 23, 2010).

178. Joe Biden, remarks (Danville, Virginia, August 14, 2012), https://www .breitbart.com/politics/2012/08/14/biden-chains-romney-response/.

179. Joe Perticone, "Tax Returns Show Many 2020 Democrats Have One Financial Habit in Common," Business Insider, April 25, 2019, https://www.business insider.com/tax-returns-show-2020-democratic-candidates-donated-little-to -charity-2019-4.

180. The younger Biden would be discharged from the U.S. Navy Reserve almost as soon as he joined, after testing positive for cocaine; he was later found to have led a troubled, drug-addled life in the fast lane, allegedly returning a rental car

with drugs in the trunk and then trying, belatedly, to recover the evidence. (Matthew Boyle, "Exclusive—2016 Arizona Police Report: Cocaine Pipe Found in Car Rented by Joe Biden's Son Hunter Biden, Authorities Declined to Prosecute," Breitbart News, May 17, 2019, https://www.breitbart.com/politics/2019/05/17/exclusive-2016 -arizona-police-report-cocaine-pipe-found-in-car-rented-by-joe-bidens-son-hunter -biden-authorities-declined-to-prosecute/.)

181. Hunter Biden also traveled with his father on Air Force Two to China, then gained access to $1.5 billion in Chinese government-controlled capital for the financial firm he cofounded with Christopher Heinz, the stepson of 2004 Democratic nominee John Kerry. (Rebecca Mansour, "NYT Confirms Hunter Biden Bank of China Deal, Leaves Out Key Details," Breitbart News, March 21, 2019, https:// www.breitbart.com/politics/2019/05/21/nyt-confirms-hunter-biden-bank-of-china -deal-leaves-out-key-details/.)

182. Joe Biden, quoted by Pollak, "Joe Biden: I'm Not a 'Moderate,'" https:// www.breitbart.com/politics/2019/04/05/joe-biden-im-not-a-moderate-its-just-that -progressive-became-socialist/.

183. Pete Buttigieg, campaign launch speech (South Bend, Indiana, April 15, 2019), https://www.nytimes.com/2019/04/15/us/politics/pete-buttigieg-speech.html.

184. Amy Klobuchar, campaign launch speech (Minneapolis, Minnesota, February 10, 2019), https://www.twincities.com/2019/02/10/amy-klobuchars-big-speech -today-heres-a-sneak-peak/.

185. Andrew Yang, "Humanity First," YouTube, February 2, 2018, https://www .youtube.com/watch?v=GhArPPmHjCs.

186. Beto O'Rourke, campaign launch speech (El Paso, Texas, March 30, 2019), https://www.elpasotimes.com/story/news/2019/03/30/beto-orourke-el-paso-rally -speech-beto-2020-donald-trump-immigration-wall/3323327002/.

187. In Afghanistan, Buttigieg—who spoke eight languages with proficiency, including Norwegian—had been an intelligence officer. He did not see combat, but he did, according to his later recollections, take "119 trips . . . outside the wire—be it driving or guarding a vehicle." Those who served with him recalled his competence and humility. The lesson he learned, he later wrote in a CNN op-ed, was "to trust my life to people completely different from me." (Pete Buttigieg, "Pete Buttigieg: The Greatest Lesson I Learned in Afghanistan," CNN.com, July 30, 2019, https://www.cnn.com/2019/07/29/opinions/pete-buttigieg-2020-national -service-plan/index.html.) Others were more skeptical of his military service. Greg Kelly and Katie Horgan, two retired marines, wrote an op-ed in the *Wall Street Journal* arguing that Buttigieg was exploiting a relatively cushy "direct commission" for full political effect: "He entered the military through a little-used shortcut: direct commission in the reserves . . . no obstacle courses, no weapons training, no evaluation of his ability or willingness to lead. Paperwork, a health exam and a background check were all it took to make him a naval officer. . . . In our experience, those who did the most in war talk about it the least. Serving in a support or noncombat role is honorable, but it shouldn't be the basis of a presidential campaign."

(Greg Kelly and Katie Horgan, "Buttigieg's War and 'The Shortest Way Home,'" *Wall Street Journal*, January 6, 2020, https://www.wsj.com/articles/buttigiegs-war -and-the-shortest-way-home-11578355312.) Either way, it was, admittedly, more experience than most of his rivals—including Trump, at least before he became commander in chief.

188. President Donald Trump, quoted by Joel B. Pollak, "Trump on Pete Buttigieg: 'Alfred E. Neuman Cannot Become President of the United States,'" Breitbart News, May 10, 2019, https://www.breitbart.com/politics/2019/05/10/trump-on-pete -buttigieg-alfred-e-neuman-cannot-become-president-of-the-united-states/.

189. Coincidentally, my own slogan for my unsuccessful congressional race in 2010 against incumbent Representative Jan Schakowsky had been "A Fresh Start."

190. He was among those who believed that President George W. Bush "was not elected president by most of the people and arguably not by the Electoral College." (Pete Buttigieg, "A Vision Thing," *Harvard Crimson*, January 14, 2004, https://www .thecrimson.com/article/2004/1/14/a-vision-thing-visitors-to-a/.) He also suggested that Bush knew, or ought to have known, about the 9/11 terror attacks beforehand, a common left-wing conspiracy theory. (Joel B. Pollak, "Pete Buttigieg's Harvard Crimson Columns Reveal Left-Wing Foundations," Breitbart News, May 21, 2019, https://www.breitbart.com/politics/2019/05/21/pete-buttigieg-harvard-crimson -columns-reveal-left-foundations/.) He showed skepticism toward Israel, and he criticized alleged war crimes committed by Americans, saying that they occurred "not because Americans are evil, but because war is the ultimate doer of evil." (Pete Buttigieg, "Seeing Is Believing," *Harvard Crimson*, May 10, 2004, https://www.the crimson.com/article/2004/5/10/seeing-is-believing-wilfred-owen-and/.)

191. Tom Ciccotta, "Yale Professor: Photo of Buttigieg and Husband Is 'Heterosexual,'" Breitbart News, May 23, 2019, https://www.breitbart.com/tech/2019/05 /23/yale-professorr-photo-of-buttigieg-and-husband-is-heterosexual/.

192. Elena Schneider, "Buttigieg Fights to Lock Down Iowa LGBTQ Vote," *Politico*, September 21, 2019, https://www.politico.com/story/2019/09/21 /buttigieg-iowa-lgbtq-vote-1507049.

193. Pete Buttigieg, interview with Clay Cane, *The Clay Cane Show*, SiriusXM Urban View channel 126, September 18, 2019, https://twitter.com/claycane/status /1174411716861603842.

194. Jesús A. Rodgríguez, "When Pete Buttigieg Ripped America's Missionary Zeal," *Politico*, June 11, 2019, https://www.politico.com/magazine/story/2019 /06/11/pete-buttigieg-undergraduate-thesis-227104.

195. Brian Anderson, "Buttigieg Battles Mike Pence, or So He Imagines," *Wall Street Journal*, April 25, 2019, https://www.wsj.com/articles/buttigieg-battles-mike -pence-or-so-he-imagines-11556232516. The *Journal* also noted that Buttigieg had previously recorded different impressions of Pence: "On meeting Mr. Pence for the first time in 2011, Mr. Buttigieg wrote, 'I was surprised by how affable, even gentle he seemed.'...By contrast, last month the mayor wondered aloud if Mr. Pence 'stopped believing in Scripture when he started believing in Donald Trump.'"

196. Pete Buttigieg, second Democratic presidential debate (Detroit, Michigan, July 30, 2019).

197. Trip Gabriel and Alexander Burns, "Pete Buttigieg Fired South Bend's Black Police Chief. It Still Stings," *New York Times,* April 19, 2019, A1, https://www.nytimes.com/2019/04/19/us/politics/buttigieg-black-police-chief-fired.html.

198. Shawn White, quoted by Tucker Higgins, "'I Ain't Ever Seen the Dude'—Residents of South Bend's Poor Neighborhoods Say Democratic Presidential Hopeful Pete Buttigieg Left Them Behind," CNBC.com, April 22, 2019, https://www.cnbc.com/2019/04/22/south-bend-poor-say-democrat-pete-buttigieg-left-them-behind.html.

199. Quinnipiac University Poll, "Biden Dominates South Carolina Dem Primary, Quinnipiac University Poll Finds; Undecided Is in Second Place," press release, November 18, 2019, https://poll.qu.edu/south-carolina/release-detail?ReleaseID=3649. (See also SSRS, "CNN Poll results," CNN, July 1, 2019, http://cdn.cnn.com/cnn/2019/images/07/01/rel8a.-.democrats.and.healthcare.pdf.)

200. President Donald Trump, tweet, February 10, 2019, https://twitter.com/realDonaldTrump/status/1094718856197799936.

201. "Klobuchar Celebrates as She's 'Still Standing' on Debate Stage," Radio Iowa, January 14, 2020, https://www.radioiowa.com/2020/01/14/klobuchar-celebrates-as-shes-still-standing-on-debate-stage/.

202. Lucien Bruggeman, "Amy Klobuchar's Mentor, a Former Vice President, Sees a Path Forward—and a Plan B," ABC News, August 26, 2019, https://abcnews.go.com/Politics/amy-klobuchars-mentor-vice-president-sees-path-forward/story?id=65147449.

203. Peter Schweizer, *Profiles in Corruption* (New York: HarperCollins, 2019), 216–18.

204. Schweizer, *Profiles in Corruption*, 225–28.

205. Hunter Schwarz, "This Is the Reason Amy Klobuchar Chose Green as Her Campaign Color," Yello, February 22, 2020, https://yello.substack.com/p/this-is-the-reason-amy-klobuchar.

206. Andrew Yang, Political Soapbox remarks (Iowa State Fair, Des Moines, Iowa, August 9, 2019).

207. Andrew Yang, "Meet Andrew," Yang2020.com, accessed March 9, 2020, https://www.yang2020.com/meet-andrew/.

208. Andrew Yang, "Humanity First."

209. Andrew Yang, "Meet Andrew."

210. Mark Zuckerberg, Harvard commencement speech (Cambridge, Massachusetts, May 25, 2017), https://news.harvard.edu/gazette/story/2017/05/mark-zuckerbergs-speech-as-written-for-harvards-class-of-2017/.

211. Joel B. Pollak, "City of Stockton to Consider America's First Basic Income Grant," Breitbart News, October 19, 2017, https://www.breitbart.com/local/2017/10/19/city-stockton-consider-americas-first-basic-income-grant/.

212. "California City Experiments with Andrew Yang-Style Universal Basic Income," Breitbart News, September 3, 2019, https://www.breitbart.com/news /california-city-experiments-with-andrew-yang-style-universal-basic-income/.

213. Kamala Harris also claimed that distinction, given her mother's birth in India.

214. Andrew Yang, Political Soapbox remarks (Iowa State Fair).

215. Andrew Yang, CNN climate town hall, CNN, September 4, 2019.

216. Andrew Yang, interviewed by Ali Velshi, MSNBC, September 19, 2019, https://www.youtube.com/watch?v=gP16mUl9zoU&feature=youtu.be.

217. Penny Starr, "Andrew Yang Says Only U.S. Citizens Would Get $1,000 per Month He Vows," Breitbart News, August 9, 2019, https://www.breitbart.com/2020 -election/2019/08/09/andrew-yang-says-only-u-s-citizens-get-1000-month-vows/.

218. Andrew Yang, second Democratic presidential debate (Detroit, Michigan, July 31, 2009), https://www.breitbart.com/2020-election/2019/07/31/andrew-yang -too-late-to-stop-global-warming-move-to-higher-ground/.

219. One poem, penned when O'Rouke was 16 years old, involved asking a cow to "Wax my ass,/Scrub my balls." Beto O'Rourke, quoted in Joseph Simonson, "Beto O'Rourke Wrote Poem Asking Cow to 'Wax My Ass' and 'Scrub My Balls,'" *Washington Examiner*, March 15, 2019, https://www.washingtonexaminer.com /news/beto-orourke-wrote-poem-asking-a-cow-to-wax-my-ass-and-scrub-my-balls.

220. Will Weissert and Ryan J. Foley, "Rich Father-in-Law Has Helped, Complicated O'Rourke's Career," Associated Press, July 5, 2019, https://apnews .com/84ca432974f04a699e4b2f7eaf0c74a1.

221. Dermot McEvoy, "Is Beto O'Rourke the New Bobby Kennedy?," Irish Central.com, August 31, 2018, https://www.irishcentral.com/news/politics/beto -orourke-bobby-kennedy.

222. Joe Hagan, "Beto O'Rourke: 'I'm Just Born to Be in It,'" *Vanity Fair*, March 13, 2019, https://www.vanityfair.com/news/2019/03/beto-orourke-cover-story.

223. Ben Kew, "Jimmy Kimmel Begs Audience to Vote for Beto O'Rourke: 'Imagine How Hilarious It Will Be,'" Breitbart News, October 23, 2018, https://www.breitbart.com /entertainment/2018/10/23/jimmy-kimmel-begs-audience-to-vote-beto-orourke/.

224. Beto O'Rourke, quoted in Warner Todd Huston, "Sen. Ted Cruz Slams Opponent for Supporting NFL Anthem Protesters," Breitbart News, August 20, 2018, https://www.breitbart.com/sports/2018/08/21/sen-ted-cruz-slams-opponent-for -supporting-nfl-anthem-protesters/.

225. LeBron James, tweet, August 23, 2018, https://twitter.com/KingJames /status/1032632419550023680.

226. Charlie Spiering, "Donald Trump Mocks Beto O'Rourke Hand Move-ment: 'Is He Crazy?,'" Breitbart News, March 14, 2019, https://www.breitbart.com/po litics/2019/03/14/donald-trump-mocks-beto-orourke-hand-movement-is-he-crazy/.

227. Caplan, "Reporters Mock Beto O'Rourke for Live-Streaming Dental Cleaning."

228. Eric Bradner, "Beto O'Rourke's Launch: Big Promises, Apologies, and Unanswered Questions," CNN, March 17, 2019, https://www.cnn.com/2019/03/17/politics/beto-orourke-2020-campaign-first-days/index.html.

229. Tom Steyer, "Fundamental Change," YouTube, July 9, 2019, https://www.youtube.com/watch?v=Q0pFvLtryd0.

230. Mike Bloomberg, "Rebuild America: Join Mike Bloomberg's 2020 Presidential Campaign," YouTube, November 24, 2019, https://www.youtube.com/watch?v=j_1T_xPpAwo.

231. John Hickenlooper, campaign launch speech (Denver, Colorado, March 8, 2019), https://www.cpr.org/2019/03/08/transcript-john-hickenloopers-presidential-kick-off-speech-from-civic-center-park/.

232. Marianne Williamson, "Marianne 2020 Official Announcement," YouTube, January 29, 2019, https://www.youtube.com/watch?v=SIBNOro0vks.

233. Joshua Caplan, "2020: Former Starbucks CEO Howard Schultz Rules Out Independent Bid," Breitbart News, September 6, 2019, https://www.breitbart.com/politics/2019/09/06/former-starbucks-ceo-howard-schultz-rules-out-independent-bid/.

234. Tom Steyer, quoted in Alexander Burns, "Tom Steyer, Billionaire Impeachment Activist, Won't Run Against Trump," *New York Times*, January 9, 2019, https://www.nytimes.com/2019/01/09/us/politics/tom-steyer-trump-2020.html.

235. Michael Bloomberg, "Our Highest Office, My Deepest Obligation," Bloomberg News, March 5, 2019, https://www.bloomberg.com/opinion/articles/2019-03-05/our-highest-office-my-deepest-obligation.

236. Michael Bloomberg, "Our Highest Office."

237. Edward-Isaac Dovere, "Tom Steyer's $110 Million Plan to Redefine the Democrats," *Politico*, July 31, 2018, https://www.politico.com/story/2018/07/31/steyer-democrats-millions-midterms-751245.

238. *Terry v. Ohio*, 392 U.S. 1 (1968).

239. Bonnie Rochman, "Bloomberg's Breast-feeding Plan: Will Locking Up Formula Help New Moms?," CNN, August 28, 2012, https://www.cnn.com/2012/08/02/health/time-bloomberg-breast-feeding/index.html.

240. Joel B. Pollak, "Mike Bloomberg Changed Rules to Run for Third Term in New York," Breitbart News, February 18, 2020, https://www.breitbart.com/politics/2020/02/18/mike-bloomberg-changed-rules-to-run-for-third-term-in-new-york/.

241. Kara Voght, "How Michael Bloomberg Bought the Gun Control Movement," *Mother Jones*, March 3, 2020, https://www.motherjones.com/politics/2020/03/how-michael-bloomberg-bought-the-gun-control-movement/.

242. Joel B. Pollak, "Rule of Law: Mike Bloomberg Funded 'Special' Prosecutors on Climate Change," Breitbart News, February 14, 2020, https://www.breitbart.com/environment/2020/02/14/rule-of-law-mike-bloomberg-funded-special-prosecutors-on-climate-change/.

243. Sean Moran, "Michael Bloomberg: 'You Could Never Afford' Medicare for All," Breitbart News, January 29, 2019, https://www.breitbart.com/politics/2019/01/29/michael-bloomberg-you-could-never-afford-medicare-for-all/.

244. Michael Bloomberg, quoted by Al Weaver, "Bloomberg Calls for 'Achievable' 'Green New Deal,'" *Washington Examiner*, January 29, 2019, https://www.washingtonexaminer.com/news/congress/bloomberg-calls-for-achievable-green-new-deal.

245. Michael Bloomberg, speech at Bermuda Executive Forum (New York, New York. March 21, 2020), https://www.breitbart.com/clips/2019/03/22/bloomberg-mocks-biden-orourke-joe-apologized-for-being-male-beto-apologized-for-being-born/.

246. billinsi, "Mike Gravel—Rock," YouTube, May 27, 2007, https://www.youtube.com/watch?v=0rZdAB4V_j8.

247. Shmuley Boteach, "Rabbi Shmuley: AIPAC Honors Cory Booker for Abandoning Israel," March 1, 2020, https://www.breitbart.com/politics/2020/03/01/rabbi-shmuley-aipac-honors-cory-booker-for-abandoning-israel/.

248. Joel B. Pollak, "'Spartacus' Cory Booker 'Broke Rules' to Release Emails Already Cleared for Publication," Breitbart News, September 6, 2018, https://www.breitbart.com/politics/2018/09/06/spartacus-cory-booker-broke-rules-to-release-emails-already-cleared-for-publication/.

249. Julián Castro, interview, *Firsthand*, NBC News, July 27, 2015, https://www.nbcnews.com/video/hud-secretary-julian-castro-on-speaking-spanish-490886723833.

250. Jay Inslee, "Our Moment," YouTube, March 1, 2019, https://www.youtube.com/watch?v=mlgdlWO-4yI&feature=youtu.be.

251. Alexandria Ocasio-Cortez, quoted in Miranda Green, "Ocasio-Cortez Calls Jay Inslee's Climate Plan the 'Gold Standard,'" *The Hill*, June 4, 2019, https://thehill.com/policy/energy-environment/446954-ocasio-cortez-calls-jay-inslees-climate-plan-the-gold-standard.

252. Jay Inslee, quoted in "Inslee: I Have 'Humility about Being a Straight White Male,'" *Washington Free Beacon*, March 10, 2019, https://freebeacon.com/politics/inslee-i-have-humility-about-being-a-straight-white-male/.

253. Gabriella Debenedetti, "Gillibrand Remark on Clinton Sends Shockwaves through Democratic Party," *Politico*, November 17, 2017, https://www.politico.com/story/2017/11/17/kirsten-gillibrand-bill-clinton-democrats-247427. She also led calls for Senator Al Franken (D-MN) to resign over sexual harassment allegations. (Amber Phillips, "The Undeniable Al Franken Connection to Kirsten Gillibrand's Failed Presidential Bid," *Washington Post*, August 29, 2019, https://www.washingtonpost.com/politics/2019/08/29/undeniable-al-franken-connection-kirsten-gillibrands-failed-presidential-bid/.)

254. Bo Erickon, "2020 Contender Kirsten Gillibrand Backs Third Gender Classification at Federal Level," CBS News, February 16, 2019, https://www.cbsnews.com/news/kirsten-gillibrand-2020-democratic-contender-backs-third-gender-classification-at-federal-level/.

255. Kirsten Gillibrand, quoted by Kyle Morris, "Kirsten Gillibrand: White Privilege Keeps Whites from 'Being Shot,'" Breitbart News, July 31, 2019, https://www.breitbart.com/politics/2019/07/31/kirsten-gillibrand-white-privilege-keeps-whites-being-shot/.

256. Agence France-Presse, "NY Mayor Takes Protest to Trump Tower," Breitbart News, May 13, 2019, https://www.breitbart.com/news/ny-mayor-takes-protest-to-trump-tower/.

257. Marcus Lim, "De Blasio Shouts Cuban Revolutionary Slogan at Miami Rally," Associated Press, June 27, 2019, https://www.apnews.com/e875acdcaa934755a71e0bae18076587.

258. Eric Swalwell, tweet, June 2, 2019, https://twitter.com/ericswalwell/status/1135275685835137025.

259. Eric Swalwell, tweet, May 21, 2016, https://twitter.com/ericswalwell/status/1131055844387434496.

260. Hickenlooper, campaign launch speech.

261. Hickenlooper, campaign launch speech.

262. Tim Ryan, campaign launch speech (Youngstown, Ohio, April 6, 2019), https://www.c-span.org/video/?459588-1/ohio-democrat-tim-ryan-launches-presidential-bid.

263. Tim Ryan, *Meet the Press*, November 27, 2016, https://www.nbcnews.com/meet-the-press/meet-press-november-27-2016-n688791.

264. Michael Bennet, quoted in Dan Merica and Jeff Zeleny, "With Viral Speech as His Introduction, Sen. Michael Bennet Tests the Waters in Iowa," CNN.com, February 24, 2019, https://www.cnn.com/2019/02/24/politics/michael-bennet-presidential-consideration-iowa/index.html.

265. Michael Bennet, quoted in John Frank, "Michael Bennet Says He's Shifting National Health Care Debate. But Even in His Home State, There's Pushback," *Colorado Sun*, December 3, 2019, https://coloradosun.com/2019/12/03/michael-bennet-health-care-medicare-for-all/.

266. Associated Press, "2020 Democrat Bennet Knocks Green New Deal with $6 Trillion 'Real Deal,'" Fox News, January 2, 2020, https://www.foxbusiness.com/money/2020-democrat-bennet-knocks-green-new-deal-with-6-trillion-real-deal.

267. John Delaney, "John Delaney: Why I'm Running for President," July 28, 2017, https://www.washingtonpost.com/opinions/john-delaney-why-im-running-for-president/2017/07/28/02460ae4-73b7-11e7-8f39-eeb7d3a2d304_story.html.

268. John Hickenlooper, quoted by Joshua Caplan, "John Hickenlooper Booed at CA Democrat Convention for Denouncing Socialism," Breitbart News, June 1, 2019, https://www.breitbart.com/politics/2019/06/01/john-hickenlooper-booed-at-ca-democrat-convention-for-denouncing-socialism/.

269. Brian Pascus, "Democrats Pick Hillary Clinton as 2020 Front-runner in New Party Poll," *New York Post*, December 9, 2019, https://nypost.com/2019/12/09/democrats-pick-hillary-clinton-as-2020-frontrunner-in-new-party-poll/.

270. Charlie Spiering, "Drudge: Michael Bloomberg Considering Hillary Clinton as Running Mate," Breitbart News, February 15, 2020, https://www .breitbart.com/politics/2020/02/15/drudge-michael-bloomberg-considering-hillary -clinton-running-mate/.

271. Lauren Gambino, "Stacey Abrams: Georgia Democrat Will Not Run for President in 2020," *Guardian*, August 13, 2019, https://www.theguardian.com /us-news/2019/aug/13/stacey-abrams-president-2020-not-running.

272. Tony Lee, "John Kerry on 2020: 'I Want to See What Joe Is Going to Do,'" Breitbart News, April 17, 2020, https://www.breitbart.com/politics/2019/04 /17/john-kerry-on-2020-i-want-to-see-what-joe-is-going-to-do/.

273. Kyle Morris, "Sherrod Brown Kicks Off 'Dignity of Work' Tour, Criticizes Trump's 'Phony Populism,'" Breitbart News, January 30, 2019, https://www .breitbart.com/politics/2019/01/30/sherrod-brown-kicks-off-dignity-of-work-tour -criticizes-trumps-phony-populism/.

274. Daniel Strauss, "Sherrod Brown Separates from Dem Pack on Medicare, 'Green New Deal' Proposals," *Politico*, February 12, 2019, https://www.politico .com/story/2019/02/12/sherrod-brown-medicare-green-new-deal-1165560.

275. Joel B. Pollak, "Sherrod Brown Drops Out of 2020 Presidential Race; Only Democrat Candidate Not to Back 'Medicare for All' and 'Green New Deal,'" Breitbart News, March 7, 2019, https://www.breitbart.com/politics/2019/03/07 /sherrod-brown-drops-out-of-presidential-race-only-democrat-candidate-to-decline -medicare-for-all-and-green-new-deal/.

276. Sherrod Brown, interview with Chris Matthews, *Hardball*, MSNBC, March 11, 2019, http://www.msnbc.com/transcripts/all-in/2019-03-11.

277. John Binder, "PHOTOS: Obama Used Same So-Called 'Cages' to Detain Child Border Crossers," Breitbart News, June 18, 2018, https://www.breitbart.com /politics/2018/06/18/photos-obama-used-same-so-called-cages-to-detain-child -border-crossers/.

278. Brandon Darby, "Leaked Images Reveal Children Warehoused in Crowded U.S. Cells, Border Patrol Overwhelmed," Breitbart News, June 5, 2014, https://www.breitbart.com/border/2014/06/05/leaked-images-reveal-children -warehoused-in-crowded-us-cells-border-patrol-overwhelmed/.

279. Bob Price, "PHOTO: Migrant Father-Daughter Pair Found Dead on Border Riverbank," Breitbart News, June 25, 2018, https://www.breitbart.com/border /2019/06/25/photo-migrant-father-daughter-pair-found-dead-on-border-riverbank/.

280. "Lea," quoted by Elizabeth Warren, tweet, June 26, 2018, https://twitter .com/ewarren/status/1143985808468299776.

281. Democratic National Committee, "DNC Announces Details for the First Two Presidential Primary Debates," February 14, 2019, https://democrats.org /news/dnc-announces-details-for-the-first-two-presidential-primary-debates/.

282. President Donald Trump, tweet, June 26, 2018, https://twitter.com/real DonaldTrump/status/1144056731653169152.

283. Cory Booker, quoted by Morgan Gstalter, "Booker Explains Viral Side-Eye Look at O'Rourke during Spanish-Speaking Moment," *The Hill*, June 27, 2019, https://thehill.com/homenews/campaign/450593-booker-explains-viral-side-eye-look-at-orourke-during-spanish-speaking.

284. Julián Castro, quoted in Ian Hanchett, "Julián Castro: My Healthcare Plan Would Cover 'Trans Female' Abortions," Breitbart News, June 26, 2019, https://www.breitbart.com/clips/2019/06/26/castro-my-government-healthcare-plan-would-cover-abortion/.

285. President Donald Trump, tweet, June 26, 2018, https://twitter.com/realdonaldtrump/status/1144064520152739840.

286. Jonathan Martin and Alexander Burns, "Democrats Split on How Far Left to Nudge Nation." *New York Times*, June 26, 2019, 1, https://www.nytimes.com/2019/06/26/us/politics/debate-recap.html.

287. Janet Hook, "This Is Not Your Father's Democratic Party: Debate Shows How Leftward It Has Moved," *Los Angeles Times*, June 26, 2019, https://www.latimes.com/politics/la-na-pol-2020-democratic-debate-miami-analysis-20190626-story.html.

288. John F. Harris, "Democrats Lead with Their Left," *Politico*, June 27,2019, https://www.politico.com/story/2019/06/27/democrats-lead-with-their-left-1385147.

289. Peggy Noonan, "The 2020 Democrats Lack Hindsight," *Wall Street Journal*, June 29, 2019, A15.

290. Noonan, "The 2020 Democrats Lack Hindsight."

291. Eric Swalwell, first Democratic debate remarks (Miami, Florida, June 27, 2019), https://www.washingtonpost.com/politics/2019/06/28/transcript-night-first-democratic-debate/.

292. Joe Biden, quoted in Katie Glueck, "Biden, Recalling 'Civility' in Senate, Invokes Two Segregationist Senators," *New York Times*, June 19, 2019, https://www.nytimes.com/2019/06/19/us/politics/biden-segregationists.html.

293. Editorial Board, "Bernie Sanders Won the Debate," *Wall Street Journal*, June 29, 2019, https://www.wsj.com/articles/bernie-sanders-won-the-debate-11561763598.

294. President Donald Trump, press conference (Trump Tower, New York City, New York, August 15, 2017), https://www.politico.com/story/2017/08/15/full-text-trump-comments-white-supremacists-alt-left-transcript-241662.

295. Joe Biden, campaign launch video, YouTube, April 25, 2019, https://www.youtube.com/watch?v=VbOU2fTg6cI.

296. Kamala Harris, interview with Jimmy Kimmel, *Jimmy Kimmel Live*, March 19, 2019, https://www.youtube.com/watch?v=B65bZOOH2BI.

297. Rachel Frazin, "Harris Campaign Sells 'That Little Girl Was Me' Shirts after Debate Confrontation with Biden," *The Hill*, June 28, 2019, https://thehill.com/homenews/campaign/450831-harris-campaign-sells-that-little-girl-was-me-shirts-after-debate-comments."There was a little girl in California who was bussed to school. That little girl was me. #DemDebate," her campaign tweeted, as

she was still at the lectern. (Kamala Harris, tweet, June 27, 2019, https://twitter.com/KamalaHarris/status/1144427976609734658.)

298. Hannah Bleau, "Kamala Harris Raises $2 Million 24 Hours after First Debate," Breitbart News, June 29, 2019, https://www.breitbart.com/politics/2019/06/29/kamala-harris-raises-2-million-24-hours-first-debate/

299. Adam Edelman, "Biden, Harris in Virtual Tie after Dramatic Shift in Black Support, Poll Shows," NBC News, July 2, 2019, https://www.nbcnews.com/politics/2020-election/joe-biden-kamala-harris-virtual-tie-democratic-nomination-new-poll-n1025656. Likewise, a CNN poll showed Harris surging into second place after the debate with 17 percent, while Joe Biden crashed to 22 percent. (Jennifer Agiesta, "CNN Poll: Harris and Warren Rise and Biden Slides after First Democratic Debates," CNN, July 1, 2019, https://www.cnn.com/2019/07/01/politics/2020-democratic-candidates-poll/index.html.)

300. President Donald Trump, quoted by Carly Sitrin, "Read: President Trump's Remarks Condemning Violence 'on Many Sides' in Charlottesville," Vox, August 12, 2017, https://www.vox.com/2017/8/12/16138906/president-trump-remarks-condemning-violence-on-many-sides-charlottesville-rally.

301. President Donald Trump, "Statement by President Trump," August 14, 2017, https://www.whitehouse.gov/briefings-statements/statement-president-trump/.

302. *Politico* staff, "Full Text: Trump's Comments on White Supremacists, 'Alt-Left' in Charlottesville," *Politico*, August 15, 2017, https://www.politico.com/story/2017/08/15/full-text-trump-comments-white-supremacists-alt-left-transcript-241662.

303. Dan Merica, "Trump Says Both Sides to Blame amid Charlottesville Backlash." CNN, August 16, 2017, https://www.cnn.com/2017/08/15/politics/trump-charlottesville-delay/index.html.

304. Joel B. Pollak, "Blue State Blues: 'Facts First' CNN Must Retract Charlottesville Hoax," Breitbart News, March 15, 2019, https://www.breitbart.com/the-media/2019/03/15/blue-state-blues-cnn-must-correct-retract-charlottesville-hoax/.

305. Jeremy W. Peters, Jonathan Martin, and Jack Healy, "Trump's Embrace of Racially Charged Past Puts Republicans in Crisis," *New York Times*, August 16, 2017, A1, https://www.nytimes.com/2017/08/16/us/politics/trump-republicans-race.html.

306. Kamala Harris, town hall, CNN, January 28, 2019.

307. Kamala Harris, interview with Jimmy Kimmel.

308. Kamala Harris, quoted in Scott Detrow, "Harris: Justice Dept. 'Would Have No Choice' but to Prosecute Trump after Presidency," National Public Radio, June 12, 2019, https://www.npr.org/2019/06/08/730941386/harris-justice-dept-would-have-no-choice-but-to-prosecute-trump-after-presidency.

309. Kristina Wong, "James Comey Admits He Leaked Memos to Friend to Start Independent Investigation," Breitbart News, June 9, 2017, https://www.breitbart.com/politics/2017/06/09/comey-admits-leaked-memos-friend-start-independent-investigation/.

310. Tom Rogan, "Whoever Convinced Most Democrats That Putin Hacked the Election Tallies Is Doing Putin's Bidding," *Washington Examiner*, November 19, 2018, https://www.washingtonexaminer.com/opinion/whoever-convinced-most -democrats-that-putin-hacked-the-election-tallies-is-doing-putins-bidding.

311. One early casualty was incoming National Security Adviser Michael Flynn, who was caught speaking on the telephone to the Russian ambassador; Obama officials invoked the rarely-enforced Logan Act of 1799, which prevents private citizens from conducting diplomacy, to set a trap for Flynn, who eventually pleaded guilty to lying to the FBI.

312. One had represented the Clinton Foundation; another attended the Clinton victory party on Election Night. There was not one conservative or Republican among them.

313. William Barr, "Special Counsel: No Russia Collusion 'Despite Multiple Offers,'" Breitbart News, March 24, 2019, https://www.breitbart.com/politics/2019 /03/24/special-counsel-no-russia-collusion-despite-multiple-offers/.

314. The Department of Justice has determined that sitting presidents cannot be prosecuted while in office, but they can be prosecuted after leaving office, theoretically.

315. William Barr, quoted in Joel B. Pollak, "Barr on Mueller Report: No Obstruction; Trump Had 'Non-corrupt Motives,'" Breitbart News, April 18, 2019, https://www.breitbart.com/politics/2019/04/18/mueller-report-attorney-general -william-barr-no-obstruction-non-corrupt-motives/.

316. Special Counsel Robert Mueller, letter to Attorney General William Barr, March 27, 2019, https://assets.documentcloud.org/documents/5984398/Mueller -letter.pdf.

317. I found that interesting. If anyone would benefit from "hierarchies among immigrants," it would be Asian immigrants, who typically brought high levels of skill to the country, along with a culture that prized education and hard work. Yet the politically organized Asian American community in Nevada seemed to see itself in solidarity with other communities. It also did not see any value in distinguishing between legal and illegal immigrants; an attack on the latter was an attack on all.

318. As featured in the History Channel show *Pawn Stars*.

319. Paul Bedard, "Boom: Bookies Boost Kamala Harris to 5-to-2 Favorite, Trump's Odds to Win Jump to Best Ever," *Washington Examiner*, June 28, 2019, https://www.washingtonexaminer.com/washington-secrets/boom-bookies-boost -kamala-harris-to-5-to-2-favorite-trumps-odds-to-win-jump-to-best-ever.

320. President Donald Trump, State of the Union address (Washington, DC, February 4, 2020), https://www.whitehouse.gov/briefings-statements/remarks -president-trump-state-union-address-3/.

321. Aaron Bycoffe et al., "The 2020 Endorsement Primary," FiveThirtyEight, accessed March 14, 2020, https://projects.fivethirtyeight.com/2020-endorsements /democratic-primary/.

322. Gavin Newsom, quoted by Carla Marinucci, "Newsom Touts Harris, but Says Buttigieg Is 'Many People's Second Choice,'" *Politico*, May 10, 2019, https://www.politico.com/states/california/story/2019/05/10/newsom-touts-harris-but-says-buttigieg-is-many-peoples-second-choice-1013442.

323. Joel B. Pollak, "Pete Buttigieg Courts Latino Voters in California's Central Valley," Breitbart News, June 4, 2019, https://www.breitbart.com/politics/2019/06/04/pete-buttigieg-courts-latino-voters-in-californias-central-valley/.

324. Michelle Moons, "Family Ties: Kamala Harris Plants Sister at Heart of 2020 Campaign," June 7, 2019, https://www.breitbart.com/politics/2019/06/07/family-ties-kamala-harris-plants-sister-heart-2020-campaign/.

325. Washington Post, second Democratic debate transcript (Detroit, Michigan, July 31, 2019), https://www.washingtonpost.com/politics/2019/08/01/transcript-night-second-democratic-debate/.

326. Frank Bruni, "Debate Disappointment: I Wanted So Much More from Joe Biden," *New York Times*, August 1, 2019, https://www.nytimes.com/2019/08/01/opinion/democratic-debate-biden-harris.html.

327. President Donald Trump, "Remarks by President Trump at a Salute to America," July 4, 2019, https://www.whitehouse.gov/briefings-statements/remarks-president-trump-salute-america/.

328. Joel B. Pollak, "Black Democrats Blast Alexandria Ocasio-Cortez and Chief of Staff," Breitbart News, July 11, 2019, https://www.breitbart.com/politics/2019/07/11/black-democrats-blast-alexandria-ocasio-cortez-and-chief-of-staff/.

329. Nancy Pelosi, quoted by Dowd, "It's Nancy Pelosi's Parade."

330. Joel B. Pollak. "Alexandria Ocasio-Cortez Calls Pelosi Racist: 'Singling Out…Women of Color,'" Breitbart News, July 10, 2019, https://www.breitbart.com/politics/2019/07/10/alexandria-ocasio-cortez-calls-pelosi-racist-singling-out-women-of-color/.

331. Joel B. Pollak. "Black Democrats."

332. President Donald Trump, quoted by Joel B. Pollak, "Donald Trump to Democrat 'Squad': 'Why Don't They Go Back and Help Fix the…Places from Which They Came,'" Breitbart News, July 14, 2019, https://www.breitbart.com/politics/2019/07/14/donald-trump-to-democrat-squad-why-dont-they-go-back-and-help-fix-the-places-from-which-they-came/.

333. Joshua Caplan, "Trump Jabs Nancy Pelosi for 'Very Racist' Phrase 'Make America White Again,'" Breitbart News, July 15, 2019, https://www.breitbart.com/politics/2019/07/15/trump-jabs-nancy-pelosi-for-very-racist-phrase-make-america-white-again/.

334. Caplan, "Trump Jabs Nancy Pelosi."

335. President Donald Trump, tweet, July 15, 2019, https://twitter.com/realDonaldTrump/status/1150879404593205249.

336. President Donald Trump, tweet, July 27, 2019, https://twitter.com/realdonaldtrump/status/1155073965880172544.

337. At first, critics claimed Trump never used such language for white people—until it was pointed out he had used it to describe largely white New Hampshire as "infested" with drugs. Then video emerged of Cummings using similar language about his own district. (Hannah Bleau, "Watch: 1999 Video Shows Cummings Calling His Baltimore District 'Drug-Infested,'" Breitbart News, July 31, 2019, https://www.breitbart.com/politics/2019/07/31/watch-1999-video-shows-cummings-calling-his-baltimore-district-drug-infested/.)

338. *USA Today Sports Weekly,* July 24–30, 2019.

339. Ed White, "28 Years in Prison for Corrupt Ex-Detroit Mayor," Associated Press, October 10, 2013, https://www.breitbart.com/politics/2013/10/10/28-years-in-prison-for-corrupt-ex-detroit-mayor/.

340. Richard Feloni, "Billionaire Dan Gilbert Has Already Bet $5.6 Billion on Detroit's Future, but Money Can't Solve His Biggest Challenge," Business Insider, August 18, 2014, https://www.businessinsider.com/quicken-loans-dan-gilbert-detroit-2018-8.

341. Joel B. Pollak, "Jay Inslee Meets Detroit Muslim Leaders Ahead of Democratic Debate; Denounces Trump's 'Attack,'" Breitbart News, July 30, 2019, https://www.breitbart.com/politics/2019/07/30/muslim-islamic-detroit-democratic-debate-jay-inslee/.

342. Unfortunately for CNN, the theater had not allowed it to cover up the giant FOX logo on the marquee, so the logo remained—dominating the CNN logos that flickered on electronic screens on either side of it.

343. Bullock replaced Eric Swalwell, who had dropped out.

344. Elizabeth Warren, quoted by Thomas Kaplan, "Elizabeth Warren's Slam on John Delaney Was Called the Line of the Night. Here's What She Said," *New York Times,* July 30, 2019. https://www.nytimes.com/2019/07/30/us/politics/elizabeth-warren-debate.html.

345. Marianne Williamson, quoted in The Fix, "Transcript: The First Night of the Second Democratic Debate," *Washington Post,* July 30, 2019, https://beta.washingtonpost.com/politics/2019/07/31/transcript-first-night-second-democratic-debate/.

346. The comment was tweeted by Annie Karni; she appeared to delete the tweet later, writing a more accurate article instead (see Karni and Peters, "Marianne Williamson Has Her Moment").

347. Annie Karni and Jeremy W. Peters, "Marianne Williamson Has Her Moment. And Republicans Are Gleefully Trumpeting It," *New York Times,* July 31, 2019, https://www.nytimes.com/2019/07/31/us/politics/marianne-williamson-democratic-debate.html.

348. Cory Booker, quoted in The Fix, "Transcript: Night 2 of the Second Democratic Debate," *Washington Post,* July 31, 2019, https://www.washingtonpost.com/politics/2019/08/01/transcript-night-second-democratic-debate/.

349. Garner's chilling last words were "I can't breathe." Panatela was fired within weeks of the debate.

350. Harris's own father, an emeritus professor of economics at Stanford University, publicly criticized his daughter when she attempted to defend marijuana use as a cultural norm in Jamaica: "My dear departed grandmothers (whose extraordinary legacy I described in a recent essay on this website), as well as my deceased parents, must be turning in their grave right now to see their family's name, reputation and proud Jamaican identity being connected, in any way, jokingly or not with the fraudulent stereotype of a pot-smoking joy seeker and in the pursuit of identity politics. Speaking for myself and my immediate Jamaican family, we wish to categorically dissociate ourselves from this travesty." Donald Harris, quoted in Penny Starr, "Kamala Harris's Dad Calls Her Out for Perpetuating Pot-Smoking Jamaicans Stereotype," Breitbart News, February 20, 2019, https://www.breitbart.com /politics/2019/02/20/kamala-harriss-dad-calls-her-out-for-perpetuating-pot -smoking-jamaicans-stereotype/.

351. Second Democratic debate.

352. Second Democratic debate.

353. Frank Bruni, "Debate Disappointment."

354. Michael Moore, quoted by Ben Kew, "Michael Moore: America Needs 'Street Fighter' Michelle Obama to Run and 'Crush' Trump," Breitbart News, August 1, 2019, https://www.breitbart.com/entertainment/2019/08/01/michael-moore -america-needs-street-fighter-michelle-obama-to-run-and-crush-trump/.

355. Joe Biden, Political Soapbox remarks (Iowa State Fair, Des Moines, Iowa, August 8, 2019).

356. Bernie Sanders, town hall meeting remarks (Berlin, New Hampshire, August 13, 2019), https://www.youtube.com/watch?v=mLrKZsE40ZA.

357. Elizabeth Warren, first Democratic presidential debate remarks (Miami, Florida, June 26, 2019), https://www.washingtonpost.com/politics/2019/06/27 /transcript-night-one-first-democratic-debate-annotated/.

358. Some peculiar examples: fried Oreos, fried pickles, maple bacon ice cream, and apple strudel funnel cakes.

359. Trump did leave Iowa with a potent weapon. The Cruz campaign had spread a rumor that Ben Carson, a favorite among evangelicals, had dropped out of the race. The misinformation undermined Carson's representatives in caucus meetings. It was, Carson later said, a dirty trick. And it gave weight to the nickname "Lyin' Ted," which Trump used for Cruz for the duration of the campaign.

360. Oprah Winfrey, speech endorsing Barack Obama (Hy-Vee Hall, Des Moines, Iowa, December 8, 2007), https://www.c-span.org/video/?c4544950/user -clip-oprah-endorses-obama.

361. Barack Obama, quoted in Chris Liddell-Westefeld, "'They Said This Day Would Never Come,'" crooked.com, January 3, 2018, https://crooked.com /articles/said-day-never-come/.

362. In fact, Trump had called her murder an act of "terrorism."

363. Rush Limbaugh, for example, congratulated me on the air, calling me "a conservative reporter traveling around trying to set the record straight." Rush Limbaugh,

"Biden Gaffes Embarrass Democrats," *Rush Limbaugh Show*, August 9, 2019, https://www.rushlimbaugh.com/daily/2019/08/09/biden-gaffes-embarrass-democrats-2/.

364. Joe Biden, quoted in Matt Stevens, "Joe Biden Says 'Poor Kids' Are Just as Bright as 'White Kids,'" *New York Times*, August 9, 2019, https://www.nytimes.com/2019/08/09/us/politics/joe-biden-poor-kids.html.

365. Kamala Harris, quoted by Matt Laslo, tweet, September 18, 2019, https://twitter.com/MattLaslo/status/1174363966614773760.

366. Natasha Korecki, "Biden Campaign Says Iowa Is Not a Must-win State," *Politico*, September 3, 2019, https://www.politico.com/story/2019/09/03/joe-biden-iowa-super-tuesday-1479854.

367. This section is adapted from Joel B. Pollak, "Bernie Sanders Barnstorms New Hampshire," Breitbart News, August 12, 2019, https://www.breitbart.com/2020-election/2019/08/12/bernie-sanders-barnstorms-new-hampshire/.

368. Senator Barack Obama, speech (University of Missouri, Columbia, Missouri, October 30, 2008), https://www.realclearpolitics.com/articles/2008/10/obama_rallies_columbia_missour.html.

369. Bernie Sanders, quoted in John Hayward, "Sanders Boasts He Has Better Chance against Trump Than Clinton," Breitbart News, January 19, 2016, https://www.breitbart.com/politics/2016/01/19/sanders-boasts-he-has-better-chance-against-trump-than-clinton/.

370. Straw purchases—purchases made by one person for another—are already illegal under federal law.

371. Adam Sexton, "Warren Speaks to Crowd of Hundreds in Franconia," WMUR, August 14, 2019, https://www.wmur.com/article/warren-speaks-to-crowd-of-hundreds-in-franconia/28704327.

372. Warren's plans, on closer examination, were often retreads of ideas from Sanders, and some quite obviously so. Sanders did not seem to mind: asked by a voter at a town hall in Berlin why he did not "call out" candidates who stole his ideas, Sanders said he was proud to have spread his message. Later, Sanders would copy Warren's wealth tax with one of his own, which went even further and called for the elimination, through taxation, of billionaires. (Thomas Kaplan, "Bernie Sanders Proposes a Wealth Tax: 'I Don't Think That Billionaires Should Exist,'" *New York Times*, September 24, 2019, https://www.nytimes.com/2019/09/24/us/politics/bernie-sanders-wealth-tax.html.)

373. Adam K. Raymond, "Elizabeth Warren Even Has a Selfie Plan," *New York*, June 10, 2019, http://nymag.com/intelligencer/2019/06/elizabeth-warren-even-has-a-selfie-plan.html.

374. Beto O'Rourke campaign, quoted in Eric Wemple, tweet, August 28, 2019, https://twitter.com/ErikWemple/status/1166781426886488065.

375. As the *Wall Street Journal* noted in January that year, Obama had to go around the party machine to win: "Mr. Obama . . . is trying something many observers say has never been done here: He is circumventing entrenched local leadership and building a political machine from scratch." (Christopher Cooper, Valerie

Bauerlein, and Corey Dade, "In South, Democrats' Tactics May Change Political Game," *Wall Street Journal*, January 23, 2008, https://www.wsj.com/articles /SB120105705756408791.)

376. His political career had not yet imploded; the affair discovered by the *National Enquirer* months before had not yet made its way into mainstream media.

377. Bill Clinton, quoted by Kevin Cirilli, "Bill Clinton's 8 Digs at Obama," *Politico*, September 5, 2012, https://www.politico.com/story/2012/09/bill-clintons -8-digs-at-obama-080728.

378. Bill Clinton would also later be accused of trying to "suppress" the black vote in the state by commenting that Jesse Jackson had won it in 1984, to no avail; Hillary Clinton would likewise later be accused of racism for pointing out that she was doing well among white voters.

379. Sean Wilentz, "Race Man," *The New Republic*, February 26, 2008, https:// newrepublic.com/article/62357/race-man.

380. Wilentz also described the charges of racism as the Obama campaign's effort to regroup from losses in New Hampshire and Nevada. As Cinque Henderson would later write, also in the *New Republic*, "In times like these, when a black man is out front in the public eye, black people feel both proud and vulnerable and, as a result, scour the earth for evidence of racists plotting to bring him down.... [Obama] was helping to convince blacks that the first two-term Democratic president in 50 years, a man referred to as the first black president, is in fact a secret racist." (Cinque Henderson, "Maybe We Can't," *The New Republic*, May 27, 2008, https://newrepublic.com/article/60948/maybe-we-cant.)

381. Max Greenwood, "Biden Holds Wide Lead in South Carolina: Poll," *The Hill*, July 25, 2019, https://thehill.com/homenews/campaign/454731-biden-holds -wide-lead-in-south-carolina-poll.

382. A state legislator, who referred to himself as the "short Greek," warmed up the crowd. He joked: "You want the tall Irishman." It fell flat; evidently much of the young crowd really thought "Beto"—the Spanish diminutive for "Roberto"— was actually Latino.

383. O'Rourke failed to tell the crowd that the killer also disavowed any inspiration by Trump.

384. Beto O'Rourke, MSNBC town hall remarks (University of Houston, Houston, Texas, October 30, 2018), http://www.msnbc.com/transcripts/hardball /2018-10-30.

385. Beto O'Rourke campaign, quoted by Erik Wemble, tweet, August 28, 2019, https://twitter.com/ErikWemple/status/1166781426886488065.

386. Eric Bradner and Brian Stelter, "Amid Criticism, O'Rourke Campaign Says It Won't Ban Breitbart from Future Events," CNN, August 28, 2019, https:// www.cnn.com/2019/08/28/media/beto-orourke-breitbart/index.html.

387. I later asked the student what he thought of Biden's answer, and though he said it had been more or less what he expected from a politician, it was also satisfactory.

388. She drew criticism, and scrutiny from the military, for appearing to endorse Biden while in uniform. Kyle Rempfer. "Unit Looking into Army Major in Uniform Telling Biden She Prays He'll Be President," *Army Times*, August 29, 2019, https://www.armytimes.com/news/your-army/2019/08/29/unit-looking-into-army -major-in-uniform-telling-biden-she-prays-hell-be-president/.

389. There had been no policy of medical deferment: migrants applied for deferred action and sometimes—rarely—received it. The Department of Homeland Security resumed allowing people to apply for medical deferments a few weeks later. (Priscilla Alvarez, "Immigration Agency Will Re-allow Requests for Medi-cal Deferments to Avoid Deportation." CNN, September 19, 2019, https://www.cnn .com/2019/09/19/politics/uscis-deferred-action/index.html.)

390. Acting USCIS Director Ken Cucinelli stated that the policy "only affects children who were born outside the US and were not US citizens" and that it "doesn't deny citizenship to the children of US gov[ernment] employees or members of the military born abroad." (Ken Cucinelli, quoted by Neil Munro, "USCIS Chief Ken Cuccinelli Deflates Fake News Scare about Military Kids' Citizenship," Breitbart News, August 29, 2019, https://www.breitbart.com/politics/2019/08/29/uscis-chief -ken-cucinelli-deflates-fake-news-scare-about-military-kids-citizenship/.)

391. Matt Viser and Greg Jaffe, "As He Campaigns for President, Joe Biden Tells a Moving but False War Story," *Washington Post*, August 29, 2019, https://www .washingtonpost.com/politics/as-he-campaigns-for-president-joe-biden-tells-a-moving -but-false-war-story/2019/08/29/b5159676-c9aa-11e9-a1fe-ca46e8d573c0_story.html.

392. Karl Marx, *The Eighteenth Brumaire of Napoleon Bonaparte* (New York: Wildside Press, 2008), 15.

393. Elijah Schaeffer, tweet, September 12, 2019, https://twitter.com/Elijah Schaffer/status/1172324256371396608.

394. For the first two contests, candidates needed 65,000 individual donors or results of 1 percent or higher in least three "qualifying" polls. For the third, can-didates needed 130,000 donors and a minimum of 2 percent in four polls. (Reid J. Epstein and Matt Stevens, "Democratic Debate Rules Will Make It Harder to Get Onstage," *New York Times*, September 23, 2019, https://www.nytimes .com/2019/09/23/us/politics/democratic-debate-criteria.html.)

395. Hannah Bleau, "The Fallen: 15 Democrats Who Dropped Out before a Single 2020 Vote Was Cast," Breitbart News, January 13, 2020, https://www.breitbart .com/politics/2020/01/13/the-fallen-15-resistance-democrats-who-failed-in-2020 -white-house-bids/.

396. Hannah Bleau, "2020 Dems Rally behind Jay Inslee Following His Decision to Drop Presidential Bid," Breitbart News, August 21, 2019, https://www .breitbart.com/politics/2019/08/21/2020-dems-rally-behind-jay-inslee-following-his -decision-to-drop-presidential-bid/.

397. Representative Seth Moulton, interview with Lawrence O'Donnell, *The Last Word*, MSNBC, July 29, 2019, https://www.breitbart.com/clips/2019/07/29 /moulton-trump-is-a-domestic-enemy-of-the-constitution/.

398. President Donald Trump, tweet, August 28, 2019, https://twitter.com /realDonaldTrump/status/1166839524762296320.

399. Charlie Spiering, "Mayor Bill de Blasio Ends Presidential Campaign," Breitbart News, September 20, 2019, https://www.breitbart.com/2020-election/2019 /09/20/mayor-bill-de-blasio-ends-presidential-campaign/.

400. Elizabeth Warren and Beto O'Rourke, third Democratic debate transcript, ABC News, September 12, 2019, https://abcnews.go.com/US/read-full-transcript -abc-news-3rd-democratic-debate/story?id=65587810.

401. Castro had been referring to Biden's statement that people would be able to "buy into" Medicare under his health insurance policy. Castro said Biden wanted people to "buy in." When Biden denied it, saying he would allow people to "opt in" without paying if they could not afford the cost, Castro accused him of having forgotten his previous remarks.

402. Cory Booker, interview with Dana Bash, CNN, September 12, 2019, https://www.cnn.com/videos/politics/2019/09/13/cory-booker-post-abc-debate -biden-moments-sot-vpx.cnn.

403. The ad was placed by a Republican political action committee run by Cambodian immigrant and former congressional candidate Elizabeth Heng.

404. Elizabeth Heng, "New Faces GOP," YouTube, September 13, 2019, https:// www.youtube.com/watch?v=BG0T_hVMqLs.

405. Representative Ilhan Omar (D-MN), another democratic socialist and a close Ocasio-Cortez ally in the Squad of left-wing first-term legislators, demanded an apology—not from Heng herself but from the network, ABC, that aired the ad. (Ilhan Omar, tweet, September 13, 2019, https://twitter.com/ilhanmn/status /1172540301459755008.) The irony of telling the media what to do, in defense of socialism, was lost.

406. Representative Tulsi Gabbard, interview, *Meet the Press*, MSNBC, February 28, 2016, https://www.nbcnews.com/meet-the-press/meet-press-february-28-2016 -n527506.

407. Tulsi Gabbard, interview, *Situation Room*, CNN, April 7, 2016, https:// www.breitbart.com/clips/2016/04/07/dem-rep-gabbard-lot-of-fear-of-consequences -going-against-the-so-called-clinton-machine-in-washington/.

408. Gabbard's decision to resign from the DNC leadership was later vindicated by the Wikileaks scandal, when a trove of emails released—ostensibly with the aid of Russian hackers—on the eve of the party convention in Philadelphia revealed the degree to which party officials had tilted the primary in favor of Clinton and against Sanders. (Tulsi Gabbard, interview, *Situation Room*, CNN, June 17, 2016, https://www.breitbart.com/clips/2016/06/17/former-dnc-vice-chair-gabbard -not-prepared-to-endorse-hillary/.)

409. Howard Dean, interview, *Hardball*, MSNBC, November 21, 2016, https:// www.breitbart.com/clips/2016/11/21/howard-dean-attacks-tulsi-gabbard-extremely -ambitious-with-flexible-principles/.

410. Joel B. Pollak, "Syria—A Rogues' Gallery of Assad's Useful Idiots," Breitbart News, February 7, 2012, https://www.breitbart.com/national-security/2012/02/07/syria-a-rogues-gallery-of-assads-useful-idiots/.

411. Tulsi Gabbard, "Congresswoman Tulsi Gabbard Returns from Syria with Renewed Calls: End Regime Change War in Syria Now," press release, January 25, 2017, https://gabbard.house.gov/news/press-releases/congresswoman-tulsi-gabbard-returns-syria-renewed-calls-end-regime-change-war.

412. Joel B. Pollak, "Tulsi Gabbard Backs Ilhan Omar's Anti-Israel Bill; Also Voted for Pro-Israel Bill," Breitbart News, August 15, 2019, https://www.breitbart.com/2020-election/2019/08/15/tulsi-gabbard-backs-ilhan-omar-anti-israel-bill-also-voted-for-pro-israel-bill/.

413. Tulsi Gabbard, "Elected Leaders Who Weaponize Religion Are Playing a Dangerous Game," The Hill, January 8, 2019, https://thehill.com/blogs/congress-blog/religious-rights/424362-elected-leaders-who-weaponize-religion-are-playing-a.

414. Joel B. Pollak, "Democrat Presidential Contender Tulsi Gabbard under Fire for Past Traditional Marriage Support," Breitbart News, January 13, 2019, https://www.breitbart.com/politics/2019/01/13/democrat-presidential-contender-tulsi-gabbard-under-fire-for-past-traditional-marriage-support/.

415. Tulsi Gabbard, quoted in fourth Democratic debate (Westerville, Ohio, October 15, 2019), https://www.washingtonpost.com/politics/2019/10/15/october-democratic-debate-transcript/.

416. Gabbard, fourth Democratic debate.

417. Tulsi Gabbard, interview with Dave Rubin, Rubin Report, September 8, 2019, https://www.youtube.com/watch?v=5gy797D3cAY.

418. Tulsi Gabbard, quoted in Joel B. Pollak, "Tulsi Gabbard on Winning Drudge Debate Poll: I'm 'Most Qualified' as Commander-in-Chief," Breitbart News, June 26, 2019, https://www.breitbart.com/2020-election/2019/06/26/watch-tulsi-gabbard-speaks-to-breitbart-news-in-debate-spin-room/.

419. Kristina Wong, "Kamala Harris Campaign Blames Russia for Humiliation by Tulsi Gabbard," Breitbart News, August 1, 2019, https://www.breitbart.com/politics/2019/08/01/kamala-harris-campaign-claims-russians-are-behind-tulsi-gabbard-after-hawaii-democrat-lands-attack/.

420. In October 2019, Hillary Clinton claimed that Russia was "grooming" Gabbard to be a third-party candidate. (Hillary Clinton, interview with David Plouffe, Campaign HQ with David Plouffe, October 17, 2019, https://podcasts.google.com/?feed=aHR0cHM6Ly9mZWVkcy5tZWdhcGhvbmUuZm0vaHEtcGx vdWZmZQ&episode=OGE2M2FhMTgtZTZlMS0xMWU5LTk4YWEtNTM 4NTJiZDViMzc5&hl=en&ved=2ahUKEwjzmZSA-KXlAhXmm-AKHZsMC_AQieUEegQIABAE&ep=6&at=1571406131757.) Gabbard retorted that Clinton was "the queen of warmongers, embodiment of corruption, and personification of the rot that has sickened the Democratic Party for so long." (Tulsi Gabbard, tweet, October 18, 2019, https://twitter.com/TulsiGabbard/status/1185289626409406464.)

She later sued Clinton for defamation. (Tulsi Gabbard, "Rep. Tulsi Gabbard Files Lawsuit against Hillary Clinton over Defamatory Statements," press release, January 22, 2020, https://www.tulsi2020.com/press/2020-01-22-rep-tulsi-gabbard-files -lawsuit-against-hillary-clinton-over-defamatory-statements.)

421. The Drudge Report, quoted in Don Surber blog post, "Drudge Goes All In for Warren," August 15, 2019, https://donsurber.blogspot.com/2019/08/drudge -goes-all-in-for-warren.html.

422. Joel B. Pollak, "Fact Check: Elizabeth Warren Exaggerates Crowd Sizes for the Third Time," Breitbart News, September 18, 2019, https://www.breitbart .com/2020-election/2019/09/18/fact-check-elizabeth-warren-exaggerates-crowd -sizes-for-the-third-time/.

423. Trump filled the SNHU Arena and shattered an attendance record previously held by rock star Elton John, with thousands more outside. (Joel B. Pollak, "Fire Marshal Fact-Checks Fake News about Trump New Hampshire Rally Attendance," Breitbart News, August 18, 2019, https://www.breitbart.com /the-media/2019/08/18/fire-marshal-fact-checks-fake-news-about-trump-new -hampshire-rally-attendance/.)

424. He added, "But don't worry, we will revive it. It can be revived. It will be revived. And it can be revived very easily, and very quickly, and we're gonna have some fun in the state of New Hampshire." (President Donald Trump, speech [Manchester, New Hampshire, August 15, 2019], https://www.c-span.org/video/?463428-1 /president-trump-holds-rally-manchester-hampshire&start=650.)

425. "2020 Democratic Presidential Nomination," RealClearPolitics, accessed March 17, 2020. https://www.realclearpolitics.com/epolls/2020/president/us/2020 _democratic_presidential_nomination-6730.html.

426. Joel B. Pollak, "Bernie Sanders Ad Touts Him as 'First Jewish President,'" Breitbart News, February 17, 2020, https://www.breitbart.com/politics/2020/02/17 /bernie-sanders-ad-touts-him-as-the-first-jewish-president/.

427. Nina Turner, remarks (Santa Monica, California, July 26, 2019), https:// www.breitbart.com/2020-election/2019/07/26/bernie-sanders-california/.

428. Kristina Wong, tweet, September 12, 2019, https://twitter.com/kristina _wong/status/1172366070440747008. Buttigieg would make it through his entire campaign without answering questions on the floor of the spin room.

429. Hannah Bleau, "Bernie Sanders Cancels Campaign Events after Emergency Heart Surgery," Breitbart News, October 2, 2019, https://www.breitbart.com /politics/2019/10/02/bernie-sanders-cancels-campaign-events-after-emergency -heart-surgery/.

430. James Freeman, "Elizabeth Warren's Unconstitutional Wealth Tax," Wall Street Journal, January 25, 2019, https://www.wsj.com/articles/elizabeth-warrens -unconstitutional-wealth-tax-11548442306?mod=article_inline.

431. Brooke Singman and Justin Berger, "Warren's $52T 'Medicare-for-all' Plan Revealed: Campaign Still Claims No Middle-Class Tax Hikes Needed," Fox News,

November 1, 2019, https://www.foxnews.com/politics/warrens-52t-medicare-for-all -plan-revealed-campaign-still-claims-no-middle-class-tax-hikes-needed.

432. Sean Moran, " 'Medicare for All' Scholar: Bernie Sanders Misunderstood Study, Socialized Medicine Might Cost $38 Trillion," Breitbart News, August 2, 2019, https://www.breitbart.com/politics/2018/08/02/medicare-for-all-scholar-bernie -sanders-misunderstood-study-socialized-medicine-might-cost-38-trillion/.

433. Elizabeth Warren, interview with Stephen Colbert, *The Late Show with Stephen Colbert*, September 18, 2019, https://www.youtube.com/watch?v=J8t6oq gqGxo.

434. Ben Kew, " 'Saturday Night Live' Mocks Elizabeth Warren's $52 Trillion Medicare for All Plan," Breitbart News, November 3, 2019, https://www .breitbart.com/entertainment/2019/11/03/saturday-night-live-mocks-elizabeth -warren-52-trillion-medicare-for-all/.

435. Caitlin Emma and Connor O'Brien, "Trump Holds Up Ukraine Military Aid Meant to Confront Russia," *Politico*, August 29, 2019, https://www.politico.com /story/2019/08/28/trump-ukraine-military-aid-russia-1689531.

436. "Trump Tries to Force Ukraine to Meddle in the 2020 Election," *Washington Post*, September 5, 2019, https://www.washingtonpost.com/opinions/global -opinions/is-trump-strong-arming-ukraines-new-president-for-political-gain /2019/09/05/4eb239b0-cffa-11e9-8c1c-7c8ee785b855_story.html. There is reason to believe that Representative Adam Schiff, chair of the House Intelligence Committee, could have been the *Post*'s source. (Joel B. Pollak, "Pollak: Did Adam Schiff Out Himself as Leaker to Washington Post?," Breitbart News, January 23, 2020, https:// www.breitbart.com/politics/2020/01/23/pollak-did-adam-schiff-out-himself-as -leaker-to-washington-post/.)

437. Rebecca Balhaus, "House Panels Investigate Trump Pressure on Ukraine," *Wall Street Journal*, September 9, 2019, https://www.wsj.com/articles/house-panels -investigate-trump-pressure-on-ukraine-11568066824.

438. Dustin Volz and Siobhan Hughes, "Whistleblower Complaint Involves Trump Communication with Foreign Leader," *Wall Street Journal*, September 19, 2019, https://www.wsj.com/articles/whistleblower-complaint-involves-trump -communication-with-foreign-leader-11568898983.

439. Adam Schiff, interview with Sam Stein, *Morning Joe*, MSNBC. September 17, 2019, https://www.youtube.com/watch?v=-_QTxCTI-w0&feature=youtu .be&t=121.

440. U.S. Const. art. II, § 4.

441. In February 2017, liberal pundit Sally Kohn tweeted: "Straightforward from here: 1. Impeach Trump & Pence 2. Constitution crisis 3. Call special election 4. Ryan v Clinton 5. President Clinton." (Sally Kohn, tweet, February 15, 2017, https://twitter.com/sallykohn/status/831871003412295682.) What Pence was to be impeached for was never made clear. She later said that the tweet was meant to be sarcastic, but it reflected the fact that people on the left were really trying to

think through a way to see Trump impeached and removed. (Sally Kohn, tweet, February 15, 2017, https://twitter.com/sallykohn/status/831876258573201409.)

442. Harvard Law School professor emeritus Alan Dershowitz has observed that Republicans were also talking about impeaching a potential President Hillary Clinton in the event that she won the 2016 election, based on her past alleged violation of federal laws on the handling of classified information and federal records with her use of an illicit private email server.

443. "'Impeachment' is already on the lips of pundits, newspaper editorials, constitutional scholars, and even a few members of Congress. From the right, Washington attorney Bruce Fein puts the odds at 50/50 that a President Trump commits impeachable offenses as president. Liberal Florida Representative Alan Grayson says Trump's insistence on building a wall at the U.S.-Mexico border, if concrete was poured despite Congress's opposition, could lead down a path toward impeachment. Even the mainstream Republican head of the U.S. Chamber of Commerce recently tossed out the I-word when discussing the civilian backlash if Trump's trade war with China led to higher prices on everyday items sold at Walmart and Target." (Darren Samuelsohn, "Could Trump Be Impeached Shortly after He Takes Office?," *Politico*, April 17, 2016, https://www.politico.com/magazine/story/2016/04/donald-trump-2016-impeachment-213817.)

444. Laurence H. Tribe, "Donald Trump Will Violate the U.S. Constitution on Inauguration Day," *Guardian*, December 19, 2016, https://www.theguardian.com/commentisfree/2016/dec/19/donald-trump-violate-us-constitution-inauguration-day.

445. A campaign finance investigation into "hush money" payments to porn star Stormy Daniels, for example, ended with a whimper: it turned out you could not prosecute a candidate for spending his own money on a personal matter. Stormy Daniels fired her lawyer, Michael Avenatti, whom the media had elevated to a chief Trump antagonist, such that he began discussing his own presidential prospects; he was later indicted by federal prosecutors in both California and New York and convicted of extortion in the latter.

446. Representative Adam Schiff, "Congress Must Ensure That Trump Is Working for the American People—Not Foreign Interests," *Washington Post*, April 22, 2019, https://www.washingtonpost.com/opinions/adam-schiff-congress-must-assure-that-trump-is-working-for-the-american-people--not-foreign-interests/2019/04/22/ac403f06-6532-11e9-82ba-fcfeff232e8f_story.html.

447. Nancy Pelosi, "Transcript: Nancy Pelosi's Public and Private Remarks on Trump Impeachment," NBC News, September 24, 2019, https://www.nbcnews.com/politics/trump-impeachment-inquiry/transcript-nancy-pelosi-s-speech-trump-impeachment-n1058351.

448. "Memorandum of Telephone Conversation," White House, September 24, 2019, https://www.whitehouse.gov/wp-content/uploads/2019/09/Unclassified09.2019.pdf.

449. Joe Biden, quoted by John Solomon, "Joe Biden's 2020 Ukrainian Nightmare: A Closed Probe Is Revived," *The Hill*, April 1, 2019, https://thehill.com

/opinion/white-house/436816-joe-bidens-2020-ukrainian-nightmare-a-closed
-probe-is-revived.

450. Haris Alic, "Hunter Biden's $83K per Month Burisma Salary Raises Questions about Role," Breitbart News, September 25, 2019, https://www.breitbart.com /politics/2019/09/25/hunter-bidens-83k-per-month-burisma-salary-raises-questions -about-role/.

451. Rebecca Mansour, "NYT Confirms Hunter Biden Bank of China Deal, Leaves Out Key Details," Breitbart News, May 21, 2019, https://www.breitbart.com /politics/2019/05/21/nyt-confirms-hunter-biden-bank-of-china-deal-leaves-out-key -details/.

452. Kenneth P. Vogel, "Rudy Giuliani Plans Ukraine Trip to Push for Inquiries That Could Help Trump," New York Times, May 9, 2019.

453. Anonymous letter to Richard Burr and Adam Schiff, August 12, 2019, https://www.scribd.com/document/427565143/House-Intel-whistleblower -complaint#from_embed.

454. Volodymyr Zelensky, press conference (New York, New York, September 25, 2019), https://www.whitehouse.gov/briefings-statements/remarks-president -trump-president-zelensky-ukraine-bilateral-meeting-new-york-ny/.

455. President Donald Trump, tweet, September 26, 2019, https://twitter.com /realDonaldTrump/status/1177182149050609664.

456. Lisa Lerer, "What, Exactly, Is Tulsi Gabbard Up To?," New York Times, October 12, 2019, https://www.nytimes.com/2019/10/12/us/politics/tulsi-gabbard .html.

457. Tulsi Gabbard, quoted in Kristina Wong, "Tulsi Gabbard Considering Debate Boycott, Says DNC and Corporate Media 'Rigging' the 2020 Primary," Breitbart News, October 10, 2019, https://www.breitbart.com/politics/2019/10/10 /dnc-corporate-media-rigging-2020-primary/.

458. Joshua Caplan, "Climate Change Crusader Tom Steyer Enters 2020 Presidential Race," Breitbart News, July 9, 2019, https://www.breitbart.com/politics /2019/07/09/tom-steyer-enters-2020-presidential-race/.

459. He had found a way of gaming the Democrats' qualification criteria, which gave a special role to poll numbers in the early primary states. Steyer simply pumped money into advertising in Nevada and South Carolina to juice his numbers, while other candidates crowded into Iowa and New Hampshire. Critics accused him of buying his way onto the stage, but all he had done is play by the rules of the game. (Joel B. Pollak, "Impeachment Activist Tom Steyer Qualifies for October Democrat Debate," Breitbart News, September 8, 2019, https://www.breitbart.com/2020-election /2019/09/08/impeachment-activist-tom-steyer-qualifies-for-october-democrat-debate/.)

460. Washington Post, fourth Democratic debate transcript (Otterbein University, Westerville, Ohio, October 15, 2019, https://www.washingtonpost.com /politics/2019/10/15/october-democratic-debate-transcript/.

461. There were several other clashes, many centering around Buttigieg. He criticized Elizabeth Warren over Medicare for All, accusing her of leaving a "giant

multi-trillion-dollar hole" and avoiding "a yes-or-no question" on whether to raise middle-class taxes to fill it. Amy Klobuchar summed it up: "At least Bernie's being honest here and saying how he's going to pay for this and that taxes are going to go up. And I'm sorry, Elizabeth, but you have not said that." Buttigieg also quarreled with Gabbard over whether to withdraw from Syria: he opposed it, and she favored it.

462. Schiff had been one of the leading proponents of the "Russia collusion" conspiracy theory punctured by the Mueller investigation. In March 2017, Schiff— who had unique access to classified information, even as the ranking member (i.e., the leader of the opposition party in the committee)—told MSNBC that there was "more than circumstantial" evidence that Trump had colluded with Russia to win the presidency. (Adam Schiff, interview with Chuck Todd, *Meet the Press Daily*, MSNBC, March 22, 2017.) Judiciary Committee chair Representative Jerrold Nadler (D-NY) was also a potentially problematic inquisitor, known for hamfisted tactics. In November 2018, for example, shortly after Democrats won the House in the midterm elections, conservative journalist Mollie Hemingway overheard Nadler talking loudly on his cell phone on the Amtrak Acela express train about his plans to impeach Trump and newly installed Supreme Court justice Brett Kavanaugh. (Mollie Hemingway, "Incoming Democrat Chairman: Dems Will Go 'All-In' on Russia, Impeach Kavanaugh for 'Perjury,'" The Federalist, November 7, 2018, https://thefederalist.com/2018/11/07/incoming-democrat-chairman-dems -will-go-all-in-on-russia-impeach-kavanaugh-for-perjury/.)

463. The official name of the committee is the House Permanent Select Committee on Intelligence (HPSCI).

464. Catherine Croft, quoted in Joel B. Pollak, "Catherine Croft, the Key Witness Left in Adam Schiff's Basement," Breitbart News, December 13, 2019, https:// www.breitbart.com/politics/2019/12/13/catherine-croft-the-key-witness-left-in -adam-schiffs-basement/.

465. Julian E. Barnes, "Schiff Got Early Account of Accusations as Whistle-Blower's Concerns Grew," *New York Times*, October 2, 2019, https://www.nytimes .com/2019/10/02/us/politics/adam-schiff-whistleblower.html.

466. Joel B. Pollak, "WATCH: Democrat Jackie Speier Proves No Law Protects Whistleblower Identity," Breitbart News, November 20, 2019, https://www .breitbart.com/politics/2019/11/20/democrat-jackie-speier-proves-no-law-protects -whistleblower-identity/.

467. Paul Sperry, "The Beltway's 'Whistleblower' Furor Obsesses over One Name," RealClearInvestigations, October 30, 2019, https://www.realclear investigations.com/articles/2019/10/30/whistleblower_exposed_close_to_biden _brennan_dnc_oppo_researcher_120996.html.

468. H.R. Res. 660, 116th Cong. (2019), https://www.congress.gov/bill/116th -congress/house-resolution/660/text.

469. John Carney, "Unemployment Falls to Lowest Level Since 1969," Breitbart News, October 4, 2019, https://www.breitbart.com/economy/2019/10/04/the -economy-created-136000-jobs-in-september-unemployment-fell-to-3-5/.

470. President Donald Trump, "Remarks by President Trump on the Death of ISIS Leader Abu Bakr al-Baghdadi," White House, October 27, 2019, https://www.whitehouse.gov/briefings-statements/remarks-president-trump-death-isis-leader-abu-bakr-al-baghdadi/.

471. President Bill Clinton, MTV town hall meeting, MTV, April 19, 1994, https://www.c-span.org/video/?56190-1/mtv-town-hall-meeting&start=177.

472. Janell Ross, "What You Need to Know about GOP Debate Moderator Jake Tapper," *Washington Post*, September 16, 2015, https://www.washingtonpost.com/news/the-fix/wp/2015/09/16/what-you-need-to-know-about-gop-debate-moderator-jake-tapper/.

473. Joel B. Pollak, "CNN Lets Students Attack Dana Loesch as a Bad Mother at Town Hall on Guns," Breitbart News, February 22, 2018, https://www.breitbart.com/the-media/2018/02/22/jake-tapper-allows-two-students-attack-dana-loesch-mother/.

474. John Nolte, "Nolte: CNN Wins Cronkite Award for Jake Tapper's Rape Victim-Booing Town Hall," Breitbart News, March 20, 2019, https://www.breitbart.com/the-media/2019/03/20/nolte-cnn-wins-cronkite-award-for-jake-tappers-rape-victim-booing-town-hall/.

475. Joel B. Pollak, "Fact Check: Jake Tapper Correctly Explains Fracking Reduces U.S. Emissions," Breitbart News, March 15, 2020, https://www.breitbart.com/politics/2020/03/15/fact-check-jake-tapper-correctly-explains-fracking-reduces-u-s-emissions/.

476. CNN climate town hall, CNN, September 4, 2019.

477. Kristina Wong, "Joe Biden's Eye Fills with Blood While Onstage During Climate Town Hall," Breitbart News, September 4, 2019, https://www.breitbart.com/politics/2019/09/04/joe-bidens-eye-fills-with-blood-while-onstage-during-climate-town-hall/.

478. This was the only time in the entire election cycle that I was denied credentials to an event.

479. Elizabeth Warren, appearance on CNN equity town hall, October 10, 2019, https://www.breitbart.com/videos/v/XiMKh0qa/.

480. Cooper felt compelled to explain to those watching at home: "Let me just point out there is a long and proud tradition and history in the gay and lesbian and transgender community of protest and we applaud them for their protest. They are absolutely right to be angry and upset at the lack of attention, particularly in the media, on the lives of transgender[s]." (Matt Perdie, "Watch—Trans Activists Disrupt CNN LGBTQ Town Hall," Breitbart News, October 10, 2019, https://www.breitbart.com/politics/2019/10/10/watch-trans-activists-disrupt-cnn-lgbtq-town-hall/.)

481. Alexandria Ocasio-Cortez, tweet, February 19, 2020, https://twitter.com/AOC/status/1230340518418186240.

482. Representative Mike Turner, hearing, House Intelligence Committee, September 26, 2019, https://www.justsecurity.org/wp-content/uploads/2019/11/ukraine-clearinghouse-maguire-testimony-transcript-2019.09.26.pdf.

483. Robert Kraychik, "Drag Queen 'Pissi Myles' Crashes Impeachment Hearing," Breitbart News, November 13, 2019, https://www.breitbart.com/pre-viral/2019/11/13/drag-queen-pissi-myles-crashes-impeachment-hearing/.

484. Officially, his title is deputy assistant secretary in the European and Eurasian Bureau.

485. Representative Adam Schiff, hearing, House Intelligence Committee, September 26, 2019, https://www.justsecurity.org/wp-content/uploads/2019/11/ukraine-clearinghouse-maguire-testimony-transcript-2019.09.26.pdf.

486. Representative Mike Turner, hearing, September 26, 2019.

487. Hannah Bleau, "'Disgrace': GOP Rips Adam Schiff for Making Up Trump Quote, Then Claiming 'Parody,'" Breitbart News, September 26, 2019, https://www.breitbart.com/politics/2019/09/26/gop-disgrace-adam-schiff-made-up-trump-quote-claimed-parody/.

488. My reaction at the time in a tweet: "This guy used to be a prosecutor? Lost in detail about foreign policy, conspiracy theories..." (Joel B. Pollak, November 13, 2019, https://twitter.com/joelpollak/status/1194634711185780740.)

489. Nick Ackerman, quoted in Robert Kraychik, "Watergate Prosecutor Fumbles in Debate with Joel Pollak: 'Impeachment Does Not Center on Legal-Illegal,'" Breitbart News, November 14, 2019, https://www.breitbart.com/politics/2019/11/14/watergate-prosecutor-fumbles-in-debate-with-joel-pollak-impeachment-does-not-center-on-legal-illegal/.

490. Joshua Caplan, "Beto O'Rourke Quits 2020 Race," Breitbart News, November 1, 2019, https://www.breitbart.com/2020-election/2019/11/01/beto-orourke-quits-2020-race/.

491. Alexander Burns, "Warren Leads Tight Iowa Race as Biden Fades, Poll Finds," New York Times, November 1, 2019, https://www.nytimes.com/2019/11/01/us/politics/iowa-poll-warren-biden.html.

492. Joe Biden campaign, quoted in Rick Klein, tweet, November 1, 2019, https://twitter.com/rickklein/status/1190277878501593088.

493. Gregory Korte and Tyler Pager, "Warren Derides Biden as Running in 'Wrong Presidential Primary,'" Bloomberg News, November 1, 2019, https://www.bloomberg.com/news/articles/2019-11-01/warren-derides-biden-as-running-in-wrong-presidential-primary.

494. Greg Schultz, tweet, November 1, 2019, https://twitter.com/schultzohio/status/1190389602466615296.

495. It was neither the first time, nor the last, that he would mix up his states. (Joe Biden, quoted in GOP War Room, "While in Iowa, Joe Biden Says He Is in 'Ohio,'" November 2, 2019, https://www.youtube.com/watch?v=3MHFZMLyNwg.)

496. Deval Patrick, "Deval Patrick Announcement Video," YouTube, November 14, 2019, https://www.youtube.com/watch?v=IJCY7qN48hU.

497. Caroline Kelly and Dan Merica, "Steyer Aide at Center of Iowa Pay for Endorsement Controversy Resigns," CNN, November 8, 2019, https://www.cnn.com/2019/11/08/politics/steyer-aide-resigns-iowa/index.html.

498. Tucker Higgins, "Pete Buttigieg Makes Big South Carolina Ad Buy as Campaign Seeks Elusive Black Support," CNBC, November 14, 2019, https://www.cnbc.com/2019/11/14/buttigieg-makes-south-carolina-ad-buy-as-campaign-seeks-black-support.html.

499. Joel B. Pollak, "Mayor Pete Buttigieg under Fire for Exaggerating Black Support," Breitbart News, November 17, 2019, https://www.breitbart.com/2020-election/2019/11/17/mayor-pete-buttigieg-under-fire-for-exaggerating-black-support/.

500. Stephanie Saul, "Buttigieg Campaign Used Stock Photo of Kenyan Woman to Illustrate Plan for Black America," *New York Times*, November 18, 2019, https://www.nytimes.com/2019/11/18/us/politics/buttigieg-stock-photo-kenya.html. Frederick Douglass, the great abolitionist, was a Republican.

501. Jonathan Martin et al., "How Kamala Harris's Campaign Unraveled," *New York Times*, November 29, 2019, https://www.nytimes.com/2019/11/29/us/politics/kamala-harris-2020.html.

502. Kyle Morris, "Ilhan Omar: Bernie Sanders 'a President Who Will Fight against Western Imperialism,'" Breitbart News, November 3, 2019, https://www.breitbart.com/politics/2019/11/03/ilhan-omar-bernie-sanders-a-president-who-will-fight-against-western-imperialism/.

503. Averi Harper, "Sanders, Campaigning with AOC, Says Potential Bloomberg Bid Shows 'the Arrogance of Billionaires,'" ABC News, November 10, 2019, https://abcnews.go.com/Politics/sanders-campaigning-aoc-potential-bloomberg-bid-shows-arrogance/story?id=66881233.

504. Barack Obama, quoted in Isabella Nikolic, "Bernie Sanders Hits Back at Obama, Insisting He Is 'Not Tearing Down the System,' after Former President Warned Democrat White House Hopefuls Not to Alienate Voters by Veering Too Far to the Left," *Daily Mail*, November 18, 2019, https://www.dailymail.co.uk/news/article-7697543/Bernie-Sanders-hits-Barack-Obama-insisting-not-tearing-system.html.

505. Obama, quoted in Nikolic, "Bernie Sanders Hits Back."

506. Lt. Col. Alexander Vindman, closed-door testimony at House Permanent Select Committee on Intelligence, October 29, 2019, https://www.npr.org/2019/11/08/777514772/read-testimony-of-alexander-vindman-the-white-houses-ukraine-specialist.

507. Ironically, Schiff had once pressed for the whistleblower to testify. (Adam Schiff, quoted in Josh Mitchell, "Whistleblower Is Expected to Testify Soon, House Intelligence Chairman Schiff Says," *Wall Street Journal*, September 29, 2019, https://www.wsj.com/articles/whistleblower-is-expected-to-testify-soon-house-intelligence-committee-chairman-says-11569768797.)

508. Joel B. Pollak, "Read: Alexander Vindman on 'Individual in the Intelligence Community,'" Breitbart News, November 19, 2019, https://www.breitbart.com/national-security/2019/11/19/read-vindman-refuses-to-name-individual-in-intelligence-community-he-gave-transcript/.

509. Sondland was a former Never Trump Republican who bought his way back into the party's good graces with a $1 million donation to the inauguration committee. (Joel B. Pollak, "Gordon Sondland: Jeb! Donor, Never Trumper, Key Impeachment Witness," Breitbart News, November 24, 2019, https://www.breitbart.com /politics/2019/11/24/gordon-sondland-jeb-donor-never-trumper-key-impeachment -witness/.)

510. Rachel Bade et al., "Sondland Acknowledges Ukraine Quid Pro Quo, Implicates Trump, Pence, Pompeo and Others," *Washington Post*, November 20, 2019, https://www.washingtonpost.com/politics/sondland-was-there-a-quid-pro-quo -the-answer-is-yes/2019/11/20/34741e3c-0b92-11ea-8397-a955cd542d00_story .html.

511. Gordon Sondland, testimony before House Intelligence Committee, November 20, 2019, https://www.washingtonpost.com/politics/2019/11/20/transcript -sondlands-nov-public-testimony-front-house-intelligence-committee/.

512. Joel B. Pollak, "WATCH: Pete Buttigieg Supporters Cannot Name Any Achievements," Breitbart News, November 20, 2019, https://www.breitbart.com /2020-election/2019/11/20/watch-pete-buttigieg-supporters-cannot-name-any -achievements/.

513. Joel B. Pollak, "Democrats Court Al Sharpton; Ignore Past of Racism, Antisemitism, Incitement," Breitbart News, April 3, 2019, https://www .breitbart.com/politics/2019/04/03/democrats-court-al-sharpton-ignore-past-of -racism-antisemitism-incitement/.

514. Matt Pearce, "Black Residents of South Bend Unload on Mayor Pete Buttigieg," *Los Angeles Times*, June 23, 2019, https://www.latimes.com/politics/la-na -pol-2020-pete-buttigieg-mayor-police-shooting-black-voters-20190624-story.html.

515. Aaron Franco, tweet, June 23, 2019, https://twitter.com/AFrancoTX /status/1142892119348121601.

516. Pete Buttigieg, quoted by Joshua Caplan, "South Bend Police Blast Pete Buttigieg for Using Shooting 'Solely for His Political Gain,'" Breitbart News, June 25, 2019, https://www.breitbart.com/2020-election/2019/06/25/south-bend-police-bl ast-pete-buttigieg-for-using-shooting-solely-for-his-political-gain/.

517. The local police union declared: "Mayor Buttigieg's comments have already and will continue to have a detrimental effect on local law enforcement officers and law enforcement officers nationwide." (Fraternal Order of Police Lodge No. 36, quoted by Jessica Campisi, "South Bend Police Union Says Buttigieg Using Police Shooting 'Solely for His Political Gain,'" *The Hill*, June 25, 2019, https://thehill.com/homenews/campaign/450190-south-bend-police-union-accuses -buttigieg-of-using-police-shooting-solely.)

518. Nina Turner, quoted in Hayley Miller, tweet, November 20, 2019, https:// twitter.com/hayleymiller01/status/1197178908988366848.

519. Pete Buttigieg, fifth presidential debate remarks (Atlanta, Georgia, November 20, 2019), https://www.nbcnews.com/politics/2020-election/read-democratic -debate-transcript-november-20-2019-n1088186.

520. Kamala Harris, quoted in Marina Pitofsky, "Harris: Buttigieg Comparing 'Struggles' between Black, LGBTQ Communities Is 'a Bit Naïve,'" *The Hill*, November 21, 2019, https://thehill.com/homenews/campaign/471554-harris -accuses-buttigieg-of-comparing-struggles-between-black-lgbtq.

521. Jerrold Nadler, quoted by Lisa Getter and Alan C. Miller, "Records Give Rare Glimpse into Cost of Starr's Probe," *Los Angeles Times*, October 29, 1998, https://www.latimes.com/archives/la-xpm-1998-oct-29-mn-37331-story.html.

522. Representative Jerrold Nadler, speech before House of Representatives (Washington, DC, December 18, 1998), https://www.breitbart.com/politics /2019/12/04/jerry-nadler-warns-must-never-be-partisan-impeachment-effort/.

523. Representative Jerrold Nadler, speech at U.S. Capitol. (Washington, DC, December 17, 1998), https://www.c-span.org/video/?c4819316/user-clip-1998-jerry -nadler-impeachment-undoing-national-election.

524. Representative Jerrold Nadler, quoted in Caitlin Oprysko, "House Dem: Impeaching Trump on Party Lines Would 'Tear the Country Apart,'" *Politico*, November 26, 2018, https://www.politico.com/story/2018/11/26/nadler-evidence -impeachable-offense-trump-1014702.

525. Heather Caygle and Sarah Ferris, "'I'm Not Going to Take Any Sh—': Nadler Girds for Battle," *Politico*, December 3, 2018, https://www.politico.com /news/2019/12/03/nadler-judiciary-impeachment-074985.

526. House Permanent Select Committee on Intelligence, "The Trump-Ukraine Impeachment Inquiry Report," December 3, 2019, https://intelligence .house.gov/uploadedfiles/the_trump-ukraine_impeachment_inquiry_report .pdf.

527. Most striking of all, it used telephone records, subpoenaed from AT&T, to imply that Ranking Member Devin Nunes had been part of a conspiracy to smear former U.S. ambassador to Ukraine Marie Yovanovitch. Not only did Nunes deny the allegation, but he noted that his civil liberties—as well as those of a journalist, the president's lawyer, and others—had been violated by Schiff's subterfuge. (Devin Nunes, quoted in "Devin Nunes: Adam Schiff Violated My 'Civil Liberties' with Phone Snooping; Pursuing 'All Legal Options,'" Breitbart News, December 4, 2009, https://www.breitbart.com/politics/2019/12/04/devin-nunes-adam-schiff -violated-my-civil-liberties-phone-snooping-legal-options/.)

528. Joel B. Pollak, "Jerry Nadler: House Rules Don't Apply until After Impeachment," Breitbart News, December 12, 2019, https://www.breitbart.com /politics/2019/12/12/jerry-nadler-house-rules-impeachment/.

529. Russell Berman, "Is a Third Lawyer the Charm for House Republicans?," *The Atlantic*, November 18, 2014, https://www.theatlantic.com/politics /archive/2014/11/Speaker-John-Boehner-hires-Jonathan-Turley-to-sue-president -executive-overreach/382884/.

530. Noah Feldman, quoted in Joel B. Pollak, "Democrats Used Deceptively Edited Video of Trump in Judiciary Committee Impeachment Hearing," Breitbart News, December 6, 2019, https://www.breitbart.com/politics/2019/12/06/democrats

-used-deceptively-edited-video-of-trump-in-judiciary-committee-impeachment
-hearing/.

531. White House, transcript of call between President Donald Trump and
Ukrainian President Volodymyr Zelensky, July 25, 2019, https://www.whitehouse
.gov/wp-content/uploads/2019/09/Unclassified09.2019.pdf.

532. Joshua Kaplan, "Impeachment Star Witness Pamela Karlan Forced to
'Apologize' for Mocking Barron Trump," Breitbart News, December 4, 2019, https://
www.breitbart.com/politics/2019/12/04/pamela-karlan-apologizes-for-invoking
-barron-trump-but-urges-president-to-say-sorry-too/.

533. Jonathan Turley, opening statement before House Judiciary Committee (Washington, DC, December 4, 2019), https://www.breitbart.com/politics
/2019/12/04/jonathan-turleys-impeachment-testimony-democrats-setting-terrible
-precedent/.

534. Jonathan Turley, quoted in Joel B. Pollak, "Turley Warns Congress on
Impeachment for 'Obstruction': 'It's YOUR Abuse of Power,'" Breitbart News,
December 4, 2019, https://www.breitbart.com/politics/2019/12/04/impeachment
-turley-warns-congress-its-your-abuse-of-power/.

535. Joshua Caplan, "Nancy Pelosi Announces Democrats Will Begin Draft-
ing Articles of Impeachment," Breitbart News, December 5, 2019, https://www
.breitbart.com/politics/2019/12/05/nancy-pelosi-announces-democrats-will-begin
-drafting-articles-of-impeachment/.

536. Joel B. Pollak, "Democrat Counsel Daniel Goldman Refuses to Say
Who Ordered Phone Snooping," Breitbart News, December 9, 2019, https://www
.breitbart.com/politics/2019/12/09/democrat-counsel-daniel-goldman-refuses-to-say
-who-ordered-phone-snooping/.

537. James Sensenbrenner, remarks at House Judiciary Committee hearing
(Washington, DC, December 9, 2019), https://www.breitbart.com/politics/2019/12
/09/james-sensenbrenner-to-democrat-impeachment-lawyer-you-have-made-joe
-mccarthy-look-like-a-piker/.

538. Joel B. Pollak, "Democrat Counsels Barry Berke, Daniel Goldman Donated
Thousands to Hillary Clinton, Barack Obama," Breitbart News, December 9, 2019,
https://www.breitbart.com/politics/2019/12/09/democrat-impeachment-counsels
-barry-berke-daniel-goldman-donated-thousands-to-hillary-clinton-barack-obama/.

539. Representative Louie Gohmert, remarks at House Judiciary Committee hearing (Washington, DC, December 9, 2019), https://thehill.com/homenews
/house/473691-judiciary-hearing-gets-heated-as-democratic-counsel-interrogates
-gop-staffer.

540. Representative Jerrold Nadler, closing statement, House Judiciary Committee, December 9, 2019, https://www.youtube.com/watch?v=IVUn0oIVsro.

541. James Sensenbrenner, House Judiciary Committee markup, December
12, 2019, https://www.breitbart.com/politics/2019/12/11/sensenbrenner-democrat-im
peachment-weakest-case-in-history/.

542. Democrats delayed the vote from the night of December 12 to the morning of December 13 to avoid passing the articles in the dead of night and to take advantage of a larger live television audience.

543. Hill admitted having an affair with a woman in her campaign office. Her estranged husband, whom she blamed for leaking the gossip (and nude photographs), had also been part of the "throuple."

544. Hannah Bleau, "Watch: Giddy Rashida Tlaib Smiled Ear to Ear on Her Way to Impeach Trump," Breitbart News, December 19, 2019, https://www.breitbart.com/politics/2019/12/19/watch-giddy-rashida-tlaib-smiled-ear-to-ear-on-her-way-to-impeach-trump/.

545. Speaker Nancy Pelosi, "Pelosi Floor Speech in Support of Articles of Impeachment against the President of the United States," House of Representatives, December 18, 2019, https://www.speaker.gov/newsroom/121819.

546. Joshua Caplan, "Watch: Louie Gohmert Erupts after Nadler Calls His Speech 'Russian Propaganda,'" Breitbart News, December 18, 2019, https://www.breitbart.com/politics/2019/12/18/watch-louie-gohmert-erupts-after-nadler-calls-his-speech-russian-propaganda/.

547. "Here's How the House Voted on Trump's Impeachment," Politico, December 18, 2019, htttps://www.politico.com/interactives/2019/trump-impeachment-vote-count-house-results/.

548. The University of California, Los Angeles.

549. The Association of Federal, State, County, and Municipal Employees (AFSCME) asked the Democratic National Committee (DNC) not to hold the event there, in solidarity with the union's ongoing dispute with the university. (Joel B. Pollak, "DNC Bows to AFSCME Union, Won't Hold 6th Debate at UCLA," Breitbart News, November 6, 2019, https://www.breitbart.com/politics/2019/11/06/dnc-bows-to-afscme-union-wont-hold-6th-debate-at-ucla/.)

550. Unite Here Local 11 was locked in a contractual dispute with Sodexo, the campus food provider. (Joel B. Pollak, "Democrat Debate Back on in L.A. after Union Dispute Settled," Breitbart News, December 17, 2019, https://www.breitbart.com/politics/2019/12/17/democrat-debate-back-on-in-l-a-after-union-dispute-settled/.)

551. Katherine Rodriguez, "Democrat Candidates Spar over Closed-Door 'Wine Cave' Fundraisers," Breitbart News, December 19, 2019, https://www.breitbart.com/2020-election/2019/12/19/democrat-candidates-spar-closed-door-wine-cave-fundraisers/.

552. Kamala Harris, quoted in Joshua Caplan, "Kamala Harris Quits Presidential Race," Breitbart News, December 3, 2019, https://www.breitbart.com/2020-election/2019/12/03/kamala-harris-quits-presidential-race/.

553. Cory Booker, interview, Morning Joe, MSNBC, December 4, 2019, https://www.breitbart.com/clips/2019/12/04/booker-concerned-2020-field-has-more-billionaires-than-black-people/.

554. Andrew Yang, appearance at sixth presidential debate (Los Angeles, California, December 19, 2019), https://www.rev.com/blog/transcripts/december -democratic-debate-transcript-sixth-debate-from-los-angeles.

555. William Shakespeare, *Julius Caesar*, Act 3, Scene 1, Dover Thrift Edition (New York: Dover, 1991), 38.

556. John Binder, "Fashion Notes: Melania Trump Brings Fireworks in Givenchy for New Year's," Breitbart News, January 1, 2020, https://www.breitbart .com/entertainment/2020/01/01/fashion-notes-melania-trump-nye/.

557. President Donald Trump, quoted in Sarah Gray, "Trump Talks about Situation in Iraq, North Korea, and Impeachment at a New Year's Eve Bash at Mar-a-Lago," Business Insider, December 31, 2019, https://www.businessinsider .com/photos-trump-melania-giuliani-new-years-eve-mar-a-lago-2019-12.

558. Melania Trump, quoted in Kevin Liptak, "How the Trumps Spent Their New Year's Eve." CNN, January 1, 2020, https://www.cnn.com/2020/01/01/politics /trump-new-years-eve-mar-a-lago-gala/index.html.

559. Dr. Gina Loudon, livestream on Facebook, January 1, 2020, https://www .facebook.com/ggloudon/videos/10221042682286935/.

560. Later it transpired that some service members had been treated for head injuries; there were, however, no deaths. (Joel B. Pollak, "Analysts: Iran Retalia- tion a 'Win' for Trump," Breitbart News, January 8, 2020, https://www.breitbart .com/national-security/2020/01/08/analysts-iran-no-us-casualties-retaliation-a-win -for-trump/.)

561. Sho Chandra, "U.S. Growth Hits 4.1%, Fastest since 2014, in Win for Trump," Bloomberg News, July 27, 2018, https://www.bloomberg.com/news /articles/2018-07-27/u-s-gdp-growth-hits-4-1-fastest-since-2014-in-win-for-trump.

562. Neil Munro, "Black Poverty Hits Record Low under President Trump," Breitbart News, September 10, 2019, https://www.breitbart.com/economy/2019 /09/10/black-poverty-record-low-under-trump/.

563. John Binder, "Fact Check: Yes, Trump's Tight Labor Market Creates Blue- Collar Wage Boom," Breitbart News, February 4, 2020, https://www.breitbart.com /politics/2020/02/04/fact-check-yes-trumps-tight-labor-market-creates-blue-collar -wage-boom/.

564. President Donald Trump, tweet, December 31, 2019, https://twitter.com /realDonaldTrump/status/1212014713808273410?s=20.

565. "President Trump Job Approval," RealClearPolitics, accessed March 22, 2020, https://www.realclearpolitics.com/epolls/other/president_trump_job _approval-6179.html.

566. Jeffrey M. Jones, "U.S. Satisfaction Surpasses 40% for First time Since 2005," Gallup, January 24, 2020, https://news.gallup.com/poll/283958/satisfaction -surpasses-first-time-2005.aspx.

567. Laurence Tribe and Joshua Matz, *To End a Presidency: The Power of Impeachment* (New York: Basic Books, 2018).

568. Mark Leibovitch and Nicholas Fandos, "Behind the Scenes of Impeachment: Crammed Offices, Late Nights, Cold Pizza," *New York Times*, December 7, 2019, https://www.nytimes.com/2019/12/07/us/impeachment-judiciary-committee.html.

569. Laurence Tribe, "Don't Let Mitch McConnell Conduct a Potemkin Impeachment Trial," *Washington Post*, December 16, 2019, https://www.washington post.com/opinions/dont-let-mitch-mcconnell-conduct-a-potemkin-impeachment-trial/2019/12/16/71a81b30-202f-11ea-a153-dce4b94e4249_story.html.

570. U.S. Const. art. I, § 3.

571. Hamilton warned of "the injury to the innocent, from the procrastinated determination of the charges which might be brought against them; the advantage to the guilty, from the opportunities which delay would afford to intrigue and corruption." (Alexander Hamilton, *Federalist No. 65*, March 7, 1788, https://avalon.law.yale.edu/18th_century/fed65.asp.)

572. Kyle Cheney et al., "Pelosi Threatens to Delay Senate Impeachment Trial," *Politico*, December 18, 2019, https://www.politico.com/news/2019/12/18/trump-impeachment-trial-steny-hoyer-087319.

573. Speaker Nancy Pelosi, quoted in Joshua Caplan, "Pelosi Won't Say When She Plans to Send Impeachment Articles to Senate," Breitbart News, December 18, 2019, https://www.breitbart.com/politics/2019/12/18/pelosi-wont-say-when-she-plans-to-send-impeachment-articles-to-senate/.

574. Pelosi, quoted in Caplan, "Pelosi Won't Say."

575. Associated Press, "Mitch McConnell: Pelosi 'Too Afraid' to Send Impeachment Articles to Senate," December 19, 2019, https://www.breitbart.com/politics/2019/12/19/mitch-mcconnell-pelosi-too-afraid-to-send-impeachment-articles-to-senate/.

576. Senate Majority Leader Mitch McConnell, quoted in Joel B. Pollak, "McConnell Suggests Senate Will Move to Dismiss Impeachment after Opening Arguments," Breitbart News, December 17, 2019, https://www.breitbart.com/politics/2019/12/17/mcconnell-suggests-senate-will-move-to-dismiss-impeachment-after-opening-arguments/.

577. Senate Majority Leader Mitch McConnell, "McConnell Remarks on House Democrats' Impeachment of President Trump," December 19, 2019, https://www.republicanleader.senate.gov/newsroom/remarks/mcconnell-remarks-on-house-democrats-impeachment-of-president-trump.

578. Senate Majority Leader Mitch McConnell, "McConnell Updates Senate on Impeachment Procedure," December 19, 2019, https://www.republicanleader.senate.gov/newsroom/remarks/mcconnell-updates-senate-on-impeachment-procedure.

579. Senate Minority Leader Chuck Schumer, press conference remarks (Washington, DC, December 16, 2019), https://www.democrats.senate.gov/newsroom/press-releases/transcript-schumer-remarks-at-press-conference-outlining

-proposed-structure-for-a-fair-and-honest-bipartisan-impeachment-trial-if-articles
-are-approved-by-the-house.

580. Sui-Lee Wee and Vivian Wang, "China Grapples with Mystery Pneumonia-Like Illness," *New York Times*, January 6, 2020, https://www.nytimes.com/2020/01/06/world/asia/china-SARS-pneumonialike.html.

581. Wee and Wang, "China Grapples with Mystery Pneumonia-Like Illness."

582. Sui-Lee Wee and Donald G. McNeil Jr., "China Identifies New Virus Causing Pneumonialike Illness," *New York Times*, January 8, 2020, https://www.nytimes.com/2020/01/08/health/china-pneumonia-outbreak-virus.html.

583. Amy Qin and Javier C. Hernández, "China Reports First Death from New Virus," *New York Times*, January 10, 2020, https://www.nytimes.com/2020/01/10/world/asia/china-virus-wuhan-death.html.

584. World Health Organization, tweet, January 14, 2020, https://twitter.com/who/status/1217043229427761152.

585. World Health Organization, "Novel Coronavirus (2019-nCoV)," Situation Report, January 21, 2020, https://www.who.int/docs/default-source/coronaviruse/situation-reports/20200121-sitrep-1-2019-ncov.pdf?sfvrsn=20a99c10_4.

586. Cate Cadell, "Virus Casts Shadow over China's Biggest Festival, but Little Worry at Epicenter," Reuters, January 17, 2020, https://www.reuters.com/article/us-china-health-wuhan/virus-casts-shadow-over-chinas-biggest-festival-but-little-worry-at-epicenter-idUSKBN1ZH05Q.

587. Derrick Bryson Taylor, "A Timeline of the Coronavirus," *New York Times*, March 19, 2020, https://www.nytimes.com/article/coronavirus-timeline.html.

588. Frances Martel, "China Says 'No Need to Panic' as Deadly Virus Goes International," Breitbart News, January 20, 2020, https://www.breitbart.com/asia/2020/01/20/china-says-no-need-to-panic-as-deadly-virus-goes-international/.

589. Michelle L. Holshue, "First Case of 2019 Novel Coronavirus in the United States," *New England Journal of Medicine*, March 5, 2020, https://www.nejm.org/doi/full/10.1056/NEJMoa2001191.

590. President Donald Trump, "Remarks by President Trump at Signing of the U.S.-China Phase One Trade Agreement," White House, Washington, DC, January 15, 2020.

591. Vice President Mike Pence, remarks at trade agreement signing (White House, Washington, DC, January 15, 2020).

592. Vice Premier Liu He, remarks at trade agreement signing (White House, Washington, DC, January 15, 2020).

593. Joel B. Pollak, "Nancy Pelosi Claims Constitution Gives Her Equal Power to President Trump," Breitbart News, January 3, 2019, https://www.breitbart.com/politics/2019/01/03/nancy-pelosi-claims-constitution-gives-her-equal-power-to-president-trump/.

594. Stephanie Grisham, tweet, January 15, 2020, https://twitter.com/PressSec/status/1217587165829521409.

595. Michelle L. Holshue et al., "First Case of 2019 Novel Coronavirus in the United States," *New England Journal of Medicine*, March 5, 2020, https://www.nejm.org/doi/full/10.1056/NEJMoa2001191.

596. Pat Cipollone, quoted in Tim Hains, "White House Counsel Pat Cipollone: 'They're Not Here to Steal One Election, They're Here to Steal Two Elections,'" RealClearPolitics, January 21, 2020, https://www.realclearpolitics.com/video/2020/01/21/white_house_counsel_pat_cipollone_theyre_not_here_to_steal_one_election_theyre_here_to_steal_two_elections.html.

597. Jeremy W. Peters, "Inside the Biggest 2020 Advertising War against Trump," *New York Times*, December 29, 2019, https://www.nytimes.com/2019/12/29/us/politics/michael-bloomberg-trump-advertising.html.

598. Jacob Knutson, "Pete Buttigieg's Campaign Says It Raised $24.7 million in Q4," Axios, January 1, 2020, https://www.axios.com/pete-buttigieg-fundraising-4th-quarter-2019-12f3e563-5c86-4c95-a88c-15b037d15544.html.

599. Sydney Ember and Thomas Kaplan, "Bernie Sanders Raised $34.5 Million in the Fourth Quarter, Pacing the Field," *New York Times*, January 2, 2020, https://www.nytimes.com/2020/01/02/us/politics/bernie-sanders-q4-campaign-fundraising.html.

600. Max Greenwood, "Biden Rakes in $22.7 Million in Fourth Quarter of 2019," *The Hill*, January 2, 2020, https://thehill.com/homenews/campaign/476549-biden-rakes-in-227-million-in-fourth-quarter-of-2019. Biden barely raised more than Warren (Shane Goldmacher and Thomas Kaplan, "Lagging Rivals, Elizabeth Warren Raised $21.2 Million in 4th Quarter," *New York Times*, January 3, 2020, https://www.nytimes.com/2020/01/03/us/politics/elizabeth-warren-fundraising.html.) and not much more than Yang (Simon Lewis and Steve Holland, "Happy New Year for Sanders, Trump in Campaign Fundraising Hauls," Reuters, January 2, 2020, https://www.reuters.com/article/us-usa-election-fundraising/happy-new-year-for-sanders-trump-in-fundraising-hauls-idUSKBN1Z10NT), who would not even make the Iowa debate.

601. Joel B. Pollak, "Cory Booker Blames Impeachment for Early Withdrawal from 2020 Race," Breitbart News, January 13, 2020, https://www.breitbart.com/politics/2020/01/13/cory-booker-blames-impeachment-for-early-withdrawal-from-2020-race/.

602. Nicole Sganga, tweet, January 1, 2020, https://twitter.com/NicoleSganga/status/1212448598845198338.

603. Speaker Nancy Pelosi called the air strike "provocative and disproportionate," as if the United States had committed a war crime, though there had been no civilian casualties and a very limited Iranian response. (Speaker Nancy Pelosi, press release, January 5, 2020, https://www.speaker.gov/newsroom/1520-0.)

604. Daniel Marans, tweet, January 3, 2020, https://twitter.com/danielmarans/status/1213258973295632386. He also compared Trump's air strike to Russian President Vladimir Putin assassinating political dissidents. (Bernie Sanders, interview,

Anderson Cooper 360, CNN, January 6, 2020, https://twitter.com/tcpigott/status /1214375318238224385.)

605. Joel B. Pollak, "'Dreamers' Protest against Joe Biden outside Democrat Debate in Iowa," Breitbart News, January 14, 2020, https://www.breitbart.com /politics/2020/01/14/dreamers-protest-against-joe-biden-outside-democrat-debate/.

606. Abby Phillip, quoted in Joel B. Pollak, "Fact Check: CNN's Abby Phillip Parrots Elizabeth Warren's Claim about Bernie Sanders and Women," Breitbart News, January 14, 2020, https://www.breitbart.com/politics/2020/01/14/fact-check -cnn-abby-phillip-parrots-elizabeth-warrens-claim-about-bernie-sanders/.

607. Elizabeth Warren, quoted in Ian Hanchett, "Listen: After Debate, Warren Accuses Sanders of Calling Her a Liar, Sanders Says She Called Him a Liar," Breitbart News, January 15, 2020, https://www.breitbart.com/clips/2020/01/15 /listen-after-debate-warren-accuses-sanders-of-calling-her-a-liar-sanders-says-she -called-him-a-liar/.

608. Joel B. Pollak, "Julián Castro: Elizabeth Warren Brought Diversity to Debate Stage in Iowa." Breitbart News, January 15, 2020, https://www.breitbart.com /politics/2020/01/15/julian-castro-elizabeth-warren-brought-diversity-to-debate -stage-in-iowa/.

609. Representative Adam Schiff, quoted in Edwin Mora, "Schiff: Trump 'Guilty' If Senate Rejects Democrats' Demand for New Witnesses, Evidence," Breitbart News, January 21, 2020, https://www.breitbart.com/politics/2020/01/21/schiff -trump-guilty-if-senate-rejects-democrats-demand-for-new-witnesses-evidence/.

610. Joel B. Pollak, "Adam Schiff Fakes Ukraine Transcript—Again—in Senate Impeachment Trial," Breitbart News, January 21, 2020, https://www.breitbart .com/politics/2020/01/21/adam-schiff-fakes-ukraine-transcript-again-in-senate -impeachment-trial/. The president's actual words in the transcript of the call were: "I would like you to do us a favor though because our country has been through a lot."

611. Joel B. Pollak, "Chief Justice Rebukes Lawyers in Senate Impeachment Trial: Remember Where You Are," Breitbart News, January 21, 2020, https:// www.breitbart.com/politics/2020/01/21/chief-justice-rebukes-lawyers-in-senate -impeachment-trial-remember-where-you-are/.

612. Bernie Sanders, quoted in Hannah Bleau, "Bernie Sanders Rages over Senate Impeachment Trial Schedule," Breitbart News, January 21, 2020, https://www.breitbart.com/politics/2020/01/21/bernie-sanders-rages-over-senate -impeachment-trial-schedule/.

613. President Donald Trump, tweet, January 18, 2020, https://twitter.com /realDonaldTrump/status/1218668999086694400.

614. Jennifer Rubin, tweet, January 22, 2020, https://twitter.com/JRubin Blogger/status/1220073127696355330.

615. The president's team could not respond at all, save during brief recesses, when White House lawyer Jay Sekulow would hold forth in front of the press in the Capitol hallways. At one point, he quipped: "The good news is we only have 22 hours more to go of their side and we'll go." (Jay Sekulow, quoted in Tony Lee, "***Live

Updates*** Trump Impeachment Trial: Democrats Begin Opening Arguments," Breitbart News, January 22, 2020, https://www.breitbart.com/politics/2020/01/22 /live-updates-trump-impeachment-trial-democrats-begin-opening-arguments/.)

616. Senator Lindsey Graham, quoted in Dylan Stableford, "Graham Praises Schiff on Impeachment Presentation: 'You're Very Well-Spoken,'" Yahoo News, January 23, 2020, https://finance.yahoo.com/news/graham-schiff-impeachment -very-well-spoken-154244068.html.

617. Republicans had been threatening for weeks to call the former vice president and his son to testify; there had even been talk of a deal, in which the Democrats could call Bolton if Republicans could call Biden. No such deal was ever made.

618. Jay Sekulow, quoted in Joel B. Pollak, "Pollak: House Democrats Accidentally Make Case for Calling Joe, Hunter Biden as Witnesses in Senate Trial," Breitbart News, January 23, 2020, https://www.breitbart.com/crime/2020/01/23 /pollak-house-democrats-accidentally-make-case-for-calling-joe-hunter-biden -as-witnesses-in-senate-trial/.

619. Joel B. Pollak, "White House Counsel Opens with Facts Schiff Left Out of Impeachment Trial," Breitbart News, January 25, 2020, https://www.breitbart .com/politics/2020/01/25/white-house-counsel-opens-with-facts-schiff-left-out -impeachment-trial/.

620. Maggie Haberman and Michael S. Schmidt, "Trump Tied Ukraine Aid to Inquiries He Sought, Bolton Book Says," New York Times, January 26, 2020, https:// www.nytimes.com/2020/01/26/us/politics/trump-bolton-book-ukraine.html.

621. Lt. Col. Vindman's brother was the White House ethics officer in charge of clearing publications by former officials. (Joel B. Pollak and Kristina Wong, "Source: Alexander Vindman's Brother, Yevgeny, Clears Publications by NSC Officials," Breitbart News, January 26, 2020, https://www.breitbart.com/politics /2020/01/26/source-alexander-vindmans-brother-yevgeny-clears-publications-by -nsc-officials/.)

622. Alan Dershowitz, opening arguments, impeachment trial (Washington, DC, January 27, 2020), https://www.rev.com/blog/transcripts/trump-impeachment -lawyer-defense-argument-transcripts-monday-january-27-ken-starr-purpura-raskin.

623. Alan Dershowitz, quoted by Joel B. Pollak, "Dershowitz: Trump Impeachment Invalid; Requires 'Criminal-like Conduct,'" Breitbart News, January 27, 2020, https://www.breitbart.com/politics/2020/01/27/dershowitz-trump-impeachment -invalid-requires-criminal-like-conduct/.

624. Rep. Adam Schiff, quoted in Joel B. Pollak, "Fact Check: Adam Schiff Lies about What Dershowitz Said on 'Quid Pro Quo,'" Breitbart News, January 30, 2020, https://www.breitbart.com/politics/2020/01/30/fact-check-adam-schiff-lies-ab out-what-dershowitz-said-on-quid-pro-quo/.

625. Adam Kelsey, tweet, January 25, 2020, https://twitter.com/adamkelsey /status/1221173424141283329.

626. Alexandria Ocasio-Cortez, quoted in Joseph Simonson, "AOC Speaks of a Nation 'in Decline' in Speech for Bernie Sanders," Washington Examiner, January

25, 2020, https://www.washingtonexaminer.com/news/aoc-speaks-of-a-nation-in
-decline-in-speech-for-bernie-sanders.

627. Editorial Board, "Endorsement: Elizabeth Warren Will Push an Unequal
America in the Right Direction," *Des Moines Register*, January 25, 2020, https://
www.desmoinesregister.com/story/opinion/editorials/caucus/2020/01/26/elizabeth
-warren-president-democrat-iowa-caucuses-des-moines-register-editorial-board
-endorsement/4562157002/.

628. Editorial Board, "The Democrats' Best Choices for President," *New York
Times*, January 19, 2020, https://www.nytimes.com/interactive/2020/01/19/opinion
/amy-klobuchar-elizabeth-warren-nytimes-endorsement.html.

629. Joe Biden, tweet, January 25, 2020, https://twitter.com/JoeBiden/status
/1221135646107955200.

630. Gonzales Research and Media Services, "Gonzales Poll – Delaware," January 28, 2020, https://projects.fivethirtyeight.com/polls/20200128_DE.pdf.

631. Joe Biden, quoted in Marina Pitofsky, "Biden: 'I Sure Would Like
Michelle to Be the Vice President,'" *The Hill*, January 28, 2020, https://thehill
.com/homenews/campaign/480342-biden-on-michelle-obama-i-sure-would-like
-michelle-to-be-the-vice-president.

632. Joe Biden, quoted in Emily Larsen, "Biden Acknowledges He Might Die
in Office: 'I'm an Old Guy,'" *Washington Examiner*, January 29, 2020, https://www
.washingtonexaminer.com/news/biden-suggests-he-might-die-in-office-im-an-old
-guy.

633. Sydney Ember, tweet, January 25, 2020, https://twitter.com/melbournecoal
/status/1221169949059710977?s=20.

634. Pete Buttigieg, "It's Time," Pete Buttigieg for President, January 27, 2020,
https://www.youtube.com/watch?v=xROs4zWeE44&feature=youtu.be.

635. Dan Merica and Donald Judd, "Buttigieg Calls Out Biden and Sanders by Name Ahead of Iowa Caucuses," CNN, January 30, 2020, https://www.cnn
.com/2020/01/30/politics/buttigieg-calls-out-biden-sanders/index.html.

636. Specifically, Senators Ted Cruz (R-TX) and David Perdue (R-GA) asked
the House impeachment managers why, if they had wanted documents, they had
not handed over the transcript of an interview with the Intelligence Community
Inspector General (ICIG) about the political bias of the whistleblower.

637. Chief Justice Roberts refused to read a question by Senator Rand Paul
(R-KY) that named the whistleblower. He did, however, read a question from
Warren about whether the trial would "contribute to the loss of legitimacy of
the Chief Justice, the Supreme Court, and the Constitution." (Charlie Spiering,
"Elizabeth Warren Forces Chief Justice John Roberts to Read Question about His
Own Legitimacy," Breitbart News, January 30, 2020, https://www.breitbart.com
/politics/2020/01/30/elizabeth-warren-forces-chief-justice-john-roberts-to-read
-question-about-his-own-legitimacy/.)

638. Charlie Spiering, "'Jerry. Jerry. Jerry!'— Adam Schiff Tries in Vain to Stop
Jerry Nadler from Historic Impeachment Trial Moment," Breitbart News, January

30, 2020, https://www.breitbart.com/politics/2020/01/30/adam-schiff-stop-jerry-nadler-historic-impeachment-trial-moment/.

639. He would miss closing arguments due to his wife's sudden diagnosis with pancreatic cancer.

640. Senator Susan Collins (R-ME) and Mitt Romney (R-UT) crossed the aisle.

641. Joel B. Pollak, "Pam Bondi Lays Out Case against Joe Biden, Hunter Biden, Burisma," Breitbart News, January 27, 2020, https://www.breitbart.com/politics/2020/01/27/pam-bondi-lays-out-case-against-joe-biden-hunter-biden-burisma/.

642. Andy Shain, "Sanders and Steyer Closing Gap on Biden as SC 2020 Presidential Primary Nears," *Post and Courier*, February 2, 2020, https://www.postandcourier.com/politics/sanders-and-steyer-closing-gap-on-biden-as-sc-presidential/article_b27fd0ca-43c6-11ea-9805-6b054517633c.html.

643. CNN, quoted in Joel B. Pollak, "CNN: Tom Steyer Responsible for 91% of TV Ad Spending in South Carolina, 97% in Nevada," Breitbart News, January 12, 2020, https://www.breitbart.com/politics/2020/01/12/cnn-tom-steyer-responsible-for-91-of-tv-ad-spending-in-south-carolina-97-in-nevada/.

644. Jonathan Allen and Allan Smith, "John Kerry Overheard Discussing Possible 2020 Bid amid Concern of 'Sanders Taking Down the Democratic Party,'" NBC News, February 2, 2020, https://www.nbcnews.com/politics/2020-election/john-kerry-overheard-discussing-possible-2020-bid-amid-concern-sanders-n1128476.

645. Faiz Shakir, tweet, January 31, 2020, https://twitter.com/fshakir/status/1223331124035887105.

646. Charlie Spiering, "Donald Trump: Democrats Want to Kill Your Cows and 'You're Next,'" Breitbart News, January 30, 2020, https://www.breitbart.com/politics/2020/01/30/donald-trump-democrats-want-to-kill-your-cows-and-youre-next/.

647. Ryan Lizza, "The Unexpected Joy at a Trump Rally in Iowa," *Politico*, January 31, 2020, https://www.politico.com/news/2020/01/31/unexpected-joy-trump-rally-iowa-109864.

648. Stephanie Grisham, "Statement from the Press Secretary Regarding the President's Coronavirus Task Force," White House, January 29, 2020, https://www.whitehouse.gov/briefings-statements/statement-press-secretary-regarding-presidents-coronavirus-task-force/.

649. Brandon Tensley, "Coronavirus Task Force Another Example of Trump Administration's Lack of Diversity," CNN, January 30, 2020.

650. Stephanie Nebehay, "WHO Chief Says Widespread Travel Bans Not Needed to Beat China Virus," Reuters, February 3, 2020, https://www.reuters.com/article/us-china-health-who/who-chief-says-widespread-travel-bans-not-needed-to-beat-china-virus-idUSKBN1ZX1H3.

651. Joe Biden, speech (Fort Madison, Iowa, January 31, 2020), https://www.facebook.com/NowThisPolitics/videos/184485232624296/.

652. President Donald Trump, speech (Drake University, Des Pointes, Iowa, January 30, 2020), https://www.rev.com/blog/transcripts/donal-trump-iowa-rally -transcript-trump-holds-rally-in-des-moines-iowa.

653. President Donald Trump, "Remarks by President Trump in State of the Union Address," White House, February 4, 2020, https://www.whitehouse .gov/briefings-statements/remarks-president-trump-state-union-address-3/.

654. House impeachment managers led with their attack on Dershowitz, tor- turing his argument beyond recognition. "Professor Dershowitz, and the other counselors to the president, have argued that if the president thinks that some- thing is in his interest, then it is, by definition, in the interest of the American peo- ple," said Representative Jason Crow (D-CO). (Representative Jason Crow, quoted in Joel B. Pollak, "Fact Check: No, Dershowitz Did Not Say President's Interest Equals National Interest," Breitbart News, February 3, 2020, https://www.breitbart .com/politics/2020/02/03/fact-check-no-dershowitz-did-not-say-presidents-interest -equals-national-interest/.)

655. Kenneth Starr, the prosecutor who led the investigation that led to Pres- ident Bill Clinton's impeachment, rose in the president's defense. He quoted Dr. Martin Luther King Jr.: "During his magnificent life, Dr. King spoke not only about freedom, freedom standing alone, he spoke frequently about freedom and justice." And justice, Starr said, meant "playing by the rules." House Democrats, he said, had not. "Were the rules here faithfully followed?...If not...then...the prosecu- tors should not be rewarded," he argued. (Kenneth Starr, closing argument, Sen- ate Impeachment Trial, February 3, 2020, https://www.rev.com/blog/transcripts /transcript-trump-impeachment-trial-monday-february-3-2020-key-moments.)

656. Representative Adam Schiff, quoted by Joel B. Pollak, "Adam Schiff Closes Impeachment Trial with Rant against Trump: 'Decency Matters,'" Breit- bart News, February 3, 2020, https://www.breitbart.com/politics/2020/02/03/adam -schiff-closes-impeachment-trial-with-rant-against-trump-decency-matters/.

657. Roosevelt actually had three caucuses in the building: one in a cafeteria, one in a small gymnasium, and one in the main gym.

658. They could also group together to vote for one of the original, failed, can- didates. The final tally would then determine which campaigns won the most "state delegate equivalents" to the state nominating convention in March.

659. Kristina Wong, "#MayorCheat Trends after Buttigieg Campaign Is Tied to Company Behind Iowa Caucus App Failure," Breitbart News, February 4, 2020, https://www.breitbart.com/politics/2020/02/04/mayorcheat-trends-after-buttigieg -campaign-is-tied-to-company-behind-iowa-caucus-app-failure/.

660. Pete Buttigieg, quoted in Charlie Spiering, "Pete Buttigieg Claims Victory without Results: Iowa 'Shocked the Nation,'" Breitbart News, February 3, 2020, https://www.breitbart.com/politics/2020/02/03/pete-buttigieg-claims-victory -without-results-iowa/.

661. Amy Klobuchar, quoted in Kyle Morris, "Amy Klobuchar amid Iowa Cau- cus Inconsistencies: We 'Cannot Take Another Four Years' of Trump," Breitbart

News, February 3, 2020, https://www.breitbart.com/politics/2020/02/03/klobuchar -our-country-cannot-take-another-four-years-of-donald-trump/.

662. Brad Parscale, tweet, February 24, 2020, https://twitter.com/parscale /status/1232047245236764673.

663. President Donald Trump, tweet, February 4, 2020, https://twitter.com /realDonaldTrump/status/1224657196392370177.

664. Tim Hains, "President Trump Honors Widow of Navy SEAL Killed in Yemen," RealClearPolitics, February 28, 2019, https://www.realclearpolitics .com/video/2017/02/28/president_trump_honors_widow_of_navy_seal_killed_in _yemen.html.

665. Joel B. Pollak, "State of the Union: Democrat Women Give Trump Standing Ovation," Breitbart News, February 5, 2019, https://www.breitbart.com/politics /2019/02/05/state-of-the-union-democrat-women-give-trump-standing-ovation/.

666. Pollak, "State of the Union."

667. Joel B. Pollak, "Van Jones Warns Democrats: Trump Is Helping African-Americans 'In Real Life,'" Breitbart News, February 5, 2020, https://www.breitbart .com/politics/2020/02/05/van-jones-warns-democrats-trump-is-helping -african-americans-in-real-life/.

668. Democrats argued that Trump had neglected to shake Pelosi's outstretched hand at the start of the speech—though it was not clear he had seen it. Moreover, she had just impeached him; the expectation that he would shake her hand was not realistic.

669. Ed O'Keefe, tweet, February 6, 2020, https://twitter.com/edokeefe /status/1225481108164354048.

670. Jon Keller, "Exclusive NH Tracking Poll: Pete Buttigieg Stays Hot, Ties Bernie Sanders for Lead," CBS Boston, February 6, 2020, https://boston.cbslocal .com/2020/02/06/new-hampshire-primary-tracking-poll-pete-buttigieg-bernie -sanders-tied/.

671. Katherine Rodriguez, "Amy Klobuchar Lone Democrat to Raise Hand When Asked about Concerns on Socialism," Breitbart News, February 7, 2020, https://www.breitbart.com/2020-election/2020/02/07/amy-klobuchar-lone -democrat-to-raise-hand-when-asked-about-concerns-on-socialism/.

672. Amy Klobuchar, appearance at seventh Democratic presidential debate (Manchester, New Hampshire, February 7, 2020), https://www.rev.com/blog/transcripts /new-hampshire-democratic-debate-transcript.

673. President Donald Trump, tweet, February 8, 2020, https://twitter.com/real DonaldTrump/status/1226314556399591424.

674. Josh Kraushaar, tweet, February 9, 2020, https://twitter.com/hotlinejosh /status/1226718753955753984.

675. Haris Alic, "Joe Biden Calls New Hampshire Voter a 'Lying, Dog-Faced Pony Soldier,'" Breitbart News, February 9, 2020, https://www.breitbart.com/2020 -election/2020/02/09/joe-biden-calls-new-hampshire-voter-a-lying-dog-faced-pony -soldier/.

676. Joel B. Pollak, "Kevin Costner Rallies with Pete Buttigieg in New Hampshire: 'Someone Who Listens,'" Breitbart News, February 10, 2020, https://www.breitbart.com/entertainment/2020/02/10/kevin-costner-rallies-with-pete-buttigieg-in-new-hampshire-someone-who-listens/.

677. Annie Karni and Maggie Haberman, "Trump Travels to New Hampshire to Rally Republicans and Distract Democrats," *New York Times*, February 10, 2020, https://www.nytimes.com/2020/02/10/us/politics/trump-new-hampshire-rally.html

678. Tony Lee, "***Live Updates*** Trump Holds New Hampshire Rally," February 10, 2020, https://www.breitbart.com/2020-election/2020/02/10/live-updates-trump-holds-new-hampshire-rally-2/.

679. President Donald Trump, remarks at SNHU Arena rally (Manchester, New Hampshire, February 10, 2020), https://www.rev.com/blog/transcripts/donald-trump-new-hampshire-rally-february-10-2020.

680. Joel B. Pollak, "Mike Bloomberg Wins Democrat, Republican Primaries in Dixville Notch—as Write-in," Breitbart News, February 11, 2020, https://www.breitbart.com/2020-election/2020/02/10/mike-bloomberg-wins-democrat-republican-primaries-in-dixville-notch-as-write-in/.

681. Mike Bloomberg, quoted in AWR Hawkins, "Audio: Mike Bloomberg Tells Aspen Elites 'All the Crime' Is in Minority Areas; 'Throw Them against the Wall and Frisk Them,'" Breitbart News, February 11, 2020, https://www.breitbart.com/politics/2020/02/11/audio-mike-bloomberg-tells-aspen-elites-all-the-crime-is-in-minority-areas-throw-them-against-the-wall-and-frisk-them/.

682. Mike Bloomberg, quoted by Tim Perry, tweet, February 11, 2020, https://twitter.com/tperry518/status/1227271639500574721.

683. Josh Lederman, tweet, February 11, 2020, https://twitter.com/JoshNBCNews/status/1227348712248217601.

684. ""What would America do if we had a continuous country and a lot of people in that country wanted to be Americans. Does California ring a bell? We just went and took it." (Josh Rogin, tweet, February 11, 2020, https://twitter.com/joshrogin/status/1227267729524215810.)

685. Joel B. Pollak, "Electile Dysfunction: Joe Biden Pulls Out Early from New Hampshire, Breitbart News, February 11, 2020, https://www.breitbart.com/politics/2020/02/11/joe-biden-leaves-new-hampshire/.

686. Tim Malloy and Doug Schwartz, "Sanders Takes Top Spot in Primary as Biden Falls," Quinnipiac Poll, February 10, 2020, https://poll.qu.edu/images/polling/us/us02102020_uyid781.pdf/.

687. Joel B. Pollak, "Bernie Sanders Supporters Celebrate New Hampshire Win: 'We Are Unstoppable!,'" Breitbart News, February 11, 2020, https://www.breitbart.com/2020-election/2020/02/11/bernie-sanders-supporters-celebrate-new-hampshire-win-we-are-unstoppable/.

688. Evan S., quoted in Joel B. Pollak, "WATCH: Bernie Sanders Supporter Explains Democratic Socialism at New Hampshire Victory Rally," Breitbart News, February 11, 2020, https://www.breitbart.com/politics/2020/02/11/watch

-bernie-sanders-supporter-explains-democratic-socialism-at-new-hampshire-victory-rally/.

689. Joe Biden, quoted in Haris Alic, "Joe Biden Delivers Gaffe-Ridden, Defiant Message after New Hampshire Blowout," Breitbart News, February 11, 2020, https://www.breitbart.com/2020-election/2020/02/11/joe-biden-delivers-gaffe-ridden-defiant-message-after-new-hampshire-blowout/.

690. "New Hampshire Primary Results," *New York Times*, September 29, 2016, https://www.nytimes.com/elections/2016/results/primaries/new-hampshire.

691. "New Hampshire Results," NBC News, February 19, 2020, https://www.nbcnews.com/politics/2020-primary-elections/new-hampshire-results.

692. Tyson Fury, remarks at press conference with Deontay Wilder (MGM Grand, Las Vegas, Nevada, February 19, 2020), https://www.rev.com/blog/transcripts/deontay-wilder-v-tyson-fury-press-conference-transcript.

693. Nancy Pelosi, quoted in Hannah Bleau, "Nancy Pelosi Snaps after Asked If She Hates the President: 'Don't Mess with Me,'" Breitbart News, December 5, 2019, https://www.breitbart.com/politics/2019/12/05/nancy-pelosi-snaps-after-asked-if-she-hates-the-president-dont-mess-with-me/.

694. Mitt Romney, speech on the impeachment vote (February 5, 2020, U.S. Senate), https://www.romney.senate.gov/romney-delivers-remarks-impeachment-vote.

695. President Donald Trump. "Remarks at 68th Annual National Prayer Breakfast," Washington, DC, February 6, 2020, https://www.whitehouse.gov/briefings-statements/remarks-president-trump-68th-annual-national-prayer-breakfast/.

696. Not among those present: Lt. Col. Vindman and his brother, who were moved out of the White House. U.S. Ambassador to the EU Gordon Sondland, another key impeachment witness, was fired.

697. Charlie Spiering, "Donald Trump Thanks 'Incredible Warriors' Who Stood with Him Through 'Crooked' Impeachment," Breitbart News, February 6, 2020, https://www.breitbart.com/politics/2020/02/06/donald-trump-thanks-incredible-warriors-who-stood-with-him-through-crooked-impeachment/.

698. Jeanna Smialek and Ben Casselman, "Black Workers' Wages Are Finally Rising," *New York Times*, February 7, 2020, https://www.nytimes.com/2020/02/07/business/black-unemployment-wages.html.

699. Joe Walsh, interview, *New Day*, CNN, February 7, 2020, https://www.breitbart.com/2020-election/2020/02/07/never-trumper-joe-walsh-ends-presidential-campaign-he-cant-be-beat/.

700. President Donald Trump, tweet, February 7, 2020, https://twitter.com/realDonaldTrump/status/1225766149473947651.

701. Katelyn Polantz, "Appeals Court Tosses Democrats' Emoluments Lawsuit against Trump," CNN, February 7, 2020, https://www.cnn.com/2020/02/07/politics/emoluments-lawsuit-trump/index.html.

702. The following day, President Trump tweeted about the nine-year sentence Department of Justice prosecutors had recommended for former campaign associate

Roger Stone, who had been convicted of various process crimes in the Mueller investigation. (President Donald Trump, tweet. February 12, 2020, https://twitter .com/realDonaldTrump/status/1227564604177469441.) Trump was roundly criticized for supposedly interfering in the case—especially after Attorney General William Barr reined in the prosecutors, supposedly doing so independently of Trump's comments. But when the jury forewoman came forward to defend the prosecution, the country learned that she was a former Democratic candidate for Congress with a pronounced bias against Trump and Stone. Experts agreed Stone likely deserved a new trial. It was only the latest pillar of the Mueller investigation to crack. (Alan Dershowitz, quoted in Joel B. Pollak, "Alan Dershowitz: 'All Civil Libertarians' Must Defend Roger Stone," Breitbart News, February 13, 2020, https://www.breitbart .com/politics/2020/02/13/alan-dershowitz-civil-libertarians-must-defend-roger -stone/.) A week later, he commuted the fourteen-year federal prison sentence of former Illinois governor Rod Blagojevich, which even critics of "Blago" thought excessive. (Charlie Spiering, "Donald Trump Commutes Democrat Gov. Rod Blagojevich's Jail Sentence," Breitbart News, February 18, 2020, https://www.breitbart.com /politics/2020/02/18/donald-trump-commutes-democrat-gov-rod-blagojevichs-jail -sentence/). Blagojevich promptly emerged and called himself a "Trumpocrat." The theme of prosecutorial excess was clearly on the president's mind.

703. Charlie Spiering, "Donald Trump Smashes Incumbent President Primary Record in New Hampshire," Breitbart News, February 12, 2020, https://www .breitbart.com/politics/2020/02/12/donald-trump-smashes-incumbent-president -primary-record-in-new-hampshire/.

704. Daniel S. Levine, "Daytona 500: Jeff Gordon's Comments amid Donald Trump's Appearance Divide NASCAR Fans," PopCulture.com, February 16, 2020, https://popculture.com/sports/2020/02/16/daytona-500-jeff-gordon-comments -donald-trump-appearance-nascar-reactions/.

705. Frances Martel, "China Says 'No Need to Panic' as Deadly Virus Goes International," Breitbart News, January 20, 2020, https://www.breitbart.com /asia/2020/01/20/china-says-no-need-to-panic-as-deadly-virus-goes-international/.

706. Lenny Bernstein, "Get a Grippe, America. The Flu Is a Much Bigger Threat Than Coronavirus, for Now," *Washington Post*, February 1, 2020, https://www.washingtonpost.com/health/time-for-a-reality-check-america-the -flu-is-a-much-bigger-threat-than-coronavirus-for-now/2020/01/31/46a15166-4444 -11ea-b5fc-eefa848cde99_story.html.

707. Allison Aubrey, "Worried about Catching The New Coronavirus? In the U.S., Flu Is a Bigger Threat," National Public Radio, January 29, 2020, https://www .npr.org/sections/health-shots/2020/01/29/800813299/worried-about-catching-the -new-coronavirus-in-the-u-s-flu-is-a-bigger-threat.

708. Matthew Boyle, "Exclusive—Tom Cotton Urges Trump Administration to Consider Banning Travel from China over Coronavirus," Breitbart News, January 22, 2020, https://www.breitbart.com/politics/2020/01/22/exclusive-tom-cotton-urges -trump-administration-to-consider-banning-travel-from-china-over-coronavirus/.

709. Wendy Parmet and Michael Sinha, "Why We Should Be Wary of an Aggressive Government Response to Coronavirus," *Washington Post*, February 3, 2020.

710. Bob Price, "Governments Should Take 'Draconian Measures' to Stop Coronavirus Spread, Say Hong Kong Doctors," Breitbart News, January 28, 2020, https://www.breitbart.com/border/2020/01/28/governments-should-take-draconian-measures-to-stop-coronavirus-spread-say-hong-kong-doctors/.

711. House Foreign Affairs Subcommittee on Asia, the Pacific and Nonproliferation, "The Wuhan Coronavirus: Assessing the Outbreak, the Response, and Regional Implications," Washington, DC, February 5, 2020, https://www.congress.gov/event/116th-congress/house-event/110450.

712. Josh Lederman, tweet, February 12, 2020, https://twitter.com/JoshNBCNews/status/1227550700319780864.

713. Amanda Golden, tweet, February 12, 2020, https://twitter.com/amandawgolden/status/1227674335957180423.

714. The forum was sponsored by the League of United Latin American Citizens (LULAC). (Joel B. Pollak, "Democrats in Nevada Ask Candidates: How Will You Counter Trump on Economy?" Breitbart News, February 13, 2020, https://www.breitbart.com/economy/2020/02/13/economy-lulac-forum-las-vegas-nevada-caucus/.)

715. His full name is Andrés Manuel López Obrador (or AMLO, as he is colloquially known). (Joel B. Pollak, "Amy Klobuchar Can't Name President of Mexico, Despite Voting for USMCA," Breitbart News, February 14, 2020, https://www.breitbart.com/politics/2020/02/14/amy-klobuchar-cant-name-president-of-mexico-in-telemundo-interview-usmca/.)

716. "Nevada Democratic Presidential Caucus," RealClearPolitics, accessed March 25, 2020, https://www.realclearpolitics.com/epolls/2020/president/nv/nevada_democratic_presidential_caucus-6866.html.

717. Joel B. Pollak, "Nevada Wild: Sanders Has Advantage, but Vote-Counting Could Be Messy," Breitbart News, February 17, 2020, https://www.breitbart.com/politics/2020/02/17/nevada-wild-sanders-has-advantage-but-vote-counting-could-be-messy/.

718. Joel B. Pollak, "Powerful Las Vegas Culinary Union Declines to Endorse Any Particular Democrat," Breitbart News, February 13, 2020, https://www.breitbart.com/politics/2020/02/13/powerful-las-vegas-culinary-union-declines-to-endorse-any-particular-democrat/.

719. Ben Pu, tweet, February 15, 2020, https://twitter.com/BenPu_nbc/status/1228757125658136576.

720. Penny Starr, "Topless Protesters Interrupt Bernie Sanders Rally to Demand Action against 'Big Dairy,' Animal Agriculture," Breitbart News, February 17, 2020, https://www.breitbart.com/2020-election/2020/02/17/topless-protesters-interrupt-bernie-sanders-rally-demand-action-big-dairy-animal-agriculture/.

721. Abigail Marone, tweet, February 16, 2020, https://twitter.com/abigailmarone/status/1229184562418405376.

722. Joel B. Pollak, "Bernie Sanders Compares Voting for Him to Voting for Nelson Mandela," Breitbart News, February 18, 2020, https://www.breitbart.com /politics/2020/02/18/bernie-sanders-compares-voting-for-him-to-voting-for-nelson -mandela/.

723. Sam Donaldson, quoted in Team Bloomberg, tweet, February 15, 2020, https://twitter.com/Mike2020/status/1228770305784602629

724. Michael Bloomberg, "Starting with Iowa and New Hampshire Hurts Democrats and Helps Trump," CNN, January 13, 2020, https://www.cnn.com/2020/01/13 /opinions/iowa-new-hampshire-democratic-primary-bloomberg/index.html.

725. John Bowden, "Bloomberg Has Spent $124M on Ads in Super Tuesday States," *The Hill*, February 28, 2020, https://thehill.com/homenews/campaign /483427-bloomberg-spending-124m-on-ads-in-super-states.

726. Steyer's method of qualifying thus far had been to spend heavily in Nevada and South Carolina, driving up his poll numbers there, while other candidates focused on Iowa and New Hampshire. But while he had reached the 10 percent threshold in four polls prior to the Nevada debate, none of those polls—which were independent and reputable—was on the DNC's approved list. For whatever reason, the mainstream media and academic institutions favored by the party simply had not conducted any new polls in those states. (Joel B. Pollak, "Tom Steyer Hits 10% Debate Threshold in Four Polls, but None of Them Counts," Breitbart News, February 17, 2020, https://www.breitbart.com/politics/2020/02/17/tom-steyer -hits-10-threshold-in-four-polls-but-none-of-them-count/.)

727. Mike Tyson, quoted in Mike Berardino, "Mike Tyson Explains One of His Most Famous Quotes," *South Florida Sun-Sentinel*, November 9, 2012, https://www .sun-sentinel.com/sports/fl-xpm-2012-11-09-sfl-mike-tyson-explains-one-of-his -most-famous-quotes-20121109-story.html.

728. Elizabeth Warren, appearance at ninth Democratic presidential debate (Paris Hotel and Casino, Las Vegas, Nevada, February 19, 2020), https://www.nbc news.com/politics/2020-election/full-transcript-ninth-democratic-debate-las-vegas -n1139546.

729. The *New York Times* reported after the debate that the Bloomberg quotations had been compiled by his former employees. He had dismissed them as jokes, though he "has never explicitly acknowledged" saying them. (*New York Times*, "Fact-Checking the Las Vegas Democratic Debate," *New York Times*, February 19, 2020, https://www.nytimes.com/2020/02/19/us/politics/democratic-debate-nevada -fact-check.html.)

730. John Koblin, tweet, February 20, 2020, https://twitter.com/koblin/status /1230564938445275140.

731. As of the debate, 75,000 Nevada Democrats had voted early—compared to a total turnout of 86,000 in 2016. (Nevada State Democratic Party, press statement, February 19, 2020, https://twitter.com/meganmesserly/status/1230311189651107841.) Turnout would ultimately exceed 2016, but it was less than the turnout in 2008.

(Steve Sebelius, "Nevada's Caucuses See Big Turnout," *Las Vegas Review-Journal*, February 24, 2020, https://www.reviewjournal.com/news/politics-and-government/nevada/nevadas-caucuses-see-big-turnout-1965134/.)

732. "Nevada 2020: Sanders with Comfortable Lead Heading into Caucus, Tight Race for Second Place," Emerson College Polling, February 21, 2020, http://emersonpolling.com/2020/02/20/nevada-2020-sanders-with-comfortable-lead-heading-into-caucus-tight-race-for-second-place/.

733. Shane Harris et al., "Bernie Sanders Briefed by U.S. Officials That Russia Is Trying to Help His Presidential Campaign," *Washington Post*, February 21, 2020, https://www.washingtonpost.com/national-security/bernie-sanders-briefed-by-us-officials-that-russia-is-trying-to-help-his-presidential-campaign/2020/02/21/5ad396a6-54bd-11ea-929a-64efa7482a77_story.html.

734. Mike Bloomberg for President, press statement, February 21, 2020, https://twitter.com/JuliaManch/status/1230920312696471553.

735. Senator Bernie Sanders, Nevada caucuses victory speech (San Antonio, Texas, February 22, 2020, https://www.rev.com/blog/transcripts/nevada-caucus-speech-transcripts-bernie-sanders-elizabeth-warren-joe-biden-pete-buttigieg-amy-klobuchar-speak-after-nevada-results.

736. Scott Clement et al., "Entrance Polls from the 2020 Nevada Democratic Caucuses," *Washington Post*, February 24, 2020, https://www.washingtonpost.com/graphics/politics/entrance-polls-2020-nevada-caucuses/.

737. Representative Pramila Jayapal, tweet, February 22, 2020, https://twitter.com/PramilaJayapal/status/1231389809446227968.

738. Marc Caputo, "Biden Claims Comeback despite Distant Second Finish to Sanders," *Politico*, February 22, 2020, https://www.politico.com/news/2020/02/22/joe-biden-claims-victory-nevada-116756.

739. Representative James Clyburn, quoted in Peggy Noonan, "Jim Clyburn Saves the Democrats," *Wall Street Journal*, March 5, 2020, https://www.wsj.com/articles/jim-clyburn-saves-the-democrats-11583450229.

740. Winthrop University, "Results of Winthrop Poll Released on February 21, 2020 of Likely Voters in the Feb. 29 SC Democratic Presidential Primary," press statement, February 20, 2020, https://www.winthrop.edu/winthroppoll/current-findings.aspx.

741. Alexa Lardieri, "Joe Biden, Bernie Sanders Tied in South Carolina, Poll Finds," *U.S. News & World Report*, February 19, 2020, https://www.usnews.com/news/elections/articles/2020-02-19/joe-biden-bernie-sanders-tied-in-south-carolina-poll.

742. Joel B. Pollak, "Bernie Sanders Goes 1-2-3 in Early States—First Time Ever," Breitbart News, February 22, 2020, https://www.breitbart.com/politics/2020/02/22/bernie-sanders-goes-1-2-3-in-early-states-and-4th-is-possible/.

743. Marianne Williamson, quoted in Hannah Bleau, "Marianne Williamson Backs Bernie Sanders: 'The Energy Is Unquestionably' with Him," Breitbart

News, February 23, 2020, https://www.breitbart.com/politics/2020/02/23/marianne
-williamson-backs-bernie-sanders-the-energy-is-unquestionably-with-him/.

744. Bill de Blasio, tweet, February 22, 2020, https://twitter.com/BilldeBlasio
/status/1231392649384472576.

745. Senator Bernie Sanders, quoted in Paul LeBlanc and Dan Merica, "Sanders Says 'It's Unfair to Simply Say Everything Is Bad' with Fidel Castro's Cuba," CNN, February 24, 2020, https://www.cnn.com/2020/02/23/politics
/sanders-fidel-castro-cuba/index.html.

746. Senator Bernie Sanders, tweet, February 23, 2020, https://twitter.com
/berniesanders/status/1231709010430189570.

747. AIPAC, tweet, February 23, 2020, https://twitter.com/AIPAC/status/12317
53656044806144.

748. He continued: "This is South Carolina, and South Carolinians are
pretty leery about that title socialist. And so I think that that would be a real burden for us in these states or congressional districts that we have to do well in. If
you look at how well we did the last time, and look at the congressional districts,
these were not liberal or what you might call progressive districts. These were basically moderate and conservative districts that we did well in. And in those districts, it's going to be tough to hold onto these jobs if you have to make the case for
accepting a self-proclaimed Democratic socialist." (James Clyburn, interview with
George Stephanopoulos, *This Week*, February 23, 2020, https://abcnews.go.com
/Politics/week-transcript-23-20-amb-robert-obrien-rep/story?id=69146720.)

749. Critics on the left noted that Scarborough only had called on female candidates to drop out. (Chrissy Clark, "Joe Scarborough Calls on Warren, Klobuchar
to Drop Out and 'Consolidate Efforts' against Sanders," *The Federalist*, February
24, 2020, https://thefederalist.com/2020/02/24/joe-scarborough-calls-on-warren
-klobuchar-to-drop-out-and-consolidate-efforts-against-sanders/.)

750. Chris Matthews, quoted in Kristine Marsh, "Chris Matthews Begs
Bernie for Forgiveness; No Apologies for Despicable Trump Family Remarks,"
NewsBusters, February 25, 2020, https://www.newsbusters.org/blogs/nb/kristine
-marsh/2020/02/25/chris-matthews-begs-bernie-forgiveness-no-apologies
-despicable.

751. The complaints had been building for weeks. Pete Buttigieg tried to cap-
italize on the issue in the Nevada debate, telling Sanders: "We can build a movement without having legions of our supporters online and in person attacking
Democratic figures and union leaders alike." (Buttigieg, ninth Democratic presidential debate).

752. Pete Buttigieg, speech (North Charleston, South Carolina, February
24, 2020), https://www.breitbart.com/politics/2020/02/24/pete-buttigieg-to-black
-voters-i-do-not-have-that-lived-experience/.

753. Associated Press, "Pete Buttigieg Confronted by Minimum Wage, Racial
Justice Protesters at South Carolina Union Event," February 24, 2020, https://time
.com/5790037/pete-buttigieg-protesters-minimum-wage-south-carolina/.

754. Joe Biden, quoted in Joel B. Pollak, "Joe Biden Flogs 'Very Fine People' Hoax to Half-empty Gym in South Carolina," Breitbart News, February 24, 2020, https://www.breitbart.com/politics/2020/02/24/joe-biden-flogs-very-fine-people-hoax-to-half-empty-gym-in-south-carolina/.

755. Joel B. Pollak, "Tom Steyer Accused of Buying Black Support in South Carolina," Breitbart News, February 24, 2020, https://www.breitbart.com/politics/2020/02/24/tom-steyer-accused-of-buying-black-support-in-south-carolina/.

756. Matthew Mulligan and Yuliya Talmazan, "Coronavirus Quarantine on Diamond Princess Cruise Ship 'Chaotic,' Japanese Expert Claims," NBC News, February 19, 2020, https://www.nbcnews.com/news/world/coronavirus-quarantine-diamond-princess-cruise-ship-chaotic-japanese-expert-claims-n1138846.

757. Agence France-Press, "Diamond Princess: The Quarantined Cruise Ship by the Numbers," Breitbart News, February 18, 2020, https://www.breitbart.com/news/diamond-princess-the-quarantined-cruise-ship-by-the-numbers/.

758. Frances Martel, "Japan: Two 80+ Passengers Die of Coronavirus on Stranded Cruise Ship," Breitbart News, February 20, 2020, https://www.breitbart.com/asia/2020/02/20/japan-two-80-passengers-die-of-coronavirus-on-stranded-cruise-ship/.

759. Joshua Caplan, "Report: Coronavirus-Infected Americans Were Flown Home despite CDC Objections," Breitbart News, February 20, 2020, https://www.breitbart.com/health/2020/02/20/report-coronavirus-infected-americans-were-flown-home-despite-cdc-objections/.

760. The United States also flew home Americans who had tested negative, before the ship was released from quarantine.

761. Dr. Susan Berry, "Rasmussen: Most Americans 'Confident' U.S. Healthcare System Can Contain Coronavirus," Breitbart News, January 28, 2020, https://www.breitbart.com/politics/2020/01/28/rasmussen-most-americans-confident-u-s-healthcare-system-can-contain-coronavirus/.

762. John Carney, "Fed Chair Powell Says Economic Effects of Coronavirus Are 'Very Uncertain,'" Breitbart News, January 29, 2020.

763. Frances Martel, "Chinese Media: 'Racism, Profiling, Hate' a Worse Virus Than Coronavirus," Breitbart News, February 3, 2020, https://www.breitbart.com/national-security/2020/02/03/chinese-media-racism-profiling-hate-worse-virus-coronavirus/.

764. John Hayward, "China Reports, Deletes, Then Again Reports Death of Wuhan Virus Whistleblower Doctor," Breitbart News, February 6, 2020, https://www.breitbart.com/national-security/2020/02/06/china-reports-deletes-again-reports-death-wuhan-virus-whistleblower-doctor/.

765. Ron Klain, quoted in Kyle Olson, "Biden Adviser Slams Trump's Handling of Coronavirus but Claimed 'No Reason' to Panic Last Month," Breitbart News, March 23, 2020, https://www.breitbart.com/politics/2020/03/23/biden-adviser-slams-trumps-handling-of-coronavirus-but-claimed-no-reason-to-panic-last-month/.

766. Rebecca Mansour, "Coronavirus Outbreak Exposes China's Monopoly on U.S. Drug, Medical Supplies," Breitbart News, February 13, 2020, https://www.breitbart.com/asia/2020/02/13/coronavirus-outbreak-exposes-chinas-monopoly-on-u-s-drug-medical-supplies/.

767. Tom Cotton, the most aggressive legislator—by far—on dealing with coronavirus, told Breitbart News that every conversation he had had with the president since mid-January had been about coronavirus. (Joel B. Pollak, "Tom Cotton: Every Conversation with Trump over Last Month Involved Coronavirus," Breitbart News, February 24, 2020, https://www.breitbart.com/health/2020/02/24/tom-cotton-every-conversation-with-trump-over-last-month-involved-coronavirus/.)

768. John Carney, "U.S. Consumer Confidence Running Even Higher in February on Sunnier Outlook," Breitbart News, February 25, 2020, https://www.breitbart.com/economy/2020/02/25/u-s-consumer-confidence-improved-a-bit-in-february-on-sunnier-outlook/.

769. John Carney, "Dow Plunges 879 Points as Government Coronavirus Warnings Pummel Markets," Breitbart News, February 25, 2020, https://www.breitbart.com/economy/2020/02/25/dow-plunges-600-points-as-government-coronavirus-warnings-pummel-markets/.

770. Pete Buttigieg made an indirect reference to it at the New Hampshire debate: "The next president is going to face challenges from global health security, like what we're seeing coming out of China." Seventh Democratic debate. (Carney, "Dow Plunges 879 Points.")

771. Joel B. Pollak, "Democrat Debates Ignored Coronavirus Almost Entirely before Feb. 25," Breitbart News, March 16, 2020, https://www.breitbart.com/politics/2020/03/16/democrat-debate-coronavirus/.

772. Joel B. Pollak, "'Bernie Bros' Troll Democrat Debate in South Carolina: 'This Sh*t Gets Too Serious,'" Breitbart News, February 25, 2020, https://www.breitbart.com/politics/2020/02/25/bernie-bros-troll-democrat-debate-in-south-carolina/.

773. Joe Biden, appearance at ninth Democratic presidential debate (Charleston, South Carolina, February 25, 2020), https://www.cbsnews.com/news/south-carolina-democratic-debate-full-transcript-text/.

774. Associated Press, quoted in Joel B. Pollak, "AP Confirms: Democrats Are Lying to the Public about Coronavirus Readiness," Breitbart News, February 27, 2020, https://www.breitbart.com/health/2020/02/27/ap-confirms-democrats-are-lying-to-the-public-about-coronavirus/.

775. Biden would later claim to have warned the country about the pandemic in a USA Today op-ed on January 27. (Joe Biden, "Joe Biden: Trump Is Worst Possible Leader to Deal with Coronavirus Outbreak," USA Today, January 27, 2020, https://www.usatoday.com/story/opinion/2020/01/27/coronavirus-donald-trump-made-us-less-prepared-joe-biden-column/4581710002/.) He called Trump "the worst possible person to lead our country through a global health challenge," adding:

"I am concerned that the Trump administration's shortsighted policies have left us unprepared for a dangerous epidemic that will come sooner or later." He claimed that Trump had "proposed draconian cuts" to several health agencies, though he did not point out that the president ultimately signed bills that had increased their budgets. (Pollak, "AP Confirms.") Biden also claimed that Trump had "dismissed the top White House official in charge of global health security and dismantled the entire team," which was also inaccurate (ibid.) and was refuted in detail by former National Security Council (NSC) official Tim Morrison in an op-ed in the *Washington Post*. Morrison noted that the pandemic team had duplicated existing functions and that its members were reassigned to other parts of the NSC—which, he said, arguably strengthened the administration's pandemic response. (Tim Morrison, "No, the White House Didn't 'Dissolve' Its Pandemic Response Office. I Was There," *Washington Post*, March 16, 2020, https://www.washingtonpost.com/opini ons/2020/03/16/no-white-house-didnt-dissolve-its-pandemic-response-office/.) Biden also claimed in the op-ed: "Diseases do not stop at borders. They cannot be thwarted by building a wall." That argument was refuted by the success of the China travel ban that Trump declared four days later—and which Biden opposed— which scientists later acknowledged had slowed the spread of the pandemic in the United States.

776. Tom Steyer, quoted in Joel B. Pollak, "Tom Steyer: Coronavirus Proves Trump 'Incompetent' on Economy," Breitbart News, February 25, 2020, https:// www.breitbart.com/2020-election/2020/02/25/tom-steyer-coronavirus-proves -trump-incompetent-on-economy/.

777. Joel B. Pollak, "Elizabeth Warren, Surrogates Dodge Debate Question on Jerusalem Embassy," Breitbart News, February 26, 2020, https://www .breitbart.com/middle-east/2020/02/26/elizabeth-warren-surrogates-dodge -question-on-jerusalem-embassy/.

778. Joe Biden, quoted in Dareh Gregorian, "Joe Biden on Sanders: Americans 'Aren't Looking for Revolution,'" Breitbart News, February 26, 2020, https://www .nbcnews.com/politics/2020-election/joe-biden-sanders-americans-aren-t-looking -revolution-n1143681.

779. Joel B. Pollak, "Democrats Court Al Sharpton; Ignore Past of Racism, Antisemitism, Incitement," Breitbart News, April 3, 2019, https://www .breitbart.com/politics/2019/04/03/democrats-court-al-sharpton-ignore-past-of -racism-antisemitism-incitement/.

780. After a famous rabbi's motorcade accidentally struck and killed a black child, Sharpton fanned the flames of outrage until an enraged mob fatally stabbed a foreign religious student, Yankel Rosenbaum, to death. Sharpton also led protests against a Jewish-owned store in Harlem, Freddy's Fashion Mart. The store had raised the rent on a subtenant, a black-owned record store. Sharpton had allegedly referred to the Jewish owner as an "interloper." One of the protesters later shot four of the store's employees and then set it on fire, killing seven people and himself. (Paul Berman, "Medieval New York," *New Yorker*, January 8, 1996, https://www

.newyorker.com/magazine/1996/01/15/medieval-new-york.) (Pollak, "Democrats Court Al Sharpton.")

781. She claimed that a local prosecutor had been one of her assailants. But her story fell apart, and the prosecutor sued for defamation. Sharpton refused to pay the damages himself; instead, his friends and supporters paid for him. (Alan Feuer, "Sharpton's Debt in Brawley Defamation Is Paid by Supporters," *New York Times*, June 15, 2001, B6, https://www.nytimes.com/2001/06/15/nyregion /sharpton-s-debt-in-brawley-defamation-is-paid-by-supporters.html.)

782. Federal Election Commission, "FEC Reaches Settlement with Rev. Al Sharpton, Sharpton 2004 and Non-profit Corporation," April 30, 2009, https:// www.fec.gov/updates/fec-reaches-settlement-with-rev-al-sharpton-sharpton-2004 -and-non-profit-corporation/.

783. As Business Insider recalled: "Obama stayed so far away from Sharpton during the 2008 campaign that Sharpton, with Obama's blessing, never even endorsed him." (Wayne Barrett, "How Al Sharpton Became Obama's Go-to Black Leader," Business Insider, April 13, 2011, https://www.businessinsider.com /al-sharpton-obama-go-to-black-leader-2011-4.)

784. Obama faced criticism from black leaders like Cornel West and Tavis Smiley for failing to do enough to help minority communities. Sharpton took Obama's side.

785. President Barack Obama, quoted by Byron Tau, "Obama: 'If I Had a Son, He'd Look Like Trayvon,'" *Politico*, March 23, 2012, https://www.politico.com/blogs /politico44/2012/03/obama-if-i-had-a-son-hed-look-like-trayvon-118439.

786. A Gallup poll showed steady improvements until 2013, when race relations turned sharply downward. (Gallup, "Race Relations," accessed September 11, 2019, https://news.gallup.com/poll/1687/race-relations.aspx.)

787. Early in the 2020 race, Sharpton had one question for the candidates: Would you back reparations for slavery? Most agreed, at least, to study the issue.

788. When Representative Matt Gaetz (R-FL) finally challenged Sharpton during a congressional hearing in September 2019, citing a list of Sharpton's past statements, Sharpton denied a few but defended others. (Joel B. Pollak, "Matt Gaetz Exposes Al Sharpton's Racist, Antisemitic, Homophobic Rhetoric; Quotes Joe Scarborough," Breitbart News, September 19, 2019, https://www.breitbart.com /politics/2019/09/19/matt-gaetz-exposes-al-sharpton-racist-antisemitic-rhetoric -quotes-msnbc-joe-scarborough/)

789. Joel B. Pollak, "Boeing Company Funds Al Sharpton Event; Executives Refuse Comment," Breitbart News, February 27, 2020, https://www.breitbart.com /economy/2020/02/27/boeing-al-sharpton-democrats-refuse-comment/.

790. Joel B. Pollak, "Democrats Make Their Pitch at Al Sharpton Breakfast in South Carolina," Breitbart News, February 26, 2020, https://www.breitbart.com ./politics/2020/02/26/democrats-make-their-pitch-at-al-sharpton-breakfast-in-south -carolina/.

791. Representative James Clyburn, speech endorsing Joe Biden (Trident Technical College, North Charleston, South Carolina, February 26, 2020).

792. Hanna Trudo, "Majority Whip Jim Clyburn: Sanders Never Courted My Endorsement," Daily Beast, March 4, 2020, https://www.thedailybeast.com /majority-whip-jim-clyburn-sanders-never-courted-my-endorsement.

793. Noonan, "Jim Clyburn Saves the Democrats."

794. "Biden Maintains Lead," Monmouth University, February 27, 2020, https://www.monmouth.edu/polling-institute/reports/monmouthpoll_sc_022720/.

795. Andy Shain, tweet, February 27, 2020, https://twitter.com/AndyShain /status/1233074240070574081.

796. Natash Korecki and Marc Caputo, "Joe Biden's Campaign Isn't Dead Yet." Politico, February 27, 2020, https://www.politico.com/news/2020/02/27/joe-biden -south-carolina-comeback-118006.

797. Kendall Karson, tweet, February 29, 2020, https://twitter.com/kendall karson/status/1233879302053167105.

798. Cara Korte, tweet, February 29, 2020, https://www.breitbart.com/politics /2020/02/29/live-updates-south-carolina-primary-results/.

799. CBS News, tweet, February 29, 2020, https://twitter.com/CBSNews /status/1233881760280326145.

800. Joe Biden, South Carolina victory speech (Charleston, South Carolina, February 29, 2020, https://www.rev.com/blog/transcripts/joe-biden-victory-speech -transcript-biden-wins-south-carolina-democratic-primary.

801. David Halberstam, The Unfinished Odyssey of Robert Kennedy (New York: Bantam, 1968), 164.

802. "South Carolina 2020 Primary: Live Results," New York Times, accessed March 27, 2020, https://www.nytimes.com/interactive/2020/02/29/us/elections/results -south-carolina-primary-election.html.

803. Hannah Bleau, "Billionaire Tom Steyer Drops Out of the Presidential Race: 'Honestly, I Can't See a Path,'" Breitbart News, February 29, 2020, https:// www.breitbart.com/politics/2020/02/29/billionaire-tom-steyer-drops-out-of-the -presidential-race-honestly-i-cant-see-a-path/.

804. Richard A. Oppel Jr. and Richard Fausset, "Klobuchar Ramped Up Prosecutions, Except in Cases against Police," New York Times, February 26, 2020, https://www.nytimes.com/2020/02/26/us/klobuchar-prosecutor-myon-burrell.html.

805. Joel B. Pollak, "Black Lives Matter Activists Shut Down Amy Klobuchar Rally in Minnesota," Breitbart News, March 2, 2020, https://www.breitbart.com /politics/2020/03/02/black-lives-matter-activists-shut-down-amy-klobuchar-rally -minnesota/.

806. Jack Turman, "Jimmy Carter Says Buttigieg 'Doesn't Know What He's Going to Do' after South Carolina," CBS News, March 1, 2020, https:// www.cbsnews.com/news/jimmy-carter-pete-buttigieg-doesnt-know-what-hes -going-to-do-after-south-carolina/.

807. Carla Marinucci, tweet, March 1, 2020, https://twitter.com/cmarinucci /status/1234252611546570752.

808. Reuters, tweet, March 2, 2020, https://twitter.com/Reuters/status/1234551 067662340096.

809. Elena Schneider, "Klobuchar Drops Out of 2020 Campaign, Endorses Biden," *Politico*, March 2, 2020, https://www.politico.com/news/2020/03/02/klobuchar -to-drop-out-of-2020-campaign-endorse-biden-118823.

810. Rishika Dugyala, "Beto O'Rourke Endorses Biden," *Politico*, March 2, 2020, https://www.politico.com/news/2020/03/02/beto-orourke-to-endorse-biden -119100.

811. Susan Rice, tweet, March 2, 2020, https://twitter.com/AmbassadorRice /status/1234575446714523654.

812. Joe Biden, remarks (Houston, Texas, March 2, 2020), https://twitter.com /mattdizwhitlock/status/1234578328423673857.

813. Pete Buttigieg, appearance at endorsement rally for Joe Biden (Dallas, Texas, March 2, 2020), https://www.rev.com/blog/transcripts/transcript-buttigieg -klobuchar-and-orourke-endorse-biden-in-dallas-rally.

814. Dick van Dyke, speech at Bernie Sanders rally (Los Angeles, California, March 2, 2020), https://www.youtube.com/watch?v=9a4CZaGpquI.

815. Jenna Amatulli, "Dick Van Dyke Hams It Up at Bernie Sanders Rally, Crowd Chants 'We Love Dick,'" Huffington Post, March 2, 2020, https://www.huff post.com/entry/dick-van-dyke-bernie-sanders-rally_n_5e5d35c3c5b67ed38b36359d.

816. Bernie Sanders, speech (Los Angeles Convention Center, Los Angeles, California, March 1, 2020), https://www.rev.com/blog/transcripts/bernie-sanders -los-angeles-rally-transcript-before-super-tuesday.

817. Sydney Ember, "Sanders Campaign Was Caught Off Guard by Quick Massing of Opposition," *New York Times*, March 3, 2020, https://www.nytimes .com/2020/03/03/us/politics/bernie-sanders-2020-super-tuesday.html.

818. Ryan Struyk, tweet, March 1, 2020, https://twitter.com/ryanstruyk/status /1234126965562658822.

819. Rebecca Klar, "Sanders Has 13-Point Lead in North Carolina Ahead of Super Tuesday: Poll," *The Hill*, March 2, 2020, https://thehill.com/homenews /campaign/485447-sanders-leads-democratic-field-by-13-points-in-north-carolina -ahead-of.

820. Sam Levine, tweet, March 1, 2020, https://twitter.com/srl/status/1234172 136580886528.

821. Matt Sepic, "Bernie Sanders in St. Paul Calls for Klobuchar's Supporters to Join Him," MPRNews.com, March 2, 2020, https://www.mprnews.org/story/2020 /03/02/sanders-in-st-paul-calls-for-klobuchars-supporters-to-join-him.

822. Molly Hensley-Clancy, tweet, March 2, 2020, https://twitter.com/mollyhc /status/1234658376442761219.

823. Joe Biden, quoted in Charlie Spiering, "Brain Freeze: Joe Biden Urges Voters to Show Up on 'Super Thursday,'" Breitbart News, March 2, 2020, https://

www.breitbart.com/politics/2020/03/02/gaffe-alert-joe-biden-urges-voters
-to-show-up-on-super-thursday/.

824. Vice President Mike Pence, "Press Briefing by Vice President Pence and Members of the White House Coronavirus Task Force," White House, March 3, 2020, https://www.whitehouse.gov/briefings-statements/press-briefing-vice-president -pence-members-white-house-coronavirus-task-force/.

825. "U.S. Will Drop Limits on Virus Testing, Pence Says," *New York Times*, March 3, 2020, https://www.nytimes.com/2020/03/03/world/coronavirus-live-news-updates.html.

826. Dr. Anthony Fauci, quoted in John Bowden, "Fauci: Neither Trump nor CDC to Blame for Testing Delay," March 17, 2020, https://thehill.com/policy /healthcare/487985-fauci-neither-trump-nor-cdc-to-blame-for-testing-delay.

827. President Donald Trump, tweet, March 1, 2020, https://twitter.com /realDonaldTrump/status/1234211248373403648.

828. The president's full quote, with context: "Now the Democrats are politicizing the coronavirus, you know that right? Coronavirus, they're politicizing it. We did one of the great jobs. You say, 'How's President Trump doing?' They go, 'Oh, not good, not good.' They have no clue. They don't have any clue. They can't even count their votes in Iowa. They can't even count. No, they can't. They can't count their votes. One of my people came up to me and said, 'Mr. President, they tried to beat you on Russia, Russia, Russia. That didn't work out too well. They couldn't do it. They tried the impeachment hoax. That was on a perfect conversation. They tried anything. They tried it over and over. They'd been doing it since you got in. It's all turning. They lost. It's all turning. Think of it. Think of it. And this is their new hoax.'" (President Donald Trump, speech [North Charleston, South Carolina, February 28, 2020], https://www.rev.com/blog/transcripts/donald-trump-charleston -south-carolina-rally-transcript-february-28-2020.)

829. Zeke Miller, tweet, March 1, 2020, https://twitter.com/ZekeJMiller /status/1234281622482145281.

830. Richard Engel, tweet, March 2, 2020, https://twitter.com/RichardEngel /status/1234535204238352385.

831. President Donald Trump, tweet, March 2, 2020, https://twitter.com /realDonaldTrump/status/1234462291652993032.

832. Jerome M. Adams, "Surgeon General: Be Cautious, but Not Afraid of Coronavirus," CNN.com, March 3, 2020, https://www.cnn.com/2020/03/03/opinions /coronavirus-prepare-not-panic-opinion-adams/index.html.

833. Jonathan Martin and Alexander Burns, "How the Democratic Establishment Stumbled as Sanders Surged," *New York Times*, March 3, 2020, A1.

834. The *Times* added: "Top Democrats now believe that there are only two realistic paths forward in the presidential race: a dominant victory on Tuesday by Mr. Sanders that gives him a wide lead in the delegate count, or a battle for delegates over months of primary elections, that might allow Mr. Biden to pull ahead or force the nomination to be decided at the Milwaukee convention in July."

835. Jonathan Easley, "Sanders Poised for Big Super Tuesday," *The Hill*, March 3, 2020, https://thehill.com/homenews/campaign/485613-sanders-poised-for-big-super-tuesday.

836. Laura Barron-Lopez and Marc Caputo, "Biden Campaign Predicts Texas Upset over Sanders," *Politico*, March 3, 2020, https://www.politico.com/news/2020/03/03/biden-texas-sanders-super-tuesday-119207.

837. Geoff Bennet, tweet, March 3, 2020, https://twitter.com/GeoffRBennett/status/1234949237198159874.

838. Hannah Bleau, "Problems Across Super Tuesday States Have Sanders Supporters Fearing a Rigged Election," Breitbart News, March 3, 2020, https://www.breitbart.com/politics/2020/03/03/problems-across-super-tuesday-states-have-sanders-supporters-fearing-a-rigged-election/.

839. Alexia Díaz, "Street Officially Renamed Obama Boulevard in Baldwin Hills/Crenshaw Ceremony," *Los Angeles Times*, May 4, 2019, https://www.latimes.com/local/lanow/la-me-ln-obama-boulevard-dedication-ceremony-20190504-story.html.

840. The *Wall Street Journal* noted that he had run an unprecedented campaign in the territory, spending a relative fortune: "In the weeks before the election, the Bloomberg campaign hired seven staffers and opened a campaign headquarters near the movie theater." Gabbard, a native daughter, never visited the territory to campaign. (Zusha Elinson, "Mike Bloomberg's $620 Million Campaign Did Really Well—in American Samoa," *Wall Street Journal*, March 6, 2020, https://www.wsj.com/articles/mike-bloombergs-620-million-campaign-did-really-wellin-american-samoa-11583538043.)

841. Joe Biden, quoted in Joshua Caplan, "Brain Freeze: Joe Biden Mixes Up Wife Jill with His Sister," Breitbart News, March 3, 2020, https://www.breitbart.com/politics/2020/03/03/brain-freeze-joe-biden-mixes-up-wife-jill-with-his-sister/.

842. José Saramago, *Blindness* (London: The Harvill Press, 1995), 30.

843. Ian Hanchett, "Carville: There Will Be Calls for Sanders to Exit—Clyburn 'Saved the Democratic Party,'" Breitbart News, March 3, 2020, https://www.breitbart.com/clips/2020/03/03/carville-there-will-be-calls-for-sanders-to-exit-clyburn-saved-the-democratic-party/.

844. Zacks Equity Research, "Stock Market News for Mar 5, 2020," Yahoo! Finance, March 5, 2020, https://finance.yahoo.com/news/stock-market-news-mar-5-143402756.html.

845. Michaela Tindera, "Michael Bloomberg Poured Over $1 Billion into His Presidential Campaign," *Forbes*, April 20, 2020, https://www.forbes.com/sites/michelatindera/2020/04/20/michael-bloomberg-poured-over-1-billion-into-his-presidential-campaign/#361f99036b45.

846. Mike Bloomberg, quoted in Tim Perry, "Bloomberg Ends Presidential Run and Endorses Biden after Super Tuesday rejection." CBS News, March 4, 2020,

https://www.cbsnews.com/news/bloomberg-ends-presidential-bid-biden-endorsement
-super-tuesday/.

847. President Donald Trump, tweet, March 4, 2020, https://twitter.com
/realDonaldTrump/status/1235232818692792320.

848. Ilhan Omar, tweet, March 3, 2020, https://twitter.com/IlhanMN/status
/1235055956888674304. Tulsi Gabbard, still in the race, mocked Warren as a
"fake indigenous woman of color." (tweet, March 3, 2020, https://twitter.com/Tulsi
Gabbard/status/1234962318045278208.)

849. President Donald Trump, tweet, March 4, 2020, https://twitter.com
/realDonaldTrump/status/1235232818692792320.

850. Warren would eventually endorse Biden—on April 15, a day after former
President Barack Obama had already done so, when Biden was the only candidate left.

851. David Catanese, tweet, March 5, 2020, https://twitter.com/davecatanese
/status/1235755316349820928.

852. Edward-Isaac Dovere, tweet, March 6, 2020, https://twitter.com/Isaac
Dovere/status/1235936441114517504.

853. Johnny Verhovek, tweet, March 6, 2020, https://twitter.com/JTHVerhovek
/status/1236027420311982083.

854. Zack Budryk, "Kamala Harris Endorses Biden's Presidential Bid," *The
Hill*, March 8, 2020, https://thehill.com/homenews/campaign/486480-kamala-harris
-endorses-biden-presidential-bid.

855. Malachi Barrett, "John Kerry Visiting Michigan to Stump for Joe Biden
Days Before Democratic Primary," MLive.com, March 6, 2020, https://www.mlive
.com/public-interest/2020/03/john-kerry-visiting-michigan-to-stump-for-joe-biden
-days-before-democratic-primary.html.

856. Nick Corasaniti, "Cory Booker Endorses Joe Biden as Candidates Race
Toward More Primaries." *New York Times*, March 9, 2020, https://www.nytimes
.com/2020/03/09/us/politics/cory-booker-endorses-joe-biden.html.

857. Cory Booker, speech endorsing Joe Biden (Flint, Michigan, March 9,
2020), https://www.youtube.com/watch?v=551gVtWP68g.

858. Eli Yokley, "Biden Boasts 16-Point Lead Over Sanders in Democratic
Presidential Race," Morning Consult, March 6, 2020, https://morningconsult
.com/2020/03/06/democratic-primary-polling-joe-biden-bernie-sanders/.

859. Quinnipiac University, "Biden Crushes Sanders in Democratic Race,
Quinnipiac University National Poll Finds; More Disapprove of Trump's Response
to Coronavirus," March 9, 2020, https://poll.qu.edu/national/release-detail?Release
ID=3657.

860. Jim VandeHei and Mike Allen, "Joe Biden's Secret Governing Plan," Axios,
March 9, 2020, https://www.axios.com/joe-biden-cabinet-vice-president-picks-b17882
ac-3953-450f-8afb-38a3c8dcda57.html.

861. People4Bernie, tweet, March 8, 2020, https://twitter.com/People4Bernie
/status/1236633603083128832.

862. Holly Otterbein, "Sanders Backed by Justice Democrats," *Politico*, March 8, 2020, https://www.politico.com/news/2020/03/08/bernie-sanders-justice-democrats -123535.

863. Holly Otterbein, "Sanders Courts Muslim Voters for Michigan Edge," *Politico*, March 8, 2020, https://www.politico.com/news/2020/03/08/sanders-courts -muslim-voters-michigan-124034.

864. Natasha Korecki, tweet, March 5, 2020, https://twitter.com/natashakorecki /status/1235630871039930372.

865. Ruby Cramer, tweet, March 5, 2020, https://twitter.com/rubycramer /status/1235768148701392898.

866. Maggie Severns, "Biden to Get Cover from Major Super PAC as GOP Attacks Ramp Up," *Politico*, March 9, 2020, https://www.politico.com/news/2020 /03/09/biden-priorities-usa-gop-attacks-124136.

867. Senator Chuck Schumer, quoted in Ian Hanchett, "Schumer to Kavana- ugh and Gorsuch: 'You Will Pay the Price'—'Won't Know What Hit You' If You Make 'Awful Decisions,'" Breitbart News, March 4, 2020, https://www.breitbart .com/clips/2020/03/04/schumer-to-kavanaugh-and-gorsuch-you-will-pay-the-price -wont-know-what-hit-you-if-you-make-awful-decisions/.

868. Chief Justice John Roberts, quoted in Robert Barnes, tweet, March 4, 2020, https://twitter.com/scotusreporter/status/1235323171299119110.

869. Steve Herman, tweet, March 4, 2020, https://twitter.com/W7VOA/status /1235361539974148096.

870. Rosie Perper et al., "Almost All US States Have Declared States of Emer- gency to Fight Coronavirus—Here's What It Means for Them," Business Insider, March 16, 2020, https://www.businessinsider.com/california-washington-state-of -emergency-coronavirus-what-it-means-2020-3.

871. Justin McCarthy, "High Confidence in Government to Handle Corona- virus," February 20, 2020, https://news.gallup.com/poll/286277/high-confidence -government-handle-coronavirus.aspx.

872. President Donald Trump, tweet, March 5, 2020, https://twitter.com /realDonaldTrump/status/1235604572850343937.

873. Ryan Browne, "US Navy to Self-quarantine Ships in Europe Due to Coronavirus," CNN, 3 Mar. 2020, https://www.cnn.com/2020/03/03/politics/navy -coronavirus-self-quarantine-ships-europe/index.html.

874. American Conservative Union, tweet, March 7, 2020, https://twitter.com /ACUConservative/status/1236415113265102852.

875. David Brancaccio and Alex Schroeder, "273,000: A Blockbuster Num- ber for the February Jobs Report," Marketplace, March 6, 2020, https://www .marketplace.org/2020/03/06/jobs-report-coronavirus-weather/.

876. Jeff Cox, "Job Growth Smashes Expectations for February as Unemploy- ment Falls Back to 3.5%," CNBC, March 6, 2020, https://www.cnbc.com/2020/03/06 /us-jobs-report-february-2020.html.

877. As late as March 17, the "Job Openings and Labor Turnover Summary" from the Bureau of Labor Statistics reported that "hires and separations were little changed"—though the data were from late January. (U.S. Bureau of Labor Statistics, "Job Openings and Labor Turnover Summary," March 17, 2020, https://www.bls.gov/news.release/jolts.nr0.htm.)

878. MUFG Union Bank economist Chris Rupkey, quoted in Cox, "Job Growth Smashes Expectations."

879. President Donald Trump, tweet, March 9, 2020, https://twitter.com/realDonaldTrump/status/1237027356314869761.

880. Agence France-Presse, "Oil Falls Most since Gulf War as Saudi Starts Price War," Breitbart News, March 9, 2020, https://www.breitbart.com/news/oil-falls-most-since-gulf-war-as-saudi-starts-price-war/.

881. Yun Li, "Dow Sinks 2,000 Points in Worst Day since 2008, S&P 500 Drops More Than 7%," CNBC, March 8, 2020, https://www.cnbc.com/2020/03/08/dow-futures-drop-700-points-as-all-out-oil-price-war-adds-to-coronavirus-stress.html.

882. Akane Otani and Karen Langley, "Dow Jones Industrial Average's 11-Year Bull Run Ends," *Wall Street Journal*, March 11, 2020, https://www.wsj.com/articles/global-markets-calmer-after-two-hectic-days-11583899913?mod=e2tw.

883. Joshua Caplan, "Tom Hanks, Wife Rita Wilson Test Positive for Coronavirus," Breitbart News, March 11, 2020, https://www.breitbart.com/entertainment/2020/03/11/tom-hanks-wife-rita-wilson-test-positive-for-coronavirus/.

884. Tom Hanks, quoted in David Ng, "Tom Hanks, Rita Wilson Give Coronavirus Update: 'There Is No Crying in Baseball,'" Breitbart News, March 13, 2020, https://www.breitbart.com/entertainment/2020/03/13/tom-hanks-rita-wilson-give-coronavirus-update-there-is-no-crying-in-baseball/.

885. Kyle Olson, "Joe Biden Argues with Construction Workers over Guns: 'You're Full of Sh*t!,'" Breitbart News, March 10, 2020, https://www.breitbart.com/2020-election/2020/03/10/joe-biden-argues-with-construction-workers-over-guns-youre-full-of-sht/.

886. Joe Wuerzelbacher, quoted in Susan Jones, "'Spread the Wealth Around' Comment Comes Back to Haunt Obama," CNSnews.com, October 15, 2008, https://www.cnsnews.com/news/article/spread-wealth-around-comment-comes-back-haunt-obama.

887. Kyle Olson, "Watch: Joe Biden Trails Off in Victory Speech before Saying Which Office He's Running For," Breitbart News, March 11, 2020, https://www.breitbart.com/2020-election/2020/03/11/watch-joe-biden-trails-off-in-victory-speech-before-saying-which-office-hes-running-for/

888. Robert Kraychik, "First Congressional Staffer Tests Positive for Coronavirus," Breitbart News, March 11, 2020, https://www.breitbart.com/health/2020/03/11/first-congressional-staffer-tests-positive-for-coronavirus/.

889. President Donald Trump, tweet, March 11, 2020, https://twitter.com /realDonaldTrump/status/1237841878889840642.

890. President Donald Trump, remarks from the Oval Office (Washington, DC, March 11, 2020), https://www.whitehouse.gov/briefings-statements/remarks -president-trump-address-nation/.

891. John Carney, "Stocks Collapse in Worst Day for Dow since Crash of 1987," Breitbart News, March 12, 2020, https://www.breitbart.com/economy/2020 /03/12/stocks-collapse-in-worst-day-for-dow-since-crash-of-1987/.

892. Senator John McCain, quoted in John Bentley, "McCain Says 'Fundamentals' of U.S. Economy Are Strong," CBS News, September 15, 2008, https:// www.cbsnews.com/news/mccain-says-fundamentals-of-us-economy-are-strong/.

893. Kyle Olson, "Joe Biden 29 Minutes Late for Coronavirus Plan Announcement after 7 Staffers Mend Mic," Breitbart News, March 12, 2020, https:// www.breitbart.com/2020-election/2020/03/12/jjoe-biden-29-minutes-late-for -coronavirus-plan-announcement-after-7-staffers-mend-mic/.

894. Joe Biden, speech on the coronavirus pandemic (Wilmington, Delaware, March 12, 2020), https://www.youtube.com/watch?v=2QOidd8FGUM.

895. Joe Biden, "The Biden Plan to Combat Coronavirus (COVID-19) and Prepare for Future Global Health Threats," JoeBiden.com, accessed March 29, 2020, https://joebiden.com/covid19/.

896. Haris Alic, "Biden's Coronavirus Proposal Cribs Heavily from Trump Administration," Breitbart News, March 12, 2020, https://www.breitbart.com /2020-election/2020/03/12/bidens-coronavirus-proposal-cribs-heavily-from-trump -administration/.

897. John Binder, "Joe Biden's 'Combat Coronavirus' Plan Does Not Mention China," Breitbart News, March 12, 2020, https://www.breitbart.com/politics/2020 /03/12/joe-bidens-combat-coronavirus-plan-does-not-mention-china/.

898. Bernie Sanders, speech on the coronavirus pandemic (Burlington, Vermont, March 12, 2020), https://www.breitbart.com/politics/2020/03/12/bernie -sanders-calls-for-trump-to-be-replaced-on-coronavirus-by-congress-and-experts/.

899. Joel B. Pollak, "Nancy Pelosi Does Not Mention 'President' Once in Address to Nation on Coronavirus," Breitbart News, March 13, 2020, https:// www.breitbart.com/politics/2020/03/13/nancy-pelosi-does-not-mention-president -once-in-address-to-nation-on-coronavirus/.

900. Charlie Spiering, "Donald Trump Declares National Emergency over Coronavirus," Breitbart News, March 13, 2020, https://www.breitbart.com /politics/2020/03/13/donald-trump-declares-national-emergency-over-coronavirus/.

901. Joel B. Pollak, "Fact Check: No, Stephen King, Trump's Coronavirus Team Is Not 'All Male, All Old, and All White,'" Breitbart News, March 13, 2020, https://www.breitbart.com/entertainment/2020/03/13/fact-check-no-stephen-king -trumps-coronavirus-team-is-not-all-male-all-old-and-all-white/.

902. John Carney, "Hope Reborn: Stocks Skyrocket as President Presents 'All of America' Program to Fight Coronavirus," Breitbart News, March 13, 2020, https://

www.breitbart.com/economy/2020/03/13/hope-reborn-stocks-skyrocket-as-president
-presents-all-of-america-program-to-fight-coronavirus/.

903. Robert F. Kennedy, "Youth," *To Seek a Newer World* (New York: Double-day, 1967), 17.

904. Peter Wehner, "The Trump Presidency Is Over," *The Atlantic*, March 13, 2020, https://www.theatlantic.com/ideas/archive/2020/03/peter-wehner-trump -presidency-over/607969/.

905. Hannah Bleau, "DNC Changes Debate Rules after Tulsi Gabbard Reaches Previous Requirement," Breitbart News, March 6, 2020, https://www.breit bart.com/politics/2020/03/06/dnc-changes-debate-rules-after-tulsi-gabbard-reaches -previous-requirement/.

906. Tulsi Gabbard, tweet, November 19, 2020, https://twitter.com/TulsiGab-bard/status/1240650484546859008?s=20.

907. Hannah Bleau, "Mike Bloomberg Transferring $18 Million in Campaign Funds to DNC to Defeat Donald Trump," Breitbart News, March 20, 2020, https:// www.breitbart.com/politics/2020/03/20/mike-bloomberg-transferring-18-million -campaign-funds-dnc-defeat-donald-trump/.

908. Christopher Cadelago, "Bloomberg Sued by Aides for Stiffing Them on Yearlong Pay Promise," *Politico*, March 23, 2020, https://www.politico.com /news/2020/03/23/mike-bloomberg-aides-pay-lawsuits-144185.

909. James Clyburn, quoted in Domenico Montanaro, "The Democratic Nom-ination Is Now in View for Joe Biden—and 5 Other Takeaways," National Public Radio, March 11, 2020, https://www.npr.org/2020/03/11/814298678/the-democratic -nomination-is-now-in-view-for-joe-biden-and-6-other-takeaways.

910. Thomas Kaplan and Katie Glueck, "Biden, Courting Liberals, Backs Tuition-Free College for Many Students," *New York Times*, March 15, 2020, https:// www.nytimes.com/2020/03/15/us/politics/biden-backs-free-college.html.

911. Bernie Sanders, press statement, March 15, 2020, https://twitter.com /HCTrudo/status/1239308658128936960.

912. Joe Biden, appearance at eleventh Democratic presidential debate (Wash-ington, DC, March 15, 2020), https://www.breitbart.com/politics/2020/03/15/joe -biden-fumbles-coronavirus-response-n1h1-virus/.

913. Joel B. Pollak, "Fact Check Update: U.S. Never Rejected WHO Coronavi-rus Tests; They Were Never Offered," Breitbart News, March 17, 2020, https://www .breitbart.com/health/2020/03/17/fact-check-update-u-s-never-rejected-who -coronavirus-tests-they-were-never-offered/.

914. Joel B. Pollak, "Bernie Sanders on Coronavirus: First Thing, 'Shut This President Up Right Now," Breitbart News, March 15, 2020, https://www.breitbart .com/politics/2020/03/15/bernie-sanders-on-coronavirus-first-thing-shut-this-president -up-right-now-2/.

915. Bernie Sanders, appearance at Democratic presidential debate (Wash-ington, DC, March 15, 2020), CNN, http://transcripts.cnn.com/TRANSCRIPTS /2003/15/se.03.html.

916. John Binder, "Joe Biden: No Deportations for Any Criminal Illegal Aliens in My First 100 Days," Breitbart News, March 15, 2020, https://www.breit bart.com/politics/2020/03/15/joe-biden-no-deportations-for-any-criminal-illegal -aliens-in-my-first-100-days/.

917. Joe Biden, quoted in Joel B. Pollak, "Joe Biden Promises to Nominate Black Woman to Supreme Court for 'Representation,'" Breitbart News, March 15, 2020, https://www.breitbart.com/politics/2020/03/15/joe-biden-promises-to-nominate -black-woman-to-supreme-court-for-representation/.

918. Chicago Tribune Staff, "Illinois Primary Results: Marie Newman Ousts U.S. Representative Dan Lipinski; Cook County State's Attorney Kim Foxx Survives," *Chicago Tribune*, March 17, 2020, https://www.chicagotribune.com/election-2020 /ct-illinois-primary-election-day-updates-20200317-gf5morm2gzbc5j3laniwpr5kx4 -story.html.

919. Joel B. Pollak, "'Fifth Member of Squad' Marie Newman Unseats Dan Lipinski in IL-03 Democrat Primary," Breitbart News, March 17, 2020, https://www .breitbart.com/2020-election/2020/03/17/fifth-member-of-squad-marie-newman -unseats-dan-lipinski-in-illinois-03-democrat-primary/.

920. Tal Axelrod, "Axios Issues Apology after Incorrectly Reporting Sanders Suspended His 2020 Campaign," *The Hill*, March 18, 2020, https://thehill.com /homenews/media/488303-axios-issues-apology-after-reporting-sanders-suspended -his-2020-campaign.

921. Maggie Severns and James Arkin, "'It Can Be Catastrophic': Coronavirus Tanks Campaign Fundraising," *Politico*, March 20, 2020, https://www.politico.com /news/2020/03/20/coronavirus-campaign-fundraising-138381.

922. Emma Goldberg, "The Bernie Sanders Revolution Has Moved to Mom's Couch," *New York Times*, March 18, 2020, https://www.nytimes.com/2020/03/18/us /politics/bernie-sanders-young-voters.html.

923. Kyle Olson, "Amateur Hour: Joe Biden 'Virtual Town Hall' Marred by Tech Issues, Dick Durbin's Wailing Baby," Breitbart News, March 13, 2020, https:// www.breitbart.com/2020-election/2020/03/13/amateur-hour-joe-biden-virtual -town-hall-marred-by-tech-issues-dick-durbins-wailing-baby/.

924. Pam Key, "CNN's Jake Tapper Corrects 'Old School' Biden—'You Are Supposed to Cough into Your Elbow," Breitbart News, March 24, 2020, https:// www.breitbart.com/clips/2020/03/24/cnns-jake-tapper-corrects-old-school-biden -you-are-supposed-to-cough-into-your-elbow/.

925. Ken Thomas, tweet, March 23, 2020, https://twitter.com/KThomasDC /status/1242082792168722437.

926. John Sexton, "Sanders: I'm Staying in the Race and I'm Ready for the Next Debate," HotAir.com, March 24, 2020, https://hotair.com/archives/john-s-2/2020/03 /24/sanders-im-staying-race-ready-next-debate/.

927. Gabriela Schulte, "Poll: Trump Gets Low Marks on Handling Coronavirus," *The Hill*, March 12, 2020, https://thehill.com/hilltv/what-americas-thinking /487327-poll-trump-sees-high-marks-on-the-economy-low-marks-on-handling.

928. President Donald Trump, tweet, March 17, 2020, https://twitter.com /realDonaldTrump/status/1239889767267008512.

929. Cuomo continued: "They've been responsive, late at night, early in the morning, and they've thus far been doing everything that they can do, and I want to say thank you, and I want to say that I appreciate it." (Andrew Cuomo, quoted in Kristina Wong, "NY Gov. Cuomo Praises Trump: 'His Team Has Been on It'; 'President Is Doing the Right Thing,'" Breitbart News, March 17, 2020, https://www .breitbart.com/politics/2020/03/17/ny-governor-cuomo-praises-trump-his-team-has -been-on-it-president-is-doing-the-right-thing/.)

930. President Donald Trump, tweet, March 18, 2020, https://twitter.com /realDonaldTrump/status/1240355985673392128.

931. President Donald Trump, tweet, March 18, 2020, https://twitter.com /realDonaldTrump/status/1240355986541613062.

932. Gavin Newsom, quoted in Hannah Bleau, "Gavin Newsom Praises Trump's Coronavirus Cruise Ship Response: 'Every Single Thing He Said They Followed Through On,'" Breitbart News, March 9, 2020, https://www.breitbart .com/politics/2020/03/09/gavin-newsom-praises-trumps-coronavirus-cruise-ship -response-every-single-thing-he-said-they-followed-through-on/.

933. Mark Finkelstein, "Sharpton: 'To My Surprise,' President Trump Called Me to Discuss Coronavirus and the Poor," NewsBusters, March 21, 2020, https:// www.newsbusters.org/blogs/nb/mark-finkelstein/2020/03/21/sharpton-pres-trump -called-me-discuss-homeless-incarcerated-re.

934. Michael M. Grynbaum, "Trump's Briefings Are a Ratings Hit. Should Networks Cover Them Live?," New York Times, March 25, 2020, https://www.nytimes .com/2020/03/25/business/media/trump-coronavirus-briefings-ratings.html.

935. The president had already signed a bill providing $8.3 billion in coronavirus funding, more than the $2.5 billion the White House requested. The squabbles over those numbers were soon to be forgotten. On March 10, Senator Marco Rubio (R-FL) suggested $300 billion in relief. But as governors in the most populous states began issuing "shelter at home" orders, it was clear that the economic damage would be on a scale not seen since the Great Depression.

936. Senator Tom Cotton, quoted in Phil Mattingly, tweet, March 17, 2020, https://twitter.com/Phil_Mattingly/status/1239905476248252417.

937. Andrew Yang, tweet, March 17, 2020, https://twitter.com/AndrewYang /status/1239963916177772544.

938. Joe Biden, quoted in Stef Feldman, tweet, March 22, 2020, https://twitter .com/StefFeldman/status/1241898013750157313.

939. Alexandria Ocasio-Cortez, quoted in Hannah Bleau, "Alexandria Ocasio-Cortez Rages over Relief Bill: 'There Should Be Shame,'" Breitbart News, March 27, 2020, https://www.breitbart.com/politics/2020/03/27/alexandria-ocasio-cortez-rages -over-relief-bill-there-should-be-shame/.

940. Kristina Wong, "CBS News Poll: Majority of Americans Approve of Trump's Handling of the Coronavirus Outbreak," Breitbart News, March 24, 2020,

https://www.breitbart.com/politics/2020/03/24/cbs-news-poll-majority-of-americans-approve-of-trumps-handling-of-the-coronavirus-outbreak/.

941. Christopher DeMuth of the Hudson Institute argued that Trump had set a new standard for presidential responses to emergencies by decentralizing power rather than centralizing it, and deregulating rather than creating new rules—unlike his predecessors. He used the Constitution's federalist structure to give governors the flexibility to set their own policies and harnessed the energies of the private sector to manufacture necessary medical equipment—usually voluntarily—and to develop new medical treatments. (Christopher DeMuth, "Trump Rewrites the Book on Emergencies," *Wall Street Journal*, April 17, 2020, https://www.wsj.com/articles/trump-rewrites-the-book-on-emergencies-11587142872.)

942. During Trump's impeachment, for example, social media companies quashed efforts merely to report the identity of the whistleblower—a fact of legitimate public interest.

943. John Carney, "Jobless Claims Surge to 281,000," Breitbart News, March 19, 2020, https://www.breitbart.com/economy/2020/03/19/jobless-claims-surge-to-281000/.

944. John Carney, "Jobless Claims Soar to 3,283,000, Biggest Jump Ever," Breitbart News, March 26, 2020, https://www.breitbart.com/economy/2020/03/26/jobless-claims-soar-to-3283000/.

945. Stephanie Armour, "Trump Administration to Pay Hospitals to Treat Uninsured Coronavirus Patients," *Wall Street Journal*, April 3, 2020, https://www.wsj.com/articles/trump-administration-plans-to-pay-hospitals-to-treat-uninsured-coronavirus-patients-11585927877.

946. The episode calls to mind a famous Jewish folk tale. A starving man asks a rabbi if he can eat pork, violating a core prohibition in Jewish dietary laws, if it is the only food available. The rabbi says yes—"just don't suck on the bones." In other words, don't enjoy it; it should not be something pleasant and certainly should not become a norm.

947. Barack Obama, speech (University of Missouri, Columbia, Missouri).

948. Rahm Emanuel, quoted in Armour, "Trump Administration."

949. Bernie Sanders, town hall remarks (Berlin, New Hampshire).

950. James Clyburn, quoted in Mike Lillis and Scott Wong, "House Democrats Eyeing Much Broader Phase 3 Stimulus," *The Hill*, March 19, 2020, https://thehill.com/homenews/house/488543-house-democrats-eyeing-much-broader-phase-3-stimulus.

951. Libby Cathey et al., "Super Tuesday Results: Biden Sweeps the South, Sanders Strong in the West, Anemic Outcome for Bloomberg," ABC News, March 3, 2020, https://abcnews.go.com/Politics/super-tuesday-live-updates-voters-14-states-us/story?id=69354977.

952. Joe Biden, quoted in Bill Barrow and Elena Schor, "Biden: Congress Should Protect Abortion Rights, If Necessary," Associated Press, May 22, 2019, https://apnews.com/37bcf15a80a54014bd37fa4298d5d5c1.

953. Lisa Lerer, "When Joe Biden Voted to Let States Overturn Roe v. Wade," *New York Times*, March 29, 2019, https://www.nytimes.com/2019/03/29/us/politics/biden-abortion-rights.html.

954. Joe Biden, tweet, May 21, 2019, https://twitter.com/joebiden/status/11308 66163783806981.

955. Joe Biden, quoted in Nicholas Fandos, "Joe Biden's Role in '90s Crime Law Could Haunt Any Presidential Bid," *New York Times,* August 21, 2015, https://www .nytimes.com/2015/08/22/us/politics/joe-bidens-role-in-90s-crime-law-could-haunt -any-presidential-bid.html.

956. Joe Biden, quoted in Charlie Spiering, "Joe Biden: 'Mistakes Were Made' in My Nineties-Era Anti-Crime Bills," Breitbart News, May 14, 2019, https://www .breitbart.com/politics/2019/05/14/joe-biden-mistakes-were-made-in-my-nineties -era-anti-crime-bills/.

957. Biden specifically attacked Republican nominee Senator John McCain (R-AZ) for wanting the U.S. economy to make the transition from coal to "cleaner" fuels. (Joe Biden, speech [Charleston, West Virginia, October 24, 2008], https:// www.youtube.com/watch?v=j1NP8DP9uM4.)

958. Joel B. Pollak, "Joe Biden at Democrat Debate: Eliminate Coal, Fracking, Fossil Fuels," Breitbart News, July 31, 2009, https://www.breitbart.com/2020 -election/2019/07/31/joe-biden-at-democrat-debate-eliminate-coal-fracking-fossil-fuels/.

959. Joe Biden, quoted in GOP War Room, "FLASHBACK: Biden in 2006: No Amnesty, Immigrants Need to Speak English," YouTube, May 23, 2019, https:// www.youtube.com/watch?v=Kgxq3Va9Lpc.

960. Joe Biden, quoted in Tina Nguyen, "Here's a Video of Joe Biden Sounding a Lot Like Trump," *Vanity Fair,* May 10, 2019, https://www.vanityfair.com /news/2019/05/joe-biden-2006-vote-border-fence.

961. Haris Alic, "Democrat Debate: Biden Promises to Raise Taxes If Elected." Breitbart News, June 27, 2019, https://www.breitbart.com/politics/2019/06/27/democrat -debate-biden-promises-to-raise-taxes-if-elected/.

962. Kristina Wong, "Biden: I Would Not Have Killed Quds Force Leader Qasem Soleimani," Breitbart News, February 7, 2020, https://www.breitbart .com/politics/2020/02/07/biden-i-would-not-have-killed-quds-force-leader-qasem -soleimani/.

963. His supposed inspiration for running was a lie about Trump's response to the Charlottesville riots. Trump had condemned the neo-Nazis and white supremacists—"totally" and repeatedly. His sin had been to condemn violence "on many sides." That was once a core principle of the civil rights movement. It was no longer good enough.

964. Marc Caputo, "Leftward Ho! Biden pivots to progressives," *Politico,* April 9, 2020, https://www.politico.com/news/2020/04/09/biden-progressives-sanders-178073.

965. "Joe Biden Pivots...to the Left," *Wall Street Journal,* April 12, 2020, https://www.wsj.com/articles/joe-biden-pivots-to-the-left-11586718072.

966. Joe Biden, livestream with Bernie Sanders, April 13, 2020, https://www .pscp.tv/w/1vOxwoAjQVVxB.

967. Barack Obama, tweet, April 14, 2020, https://twitter.com/BarackObama /status/1250088269502709762.

968. Joe Biden, remarks to virtual town hall (Wilmington, Delaware, May 4, 2019), https://www.youtube.com/watch?v=3zWNQn9KHWI.

969. Biden promised as much when he told supporters a Green New Deal would be part of a future coronavirus relief bill. (Joe Biden, quoted in Ian Hanchett, "Biden: There Will Be Opportunity in 'Next Round' to Use 'Green Deal' to Boost Economy," Breitbart News, March 25, 2020, https://www.breitbart.com/clips/2020 /03/25/biden-there-will-be-opportunity-in-next-round-to-use-green-deal-to-boost -economy/.) He also would, he promised in April, "very much want" Sanders to be involved in his administration, advocating for his positions, "may of which I agree with." (Joe Biden, interview, Today, NBC News, April 7, 2020.)

970. President Donald Trump. "Remarks by President Trump at Naval Station Norfolk Send-Off for USNS Comfort, Norfolk, Virginia," White House, March 28, 2020, https://www.whitehouse.gov/briefings-statements/remarks-president-trump-naval -station-norfolk-send-off-usns-comfort-norfolk-va/.

971. Jeffry Bartash, "Prescription Drug Prices Aren't Rising—They're Fall- ing for the First Time in 47 years," MarketWatch, March 12, 2019, https://www .marketwatch.com/story/prescription-drug-prices-arent-rising-theyre-falling-for-the -first-time-in-47-years-2019-03-12.

972. Jonathan Easley, "Poll: Biden Leads Trump by 10 Points as Economic Pes- simism Grows," The Hill, March 30, 2020, https://thehill.com/homenews/campaign /490163-poll-biden-leads-trump-by-10-points-as-economic-pessimism-grows.

973. Pam Key, "Biden Struggles with Coronavirus Question—Trump Has to 'Wait Until the Cases Before Anything Happens,'" Breitbart News, March 30, 2020, https://www.breitbart.com/clips/2020/03/30/biden-struggles-with-coronavirus -question-trump-has-to-wait-until-the-cases-before-anything-happens/.

974. Haris Alic, "Joe Biden Faces New Sexual Assault Allegation from Former Staffer," Breitbart News, March 27, 2020, https://www.breitbart.com/2020-election /2020/03/27/joe-biden-faces-new-sexual-assault-allegation-from-former-staffer/.

975. Kamala Harris, quoted by Joel Pollak, "Kamala Harris Trolls Joe Biden: 'A Great Running Mate,'" Breitbart News, May 15, 2009, https://www.breitbart .com/2020-election/2019/05/15/kamala-harris-trolls-joe-biden-a-great-running -mate/.

976. Joe Biden, campaign launch video.

977. Robert F. Kennedy, "Day of Affirmation Address" (University of Cape Town, Cape Town, South Africa, June 6, 1966), https://www.jfklibrary.org /learn/about-jfk/the-kennedy-family/robert-f-kennedy/robert-f-kennedy-speeches /day-of-affirmation-address-news-release-version-university-of-capetown-capetown -south-africa-june-6.

978. President Donald Trump, State of the Union address (United States Cap- itol, February 5, 2019), https://www.whitehouse.gov/briefings-statements/president -donald-j-trumps-state-union-address-2/.